Unsustainable Transport

"The definitive contribution to this centrally important topic, which will remain the standard work for years to come."

Professor Sir Peter Hall
Bartlett Professor of Planning, University College London

"This brilliant analysis of the crucially important issue of sustainability further reinforces Banister's reputation as one of the world's leading authorities on the topic. He provides a thorough, highly informative, up-to-date examination of the problems and alternative solutions to transport's current unsustainability, including proposals for practical strategies to implement the necessary policy measures."

Professor John Pucher Bloustein
School of Planning and Public Policy, Rutgers University, New Jersey, USA

"This is a very important book. One of its great strengths is that is the first time a transport specialist has made the connection between sustainable cities and sustainable transport. The author explores the need not only to pursue technological innovation but the need to change our institutional structures, social behaviour and the ways we live and work if we wish to seriously pursue the notion of sustainable cities.

The book eschews the apocalyptic tone adopted by many writers and equally rejects the familiar physical determinist position taken by most transport specialists. This is a balanced exploration of the fundamental issues raised by pursuit of sustainability policy. The book should be read by all those who are concerned about urban issues and especially those who want to take part in an informed discussion of sustainability."

Professor Patrick Troy
Centre for Resource and Environmental Studies, Australian National University, Canberra ACT 0200

Transport, Development and Sustainability

*Series editor: David Banister, Professor of Transport Planning,
University College London*

European Transport Policy and Sustainable Mobility
David Banister, Dominic Stead, Peter Steen, Jonas Akerman, Karl Dreborg, Peter Nijkamp and Ruggero Schleicher-Tappeser

The Politics of Mobility: transport, the environment and public policy
Geoff Vigar

Experimenting for Sustainable Transport: the approach of Strategic Niche Management
Remco Hoogma, Rene Kemp, Johan Schot and Bernard Truffer

Transport Planning – Second Edition
David Banister

Unfare Solutions: local earmarked charges to fund public transport
Barry Ubbels, Marcus Enoch, Stephen Potter and Peter Nijkamp

Barriers to Sustainable Transport
edited by Piet Rietveld and Roger Stough

Unsustainable Transport – city transport in the new century
David Banister

David Banister

Unsustainable Transport
City transport in the new century

Routledge
Taylor & Francis Group

LONDON AND NEW YORK

First published 2005 by Routledge
2 Park Square, Milton Park, Abingdon, Oxfordshire OX14 4RN
Simultaneously published in the USA and Canada
by Routledge, 270 Madison Avenue, New York, NY 10016

Routledge is an imprint of the Taylor & Francis Group

Typeset in Sabon and Imago by PNR Design, Oxfordshire
Printed and bound in Great Britain by MPG Books, Bodmin

British Library Cataloguing in Publication Data
A catalogue record for this book is available from the British Library

Library of Congress Cataloging in Publication Data
A catalog record for this book is available

ISBN 415-35782-9 (Hbk)
ISBN 415-35790-X (Pbk)

Contents

Preface   vii

Acknowledgements   ix

Abbreviations   xi

01   Introduction   1
      1.1   Introduction   1
      1.2   Sustainable development   2
      1.3   The debate   4
      1.4   The car as an icon   5
      1.5   Car ownership and car use   7
      1.6   The structure of the book   9

Part 1

02   The global picture   11
      2.1   Introduction   11
      2.2   Proposition 1 – Transport is unsustainable   11
      2.3   Proposition 2 – Sustainable urban development is dependent upon
            the city being the centre of vitality, opportunity and wealth, and
            that transport has a major role to play   14
      2.4   The ten principles of sustainable development and transport   15
      2.5   Global trends and key concepts   19
      2.6   Conclusions   33

03   Sustainability and transport intensity   37
      3.1   The economic background   37
      3.2   The transport case   41
      3.3   Transport intensity   42
      3.4   Alternative measures of economic growth   49
      3.5   Empirical evidence from the UK and the EU15   52
      3.6   Changes in society and the economy   53
      3.7   Conclusions   55

04   Public policy and sustainable transport   58
      4.1   Introduction   58
      4.2   Global perspectives on public policy   61
      4.3   Local perspectives on public policy   65
      4.4   Barriers to implementation   70
      4.5   Conclusions   77

05   Institutional and organizational issues   80
      5.1   Policy perspectives   80
      5.2   Opportunities for change   82
      5.3   Conclusions   92

Part 2

06   Transport and urban form   97
      6.1   Introduction   97
      6.2   The key relationships between transport and urban form   99
      6.3   Case studies   121
      6.4   Conclusions   124

07   Fiscal and regulatory measures   129
      7.1   Introduction   129
      7.2   Pricing   130
      7.3   Distributional effects of congestion charging in London   140
      7.4   Regulatory incentives   145
      7.5   Carbon taxes   147
      7.6   Air travel   148
      7.7   Pricing and the United States   151
      7.8   Comments on fiscal and regulatory measures   154

08   Technology and transport   157
      8.1   Introduction   157
      8.2   The technology   158
      8.3   Freight   165
      8.4   The limits of technology   166

09   The impact of ICT on transport   169
      9.1   Introduction   169
      9.2   Production   174
      9.3   Living (and travelling)   179
      9.4   Working   183
      9.5   Conclusions   186

Part 3

10   Learning from cities with low levels of motorization   191
      10.1   Introduction   191
      10.2   Equity   193
      10.3   Innovation   201
      10.4   Institutions and governance   204
      10.5   Conclusions   208

11   Visions for the future   211
      11.1   Introduction   211
      11.2   Visioning and backcasting   212
      11.3   The scenario building process outlined   213
      11.4   Discussion of the visions within cities in OECD countries   216
      11.5   The north-south divide in perceptions of sustainable development 225
      11.6   Discussion of the visions within cities in non-OECD countries 227
      11.7   Conclusions   229

12   Conclusions   233
      12.1   Sustainable transport planning   233
      12.2   The achievement of sustainable transport objectives   237
      12.3   Importance of involving the people   240
      12.4   Sustainable urban development and transport   246

References   256

Index   281

We have not inherited the Earth from our ancestors, but we are borrowing it for our children. (Old Indian Saying)

One of the major problems facing authors when writing books is to think of a suitable title that both reflects the content of the book and will catch the eye of the potential reader. Further, all good book titles comprise no more than three words. For me, this makes inspiration difficult, as I have already used up all possible combinations of the relevant three words, hence this book has a more cryptic title that should be followed by its real content, sustainable urban development and transport.

'Unsustainable transport' is meant to suggest that we have a series of choices to make with respect to transport and sustainable development. Even making no choice needs to be placed within the same context, as that would have important implications for cities and regions. The book presents a global and local perspective on the nature of sustainable development, and the crucial role that transport has in making or breaking cities. It also presents the range of options available, together with a commentary on the barriers to implementation and explanations of why outcomes often do not match up to expectations. There is an investigation of cities in developing countries, which are growing at a phenomenal rate and where many of the same problems are now manifesting themselves. But so is a different set of innovative solutions. Visions of the sustainable city are presented, together with a summary of the packages of policy measures in transport and other sectors that could be used to move in a more 'sustainable' direction.

Throughout the book, I have taken a positive line in the argument, stating that sustainable urban development is a feasible and necessary policy objective, and that transport has a major role to play in its achievement. Even though many of the trends are in the wrong direction (unsustainable) and there are many barriers to effective implementation, this does not mean that all hope is lost. The book reflects the opportunities for a fundamental shift in thinking about the future of transport policy. Realization of that aim can be achieved if transport is placed at the centre of sustainable urban development.

Ten years ago, the influential Royal Commission on Environmental Pollution stated that the key to a sustainable transport policy is coordinated action by government and industry on several fronts. Economic growth cannot continue in a sustainable way unless transport and land use planning are integrated. Technology must be improved to cut fuel consumption and make vehicles less polluting. New residential, commercial and leisure developments should be sensibly located, so that people do not have to travel long distances, and are not forced to use cars for their journeys. The cost of private transport will have to rise because at the moment it does not reflect damage done to health and the environment. Resources should be switched from road-building to improving public transport.

Part of the thinking behind this book is to reflect on what has been achieved over this 10-year period, to see where we have gone wrong and where progress has been made. As T.S. Eliot is reported to have said 'and the end of all our exploring will be to arrive where we started and know the place for the first time'. We have now reached that point, and it is time to decide whether there is now a sufficient momentum to move towards sustainable transport.

David Banister
March 2005

Acknowledgements

Many individuals have helped me with this book. The genesis has come from the POSSUM project where I was introduced to the concepts of sustainable development and scenario building. The POSSUM Consortium (EU DGVII Strategic Research Programme) had members from University College London (Dominic Stead and Alan McLellan), The Free University of Amsterdam (Peter Nijkamp, Sytze Rienstra and Hadewijch van Delft), The National Technical University of Athens (Maria Giaoutzi and Zenia Dimitrakopoulo), the Environmental Strategies Research Group in Stockholm (Peter Steen, Karl Dreborg, Jonas Akerman, Leif Hedberg and Sven Hunhammar), EURES – Institute for Regional Studies in Europe in Freiburg (Ruggero Schleicher-Tappeser and Christian Hey), VTT – Technical Research Centre of Finland in Helsinki (Veli Himanen and Anu Touminen), Warsaw University of Technology (Wojciech Suchorewski), and the Ministry of Transportation of the Russian Federation in Moscow (Viacheslav Arsenov). This interest was continued in projects for the German government leading to the Global Conference on Urban 21 (Ulrich Pfeiffer and Peter Hall) – some of the material used in this book relates to that earlier research.

Dominic Stead also made a major contribution to Chapter 3 on transport intensity and Chapter 5 on the key relationships between transport and urban form. Chapter 3 is in part based on a paper written with Dominic Stead and presented at a STELLA Conference in Helsinki (2002) and subsequently published in the *European Journal of Transport Infrastructure Research*, 2(2/3), pp. 161–178.

Chapter 4 on Public Policy is based on a contribution to the Encyclopedia of Life Support Systems (EOLSS), which in turn used material from the EU DANTE Consortium research. This project was concerned with the barriers to implementation, and subsequent research covered the issues of public acceptability of sustainable transport futures. I would like to thank the following contributors to the DANTE project: Stephen Marshall, Daniel Mittler, Alan McLellan (again) and Nick Green of the Bartlett School of Planning, University College London, and our partners in the DANTE team – Kees Maat, Erik Louw and Hugo Priemus of Delft University; Sandra Mathers and Laurie Pickup of Transport and Travel Research Ltd.; Jens Peder Kristensen of PLS Consult A/S, Aarhus; Massimo Marciani of FIT Consulting,

Rome, Madalina Cotorogea and Ovidiu Romosan of Regia Autonoma de Transport Bucuresti; Rico Maggi and Juerg Maegerle of Zürich University.

Chapter 9 is based on a paper written with Dominic Stead (again) and published in *Transport Reviews* 24(6). The research input has come from the EU ESTO Project on the Impacts of ICT on Transport and Mobility (ICTRANS). I am grateful to all members of that team – Matthias Weber and Petra Wagner (ARC Research, Austria), Karl Dreborg (again) and Anders Eriksson (FOI, Sweden), Peter Zoche, Bernd Beckert, Martina Joisten (ISI-FhG, Germany), Anique Hommels, René Kemp, Peter Peters, Theo Dunnewijk (MERIT, the Netherlands) and Lucien Dantuma, Richard Hawkins, Carlos Montalvo (TNO-STB, the Netherlands).

This book is central to the Spon series on transport and sustainable development as it integrates all three elements. It has arisen out of a Masters course Specialism that I run at the Bartlett School of Planning in University College London, and the book has been read and commented on by the students taking the Specialism. My thanks to them all for their input, mainly complementary, but always incisive and in some cases inspirational. Thanks also to Lloyd Wright for reading the complete draft of the book and taking the trouble to engage in serious debate about the issues that it raises. Lizzie also volunteered to read the final draft – this is beyond the call of duty.

BRT	Bus Rapid Transit
CAFE	Corporate Average Fuel Efficiency
CO	Carbon Monoxide
CO_2	Carbon Dioxide
ECMT	European Conference of Ministers of Transport
EDI	Electronic Data Interchange
EJ	Exa Joules
EU (EU15)	European Union (the 15 members of the EU to 1st May 2004)
GDP	Gross Domestic Product
GHG	Greenhouse Gases
GIS	Geographical Information System
HGV	Heavy Goods Vehicles – over 3.5 tonnes gross unladen weight
ICT	Information and Communications Technologies
IPCC	Intergovernmental Panel on Climate Change
ITS	Intelligent Transport Systems
LA21	Local Agenda 21
LGV	Light Goods Vehicles – under 3.5 tonnes gross unladen weight
LPG	Liquid Petroleum Gas
LRT	Light Rail Transit
MRT	Mass Rapid Transit
NECAR	New Electric Car – made by Mercedes
NGO	Non Governmental Organization
NO_x	Nitrogen Oxides
OECD	Organisation for Economic Cooperation and Development
PM_{10}	Particulate Matter under 10 microns in diameter
RCEP	Royal Commission on Environmental Pollution
SACTRA	Standing Advisory Committee on Trunk Road Appraisal
SUV	Sports Utility Vehicle
TGV	Train à Grand Vitesse
UK	United Kingdom
UNDP	United Nations Development Programme
US (USA)	United States (of America)
VAT	Value Added Tax
VED	Vehicle Excise Duty
VOC	Volatile Organic Compounds
WHO	World Health Organisation

I would like to dedicate this book to my parents, Michael and Rachel, who have just celebrated their 60th (diamond) wedding anniversary. They are two of the most environmentally sustainable people that I know, even when it comes to transport. They may have little to learn from this book, but others I hope will have much to learn from it.

Chapter 1

Introduction

1.1 Introduction

At the beginning of the twenty-first century, there are many new challenges facing the world, but the one that has captured the headlines has been the growing instability of many natural phenomena, whether it is volcanic activity, flooding, drought, fire, and hurricanes. The climate is changing and the evidence is clear that global warming is taking place with the small but consistent increases in temperatures across the globe. Much of the world's population is located in areas that are susceptible to flooding and 20 of the 30 megacities (population of over 10 million in 2015) are located near to sea level or in river flood plains. Rising sea level and the propensity for flooding may affect all of these locations where some 500 million people will live. Such a statement may appear alarmist, but it does give an indication of the scale of change taking place. Not all parts of the cities are at sea level, but enormous investment is needed to safeguard the population. In addition to the problems of sea level rises, there seem to be increasing occurrences of other disasters, such as crop failures, new diseases, fires and storms, and threats to biodiversity. Some of these are directly caused by human activity, but in other cases their causes are not so obvious.

It is clear that this process of global warming needs to be moderated and if possible stabilized. This means that there should be a substantial reduction in all forms of carbon consumption, as it is the use of these resources that is the principal cause of global warming. The total global emissions of CO_2 (the main global warming gas) have increased by about 60 per cent (1971–2001) to nearly 24 billion tonnes (IEA, 2000 and 2001).

Transport's share of this total has increased from 19.3 per cent (1971) to 28.9 per cent (2001), so both the absolute and relative share attributable to transport consumption is increasing (EC, 2003). In addition, transport is almost totally dependent on oil for energy and there seems to be little prospect for a major change even if prices were to rise substantially (see Chapters 7 and 8). Attempts to introduce alternative fuel vehicles have so far been unsuccessful and the capital investment in petrol and diesel engined vehicles is vast. Change has to come gradually, and clear direction is also required for emerging new transport markets, such as air travel and the growth in car ownership in developing countries. Optimistically, one might be suggesting that a 20-year time horizon is needed before a significant (over 20 per cent) proportion of the vehicle fleet is run on non-carbon-based fuels (e.g. fuel cells or electricity generated from renewable sources such as wind and water power).

Apart from the search for alternative fuels and the expectation that technology will provide some of the answers (see Chapter 8), there are other actions that can be taken now. One set of actions relates to clear economic signals being given to all consumers of carbon-based energy that demand must decrease through more efficient use of that energy in transport. These actions should be complemented by high-level decisions on using the full range of economic measures to encourage efficient use of alternative fuels, to invest in the best available technology, and to reduce substantially the use of carbon-based fuels (see Chapter 7). The second set of actions relates to the cities in which the majority of the world's population will live. This is where the concept of sustainable urban development becomes important, as cities are seen as being the source of economic wealth and prosperity, and the centres of sustainable development. It is only in cities that many of the activities essential to the creation of wealth and well-being can take place.

The prime objective of sustainable urban development should be to facilitate that development whilst at the same time ensuring that the use of carbon resources are within the limits of sustainability, and that all individuals have access to that development in terms of their welfare and well-being. Within the context of cities, transport has a key role in ensuring the efficient operation of the wealth-creating activities, as well as contributing towards social well-being and providing access to those activities. But transport, as a major and increasing consumer of energy, should also contribute substantially to the environmental objective of reducing its use of these carbon-based energy sources. Achieving all three objectives may be an impossible task. The purpose of this book is to assess the options available and come to some conclusions on the most appropriate role for transport in contributing fully to sustainable urban development.

1.2 Sustainable development

Sustainable development has become part of the common language. Since the classic Brundtland report stated that 'a sustainable condition for this planet is one in which there is a stability for both social and physical systems, achieved through meeting the needs of the present without compromising the ability of future generations to meet their own needs' (WCED, 1987, p. 43), it has been used by most researchers and decision-makers interested in the environment, and like many of the terms that are used and supported, it is difficult to define precisely. Underlying the concept of sustainable development is the need to redress the balance between economic, social and environmental priorities. In the past, it was argued that economic growth was paramount and that this would take priority over all other concerns. As incomes and wealth rise, there would be trickle-down effects to help those that could not participate in the new prosperity, and that there would also be resources available to clean up the environment. In practice though, this 'natural allegiance' between the three dimensions of sustainable development was not occurring. It was realized about this time (1987) that a more positive approach was needed that redressed the balance between the overriding economic imperative and the other two components of development. The trigger for this fundamental change in priorities has been the concern over the global environment (primarily global warming), but also the other transboundary issues such as acid rain.

Much effort has been directed at trying to define sustainable development. In this book our focus is on the three basic elements already alluded to here. Economic development relates to the growth in the economy over time and how this is reflected in the wealth of individual countries. Social development addresses the question of the distribution of that wealth between individuals (social equity) and over space (spatial equity). Environment development is the protection of the environment, both in terms of maintaining the current stock of environmental resources (intragenerational) and in terms of bequeathing to subsequent generations a stock that has not been substantially depleted (intergenerational). The definition of the environment includes the global and local environment in terms of the use of resources and the generation of pollution. It also covers issues relating to biodiversity, water quality, sanitation and waste-management.

In addition to these three basic elements, there are two other important factors. Increasingly it is accepted that effective implementation of sustainable development requires all actors to be involved in that process. It must be seen as being participatory so that private individuals, companies, industries and governments all 'buy in' to the proposals being considered. Exclusion from the process means that it is much harder to develop strategies for change. Explanation, understanding and engagement are all essential elements of successful implementation, particularly with respect to sustainable development, as this requires the full co-operation of all parties.

The second factor is the role of governance in achieving sustainable development. Much of the decision-making process is carried out at all levels of government within a sectoral framework. Sustainable development is all embracing and requires new thinking so that cross-sectoral decisions can be made. This in turn means that both the responsibilities and resources should be reallocated between departments to facilitate action. There may need to be changes in the organizational structures of government so that this can take place, with the establishment of new institutional structures to implement sustainable development. It seems that stable government with appropriate structures is essential and there needs to be consistency in objectives over time. Further, it is often difficult to introduce major changes within the life span of one government, so continuity is essential. It is here that clear leadership and direction is required at all levels of government if real changes are to take place. All five aspects of sustainable development will be used in this book.

1.3 The debate

As with many new initiatives, there is substantial debate over the meaning of sustainable development and the usefulness of the concept. For example, the World Economic Forum (Esty, 2002) suggests that the Brundtland definition of sustainable development is a 'buzz word largely devoid of meaning' and that there needs to be a clearer trade-off between the environment and development. The question is raised about whether there can ever be win-win situations as someone always loses when policy choices are made. But, as stated above, sustainable development does help focus the attention of decision-makers at all levels on a wider range of indicators of well-being and it forces more integrated policy-making. More holistic forms of decision-making must be encouraged.

The experience since Brundtland has also taught us a series of other lessons that need to be addressed if the path of sustainable urban development is to be followed:

1   Reductions have to start modestly as the capital stock involved in the global energy system is vast and long-lived. It would be costly to replace that investment, but the switch to low-carbon technologies must occur when replacement takes place.

2   Clear fiscal incentives should be given to all users of carbon-based energy sources so that prices will rise (i.e. carbon taxes) and restrictions will be imposed on emissions. Industry, business and domestic users need to be given guidance and a clear framework within which to make decisions.

3   Strong action is required on research and development in the science and technology of climate change and in promoting its implications. This also includes action on clean energy research and the best means by which research can be quickly translated into practice in all parts of the world.

4   The lead for change to a low-carbon economy must come from the rich countries, but all countries must play a role. Industry is the key player in supporting research and development, and must be at the forefront of best practice.

5   Action is required now and uncertainty is not a reason for inaction or weak action. Politicians in key nations need to take on the roles of champions and demonstrate leadership.

Once such a framework has been set in place, then it becomes easier to see how urban development and transport fits into this wider picture. The imperative to reduce all forms of carbon consumption must be reflected across all sectors. It provides the context within which other key issues can be placed. The most important of these is that of 'fair shares in environmental space', where it is argued that each country should have the opportunity to consume the same amount of resources relative to its population (www.mbnet.mb.ca/linkages/consume). The estimates for a global population of 6 billion are for 2.0 tonnes of CO_2 per person to stabilize emission levels, but average levels globally are 3.9 tonnes per person and, as we shall see (Chapter 2, Table 2.3), the figures for many rich countries are much higher than this in the transport sector alone. It reflects the global distribution of income, where the top 15 per cent of population has 80 per cent of the world's income, the next 25 per cent has a further 15 per cent, and the remaining 60 per cent have only 5 per cent of the world's income (World Bank, 1998).

1.4   The car as an icon

If there is one object that has become an icon of the twentieth century, it is the car and it is difficult to see how that will change. It can be seen as a 'security' in that it is always available and never too far away. If it is parked at a distance, then people become nervous, and even if they are in the country, many do not venture too far away from that security. This is because of the desire to be 'in the car and motoring', so that one can feel safe and isolated from the dangers outside, and enjoying the luxury that it provides. As Urry (2001) argues, the car has a special combination of factors that seem to give it a dominant role as a global icon:

1   It is a *manufactured object* produced by the iconic firms that symbolize capitalism and industry from which both Fordism and post Fordism have emerged.
2   It is the main item of *individual consumption* after housing, which provides it and the user with status. But it is also represented as a family member with a name, rebellious features, and an age.
3   It has a powerful *machinic complex* through its technical and social linkages with a wide range of supply industries, including parts and accessories, petrol stations, road construction and maintenance, service areas, repair garages and car parks.

4   It provides *individual mobility* that subordinates other forms of mobility (public transport, cycle and walk) as it reorganizes the way in which people participate in work, family life, leisure and social activities.

5   It is the dominant *culture* that maintains major discourses on the quality of life from its use in films, on the news, and at the centre of much advertising.

6   It is one of the most important *users of resources* resulting from the range and scale of materials consumed, the space requirements and the power used in the manufacture of cars and roads, and in responding to the material, air quality, accidents, visual, noise and other costs of car-based travel.

Most of these attributes are well known (Whitelegg, 1997), but the power of and the addiction to the car has often been underestimated. The car offers individuals the means to 'escape' from the real environment by allowing them to have their own flexibility and freedom. The advertisements are very successful in selling that dream of individuality and convenience, and the ability to do what you want (within reason). But that same car is both socially and spatially divisive as it allows cities to spread with the consequences that all people have to travel much longer distances than before, with space becoming something that you want to pass through rather than to stop in (Urry, 2001). For those without a car, the fragmented city becomes more hostile and it can force even reluctant users into their cars, thus exacerbating the problem even further. The car is the one item of consumption that seems to give the user huge (perceived) benefits, but at the same time imposes costs on many others both directly (e.g. through pollution effects) and indirectly (e.g. through congestion and poorer access to facilities).

Perhaps the car is embedded so much within our society, that it is impossible to make any real change to that situation. If the 'car as icon' view spreads to countries where current levels of motorization are low, then what future is there for the city, the environment and for those without a car? The car may however become a victim of its own success as the means to accommodate it will never expand as fast as ownership levels, so it will become less attractive to use it as congestion increases. Urry (2001) proposes three stages where transitions have taken place in attitudes to the car. In the early days, car drivers inhabited the roads with the pioneering spirit of freedom and the image of the open road. As car ownership became more universal, this changed to inhabiting the car, where the car drivers were 'safe' in the metal boxes with complete privacy and the ability to listen to radio, cassette, or CD, as if they were in their own homes. The car was really seen as an extension of the home, as a detachable room that could be taken to different places. The third stage is inhabiting the intelligent car, where some of the routine tasks are allocated to the vehicle rather than the driver. Included here are traffic control functions, route guidance and information systems. In addition, technology has been used to 'reform' the car and make it more sustainable, through the use of materials that can be recycled, new materials, alternative propulsion systems, and the development of the 'smart car'. The car has become a more sophisticated office with mobile systems for telephones, e-mail and Internet access, so the driver can make the best use of time with even more flexibility.

The icon still remains, but it has adapted itself to the differing requirements of the congested road environment and the driver. Manufacturers and advertisers have been successful in responding to changes so that the car still remains attractive. The public transport system has struggled to compete with the car at every stage. The implications of this car culture must not be underestimated, as it helps to explain why rational behaviour in the economic sense does not prevail. Even though pricing measures are important, behavioural change requires strong complementary actions to be taken across the board if real change is to take place. Single policy measures are limited in their scope, and successful implementation requires creative packages of complementary measures (see Chapter 11) to be introduced consistently over a period of time. A crucial element of the package must be effective engagement with car drivers so that they understand why particular measures are important to the achievement of sustainable urban development, and that they are prepared to respond positively to those measures. If there is little or no support for the measures, then there is little chance of success even if they are implemented successfully. People (and particularly car drivers) are extremely resourceful in finding ways to avoid doing something that they do not support. It is small wonder that so many measures introduced with good intention have not worked as expected, as the target group (often car drivers) have found ways to get round them.

1.5   Car ownership and car use

There is a clear link between car ownership and car use, and any coherent strategy to reduce car use is doomed to failure as it is not really addressing the cause of unsustainable mobility, namely the car (Gilbert, 2000). Any increase in car ownership is likely to result in more urban sprawl, greater consumption of land for transport, and more material consumption overall. Even if technology permits the development of the Eco car,[1] this does not constitute a solution to the problem, as there is still considerable energy tied up with its production over the life of the vehicle. The only solution to sustainable transport in cities is to push hard on a low technology alternative that has a reduction of car ownership at its centre, so that individuals voluntarily give it up.

A powerful argument for this approach is presented by Gilbert (2000), but the mechanisms by which such a change can take place are difficult to envisage in any democratic society. Singapore has come closest to it through rationing the availability of new cars by auctioning the right to own them. The annual auction of the ownership permits only applies to new cars and has the effect of substantially raising the costs of ownership and making it even more exclusive. But even here, the numbers of cars are still increasing, although that increase is at a much lower rate than would be the case under normal market conditions. The alternative might be a more voluntary approach where individuals choose to live in car free locations within cities. Public transport in cities should be of a sufficiently high standard to make car ownership unattractive, particularly if the costs of ownership are high because of the city insurance premiums. Car free developments can mean that no parking space is allocated to the dwelling, or that cars are not permitted on the site at all. The space that would have been allocated to the car can be used for increasing the amount of open space, or to get higher densities on the site. There is a necessary trade-off here between the need to balance open space and homes. Such new thinking makes a clear case for car ownership to be 'voluntarily reduced'.

Car free housing can lead to wider areas of the city being designated as clear zones or areas where only non-polluting forms of transport would be allowed. Electric vehicles would be used within the area, preferably powered from renewable energy sources. All forms of polluting transport would be parked outside the area. Most travel inside would be by walk and bicycle, electric bus and tram, with electric vehicles being used for deliveries and to transport those with some mobility limitation. These areas should provide clear demonstration of the benefits of zero levels of transport pollution, and the quality aspects of city living would be considerably enhanced, as these areas would be both clean and quiet.

It is often argued that mobility should be encouraged and not discouraged, and that there is nothing unsustainable about the growth in long distance travel and the use of resources. In this book we do not take the opposite view, but argue that mobility is essential to current lifestyles and the patterns of production and consumption. It is really a matter of degree and this is why sustainable transport requires action to reduce the need to travel in cities (through development and land-use policies), to make people fully aware of the costs of travel (through fiscal and regulatory policies), and to make full use of the technological options available (through a switch to non-carbon sources of fuel). Sustainable urban development can only be achieved through less travel and better travel, and all three core strategies need to be applied effectively as a package of measures individually designed for each city. So it is not saying that mobility is bad, but that people and firms should be given the opportunity to travel less rather than being 'forced' to travel further.

1.6   The structure of the book

The focus of this book is narrower than these more ambitious objectives. It will concentrate on the links between sustainable urban development and transport. It is not a polemical piece against car ownership and use of the car in the city, as many cities have structured themselves around the use of the car. It is acknowledged that the car has a powerful iconic role in all societies and that we have learned to live with the car. But we also have to live in cities and these urban areas should be accessible and attractive to all residents. This means that we should be designing cities for people, businesses, prosperity and security as well as a high quality environment. Transport plays an essential role in creating the sustainable city, but it should not be the main agent in its destruction. So the question is 'What can transport in all its forms contribute to the sustainable city?'.

The three parts of the book address these issues. The first part places the debate within the global context, highlighting important trends and the background to the importance of sustainable urban development. There is a chapter on the links between sustainability and transport intensity that argues for the decoupling of economic growth from transport growth. The public policy context, in terms of institutional and organizational issues, is complemented by a discussion of the main barriers to implementation. This first part demonstrates the nature and scale of the problems to be addressed, together with some of the difficulties in their resolution. At this point, some might agree that it is too difficult to proceed further and accept that transport in cities can never be made more sustainable.

For the more adventurous, the second part provides the heart of the book, as it presents the three main elements of a transport strategy as it relates to sustainable urban development. There are chapters on urban form and its impacts on travel patterns and on the regulatory and fiscal options available to internalize some of the external costs of transport. It is here that creative combinations of policies can create urban areas that are highly attractive places to live, with spaces that are conducive to walking and cycling. It is also the scale at which innovative forms of public transport can offer a high quality alternative to the car. The important role that technology will play in reducing the dependence of all modes of transport on carbon-based fuels is also covered, as is the potential contribution of information and communications technologies (ICTs) to changing activity patterns and business practices.

There are three main themes in the last part of the book, which is more synthetic. The first provides a clear contrast with the main focus on cities in developed countries, as it covers thinking within cities in developing countries that are now experiencing rapid growth both in population and levels of mobility. Although some signs suggest that they are following the same paths towards motorization, there is also evidence of innovation and the possibility that they might retain a high level of commitment to public transport and providing cities for people. In the second, visioning about the future of the sustainable city provides a longer term perspective, through the application of a backcasting scenario building process. This starts from the premise that the desirable city of the future forms the vision, and transport in its weak and strong sustainability form is then fitted into that vision. The intention here is to show that futures need not be based only on trends, but that they can also be more radical and attractive in their thinking. Finally, an extended conclusion brings all the previous discussion back together, highlighting some of the main challenges presented in this book.

To put this in a slightly different way, the focus on the urban situation is natural as over half the population of the world lives in urban areas (over 25,000 population), and this number is likely to increase to 70 per cent by 2020. Already in the developed countries the levels are above 70 per cent. The argument underlying the book is that the city is central to sustainable development. As the population increases and land becomes scarcer, the most 'efficient' and 'sustainable' development type must be where economies of scale and scope exist through closer proximity, higher densities, and a full range of services, facilities and jobs. Underlying this argument is the important supporting role that transport plays in providing the links between people, firms, services, facilities and jobs. The primary aim is to maintain high levels of accessibility with trip lengths being as short as possible. In this sense sustainable development is not a goal, but a change in direction.

Note

1   The term eco-car is used in this book to describe a small passenger vehicle that is highly efficient and uses alternative fuel sources such as hydrogen and electricity generated from renewable sources. The nearest production vehicle is the hybrid vehicle that combines low energy conventional power with electric power obtained from a dynamo and regenerative energy (from the breaks) – the Toyota Prius. It is similar to what Amory Lovins (www.hypercar.com) and others have called the hyper-car.

Chapter 2

The global picture

2.1 Introduction

Transport is vital to national and international economies and it provides substantial benefits to individuals and businesses, such as its impacts on employment, prices and economic growth at all levels (ECMT, 2000). However, there is also well documented evidence that transport creates substantial externalities through congestion, urban pollution, greenhouse gas emissions, noise, accidents and a multitude of other factors (Banister, 2002*a*; Maddison *et al.*, 1996, and Table 2.1). In addition to the external costs, there are important social and distributional consequences as not everyone has or will ever have equal access to motorized transport. Such a universal requirement is unrealistic, but there are many situations where participation cannot take place because there are no adequate transport services. Subsidies to the individual or the service can be provided, but this may not help the objective of sustainability (Button and Rietveld, 2002). More recently, there has been an increasing concern over the health effects of transport-induced pollution, particularly in urban areas, and it is argued that these negative effects particularly impact on the low-income population as they suffer greater exposure to these effects (Social Exclusion Unit, 2002). Within the framework of sustainable development, it is important to balance the positive role of transport in contributing to the economic (and leisure) prosperity with these negative factors relating to the environmental, social and health implications. There are no simple solutions to these conflicting factors, but it is necessary to establish the basic parameters of the debate. To help in giving a flavour of the main aspects, two propositions will be discussed in this chapter.

2.2 Proposition 1 – Transport is unsustainable

Travel patterns in most developed countries are increasingly dependent on the car. Levels of mobility and car ownership have risen substantially over the recent past and that increase seems likely to continue to rise. In the EU15 there was an increase of over 31 per cent in the numbers of vehicles owned (1984– 1994), and it is likely that in the next 25 years (to 2020) that number will increase by a further 50 per cent (OECD, 1995).[1] By 2001, the level of vehicle

Table 2.1 Environmental impacts of transport in the United Kingdom

Environmental media	Environmental impacts	Transport's contribution (1995 unless otherwise stated)
Energy and mineral resources	› Energy resources used for transport (mainly oil-based) › Extraction of infrastructure construction materials	› 44.8 million tonnes of petroleum consumed by transport. › transport accounts for approximately one-third of the UK's total energy consumption › approximately 120,000 tonnes of aggregates per kilometre of 3-lane motorway › 78 million tonnes of roadstone extracted
Land resources	› Land used for infrastructure	› approximately 4.2 hectares of land per kilometre of 3-lane motorway › 1,725 hectares of rural land developed for transport and utilities per annum (1992)
Water resources	› Surface and groundwater pollution by surface run-off › Changes to water systems by infrastructure construction › Pollution from oil spillage	› 25 per cent of water pollution incidents in England and Wales caused by oil › 585 oil spills reported in the UK › 142 oil spills requiring clean up in the UK
Air quality	› Global pollutants (such as carbon dioxide) › Local pollutants (such as carbon monoxide, nitrogen oxides, particulate matter, volatile organic compounds)	› 25 per cent of the UK's carbon dioxide emissions (CO_2) › 76 per cent of the UK's emissions of carbon monoxide (CO) › 56 per cent of the UK's emissions of nitrogen oxides (NO_x) › 51 per cent of the UK's emissions of black smoke (particulates) › 40 per cent of UK emissions of volatile organic compounds (VOCs)
Solid waste	› Scrapped vehicles › Waste oil and tyres	› approximately 1.5 million vehicles scrapped › more than 40 million scrapped tyres
Biodiversity	› Partition or destruction of wildlife habitats from infrastructure construction	
Noise and vibration	› Noise and vibration near main roads, railway lines and airports	› approximately 3,500 complaints about noise from road traffic › approximately 6,500 complaints about noise from air traffic
Built environment	› Structural damage to infrastructure (e.g. road surfaces, bridges) › Property damage from accidents › Building corrosion from local pollutants	› more than £15 million annual road damage costs
Health	› Deaths and injuries from road accidents › Noise disturbance › Illness and premature death from local pollutants	› 3,500 deaths (2001) › 44,000 serious injuries (2001) › 49 per cent of people who can hear noise from aircraft or trains consider it a nuisance (1991) › 63 per cent of people who can hear noise from road traffic consider it a nuisance (1991) › between 12,000 and 24,000 premature deaths due to air pollution (2001) › between 14,000 and 24,000 hospital admissions and re-admissions may be associated with air pollution (2001)

Sources: Banister (1998a); Central Statistical Office (1997); Committee on the Medical Effects of Air Pollutants (1998); Department of the Environment, Transport and the Regions (1997d, e, f and g); Department of Trade and Industry (1997); Maddison *et al.* (1996); OECD (1988) and Royal Commission on Environmental Pollution (1994).

ownership in the EU15 had reached 629 vehicles per 1000 population (238 million vehicles for 378 million population), similar to the mid 1980s levels in the United States. Road capacity will not increase by the same amount, so congestion will grow, particularly in the cities. The car brings many benefits to the individual user, but its wider social costs present a fundamental challenge to sustainable urban development.

At present, about 70 per cent of all vehicles are in OECD countries, with the remaining 30 per cent being in the emerging and developing countries. However, over the next 25 years, the distribution will change as the number of vehicles increases by a further 75 per cent (to 2020), and as 43 per cent of vehicles will now be in the emerging and developing countries (Table 2.2).

Several important points relate to this table. Cars account for about 60 per cent of all vehicles in both 1995 and 2020, but they are more important in the OECD countries. In the emerging and developing countries light trucks (15 per cent) and motorcycles (32 per cent) form important elements in the vehicle fleet. In the year 2005, the global numbers of vehicles will exceed 1000 million for the first time, and before 2030 the number of vehicles in non-OECD countries will exceed that of the OECD countries. The scale of the problem is vast and increasing.

There are key differences in the problem of transport in the OECD and the non-OECD countries. In developing economies, cities are coping with rapid motorization (10–15 per cent per annum) and an urban population that is growing by 6 per cent per annum (World Bank, 1996). At comparable levels of income, industrial countries have few cars, but in developing countries car

Table 2.2 Expected growth in worldwide vehicle ownership and traffic

Thousands	1995		2020	
	Cars	Vehicles	Cars	Vehicles
OECD North America	170,460	231,557	247,328	335,056
Europe	160,215	203,429	244,720	300,054
Pacific	52,654	101,188	82,193	147,251
Total OECD	383,329	536,174	574,241	782,361
Rest of world	111,255	240,357	283,349	580,288
Global totals	494,584	776,531	857,590	1,362,649
Vehicle-kilometres – billions	7,792	12,341	13,569	21,953

Notes: All vehicles include cars, light trucks, motorcycles and heavy trucks.
OECD North America – US, Canada;
OECD Europe – Austria, Belgium, Denmark, France, Germany, Greece, Iceland, Ireland, Italy, Luxembourg, The Netherlands, Norway, Portugal, Spain, Sweden, Switzerland, Turkey, UK, Finland;
OECD Pacific – Japan, Australia, New Zealand.
Mexico is a member of OECD (since 1994) but is excluded from these OECD figures
Source: OECD (1995).

ownership rates are much higher. There is also less road space available. For example, in Bangkok and Calcutta 7–11 per cent of urban space is devoted to transport activities, but the corresponding figures in European cities are 20–25 per cent and over 30 per cent in Manhattan (World Bank, 1996).

This means that city roads in developing countries are more congested at lower levels of car ownership. Slow moving traffic and ill maintained vehicles cause greater levels of pollution than that experienced from more efficient modern vehicles operating in less congested conditions. High land and housing costs in central areas contribute to sprawling, land-consuming cities with long and slow journeys to and from work, often taking over five hours a day. This is the classic 'Bangkok Effect' where congestion and pollution are so bad that vehicles are 'abandoned' on roads as it is quicker to walk (Table 2.2).

2.3   Proposition 2 – Sustainable urban development is dependent upon the city being the centre of vitality, opportunity and wealth, and that transport has a major role to play

Society is becoming more urbanized and we have now reached the point where over half the world's population of 6 billion people live in cities (2000, EC, 2003). The number of people living in cities is growing at a rate of 60 million a year, and the level of urbanization will continue to increase, as the urban population will rise to over 61 per cent in 2025 (UNCHS, 1996). This growth is distributed unevenly over the world, and it is in the cities of the developing world that urbanization is taking place at the most rapid rate. In the northern cities, this transformation has already been seen as some 80 per cent of the population is living in cities, with the tendency now to move out from the larger urban areas to smaller places. Much of the current thinking is looking at the means by which population can be attracted back into the cities.

The scale of the changes taking place is only now being fully appreciated. Although the growth rates of urban population are declining from 3.8 per cent (1980–1985) to 2.9 per cent (2000–2005), this still means a doubling of city population every 25 years. In 1995, there were some six cities with populations over 15 million, led by Tokyo with its massive 27 million population, and a further nine cities with populations over 10 million. By 2015, it is expected that there will be 27 cities with populations over 10 million, seven of which will have reached 20 million (UNCHS, 1996). Eighteen of these cities will be in Asia, five in South America, two in North America and two in Africa. There will be none in Europe.

In addition to these individual cities, many will effectively join to form new agglomeration cities, which although having their own identity will be networked giving total populations of over 30 million. This does not mean that the built up area is continuous, as the distances between them are still substantial, but that they are becoming hugely attractive growth centres for investment and migration. The Pearl River Delta linking Hong Kong with Guangzhou is the best known example (Hall and Pfeiffer, 2000), but others include the Jakarta to Surabaya corridor in Indonesia, the east coast of Japan from Tokyo through Nagoya to Osaka, and the axis between Sao Paulo and Rio de Janeiro in Brazil. It is not just in the megacities that the growth in urban population is taking place, but across cities of all sizes. It is in the cities that jobs are located and where investment is taking place. But it does seem that the largest cities may grow at the expense of the smaller ones, at least in terms of human capital, as the best educated tend to migrate to the largest centres.

Cities have witnessed the four great transformations that have swept society over the last two hundred years, with the industrial revolution, followed by transport and telecommunications innovations, the switch to democracy, and the most recent development of the network society, with most jobs and wealth being created in the service and information sectors. It is not surprising that most of these developments have been concentrated in the cities, which themselves have become the key nodes in the global systems that are both interactive and interdependent. Although economies are now global, and the levels of communication and interaction required to service them have grown exponentially, there still seem to be strong arguments for agglomeration economies, as businesses are dependent on each other. There is still a requirement for face-to-face contact, and travel is easier over shorter rather than longer distances.

These trends provide an important framework within which to place the second proposition. The global trend towards urbanization and economic factors promoting agglomeration should support sustainable urban development. In addition to the city being the centre of vitality, opportunity and wealth, it is the necessary supporting infrastructure (water, waste, electricity, communications, and transport) that also needs to be provided so that the city can 'work'. The underlying argument here is that it is only in the city that these high levels of accessibility and proximity can be maintained, at a reasonable cost.

2.4 The ten principles of sustainable development and transport

Current trends in transport and the growing dependence on the car (and air travel) constitute one of the main challenges to sustainable development. Conventionally, there are seven key issues that need to be addressed if transport is to conform to the principles of sustainable development (EFTE, 1994; Banister, 1997a).

1   Growing congestion in many urban areas has been increasing in its

duration and intensity. On average, speeds in cities have been declining by about 5 per cent per decade (EFTE, 1994), and the severity of congestion increases with city size (Dasgupta, 1993).

2   Increasing air pollution has resulted in national air quality standards and those recommended by the World Health Organization being exceeded in many cities. Air pollution affects health, impairs visibility, and damages buildings and local ecology – it reduces the quality of urban life.

3   Traffic noise affects all city life and it is estimated by the OECD/ECMT (1995) that about 15 per cent of the population in developed countries is exposed to high levels of noise, mainly generated by traffic. Disturbance is also caused by vibration, particularly from heavy lorries, and night time deliveries.

4   Road safety is a major concern in cities and elsewhere. Worldwide, traffic accidents result in 250,000 deaths and about 10 million injuries each year (Downey, 1995). The accident rates are now declining in some countries (with high levels of motorization), but increasing in others (with low levels of motorization). This is a very high cost 'accepted' by society.

5   Degradation of urban landscapes results from the construction of new roads and transport facilities, the demolition of historic buildings, and reductions in open space. Transport contributes to the decaying urban fabric and neglect of central city areas, as well as urban sprawl (Ewing, 1997).

6   Use of space by traffic facilitates the movement of the motorist, but reduces the accessibility of others as transport routes become barriers, as parked vehicles form obstacles for pedestrians, cyclists and those with disabilities. Car dependency results in traffic domination in urban areas, sometimes splitting communities.

7   Global warming results from the use of fossils fuels. Transport (2001) accounts for 28.9 per cent of CO_2 emissions and this level is rising in relative terms as well as in absolute quantities. Transport is almost wholly dependent on oil, and this is a non-renewable energy source.

In addition, transport has also facilitated changes in the city, and three land-use and development factors need to be added to the list above.

8   Decentralization of cities has been facilitated by the car, in combination with efficient public transport. This has resulted in a substantial growth in trip lengths and patterns that are dispersed rather than concentrated on the city centre. This in turn increases car dependence and reduces the possibilities of promoting efficient public transport.

9   Development pressures have taken place around car accessible

locations which are not accessible to all people (including the edge city developments). The spatial segregation of activities in urban areas again increases trip lengths and has strong distributional consequences. High land and property prices are symbolic of a buoyant economy, but they are also socially exclusive, particularly in terms of access to low-cost city centre housing.

10 Globalization and the relocation of industry (including the information economy) have resulted in new patterns of distribution and the transport intensity of freight has increased globally, regionally and locally.

Policy options on transport in most OECD countries have changed substantially over the last 20 years with the realization that the road building option is no longer the solution to congestion, and even if it were the environmental and social costs are too high. In advanced economies with extensive road networks, additional links have only a marginal effect on accessibility (Banister and Berechman, 2000). Demand management, combined with strong policies to promote public transport and the concentration of development will both reduce congestion and have environmental and social benefits. This is the key to sustainable development.

In the non-OECD countries the situation is different as the high quality basic infrastructure is not yet available, so any new investment in roads may have a major impact on accessibility, with markets being flooded by non-local products. The case for new road construction is stronger in these countries and cities, but again it must be placed within the context of a policy towards sustainable development that also builds upon the city as the key element. It is not possible or desirable in the non-OECD countries to accommodate the expected growth in demand for car travel. Even if it were possible, it would necessitate massive reconstruction of existing cities, as road space would need to be expanded.

To establish a policy that addresses the ten principles of sustainable development listed above, there are seven basic objectives to be met:

1 reduce the need to travel;
2 reduce the absolute levels of car use and road freight in urban areas;
3 promote more energy efficient modes of travel for both passenger and freight;
4 reduce noise and vehicle emissions at sources;
5 encourage a more efficient and environmentally sensitive use of the vehicle stock;
6 improve safety of pedestrians and all road users;
7 improve the attractiveness of cities for residents, workers, shoppers and visitors.

This list (based on OECD/ECMT, 1995, pp. 133–134) would tackle the problems of congestion, air pollution, noise, safety, degradation of urban landscapes, the use of space, and global warming. In addition, objective 1 would help reduce city decentralization, whilst objective 7 would in part address the question of development pressures. The more general economic context of globalization is really external to the objectives set here. The land-use and planning strategies have a clear potential to reduce the need to travel, and both transport and land-use policies will help reduce the absolute levels of car use and promote the use of more environmentally friendly transport. Targets and standards are important tools to tackle noise and emissions at source. Road safety and the attractiveness of cities can again be addressed by transport and land-use policies, as well as by the application of targets and standards (OECD/ECMT, 1995).

The potential for change is clearly there, at least in theory. But any review of the trends and actions would suggest that in practice the achievement of sustainable development objectives listed above has been very limited. The need to travel has not been reduced, nor has there been any evidence of reductions in the use of cars and lorries. Promotion of public transport has taken place in many cities with high quality services being provided and patronage levels have increased. But, even here, the costs have been high as subsidy levels have risen and as the new patronage has come from cycling and walking. Noise levels have remained unchanged as reductions at source have been balanced by increases in traffic. Emissions levels have been substantially reduced through the use of catalytic converters, but CO_2 levels have increased as this is related directly to the carbon content of the fuel. There are only limited examples of forms of road pricing to reduce the use of the car.[2] Many countries have high levels of fuel taxation, typically set at 75–85 per cent of the pump prices. Although this level of pricing reduces consumption, it is primarily a means to raise revenues for the national Treasuries. Load factors in cars and lorries have declined, whilst high occupancy vehicle lanes have proved only a limited success. Road safety is one area of success, but even here it is limited to certain countries, often with high levels of motorization. The number of pedestrian casualties related to other accidents involving road users has also been increasing. Policies to promote city centres are taking place to produce multi-centre structures within a metropolitan region, and this may be reducing levels of out-migration, as regeneration and new development takes place.

This brief (and general) assessment makes disappointing reading but, with the exception of a limited number of cities, little progress has been made towards sustainable development and transport. Any improvement has been more than outweighed by the underlying growth in car-based mobility. There is a series of constraints that need to be addressed if a clear strategy on transport and sustainable development is to be established.

1   New organizational and institutional structures need to be established so that the appropriate powers and responsibilities can be allocated. This involves both the public and private sectors, and approaches that are multi-sector based. It also means that the support of the general public, industry (including the motor industry), commerce, business, and governments must be present (Chapters 4 and 5).

2   Policies have often been introduced as single stand-alone elements, with no clear perspective on how they link together to form a strategy. To achieve sustainable development requires a clear statement of policy, together with achievable objectives (and targets) over a period of time. Within the transport sector, this could be taken as no increase in non-renewable energy consumption as this will stabilize levels of CO_2 emissions. But if the tougher targets for global stabilization are set, then the OECD countries will have to accept substantial reductions as the non-OECD countries increase their output (Chapters 6 and 7).

3   Most progress has (naturally) been made on policies that have promoted public transport and those that have allocated new investment and development. To achieve sustainable development requires difficult as well as easy decisions to be made. The hardest decision is the role that the car should play in its current 'polluting form' and in its future 'non-polluting form' in our cities (Chapters 8 and 9).

4   More generally, we need to develop a set of visions as to how we see cities in the future. With the growth in population, the city must remain the focus of human activity with some 70–80 per cent of the world's population living in cities. Within the changing global economy, we must visualize the sustainable city of the future in terms of qualities such as density, mixed use, intensity of development, open space, safety and security, environmental priorities, the costs of living, housing type, function and vitality. Within that vision, a role for transport can be established (Chapter 11).

2.5 Global trends and key concepts

From this general analysis of the problem and the important principles that have been established, we can now focus on the key trends. The 'driving force' is car ownership growth and the increase in demand for travel. From this starting point, there are consequences for energy consumption and CO_2 emissions, as well as local air quality. This in turn has distributional consequences, both globally, and for the city. Finally, the resolution has to be examined in terms of what technology and reduced levels of growth in travel can offer.

2.5.1   Growth in car ownership and travel

Rising levels of income and affluence, the dispersal of urban activities, and the growth in urban population have all contributed to the doubling of levels of car ownership and travel (1975–1995). This growth has been compounded by the low costs of using the car and the perceived advantages inherent in the car. Similar trends can be observed in the freight sector. One of the fundamental 'laws' used in much of transport forecasting has been the close link between travel growth and increases in GDP. Recently, however, travel has been increasing at a rate substantially higher than GDP growth (in the OECD countries, GDP growth 1970–1990 was 2.8 per cent per annum, traffic growth was 3.3 per cent per annum, and car ownership increased by 3.5 per cent per annum – OECD/ECMT, 1995). Transport intensity has increased substantially (Chapter 3). Over the next 25 years (to 2020), we are likely to see a further increase of 75 per cent in car ownership levels and a growth of 56 per cent in traffic levels globally (Table 2.2). In developed countries, there is some stability in the patterns of travel, with car ownership expected to increase by 45 per cent (North America) and 54 per cent in the other OECD countries. But it is in the rest of the world where the real growth will take place (+155 per cent, Table 2.2). The corresponding growth figures for vehicle ownership are 45 per cent, 47 per cent, and 141 per cent in North America, the rest of the OECD and the rest of the world, respectively.

2.5.2   Energy consumption and CO_2 emissions

The same patterns are reflected in energy consumption and emissions of CO_2, which is directly linked to fuel consumption. In 1990, the 65 EJ[3] consumed by transport is heavily concentrated in 23 countries. The United States consumes 20.3 EJ (31.2 per cent of the total), followed by Russia 3.5 EJ (5.4 per cent), Japan 3.2 EJ (4.9 per cent) and Germany 2.5 per cent EJ (3.8 per cent). Nine[4] other countries consume between 1.0 and 1.9 EJ (20.5 per cent), and a further seven countries have levels of consumption over 0.4 EJ (6.1 per cent). The rest of the world (over 100 countries) consumes just 12.1 per cent of transport energy use (Michaelis *et al.*, 1996). The vast majority of that energy use (80 per cent) is for road transport, with air travel accounting for a further 13 per cent, rail 4.4 per cent, and inland water transport 2.6 per cent. The fastest growing sectors are road (+2.4 per cent per annum) and air (+6 per cent per annum, although recently this level of growth has halved). The focus here is on the urban scale and sustainable road transport, so only limited coverage is made of air travel, which must also make a substantial contribution to energy and emissions reductions (Chapter 7.6).

Two-thirds of transport energy consumption was in just thirteen countries and the US alone accounts for over one-third of all consumption (1990). Most countries were committed to stabilization of CO_2 emissions at 1990 levels by the year 2000 (the Rio Summit, 1992). Only two countries in the EU actually met that stabilization target. Germany achieved it through unification, and the UK achieved it through the coincidental switch from coal power generation. In both cases, reductions have taken place in other sectors (e.g. energy, housing, and industry), but in the transport sector there has been a steady increase in the consumption of oil and in the levels of global emissions. Outside the EU, other countries have achieved stabilization through the contraction of their economies (e.g. the former Soviet Union). The Rio agreement had no legal status for those countries that failed to achieve the stabilization targets.

As part of the more recent Kyoto Protocol (1997), some countries (e.g. UK and the Netherlands) have committed themselves to reductions of 20 per cent over the next 20 years, with a more general target in the EU15 of 15 per cent (to 2010) (Table 2.3). This will be increasingly difficult to achieve as transport will have to take a much larger share of any reduction. The US with 5 per cent of the world population produces 24.2 per cent of greenhouse gas emissions (2000). The US Government has renounced the Kyoto Protocol and is in favour of a much looser objective to achieve stabilization between 2008 and 2012. But even here there is no commitment from the US. The Kyoto Protocol (Fact Box 2.1) set a range of mandatory targets for the 40 Annex 1 countries, ranging from a reduction of 8 per cent in CO_2 emissions in the EU, 7 per cent in the United States, and 6 per cent in Canada, to an increase in other countries (Table 2.3). The US target means the 5.8 billion tonnes of carbon (1990) should be reduced to 5.4 billion tonnes (2010). But the expectation now is that the level in 2010 will be 7.4 billion tonnes (+24 per cent), and through using best available technology this might be reduced to 6.6 billion tonnes (+14 per cent) (Dobes, 1999).

Fact Box 2.1   Kyoto 1997

The Kyoto Protocol lists 40 Annex 1 countries and their 'quantified emission limitation or reduction commitment' as a percentage of the base year (1990). Each country is expected to reduce its own emissions levels by an agreed amount (Table 2.3) by the 'commitment period' of 2008–2012 – this is a mandatory target.

Overall, the 40 countries are to reduce CO_2 equivalent emissions of six specified greenhouse gases by 5.2 per cent below 1990 levels. The six greenhouse gases are carbon dioxide (CO_2), methane (CH_4), nitrous oxide (N_2O), hydrofluorocarbons (HFCs), perfluorocarbons (PFCs), and sulphur hexafluoride (SF_6). All are radiatively active as they are direct greenhouse gases that absorb infrared radiation from the Earth (as a result of warming from solar radiation), and then re-emit it upwards (and ultimately out of the Earth's atmosphere) and downwards to heat the atmosphere (the warming effect) (Dobes, 1999).

continued on page 22

continued from page 21

The Protocol will enter into force 90 days after 55 countries have ratified it. This must include sufficient Annex 1 countries so that at least 55 per cent of the 1990 greenhouse emissions are accounted for. Russia signed in November 2004, meaning that the threshold has now been exceeded (63 per cent in total), and the Protocol came into operation on 16th February 2005.

The UN Environment Programme suggests that economic damage from global warming is doubling every decade and that climate-related disasters are occurring with an increasing frequency.

Carbon Dioxide Emissions – tonnes CO_2 per person

	1990	2000	% change		1990	2000	% change
USA	19.30	20.57	+7%	Japan	8.25	9.10	+10%
Australia	15.20	17.90	+18%	UK	9.73	8.89	-9%
Canada	15.53	17.13	+10%	China	2.01	2.37	+18%
Germany	12.15	10.14	-17%	Brazil	1.31	1.78	+36%
				India	0.69	0.92	+33%

Source: IEA (2002).

CO_2 from transport increased globally from 19.3 per cent to 22.7 per cent in the 1990s (+18 per cent), and this figure is expected to further increase to 26 per cent by 2010 (+34 per cent since 1997).

Since April 2004, the 1997 Kyoto Protocol is legally binding on all EU Member States – it relates mainly to the monitoring and reporting of emissions, and it reaffirms the EU's leadership in fighting climate change and implementing the Protocol.

Source: UNFCCC (2003).

There is a basic divergence of views between Europe and the United States. The European view is that global warming is a real issue and that the precautionary principle should be adopted now with clear targets being set, that are tough yet achievable. Europe should take the lead. The US view is that global warming is not proven and no real action is needed now. In the near future technology will 'solve' the global warming issue. Even though the new (2004) US government is now beginning to acknowledge the problem, they are under considerable pressure from industry not to 'act hastily'.

The contribution made by transport to the Kyoto Protocol will be minimal as growth in demand continues. Although technology has a major role to play in reducing emissions generally, CO_2 is directly related to the carbon content of the fuel, and at present there is no known technological fix available. Technology can help in reducing levels of emissions from other pollutants. More efficient engines will help, but this is again outweighed by the growth in the number of vehicles and travel. In 2020 the same oil-based technology will still be in use, even though alternatives (e.g. electric cars using renewable energy and fuel cell vehicles) will also be available. Alternative fuels can reduce reliance on oil (e.g. ethanol), and other sources (e.g. compressed natural gas and liquid petroleum gas) have lower levels of carbon content, but the scale and time necessary for a significant change in the vehicle fleet means that environmental targets cannot be met by technology alone.

It takes 10 years to change production processes and another 15 years to replace the existing car fleet. There is too much inertia in the system, and with

Table 2.3　The good guys and the bad guys

		Tonnes CO_2 per person per year from Transport 1998	Percentage change 1990–1998	Kyoto Target (1990–2010) for reductions in greenhouse gas emissions
Bad guys	USA	5.967	+13.7%	−7%
>3 tonnes/person/year	Canada	5.867	+19.5%	−6%
	Australia	3.802	+15.5%	+8%
	Norway	3.198	+18.0%	+1%
	New Zealand	3.176	+32.0%	No change
2–3 tonnes/person/year	Ireland	2.505	+76.8%	+13%
	Belgium	2.445	+19.9%	−7.5%
OECD average =	Finland	2.412	−1.5%	0%
2.555 tonnes	Sweden	2.402	+13.4%	+4%
	Denmark	2.388	+15.6%	−21%
EU15 average =	France	2.367	+13.8%	0%
2.183 tonnes	Netherlands	2.226	+21.6%	−6%
	Germany	2.206	+11.5%	−21%
	UK	2.115	+5.3%	−12.5%
	Austria	2.068	+23.5%	−13%
	Switzerland	2.040	+3.9%	−8%
	Japan	2.005*	+22.2%*	−6%
1–2 tonnes/person/year	Spain	1.975	+35.1%	+15%
	Italy	1.926	+15.2%	−6.5%
	Greece	1.885	+28.8%	+25%
	Portugal	1.651	+41.8%	+27%
	Czech Republic	1.056	+35.4%	−8%
	Lithuania	1.015	−35.0%	−8%
Good Guys	Latvia	0.850	−63.0%	−8%
<1 tonnes/person/year	Hungary	0.838	+8.3%	–
	Estonia	0.824	−54.0%	–
	Bulgaria	0.762	−49.0%	–
	Poland	0.729	–	−6%
	Slovakia	0.600	–	–

Notes:　* 1997 figures.

Included in this list are 29 of the 37 countries agreeing to specific targets at Kyoto (Turkey and Mexico have no specific targets from Kyoto). The missing Kyoto signatories are Iceland, Slovenia, Russia, Mexico, Turkey, Romania, Ukraine, Croatia, Monaco and Luxembourg. The overall target for Kyoto was 5.2 per cent reduction 1990–2008/12 for the thirty-nine developed countries.

The EU target of 8 per cent reduction is for the 15 countries as a whole and these have been reallocated as shown above.

Source: UN Environment Programme (2002).

the cascading of current day technologies to developing countries, the time necessary to move to lean-burn technologies on a global scale is substantial. Interventions such as pricing may help, but the effectiveness of such actions are limited as elasticities of demand are low and as the world economic system has developed with high levels of transport intensity, which in turn is based on the availability of cheap fuel (Schipper *et al.*, 1993; Scholl *et al.*, 1994).

The recent concern about global warming and the substantial (and growing) impact that transport has had on the emission of CO_2 is a new dimension that requires a fundamental rethinking of the ways in which we carry out our activities at all levels (global, national, regional, and local). This may seem to be a problem with no solution. Hence the interest in demonstrating that there is uncertainty over the causes and effects of global warming, and in pushing environmental issues (particularly difficult ones) down the political agenda.

2.5.3   Air quality

At the urban level, there is a range of pollutants which cause poor air quality and health problems, and transport is a major contributor to this pollution.

Nitrogen oxides when combined with other air pollutants can lead to respiratory difficulties and reduced lung function, particularly in urban areas. Volatile organic compounds and NO_x are the principal components of ground level ozone, the major constituent of smog. It is formed in the lower atmosphere by a photochemical reaction promoted by heat and sunlight. Transport accounts for about 65 per cent of NO_x emissions in the EU15 (1999) and its share is rising as stationary sources are now producing less pollution.

Volatile organic compounds (VOCs) comprise a wide variety of hydrocarbons and other substances (e.g. methane and ethylene) that result from the incomplete combustion of fossil fuels. When combined with NO_x in heat and sunlight, hydrocarbons and VOCs generate ground level ozone, a main contributor to photochemical smog. Their impact has a measurable effect on respiratory functions and as an irritation, with transport contributing about 37 per cent of the total levels in the EU15 (1999), but these levels are declining as technologies improve (EC, 2003).

Carbon monoxide is an odourless and colourless gas, which is very toxic as it combines with haemoglobin thus inhibiting the absorption of oxygen. This in turn can lead to increased morbidity and can affect fertility and general levels of health. It is particularly dangerous in urban areas where 'cocktails' of pollutants result in photochemical smog and surface ozone. About 64 per cent of the EU15 CO comes from the transport sector, again principally from the incomplete combustion of fuel, but this level is reducing (EC, 2003).

Particulates, particularly those very small particles under 10 microns in diameter (PM_{10}) from diesel fuels, are the focus of current concern. The level of detailed knowledge of the science of particulates is not well known, but it can worsen heart and breathing problems for sensitive groups and may lead to premature mortality.

Benzene and 1,3-butadiene are both classified as 'probable' carcinogens and may cause leukaemia in those with high levels of exposure.

Other pollutants (e.g. lead and sulphur dioxide) also have transport connections, but are less important than those listed above, as they are being reduced through the switch to different and 'cleaner' fuels (British Medical Association, 1997).

Add-on technology (principally the catalytic converter), cleaner fuels, and more efficient and lighter vehicles will all help reduce the levels of these pollutants from petrol engine vehicles by 80 per cent. However, there are questions not only about whether the technology is working efficiently but also the rate of change in the existing vehicle fleet, particularly in those cities with the most rapid rise in car ownership. The potential benefits are substantially reduced when set against the expected growth in numbers of cars, traffic and congestion, so the achievement of half this level in cities is more realistic. There are still concerns over whether the same levels of air quality improvement can be achieved through the add-on technology in diesel vehicles, and only a 40 per cent reduction seems likely (in NO_x, CO, VOC and PM_{10}). Nevertheless, it is important that the best add-on technology is used in all possible situations,

The belief that add-on technology can 'solve' the air quality issue is too simple. As noted above, there are important limitations relating to whether the catalytic converters are working, whether diesel emissions can be controlled effectively, the time taken for all vehicles to be fitted, and the slow switch to alternative fuels. When set against the growth in car ownership and use, the catalytic converter really only gives a maximum of 10 years 'breathing space' before pollution levels start to rise again. In the US, for example, the catalytic converter has been compulsory since 1979 and so the full benefits have already worked their way into the entire car fleet. The CO_2 problem has not been addressed, as increased vehicle efficiency is not apparent in the vehicles stock (Acutt and Dodgson, 1998).

2.5.4 Distributional and equity issues

A further complication is the uneven distribution of the use of energy in transport across the world. If we set a global target (as was suggested at the 1992 Rio Summit) of stabilization of CO_2 emissions over the period from

1990–2020, the implications are not encouraging. Over the 30-year period, it is likely that vehicle ownership will double from 650 million vehicles to over 1300 million vehicles (Table 2.2), with the greatest part of that increase being concentrated in the non-OECD countries. It should also be noted that cities in developing countries are growing fast (3–4 per cent per annum – see Chapter 3), mainly as a result of inward migration. Car ownership is also growing rapidly at about 6 per cent per annum. At comparable levels of income, cities in developing countries have higher levels of car ownership and higher levels of congestion than cities in the developed world.

To achieve global stabilization targets, it is necessary to allow developing countries and emerging countries to increase their output of CO_2 so that development can take place. It is only when a sufficient level of development is reached that countries 'flip' from being developing or emerging economies to a developed economy. At this stage, it would be expected that these newly developed countries would then contribute to the stabilization process by levelling off and then reducing their CO_2 emissions, particularly in the transport sector. The net effect of this argument is that the existing developed countries (the OECD) must reduce their CO_2 emissions levels now to allow the developing and emerging countries to increase their emissions so that the global target can be reached. The implications of this argument are profound and the scale of changes required is substantial (Table 2.4).

With no intervention and current targets, it means that CO_2 emissions in the transport sector will increase by 40 per cent globally. It is assumed that the United States and Canada can achieve a stabilization target, and that the other OECD countries make a 15 per cent reduction, as was suggested by some politicians at the Rio +5 Conference in New York (1997). If a global stabilization target is imposed and the emerging and developing countries are allowed to increase their output of CO_2 but at a reduced level of the current targets, then the OECD countries must have a major reduction target imposed – the figure suggested here is 50 per cent.

Although the assumptions can be manipulated in a variety of ways, the underlying message is the same. Even with the current targets in the transport sector, there will be a substantial increase in CO_2 emissions to 2020, resulting mainly from the continued worldwide growth in car ownership, particularly in those countries that currently have low levels of ownership. To achieve a stabilization target, the OECD countries must reduce their emissions by about 50 per cent from over 60 per cent (1990) to about 30 per cent (2020) of the global total. This will allow the emerging and developing countries to increase their emissions levels over this period to assist their economic development so that they in turn can switch to a developed status and then contribute to the reduction target. Not all countries will achieve the switch status by 2020, and some will get there before 2020. The key question is whether the

Table 2.4 Targets required to stabilize global CO$_2$ emissions in transport 1990–2020

Emissions measured in millions of tonnes of carbon	1990 Emissions	%	Current targets	2020 Emissions	%	Stabilization	Emissions	%
USA and Canada	440	35	−1%	435	25	−50%	220	18
EU and other OECD	340	27	−15%	290	17	−50%	170	14
Emerging countries	160	13	+60%	255	15	+50%	240	18
Developing countries	310	25	+150%	775	44	+100%	620	50
Total CO$_2$ emissions	1250		+40%	1755		+0%	1250	

Notes:
(a) Figures are all approximate – the stabilization figures are illustrative of the scale of change required in the four country groupings if a global zero increase target is to be achieved.
(b) It has been assumed that the transport sector has to make a full contribution and cannot be 'subsidized' by other sectors.
(c) It has been assumed that the increases in car ownership will take place as described in Table 2.2. The OECD countries are also listed in Table 2.2. The emerging countries are the middle income group of about 1.5 billion population and an average GNP of $3000 per person (1999). Developing Countries are the poorest 42 countries with 3.5 billion population and an average GNP of about $500 per person (1999).
(d) The current targets are optimistic and in line with the Environmentally Compatible Energy Strategies (ECS). The Intergovernmental Panel on Climate Change – Energy Industry System (IPCC-EIS) suggest there will be a doubling of carbon emissions with no action (1990–2020).
(e) The US and Canada have a weighted figure of 1% to acknowledge the 6% target in Canada and the 0% target in the US – weighted for the relative size of the transport sectors in both countries.

Source: Based on Michaelis *et al.* (1996) figure 21.2.

OECD countries, in particular the US, would contemplate reductions of 50 per cent in their emissions levels. If not, then the global stabilization target is impossible, at least in the transport sector.

A similar approach would be the contraction and convergence argument, as proposed by Meyer (2001). Here it is accepted that there is some right to emit CO$_2$ and that this right should be allocated to all equally. Three stages are identified in the process:

1   Agreement on a maximum level of CO$_2$ emissions globally before environmental damage becomes too great and irreversible damage is done, and when this will occur;

2   Estimation of the proportion of the gas that is retained in the atmosphere so that the speed at which reduction has to take place to meet the deadline can be determined.

3   Allocation of fossil fuel consumption levels nationally so that the agreed targets can be reached at the allotted times.

Such an approach is premised on the ability to get global agreement and to involve all nations. This proved enormously difficult in Kyoto (1997). But it then allows flexibility and market mechanisms to work as there would be trading between the richer countries and the poorer ones, as the polluters pay for the other's allocations. Meyer suggests that the flow of funds from the rich to the poor countries should not be related to debt relief, and that such an approach should encourage the poorer countries to run their economies efficiently to maintain the inward flow of funds from the richer countries. It would also provide the necessary boost for the richer countries to develop sophisticated environmental technologies. The overall limits set can be reduced over time to ensure that agreed (or subsequently changed) targets are met. However, it does require all nations to participate and a willingness to co-operate through a long-term commitment to stabilization and reduction targets.

There are similarities between the flip theory and the contraction and convergence theory, as both involve all nations, with the developed countries stabilizing and reducing their emissions now, and the developing countries increasing their emissions in the short term. The key to both approaches is the requirement for global and individual targets that can then be translated into programmes of carbon reduction strategies at the national and city levels.

If a slightly longer term view is taken, the actions required also increase substantially. The World Wildlife Fund report (WWF, 2001) has concluded that in the UK, CO_2 emissions will stabilize if the average fuel efficiency of the vehicle stock is increased from 31 to 60 miles per gallon (11 to 20 kilometres per litre). Globally, this means that the vehicle stock should increase efficiency to 150 miles per gallon (50 kilometres per litre) by 2020 to cut CO_2 emissions by 40 per cent, thus making a substantial contribution to that 2050 target of a 60 per cent reduction in CO_2 emissions (this must be set against an expected increase of 70 per cent in CO_2 emissions from 1990 to 2050). The WWF conclusion was that 'improvements in vehicle technology and adoption of alternative fuels cannot on their own reduce transport's CO_2 emissions to a sustainable level, whether in 20 years or over a longer timescale'.

Their package for the UK (to 2020) would consist of reducing the growth in motorized journeys to a 30 per cent increase (rather than a 50 per cent increase), to halve the increase in journey lengths, to increase the fuel efficiency of vehicles to 2.75 times (to 85 mile per gallon – 30 kilometres per litre), and to change substantially the modal split, with the car proportion being reduced from 85 per cent to 65 per cent, bus increased from 10 per cent to 25 per cent, and rail from 2 per cent to 10 per cent. Although the WWF report does not say how such changes can take place, two important messages come from their research. The first is that the scale of change required is very large. The achievement of cutbacks to 40 per cent in CO_2 emissions is not an easy task and the necessary actions require new thinking. Incremental change will not achieve the desired outcomes. The second message is that all available policy instruments should be packaged together in mutually reinforcing ways to achieve change. These instruments include economic incentives, location decisions, and technological innovation – these important themes are taken up in Parts 2 and 3 of the book.

2.5.5   Green taxes

The consumption of goods imposes costs on other people, so it is necessary to find ways to internalize these externalities. Car driving is a prime target for green taxation or taxation on consumption as it brings clear benefits to those using the car, but costs to others – through congestion, damage to roads, noise, accidents, local air pollution and its effects on climate change. The main means by which these externalities are being priced is through real increases in fuel prices. For example, in the UK tax on fuel was increased by at least 5 per cent in real terms by the previous Conservative government, and this has been increased to 6 per cent by the current Labour government. These are substantial increases in already high levels of taxation. Fuel duties, excluding VAT, already raise one-quarter as much as income tax. As travel increases, these provide a secure and increasing source of revenue for governments. The security of these taxes is important, both because of their scale and because of the relative insensitivity of consumption to price. The fuel tax increase alone is equivalent to an increase of £7 billion per annum by the end of the current UK Parliament – about 4 pence on the basic rate of income tax (Blow and Crawford, 1997).

However, the use of fuel taxes is not the most appropriate means to tackle congestion as this varies substantially by time and location. Similarly, road taxes do not reflect damage to the road surface as this is dependent on axle weights and road surface type. Local air pollution differs between vehicles, as it relates to type of fuel, the use of the catalytic converter, whether the engine is operating under cold conditions, the speed of travel, and other factors. The actual pollution effects also relate to location, weather conditions, dispersal of pollutants and the mixture of pollutants into cocktails. It is only the global warming gas (carbon dioxide) that is well targeted by fuel tax, as the levels of CO_2 emissions are directly related to fuel consumed. Increases in VAT on all carbon-based fuel would act as tax on CO_2 emissions, but this has been ruled out in the UK, and the EU proposal for a carbon tax has not been supported.

The reason used for opposing tax increases on fuel is that it has most impact on low-income households, but those on the lowest incomes are less likely to have a car, and those that do make less use of the car. At low levels of total expenditure, the fuel share is low, then climbs sharply, before peaking and falling at higher income and expenditure levels. If fuel prices rise, then this is the expected pattern of losses. However, if the same analysis is carried out only for those households with cars, a very different pattern emerges. The share of road fuels in total spending falls steadily as total expenditure rises. Poor households who can only just afford to purchase and use a car are hardest hit by any increases in price – this is particularly true for households in rural areas (Blow and Crawford, 1997). If prices are used to reduce levels of demand, it must be made clear what the purpose of those price increases is – whether it is to reduce congestion, to pay for road damage, or to reduce levels of local and global pollution. Distributional consequences can be compensated for, but good environmental taxes need to be targeted effectively at specific problems (Chapter 7.3 and 7.5).

2.5.6   Tradable permits

The concept behind tradable permits is very simple. A right is granted by government to the permit holder to emit a specified quantity of pollution. By limiting the total number of permits, it is possible to keep control over the total level of emissions and gradually to reduce the total amount (if desired). As there is a limit, the right to emit becomes a valuable commodity and a market price is established through trading. At the national level, there seems to be little difficulty in controlling levels of pollution by permits, but even here it may increase the costs and make exports less competitive. On the international level, it is much harder to introduce tradable permits, as there are problems such as carbon leakage where production switches to another country with less restrictions. This is where the US was adamant, in that an agreement on greenhouse gases should include all countries (Dobes, 1999).

The issue that caused disagreement was the extent to which investment in carbon sinks could be used to offset tradable permits. Rather than producing less CO_2, the carbon sink is additional woodland that can then 'absorb' the carbon from the atmosphere. Credits are given for planting trees so that the value of forests is increased (Fact Box 2.2). Again there is uncertainty over the science and whether all of the carbon fixing is a net gain over the life of the forest, as some may be burnt to release the stored carbon. There are also questions of biodiversity, as those trees that grow the fastest (e.g. eucalyptus and poplar) do not provide the best habitat or diversity. The US again does not want any cap on the credits for sinks, but the EU wants all countries to achieve at least 50 per cent of their targets from domestic action. The EU has again taken the lead here with the introduction of a Directive on Trading Emissions (CEC, 2003). Although this was initially blocked (Fact Box 2.3), it has now been signed and for the first time a value is placed on each tonne of CO_2 emitted.

In transport, tradable emissions permits could operate in different ways. Manufacturers could be targeted so that if they produced vehicles of low

Fact Box 2.2 Sequestration in the UK

To sequester 150–160 MtC per year emitted from fossil fuels in the UK, about 51 million hectares of forest would need to be planted, or twice the land area of the UK. The annual emission of an average car is about 1.1 tonnes of carbon per year, and this needs 0.4 hectares of conifer forest or about 40 widely spaced broadleaf trees (every year averaged from planting to maturity) www.open.gov.uk/panel-sd/position/CO_2/ana.htm.

The UK current forest biomass sink of 2 MtC per year could be maintained if the forest area continued to expand by 30,000 ha per year, and all harvested areas were restocked. One tree sequesters about 30 kg of carbon per year over its lifetime, but this varies with species (Cannell, 1999).

energy efficiency, they would then have to acquire permits from the producers of high energy efficiency vehicles. Such an initiative seems attractive, but might be difficult to introduce in an international market as it would only affect the new car fleet. Old vehicles pollute more than new vehicles, and one strategy adopted in the US has been to early retire vehicles. Emissions credits are created by any source that acquired and retired high emissions vehicles. In California, one corporation (UNOCAL) in conjunction with the California Air Resources Board offered $700 for each pre-1971 vehicle early retired, and over 8000 were scrapped. Such schemes can also be targeted at manufacturers, so that credits are gained if the vehicles produced are cleaner than required by law (Rubin and Kling, 1993). In Bogotá, for every new articulated bus introduced in the TransMilenio, the contracted operator was obliged to scrap three older buses. In Phase II of the TransMilenio, the scrappage level has been raised to between 7 and 10 older buses.

Fact Box 2.3 EU Trading Emissions Directive

This Directive establishes the means to achieve the 8 per cent target set at Kyoto for the EU – heavy polluters (chemical, cement, iron and steel, pulp and paper, power plants) have to buy the right to pollute. The Directive is mandatory and was initially delayed in July 2001 by the German BDI (their counterpart to the UK CBI), BP and UNICE (a corporate lobby). It was eventually agreed – Directive 2003/87/EC – giving the rights to 100,000 EU companies to buy and sell Green House Gas permits from 1st January 2005. The first step was to produce national allocation plans (March 2004) to distribute emissions allowances between sectors and industrial installations.

It was signed in July 2003 and has the following main components:

1   Three year mandatory initial plans (2005–2007), followed by a five year Kyoto phase (2008–2012).

continued on page 32

continued from page 31

2   Applies to five main sectors and concentrates on CO_2 emissions – Combustion installations over 20 MW, oil refineries, minerals, pulp and paper, and ferrous metals.
3   Member states can auction up to 5 per cent (2005–2007) and 10 per cent (2008–2012) of their allocation. This allocation plan must be drawn up in advance, and be subject to public debate and scrutiny by the EU.
4   All emissions need to be monitored by companies and emissions reports will be subject to independent verification.
5   Member states and the EU will establish and maintain electronic registries to track allowances.
6   For every tonne of emissions that is not covered by an allowance, a company will have to pay a penalty of €40 in 2005–2007 and €100 after 2007. Companies will also have to give a compensating amount of allowance in the subsequent year.

Those countries participating in the EU Emissions Trading Scheme will be able to use the Kyoto's Clean Development Mechanism to implement carbon reduction projects in developing countries that can be counted as part of their own CO_2 reduction targets.

Alternatively, the source of emissions could be defined as the destination of the trip, whether it is the office, the shopping centre or the school. If the number of people going to each destination was known, then those responsible for that destination activity would have to reduce visitors' vehicular emissions, through parking restrictions (including charging) or through providing public transport. This logic seems attractive, but it would be difficult to enforce or even introduce in an effective way.

The greatest potential for tradable permits in the transport sector seems to be for individuals and producers of fuel (Dobes, 1999). Individual permits provide a direct incentive to reduce fuel consumption through the choice of vehicle, driving and travel behaviour, and residential location. But even with advanced technology, such a scheme has high costs of implementation, administration, monitoring and enforcement. For fuel wholesalers and producers, there are lower transaction costs and these can be passed onto the operators as additional costs. As there are no real alternatives or substitutes, and demand is inelastic, consumers would have to pay higher prices. Permits could be allocated to the companies as grandfather rights, and any windfall gain could be recouped through taxation. Alternatively, the permits could be auctioned and there would be a direct return to government.

Baumol and Oates (1988) suggest that the difference between tradable permits and carbon taxes is difficult to determine, as the benefits and abatement functions are not known. If the abatement cost function is not known, the tradable permits may be preferable as the total quantity of abatement is known. There are also transaction costs, probably higher for tradable permits (Stavins, 1995). This is particularly true if the permits are allocated to individuals. If permits are allocated to fuel sellers, these costs are reduced, but the resulting price effects on motorists and other fuel users would be similar to a carbon tax. But assuming that the level of the carbon tax equals the discounted future marginal damage caused by the greenhouse effect (a Pigouvian tax – the internalization of an externality), then the revenue raised should not be recycled to the victims (Baumol and Oates, 1988, pp. 23–25). The tax corrects the externality through the prices imposed on the polluters. But the polluters are also the victims (the community), and so they would be the beneficiaries if the tax is recycled by the government in some form. The reality is somewhat different, as the transaction costs have already proved to be a major disadvantage. This has been demonstrated with upstream sources (such as fuel sellers) and with the current carbon markets (e.g. in Canada). At present, individual permits are not a possibility as administration costs and enforcement costs would be prohibitive.

2.6 Conclusions

Current thinking suggests that greenhouse gas reduction targets mean that there should be 60 per cent less emissions by 2050 (measured over the period 1990–2050). This means that the greatest cuts should come in the developed countries, and that the developing countries should actually be allowed to increase their per capita output of greenhouse gases at least in the short term. The argument here is that each country should have a carbon budget and that these allowances should be tradable. By including all nations in the debate, responsibility is shared, but this proved to be one of the main stumbling blocks in Kyoto, which eventually led to a partial solution with only 37 nations having targets set (Table 2.3).

In the negotiations, it was only the US that was pushing for developing country mandates in the first phase. But there does seem to be language in both the Rio and Kyoto documents that allude to the responsibilities of developing countries, and it is implied that they will be included in the future. They are committed to producing inventory and national reduction strategies, and involvement may be increased through one of the opt in mechanisms, such as the Clean Development Mechanisms (CDMs) or the Joint Implementation (JI) alternatives. In the immediate term, however, the disagreement on mandatory targets for all countries has been used to delay ratification of the Kyoto Protocol to February 2005.

This long term perspective means that reductions should begin to take place now as there are potentially enormous implications for health and the environment, as well as the direct effects of climate change. The alternative is to do nothing and let the increasing numbers of natural disasters work their way through the legal system in terms of the costs of insurance, the growth in uninsurable losses, and litigation. The increasing frequency and scale of recent natural disasters has already been labelled as a 'weapon of mass destruction' by Sir John Houghton (a leading scientist in the UK and the former Chairman of the Royal Commission on Environmental Pollution – August 2003).

The two main ways to address climate change is through regulation and pricing. Economic instruments (Chapter 7) have been favoured as the effects of global warming are independent of location and migration has an equalizing effect, so the cost comparisons become less important. The key objective is to reduce emissions at lowest costs to society as a whole. Carbon taxes match the private costs of emitting CO_2 with the social costs of global warming, and by raising the costs there may be greater innovation and substitution. The equity effects (Chapter 7.3 and 7.5) can be mitigated through compensation provided that the welfare benefits can be identified. Politically though, they have been unpopular and they have only been introduced in the form of energy taxes in a few EU countries (Finland, Norway, Sweden, Denmark and the Netherlands – for example a sulphur tax was introduced in Sweden (1991), which reduced output of sulphur by 50 per cent, and the carbon tax in Norway (1991), which reduced emissions from power stations by 21 per cent).

The alternative tradable permits were much discussed at Kyoto, but with little agreement. There seems to be a general agreement over the use of market mechanisms to allow free trading of emissions, as evidenced by the recent EU Directive (Fact Box 2.3), but the use of 'sinks' has created less agreement (Fact Box 2.2). It was also felt (at least by the EU delegations) that all nations should commit themselves to a reduction in the national level, as well as trading internationally. The economic arguments were moderated by a moral responsibility.

Annex

This is based on OECD (2002*a*).

Transport accounts for 4–8 per cent of GDP and some 2–4 per cent of the labour force in the OECD countries. In addition to the direct costs of transport, it is estimated that a further 4 per cent of GDP relates to the external costs of transport (in the EU), including the costs of accidents, congestion, and environmental costs.

Emissions proportions by mode – OECD 2000

%	CO	NO_x	VOC	PM_{10}	CO_2
Cars	58	38	50	32	51
Light Trucks (+SUV)	36	23	38	14	23
Motorcycles	2	1	7	2	2
Heavy Trucks	4	38	5	52	24

1 gallon of petrol = 2.4 kg of CO_2 1 gallon of diesel = 2.95 kg of CO_2

Levels of emissions by mode – grammes/passenger-km of travel

Mode	CO_2	C	NO_x	PM_{10}	Fuel
Car					
Petrol	186	51	0.59	0.063	10 km/litre
Diesel	141	38	1.39	0.188	13.5 km/litre
Hybrid	125	34	0.19	–	
Rail	73	20	–	–	
Air	213	58	0.54	–	
Taxi	223	61	1.52	0.413	
Coach/bus	56	16	0.19	0.019	
Metro/Tube	107	29	0.075	–	

Notes: 1 g of carbon emitted is equivalent to 0.2727 g of CO_2.
The warming potential of all aircraft emissions (CO_2, NO_x and water vapour) is about 3 times the CO_2 emissions alone – www.chooseclimate.org/flying.

Ozone is the main component of smog, and is caused by the chemical reaction between volatile organic compounds and the oxides of nitrogen (NO, NO_2, N_2O) in the presence of heat and sunlight. It contributes to eye irritations, coughs, chest discomfort, headaches, respiratory illness, asthma and reduced pulmonary functions. The World Health Organization maximum 8-hour values are 120 µg m^{-3}. The levels in Western Europe have increased by 15 per cent since the late 1980s, whilst the increase in Japan has been 5 per cent. The levels in the United States have decreased by 4 per cent over the same period, albeit from higher historic levels. In urban areas, the levels of ozone sometimes reach twice the recommended maximums. In Europe, about 330 million people are exposed to ozone levels above the threshold in each year, and there are 33 million people living in areas with excessive levels on more than 25 days each year.

Emissions standards

NO_x g/km	Petrol					Diesel				
	1990	1996	2000	2004	2008	1990	1996	2000	2004	2008
USA	0.6	0.4	0.4	0.2	0.05	0.8	0.8	0.8	0.2	0.05
Japan	0.25	0.25	0.25	0.1	0.1	0.5	0.5	0.4	0.3	0.3
EU	0.8	0.4	0.15	0.15	0.1	0.8	0.8	0.5	0.5	0.25

PM g/km Cars – diesel	1990	1996	2000	2004	2008
USA	0.12	0.05	0.05	0.05	0.0
Japan	0.2	0.2	0.07	0.05	0.05
EU	0.18	0.18	0.05	0.05	0.02

Percentage change in emissions 2000–2030

OECD			Non-OECD		
NO$_x$	–81%	Reflects the impact of	NO$_x$	+100%	
CO	–70%	catalytic converters,	CO	+100%	Reflects levels in
VOC	–73%	designs and standards	VOC	+100%	OECD countries in 1990
PM	–89%		PM	+65%	

Most reductions in OECD countries will take place up to 2020, but heavy diesel trucks and motorcycles are still a problem.

Petrol and diesel use

	Petrol (mtoe)		Diesel (mtoe)	
	OECD	Non-OECD	OECD	Non-OECD
1990	540	160	240	150
2000	620	220	280	210
2010	710	330	320	330
2020	780	500	360	520
2030	830	620	400	710
Increase	+154%	+387%	+167%	+473%

The EU has set limits on CO_2 emission from new cars at 140 g/km in 2008, a 25 per cent reduction on 1995 levels. In OECD countries, CO_2 emissions from transport were 2.25 billion tonnes in 1995 and this will increase to 3.6 billion tonnes in 2030 (+160 per cent). In Non-OECD countries the corresponding figures are 0.9 billion tonnes of CO_2 in 1995 and 4 billion tonnes in 2030 (+440 per cent), reflecting the huge growth in vehicles and travel, the low prospects for effective emissions controls, and the rapid growth in the use of diesel vehicles. Non-OECD emissions of CO_2 overtake OECD levels in 2025.

Notes

1   The actual increase in vehicles owned (1994-2001) in the EU15 was 19 per cent, so that these figures may be underestimates (EC, 2003).
2   The Norwegian examples of cordon pricing are used to raise revenue for road construction and investment in public transport. The London cordon pricing system both tackles road congestion and raises revenue for further investment in transport. Singapore is the only city to introduce road pricing in a pure form.
3   EJ = Exa joules. A joule is a measure of energy (kg m^2 s^{-2}) and Exa is 10^{18}.
4   The Nine are the UK, France, Canada, China, Italy, Brazil, Mexico, India and Spain.
    The Seven Australia, Ukraine, South Korea, Thailand, South Africa, the Netherlands and Indonesia.

Chapter 3

Sustainability and transport intensity

3.1 The economic background

The sustainability debate has been threatened by the many different interpretations of the concept. As stated in Chapter 2, we have taken a framework of sustainable development as the starting point and argued for the social and environmental dimensions of the framework to be given a stronger role to balance the primary concern over the economic dimension. It has also been emphasized that there is no single goal, but that sustainable development is a direction or a path that needs to be followed and that there are many different means to pursue that path. However, it is important to place the sustainable development argument within the wider framework of sustainability.

Here, there are two basic perspectives. One is rooted in neo-classical economics where overall capital maintenance can be achieved largely by replacing depleted or degraded natural capital with human or produced production factors. This is economic sustainability or one form of weak sustainability. Set against the economic arguments are those that relate to environmental sustainability where the full protection and preservation of vital environmental assets and their services need to be maintained. This is sometimes known as strong sustainability or the maintenance of natural capital. In addition to these two basic constructs a third can be added, namely social sustainability, which is conditional upon common values, participation and a fair society. All three are usefully summarized by Goodland (2002) and shown in Table 3.1. Ecological economists suggest that it is important to examine processes of change through interactions between systems, in particular the links between human activities and nature (Constanza et al., 1997). Their starting point is that standard equilibrium analysis does not represent the evolutionary nature of many processes, such as technological and socio-economic change. Implicit in this approach is the argument that many outcomes are uncertain and that it is necessary to adopt precautionary principles and clear standards or thresholds to limit environmental costs. More fundamentally, they argue that there are limits to solutions being found in science and technology, and that consumption must be reduced. Ethical

Table 3.1 Comparison of social, economic and environmental sustainability

Social sustainability – SS	Economic sustainability – EcS	Environmental sustainability – EnS
This can be achieved only by systematic community participation and strong civil society. Cohesion of community, cultural identity, diversity, solidarity, comity, tolerance, humility, compassion, patience, forbearance, fellowship, fraternity, institutions, love, pluralism, commonly accepted standards of honesty, laws, discipline, etc. constitute the part of social capital least subject to rigorous measurement, but essential for SS. The 'moral capital', as some call it, requires maintenance and replenishment by shared values and equal rights, and by community, religious and cultural interactions. Without such care it depreciates as surely as does physical capital Human or social capital – investments in education, health and nutrition of individuals – is now accepted as part of economic development, but the creation and maintenance of social capital as needed for SS is not yet adequately recognized.	Economic capital should be stable. The widely accepted definition of EcS is 'maintenance of capital', or keeping capital intact. Thus Hick's definition of income – 'the amount one can consume during a period and still be as well off at the end of the period' – can define EcS, as it devolves on consuming interest, rather than capital. Economics has rarely been concerned with natural capital (e.g. intact forests, healthy air). To the traditional economic criteria of allocation and efficiency must now be added a third, that of scale (Daly, 1992). The scale criterion would constrain throughput growth – the flow of material and energy (natural capital) from environmental sources to sinks. Economics values things in monetary terms, and is having major problems in valuing natural capital, intangible, intergenerational and especially common access resources, such as air. Because people and irreversibles are at stake, economics needs to use anticipation and the precautionary principle routinely, and should err on the side of caution in the face of uncertainty and risk.	Although EnS is needed by humans and originated because of social concerns, EnS itself seeks to improve human welfare by protecting the *sources* of raw materials used for human needs, and ensuring that the *sinks* for human wastes are not exceeded, in order to prevent harm to humans. Humanity must learn to live within the limitations of the biophysical environment. EnS means natural capital must be maintained, both as a provider of inputs (sources), and as a sink for wastes. This means holding the scale of the human economic subsystem to within the biophysical limits of the overall ecosystem on which it depends. EnS means sustainable consumption by a stable population. On the sink side, this translates into holding waste emissions within the assimilative capacity of the environment without impairing it. On the source side, harvest rates of renewables must be kept within regeneration rates. Non-renewables cannot be made sustainable, but quasi EnS can be approached for non-renewables by holding their depletion rates equal to the rate at which renewable substitutes can be created.

Source: Goodland (2002), pp. 710–711.

issues become central and the distribution of costs and benefits should include notions of community, social norms and societal preferences.

There seem to be two basic arguments. One is based on the belief that economic growth is the driving force for all development, and that human ingenuity and scientific progress will always delay the time at which the exploitation of future resources of the world would exceed the benefits derived from them. The sustainability debate is really just another way for the continuation of the economic efficiency arguments (Toman, 1994). Throughput growth arguments are still central to many economists such as Beckerman (1994 and 1995), where scarce environmental services relating to natural resources of supply and waste absorption can be incorporated into the monetary value system. Provided that these 'new' externalities can be valued, there are market-oriented instruments that can be used to establish property rights over these natural assets. These instruments would include pollution charges, fees and tradable permits. Essentially, the social costs are being converted to private costs so that individuals can make a choice over whether they should pay the 'full' costs or not. It is also argued that further environmental damage would be discouraged as the costs have risen substantially and that there would be incentives for providing environmentally sound production and consumption patterns. This conforms to the positivistic value laden view promoted by neo-classical economists.

Much of this reaction has evolved relatively recently and is consistent with the post Rio (1992) debates over the future of the planet and the need not only to price the global externalities correctly, but also to seek the means by which the rate of exploitation can be reduced. This returns to the essence of sustainable development where the economic imperative for growth needs to be moderated by other concerns (i.e. social and environmental). In part, it reflects the belief of some economists that all goods can be priced appropriately and that the 'solution' to the problem is getting these prices to reflect the full social costs. It also reflects the wider debate of the limits to growth (Meadows *et al.*, 1972; 1992), where it was concluded 'that it is possible to alter these growth trends and establish a condition of ecological and economic stability that is sustainable into the future'. Those promoting stronger sustainability were arguing that it was necessary to go beyond the simple economics, as the scale of population growth, increasing affluence and consumption required a more fundamental review of priorities.

The neo-Malthusian perspective (Ehrlich and Ehrlich, 1989; Hardin, 1968; 1993) again emphasized the mismatch between the pressures of the exponential population growth and the finite resource base. They argued for the environment to be protected against unconstrained growth to preserve human welfare as diminishing returns set in. Current generations should be content with existing levels of prosperity, so that future generations can also benefit. This was really a kind of steady state position, effectively taking the foot off the economic growth accelerator (Daly, 1972). Daly's steady state economics (1977) tries to integrate population and consumption pressures on the environmental sources and sinks, so that they can be measured through a single factor of scale. The basis for sustainability is the scale of throughput of matter and energy from the environment that is used by the human economy and then released back into the environment as waste.

The limits to growth conclusions were further reinforced by the classic Daly and Cobb (1989) analysis of the US economy. Here, it was concluded that GDP growth in the US had become decoupled from all measures of well being, and that this finding is reflected in other developed countries. It argued that man-made capital should be separated from natural capital, as the environment cannot be treated as a commodity. The environment is really an invisible heritage about which people hold beliefs and convictions. This means that it cannot be reduced to monetary valuation. Such an approach is normative and judgmental, and requires those in power to make collective decisions on priorities and the way in which natural capital should be used. Growth implies quantity to physical or material increase, but development implies qualitative change and improvement. Development should take place without throughput growth. Goodland (2002, p. 715) comments

> historically, an economy starts with quantitative throughput growth as infrastructure and industries are built, and eventually it matures into a pattern with less throughput growth but more qualitative development. While this pattern of evolution is encouraging, qualitative development needs to be distinguished from quantitative throughput growth if environmental sustainability is to be approached. For sustainability, development needs to replace throughput growth to the fullest extent possible.

The main differences between the various economic perspectives on strong and weak sustainability are the problems of aggregation, measurement and valuation. There are enormous difficulties in aggregating natural and produced capital, and there are more fundamental problems as to whether the two are really substitutable (Daly and Cobb, 1989). Weak sustainability assumes perfect substitutability and the maintenance of an aggregate capital stock over time are both a necessary and sufficient condition for sustainable economic development (Turner, 2002). Strong sustainability separates natural capital from other forms of capital, so that the critical natural capital can be maintained. The risks of irreversible loss are too high and the possibility of substitution should not be considered, particularly where there are high levels of uncertainty over the nature of the processes at work (e.g. global warming).

3.2 The transport case

This contextual discussion is both informative and interesting as it provides a framework within which the transport debate can be placed. Although the different interpretations of strong and weak sustainability can be applied to transport, the perspective adopted here combines the two concepts into a more pragmatic framework that attempts to reconcile the demands of the transport system with its resource requirements. The intention is to allow the output from transport to be maintained or increased, but at the same time to reduce the energy inputs, particularly in terms of the use of non-renewable resources. In a sense, it is a sector specific version of the factor four type of thinking (Von Weizsacker *et al.*, 1997), where wealth is doubled (i.e. transport performance) and the resource inputs are halved (i.e. non-renewable resource consumption).

Historically, there has been a close relationship between the growth in demand for freight and passenger traffic and economic growth, as measured by gross domestic product (GDP). The question raised here is related to the underlying rationale for this statistical relationship and whether that relationship should (or would) continue into the future. There seems to be no reason why we should have transport growth in line with economic growth. Indeed, there are strong efficiency and environmental sustainability arguments for breaking that link. We should be seeking to reduce the transport intensity of activities whilst at the same time maintaining economic growth – this is the decoupling argument. Efficiency and intensity in transport are closely related and, in a narrow sense, transport intensity could be seen as the inverse of transport efficiency. But transport efficiency is a much wider concept than transport intensity.

Travel can be broken down into three component parts – volume, distance, and efficiency. The first two components are usually combined to give measures of performance (i.e. passenger-kilometres or tonne-kilometres), but the third element is equally important as it relates to modes, travel time and price, the use of resources, technology and organizational factors. For example, in the freight sector efficiency can be increased through the use of logistics, flat organizational structures, new forms of handling, minimization of warehouse requirements, and spatial organization to reduce distribution costs. All these measures can increase efficiency, and reduce the volumes and distances travelled. However, they can also work to increase efficiency *and* the volumes/distances travelled – the arguments work in both directions. In terms of transport intensity, the main interventions are through reducing travel distance, increasing load factors (occupancy or effective use of freight capacity), and reducing consumption of fossil fuels.

3.3 Transport intensity

The concepts of decoupling economic growth and transport intensity are of more concern in Europe than in North America (Gilbert and Nadeau, 2002). In a narrow sense, this process is already taking place in the freight sector as the tonne-kilometres carried has increased at a rate substantially below the growth in GDP (Figures 3.1 and 3.2). This trend is true both for the last 40 years (since 1960) and for the more recent past (since 1985). The argument used in the US is that good transport (especially good freight transport) is essential for economic development. The adverse impacts of transport should be reduced, but not at the expense of economic growth.

The comparison between the US and the EU is informative, as there seems to be a convergence between the curves for passenger-kilometres per

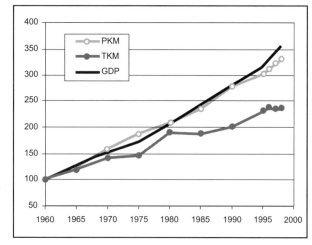

Figure 3.1 Transport and GDP growth in the US between 1960 and 1998.

Note: GDP has been adjusted for Purchasing Power Parity (PPP) with 1960 = 100.
Source: Gilbert and Nadeau (2002), Figure 1.

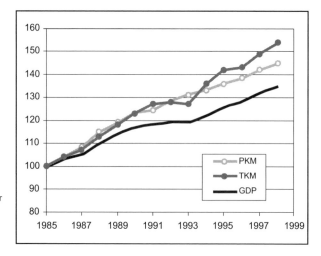

Figure 3.2 Transport and GDP growth in the EU15 between 1985 and 1998.

Note: GDP has been adjusted for Purchasing Power Parity (PPP) with 1985 = 100.
Source: Gilbert and Nadeau (2002), Figure 3.

unit of GDP. This convergence is despite substantial differences between the two continents in terms of car ownership levels (EU 629 vehicles[1] per 1000 population in 2001; US 940 vehicles per 1000 population in 2001) and in terms of land area (EU = 3.24 million km²; US = 9.36 million km²). The clear difference between the freight curves indicates the longer distances travelled in the US, but even here there is a narrowing of the gap. This may relate to space, but also to the economic restructuring that is taking place in both economies. At one level these comparisons suggest that the EU should be more concerned about decoupling than the US, partly because the EU levels of transport intensity are as high as those in the US for passenger travel, but also because the curves are rising in the EU.

There are some striking differences between the recent trends in passenger and freight transport and economic activity in the EU and the US (Tables 3.2 and 3.3). Between 1985 and 2000, there were broadly similar increases in passenger-kilometres travelled in the EU and the US (44 per cent and 55 per cent respectively) but different increases in freight transport (67 per cent and 20 per cent respectively). GDP grew at a faster rate in the US than in the EU during this period (70 per cent in the US and 43 per cent in the EU). Gilbert and Nadeau (2002) suggest that declining transport intensities in the US and rising levels in the EU may result from the stage of economic development as transport intensity may at first rise with increasing real GDP and then fall.

Table 3.2 Trends in passenger, freight and economic activity in the US and EU15 between 1985 and 2000

	1985	2000	Increase
US passenger-kilometres (billions)	4,920	7,625	55%
EU15 passenger-kilometres (billions)	3,316	4,779	44%
Ratio US/EU	1.48	1.56	
US freight-kilometres (billions)	4,305	5,177	20%
EU15 freight-kilometres (billions)	1,859	3,108	67%
Ratio US/EU	2.32	1.67	
US GDP (billions of 2000 €)	7,780	13,212	70%
EU15 GDP (billions of 2000 € PPP)	5,950	8,524	43%
Ratio US/EU	1.31	1.55	

Source: Updated version of Gilbert and Nadeau (2002), Table 1.

Table 3.3 US and EU15 comparative statistics for 2000

	US	EU15	Difference
Population (million)	282	378	EU15 +34%
Area (million km²)	9.36	3.24	US + 189%
Passenger-kilometres per capita	27,039	12,643	US + 114%
Tonne-kilometres per capita	18,358	8,206	US +124%
GDP per capita (adjusted for PPP in 2000 €)	€46,851	€22,550	US +108%

Source: EC (2003).

They further examine this proposition through plotting the transport intensity (passenger-kilometres per unit GDP) for 61 urban regions with populations over one million against GDP per capita. According to their analysis, there is 'a uniform decline in passenger transport intensity with increases in GDP for urban regions in developing and developed countries, other than those in North America and Australia' (Gilbert and Nadeau, 2002). In the US and Australia, transport intensity is much greater than in urban regions with comparable GDP and the values do not decline with increasing regional GDP. Gilbert and Nadeau's conclusion is that GDP differences do not explain the differences in transport intensity at the regional level, and that the structural development of the economy may help explain the differences.

The White Paper on EU Transport Policy (CEC, 2001*a*) has identified decoupling as a *primary objective*. The press release stated that the White Paper is 'proposing a strategy designed to gradually break the link between constant transport growth and economic growth . . .'. However, it is really only a *secondary objective* of the document, in contrast to the European Commission's Sustainable Development Strategy, in which decoupling transport growth and economic growth is the headline objective for transport (CEC 2001*b*). The White Paper recognizes that energy consumption in transport is increasing and that 28 per cent of CO_2 emissions are transport related (CEC, 2001*a*, p. 10). The absolute figures for transport were 739 million tonnes in 1990, rising to 900 million tonnes in 2000, with the expectation of further increases to 1113 million tonnes in 2010. Road transport accounts for 84 per cent of the figure (2000), and the total will increase substantially following enlargement in 2004, even though the levels of motorization in the new EU member states is lower. The White Paper is optimistic and three options are described (CEC, 2001*a*, p. 11 and annex) to provide a framework within which policy options can be assessed. The three options explore pricing (Option A), pricing and efficiency increases (Option B), and pricing, revitalization of alternatives and targeted investment in the Trans European Networks (Option C). The recommendations build on Option C where the market share for the individual modes returns to the 1998 levels in 2010 as a result of the measures implemented in the White Paper – 'By implementing the 60-odd measures set out in the White Paper there will be a marked break in the link between transport growth and economic growth, although without there being any need to restrict the mobility of people and goods' (CEC, 2001*a*, p. 11). These options were grouped under eight headings, covering passengers' rights (including compensation), road safety, congestion (covering intermodal transport), sustainable mobility (covering road pricing), harmonized taxation, transport services (including service quality and best practice), infrastructure (including 'missing links' and high-speed rail investment), and radio-navigation.

In their analysis of alternative futures, the EU presents their three options against the trend-based future (1998–2010). As can be seen from Table 3.4, the total passenger-kilometres and tonne-kilometres do not change as compared with the trend, but there are reductions in the vehicle-kilometres for both passenger and freight transport as the impact of pricing, greater efficiency and the other measures take effect. So the transport intensity as conventionally measured is expected to fall over this period. GDP is assumed to increase by 3 per cent per annum (+43 per cent over the 12-year period – rather high when compared with actual performance in the recent past), whilst trends in passenger-kilometres and tonne-kilometres increase by 24 per cent and 38 per cent respectively (Table 3.5). Transport intensity reduces by 13 per cent for passenger travel and 3 per cent for freight transport. This is where circularity is introduced as the scale of reduction is based on the assumed increase in GDP, which in turn influences the expected growth in passenger and freight travel. Provided that GDP increases at a higher rate than travel, then transport intensity will reduce.

Of more interest in the EU options (Table 3.4) are the reductions of the vehicle-kilometres by passenger and freight, and the subsequent reductions in CO_2 emissions. The policy instruments proposed in the White Paper are

Table 3.4 The base, trend and three options for the EU (1998–2010)

	1998	Trend 2010	Option A 2010	Option B 2010	Option C 2010
Passenger					
Passenger-km (billions)	4772	5929	5929	5929	5929
Vehicle-km (billions)	2250	2767	2518	2516	2470
CO_2 (million tonnes)	518.6	593.1	551.9	539.1	523.8
Freight					
Freight-km (billions)	2870	3971	3971	3971	3971
Vehicle-km (billions)	316	472.8	430	430	397
CO_2 (million tonnes)	300.9	445.4	408.5	405.1	378.6
Total					
Vehicle-km (billions)	2566	3240	2948	2946	2867
CO_2 (million tonnes)	819.5	1038.5	960.4	944.2	902.4

Source: Based on CEC (2001*a*), Table 3 in Annex.

Table 3.5 Expected changes in EU transport intensity (1998–2010)

EU	1998	2010	Change
GDP € billion	8,000	11,400	+43%
Passenger-kilometres	4,772	5,929	+24%
Tonne-kilometres	2,870	3,971	+38%
Transport intensity			
Passenger	0.5965	0.5201	−12.8%
Freight	0.3588	0.3483	−2.9%

Source: Based on CEC (2001*a*).

aimed at making more efficient use of the vehicle fleet by raising occupancy levels in all modes, by reducing vehicle-kilometres, and by encouraging modal shift (Option C). The impact is less apparent in the passenger sector (–10 per cent) than in the freight sector (–16 per cent), but this balance is redressed when the changes in CO_2 emissions are viewed, where there are about 10 per cent reductions in both sectors. The improvement in CO_2 emissions relates to expected gains in vehicle efficiency from the voluntary agreements with the car industry. It should also be noted that all these reductions are taken against the trend, not the 1998 levels. In each option for 2010 there is a substantial increase in travel and CO_2 emissions as compared with the 1998 levels.

Turning now to the UK evidence and the influential SACTRA (1999) report, which was primarily concerned with understanding the link between transport and the economy, but also investigated transport intensity. Over the period 1965–1995, a strong positive correlation was found between GDP growth and traffic growth, with the intensity of car and light goods vehicle traffic (LGVs) increasing and that of HGVs (heavy goods vehicles) decreasing. These changes were plotted as 5-year moving averages of the percentage difference between GDP change and traffic change (Figures 6.1–6.3 in SACTRA, 1999). The main conclusions are summarized here in Table 3.6.

There is a considerable variation between the modes and the different points of time, both in terms of size and direction of the difference. But in all cases the recent evidence (1985–1995) has resulted in traffic growing at

Table 3.6   Differences in GDP growth and traffic growth in Great Britain (1965–2025)

	1965–1975	1975–1985	1985–1995	Forecast 1995–2025
Car passenger-kilometres	Declining positive +1.6% to 0.2%	Constant variable +0.4%	Constant variable +0.5%	Constant negative –0.1%
	Car traffic growth > GDP growth	Car traffic growth > GDP growth	Car traffic growth > GDP growth	Car traffic growth < GDP growth
HGV tonne-kilometres	Variable negative –0.4% to –0.1%	Variable negative –0.3% to –0.1%	Variable positive +0.1% to +0.5%	Increasing negative 0.0% to –0.3%
	HGV traffic growth < GDP growth	HGV traffic growth < GDP growth	HGV traffic growth > GDP growth	HGV traffic growth < GDP growth
LGV tonne-kilometres	Variable negative and positive –0.4% to +0.2%	Volatile About 0.0%	Volatile positive +0.2% to +1.0%	No Forecast
	LGV traffic growth < GDP growth	Neutral	LGV traffic growth > GDP growth	

Notes: Positive means traffic growth is higher than GDP growth and negative means that traffic growth is less than GDP growth.
HGV = heavy goods vehicles > 3.5 tonnes gross unladen weight.
LGV = light goods vehicle < 3.5 tonnes gross unladen weight.

a faster rate than GDP. For car traffic, this pattern can be traced back much further. It is not just in the UK that this is occurring, as the SACTRA team also reviewed similar evidence from France, Sweden, the Netherlands and Italy for both car and freight traffic (1970–1994). In all cases, car traffic growth was substantially higher than GDP growth – the case for freight transport is less clear. There were also substantial differences between the national figures, and within individual countries over time, suggesting that different factors were influencing the relationship between traffic growth and GDP growth. From the perspective of reducing the transport intensity of the economy, the picture is bleak. As traffic growth is substantially higher that GDP growth, this means that some 'flip process' is required to put the curve in the future below the GDP curve.

However, the forecasts suggest that this will take place as both the car and HGV levels demonstrate that traffic growth is less than GDP growth (Table 3.6). But there seems to be a flaw in the argument here as pointed out by SACTRA (1999, p. 295). There is a clear reason why transport intensity should decrease over time as the traffic forecasts are driven by growth in car ownership, not by distance travelled per vehicle. Car ownership forecasts in turn are determined by income which itself is assumed to be linked to GDP growth (assumed to rise by 3 per cent per annum). The relationship between car ownership and income is assumed to lead to eventual saturation. These three factors together mean that intensity will decline in the future. Paragraph 17 (SACTRA, 1999, p. 296) concludes that the difference between 'periods of increasing and reducing intensity will be indications of the maturity of the car ownership growth curve rather than the success or otherwise of policies intended to influence traffic growth'.

The implications of this technical explanation are potentially profound:

1   The intensity of car traffic should fall with time as the elasticity of traffic with respect to income falls, but this has not happened yet. Transport intensity grows when the elasticity of traffic with respect to income is greater than one and declines when the elasticity is less than one. The cross sectional evidence suggests that there are substantial differences in car use, which are not related to either car ownership or income (SACTRA, 1999, p. 297). This intriguing statement is not developed further in the report, but there is an extensive literature on elasticities (e.g. Goodwin *et al.*, 2004; Graham and Glaister, 2004), and there is evidence that short-term elasticities are higher than expected from the preliminary results of the London congestion charging scheme (Banister, 2003).

2   There is circularity in the use of this approach to the measurement of transport intensity, as car ownership, income and GDP are all assumed

to be closely related when forecasting travel demand. GDP growth is often assumed given and this determines income growth and car ownership growth, which in turn are used to forecast increases in traffic. Such a close relationship means that it is difficult to unravel what is actually causing change. It seems that car use must be separated from car ownership and that other factors (e.g. pricing, regulation, technology) should all be influences in the use of the car.

3   GDP may also be too limiting a variable if the intention is to reduce transport intensity. Other measures of the economy could be used (Section 3.4).

More generally, there are other important implications:

1   Income may become less important than other factors in driving the growth in travel. Car ownership is now relatively cheap compared with income levels and it is not a real constraint. Car use has become more expensive over time (Table 3.7) as the costs of fuel and tax/insurance have all risen at a substantially higher rate than the cost of ownership. A clearer understanding is required on the motivations for car use apart from the costs (see Chapter 1).

Table 3.7 The costs of travel in the UK

Costs of travel	% change 1992–2002
Retail price index	+27.3
Car	+28.9
Purchase	−5.5
Fuel	+62.2
Maintenance	+51.5
Tax and insurance	+61.4
Bus fares	+42.8
Rail fares	+44.5

Source: ONS (2003*c*).

2   The figures used throughout reflect national travel patterns, not the growth in the longer distance and international travel markets. These two sectors are both growing substantially and further increases are expected in the future. They cannot be ignored, but the additional question here is whether GDP measured on a national basis is appropriate for international travel changes.

3   As noted above, the car traffic figures (and those for LGV) are above the GDP levels, so the transport intensity is increasing, yet the future

expectations (apart from the logic of the SACTRA saturation argument noted above) continue to put the case for curve reversal. The basic question here is that income growth is very important in determining traffic levels, but that other policy interventions (e.g. price, speed and quality of transport) must also have a key role to play in curbing traffic growth. In the past, these interventions do not seem to have been particularly successful in achieving that aim, yet both the EU and SACTRA are optimistic that this can be achieved, particularly if prices are set at marginal social cost levels.

4   The presentation of the data can be misleading in that transport intensity can be decreasing (if GDP growth is greater than traffic growth), but traffic growth is still increasing substantially. From the perspective of sustainable development, this is not acceptable as sustainable transport requires a net reduction in the environmental impact of transport as measured by emissions and the use of non-renewable resources. The headline figures from the new US statement that 'an aggressive strategy to cut greenhouse gas intensity by 18 per cent over the next 10 years' oversimplifies the challenge (*The Economist*, 16 February 2002, p. 49). There is no reduction in emissions even proposed in this statement, only the levels of emissions per unit of economic output. This is merely a continuation of the established pattern of change in the US (Gilbert and Nadeau, 2002).

3.4 Alternative measures of economic growth

In reviewing the alternative measures to present the decoupling of transport growth from economic growth, it seems that further fundamental thinking is required. In his research on the similarities between the energy sector and the transport sector, Peake (1994) made two important contributions. One was to place passenger and freight movement on a common basis (tonne-kilometre equivalent – tkme) by developing the concept of mass movement. This means that each passenger is given a gross weight (made up of their own weight and their luggage), so that passenger-kilometres can be converted to tonne-kilometres.

The second was to develop the notions of gross mass movement (GMM) to capture all transport movements in the economy and net mass movement (NMM) to capture the useful elements of activity. From these aggregate measures, indicators of gross transport intensity (GTI) and net transport intensity (NTI) can be obtained through linking them to GDP change. The GMM/GDP ratio is a proxy for transport efficiency (Peake, 1994, p. 69), and NMM/GDP is a measure of 'useful' transport activity. He found that over time (1952–1992), the NMM/GMM ratio was falling in the UK, indicating that the mass productivity of transport was declining by some 20 per cent. NTI was constant over time (0.7 tkme per £1 of GDP), and GTI was increasing over time, particularly after 1973 from 2.6 tkme per £1 of GDP (1973) to 3.1 tkme per £1 of GDP (1992) – an increase of 19 per cent.

Peake concludes that transport intensity is becoming less sustainable, and that 77 per cent of mass movement in 1992 resulted from the incidental movement of carriers, not the real movement of people and freight (Peake, 1994, p. 73). In all of this analysis, the freight sector dominated, as it accounted for 86 per cent of the NMM, and the huge increase in the unladen weight of HGVs (a 4-fold increase 1952–1992) added to this dominance. The 'average weight' of the passenger was set at 50 kg and this seems to be rather low, but even increasing this to a more realistic 90 kg for 'average' weight (including luggage) would probably not affect the results significantly (see Tables 3.8, 3.9 and 3.10). Peake also found measurement and data problems may have limited the accuracy of his results, but his work does begin to include efficiency variables in the analysis of transport intensity.

Measures of transport energy efficiency can be developed that enhance the traditional measures of transport intensity, as they include the means by which to include the efficiency of different modes of transport. They also address the issue of emissions and the use of resources, as they can be adapted to give estimates of CO_2 levels. In this way it is possible not only to view the transport implications, but also the environmental impacts of adopting particular policy packages (see Fact Box 3.1).

Such a conceptualization allows policy to impact on the volume of traffic, trip distances and the relative efficiencies of particular modes. The primary energy consumption can be converted into emissions levels for the key pollutants (including CO_2) through analysis of the carbon content of the different fuels used. As transport is almost entirely sourced from oil, this is easy to calculate, and even over a 10-year period where alternative fuels may be increasingly used, it is not difficult to estimate (Hoogma *et al.*, 2002).

Most of the components related to transport and the environment are encapsulated in these simple equations and the impacts of the different policy alternatives can be tested, together with their feedback components. As Schipper (2001) states,

> the key purpose of ASIF identity is to show policy makers how the components of transport and emissions fit together, and make sure that the potential – and actual – impacts of their actions on each component are noted . . . It helps remind analysts of some of the linkages.

The second set of issues relates to whether GDP is the most appropriate or only means to measure changes in economic activity. GDP provides a way of comparing economic activity in different countries. However, this measure has

Fact Box 3.1   Measures of transport energy efficiency

1.   Primary energy consumption = volume * distance * energy

                      trips   occupancy   MJ/km by mode
                      or load   of transport

Note that occupancy and load can be combined into mass (Peake, 1994).

2.   The ASIF equation (Ehrlich and Holdren, 1971, Schipper, 2001, Schipper and Marie-Lilliu, 1999 and Scholl et al., 1996).

$$G = A * S_i * I_i * F_{ij}$$

Where: G is the emission of any pollutant summed over modes i;
           A is the total travel activity in passenger kilometres (or tonne kilometres) across all modes;
           S converts from passenger travel (or freight) to vehicle travel by mode;
           I is the energy intensity of each mode (in fuel/passenger or tonne-km) and is related to the inverse of the actual efficiency of the vehicle, but depends on vehicle weight, power and driver behaviour;
           F is the fuel type j in mode i.

a number of limitations when considering issues of welfare or sustainability, since the calculation of GDP includes spending on actions such as pollution clean-up and medical treatment for road accident victims (for more detail, refer to Anderson, 1991; Jackson and Marks, 1994; and Cobb *et al.*, 1999). GDP does not take account of unpaid household production, even though this supplies services to the economy. All these factors make long-term analysis of GDP trends even more difficult.

1   GDP figures do not show how economic activity is distributed across society (the genuine progress indicator (GPI) attempts to address this – see below).

2   Exchange rate fluctuations and cost of living differences in different countries make comparisons of GDP trends between countries problematic.

3   GDP does not take account of unpaid activities, including many household activities (such as caring, preparing meals, education and housework), even though these are services to the economy.

Hanley *et al.* (1999) identify a number of alternative measures of economic activity such as net national product (NNP), genuine savings, net primary productivity, the index of sustainable economic welfare (ISEW) (Daly and

Cobb, 1989) and the genuine progress indicator (GPI). For example, the
GPI corrects some of the anomalies in the formulation of GDP and shows
that in the US, GPI rose by 23 per cent per capita (1950–1998) compared
with the 164 per cent increase in GDP. Apart from addressing some of the
limitations of the GDP measure, GPI explicitly includes income inequality and
people's perceptions of progress (or lack of it). The team (Redefining Progress)
producing it in San Francisco (Cobb *et al.*, 1999) also claim that the focus on
GDP encourages short term benefits rather than longer term costs in terms
of debt and loss of resources. Stead (2001*a*) compares trends in transport
efficiency in the UK between 1975 and 1990 relative to both GDP and ISEW
and shows that there is a big difference between the two.

3.5 Empirical evidence from the UK and the EU15

A substantial amount of empirical evidence has already been cited at the
aggregate level (Section 3.3). Here the focus is more on the variations within
EU countries and how these have changed over time. Data are presented for
all EU countries on the transport energy efficiency and transport economic
efficiency by passenger-kilometre and tonne-kilometre and net mass movement
(NMM). In addition to these indicators, data are given to illustrate trends for
the UK and the EU as a whole between 1970 and 1995 (Tables 3.8 and 3.9).
There are clear similarities between the two tables, with equivalent increases
in GDP per capita, but transport energy consumption in the UK rose at a
slower rate than in the EU, but it is still higher than the EU average. Travel
distance per capita in the UK was higher than the EU average in 1970, but
converged to the EU average by 1995. Freight transport per capita in the UK
increased at a slower rate than the EU average and there is still a substantial
difference in 1995 with the UK figure being some 30 per cent lower than the
EU average. The net mass movement figures in the UK are consistently lower
than those in the EU.

Between 1970 and 1995, GDP per capita in the EU increased by 65 per cent
– similar to the rate of increase in freight transport per capita and the net mass
movement per capita (Table 3.9). Transport energy consumption per capita
and passenger travel distance per capita increased more rapidly, the former by
91 per cent and the latter by 94 per cent.

Some data indicate reductions in transport intensity whilst others indicate
little overall change. The ratio of transport energy consumption per passenger-
kilometre remained fairly constant between 1970 and 1990, whilst the ratios
of transport energy consumption per tonne-kilometre and transport energy
consumption per net mass movement increased, indicating that transport
energy efficiency decreased.[2] Between 1970 and 1995, the ratios of GDP
per tonne-kilometre and GDP per NMM remained fairly constant, whilst

Table 3.8 Transport and economic trends in the UK (1970–1995)

Measure	Units	1970	1995	% change
GDP per capita	Constant 1987 US$	8,463	13,431	+59%
Transport energy use per capita	Tonnes of oil equivalent	0.48	0.82	+69%
Travel distance per capita	'000 kilometres per person per year	7.10	12.27	+73%
Freight transport per capita	Tonne-kilometres per person per year	2.02	2.93	+45%
NMM per capita	Tonne-kilometres per person per year	2.67	4.03	+51%

Note: The distance figures are all '000 of kilometres. Net mass movement converts travel distance to weight so that freight and passenger units can be measured together. The figure used here is not the low Peake figure of 50 kg, but a more realistic one of 90 kg per person (including luggage).
Source: Stead (2000*a*).

Table 3.9 Transport and economic trends in the EU15 (1970–1995)

Measure	Units	1970	1995	% change
GDP per capita	Constant 1987 US$	8,787	14,527	+65%
Transport energy use per capita	Tonnes of oil equivalent	0.40	0.77	+91%
Travel distance per capita	'000 kilometres per person per year	6.20	12.04	+94%
Freight transport per capita	Tonne-kilometres per person per year	2.61	4.10	+57%
NMM per capita	Tonne-kilometres per person per year	3.17	5.18	+63%

Note: The distance figures are all '000 of kilometres. Net mass movement converts travel distance to weight so that freight and passenger units can be measured together. The figure used here is not the low Peake figure of 50 kg, but a more realistic one of 90 kg per person (including luggage).
Source: Stead (2000*a*).

the ratios of GDP per passenger-kilometre and GDP per unit of transport energy consumption decreased, indicating that transport economic efficiency decreased. Thus, the overall picture of transport intensity using this selection of indicators is one of stability or decline, depending on the choice of indicators (Table 3.10).

3.6 Changes in society and the economy

Much of the material presented here relates to changes in a series of transport intensity indicators over time, or at one point in time. There are other changes taking place within economies that are likely to have an impact on the efficiency dimension of travel, perhaps reducing or increasing transport intensity. Included here are dematerialization, new production processes (e.g. flexible specialization), customer driven networks and globalization. These will all influence transport intensity in the freight sector and some of the important ideas are briefly outlined here.

Dematerialization can make a more fundamental impact on transport intensity. However, although the material intensity of products may decrease, material consumption can still increase as the economy grows and demand

Table 3.10   Indicators of transport intensity in the EU15[1]

Type of measure	Indicator of transport intensity	1970	1995	% change
Transport energy efficiency[2]	Transport energy consumption per passenger-kilometre	64.8	63.6	−2%
	Transport energy consumption per tonne-kilometre	153.6	186.8	+22%
	Transport energy consumption per Net Mass Movement	159.4	192.5	+21%
Economic efficiency[3]	GDP per passenger-kilometre	1.47	1.19	−19%
	GDP per tonne-kilometre	3.74	3.82	+2%
	GDP per NMM	3.87	3.93	+2%
	GDP per unit of transport energy consumption	22.6	19.1	−15%

Notes: Net mass movement converts travel distance to weight so that freight and passenger units can be measured together. The figure used here is not the low Peake figure of 50 kg, but a more realistic one of 90 kg per person (including luggage).

1   Only 6 countries were part of the European Community in 1970 but for comparison purposes, the data for 1970 and 1995 relate to the 15 countries that are currently members of the European Union.
2   Note that these figures refer to total transport energy consumption (across both passenger and freight transport sectors) and further disaggregation of the energy consumption data is obviously necessary in order to determine energy efficiency trends in the freight and passenger sectors.
3   The four economic efficiency measures were calculated using data for all countries that are currently members of the European Union with the exception of Germany, where comparable GDP data for 1970 was not available.

Source: Stead (2000*a*).

expands. According to one estimate, dematerialization could result in a 15–20 per cent reduction in freight volumes in the period between 1995 and 2020 (Schleicher-Tappeser *et al.*, 1998). Further reductions could be achieved by raising the durability of products so that they last longer but here there is a trade off between lasting quality and the need to take advantage of technological innovations.

Another significant impact on transport intensity might be made as a result of a move from global to 'glocal'[3] production. Traditional arguments strongly favour concentration of production to take advantage of agglomeration economies. However, the development of flexible specialization has created a new 'complementarity' between global networks and regional production for regional markets in which products are locally sourced (see for example Piore and Sabel, 1984). Production units are small-scale so that the new lean production methods can be introduced. For example, in the state of Baden-Wurttemberg in south Germany, most suppliers of the Mercedes car manufacturing plant are based in and around Stuttgart. Many components are sourced within a radius of 100 kilometres from the plant and are ordered virtually to the hour (Schleicher-Tappeser *et al.*, 1998). Local production networks provide the opportunity for short travel distances and a reduction in freight traffic. However, such just-in-time sourcing can also mean more journeys. The potential reduction in freight traffic through the use of regional markets, regional production, and the reduction in international flow of goods (that have been produced for local markets) could amount to between 20–30 per cent over a period of 25 years (Schleicher-Tappeser *et al.*, 1998).

There is substantial potential for decoupling in the freight sector as a result of new forms of production. The economy of scale arguments, together with economies related to specialization and the comparative cost advantages of producing large quantities for large markets, are now being questioned. Customer-driven requirements mean that products are now tailored to individual specifications so that smaller scale production for regional markets become possible, provided that the knowledge and skills are available.

However, there is still a long way to go, as global cultures and inter-nationalization have been instrumental in producing similar values, tastes and lifestyles, with the consequent loss of community and locality. Similarly, most changes in policy have tended to encourage greater internationalization through trade liberalization, market based strategies, subsidies to farmers and other groups, deregulation in transport, privatization, and even markets for environmental and consumer protection. Boundaries are no longer drawn to coincide with national frontiers, but are much wider, and any true investigation of transport intensity should recognize this. This is in part related to the 'leakage' issue, as the environmental costs may well be incurred in a different location (or country or even continent) to where consumption takes place. The most optimistic view is that in the freight sector, transport demand could remain constant over the next 20 years (to 2020), with the strong implementation of decoupling strategies.

In the passenger sector, the opportunities for stabilization in demand seem harder to envisage, particularly within the context of increased affluence and leisure time. Decoupling must again be seen as a combination of strategies to reduce the volume of traffic, the distance travelled, and measures to increase efficiency, but at the same time maintaining economic growth. The decoupling arguments follow the same structure as in the freight sector with dematerialization of travel through less travel or travel by more efficient modes, and by establishing local travel patterns through the reorganization of the production and consumption patterns based on local and regional networks (Banister *et al.*, 2000).

3.7 Conclusions

Transport intensity does seem to offer the means to monitor progress towards maintaining and increasing economic growth, but at the same time ensuring the most efficient use of transport resources. As noted earlier, there is a range of policy interventions that can be used to improve load factors in both passenger and freight transport, to reduce trip lengths, and to use the most efficient technology. All these factors are discussed in detail in Part 2.

Public policy intervention is important and transport intensity is responsive, whether it is through raising user costs to reflect the environmental costs, or to designate development in locations that are accessible to public transport. The main limitation has been the reluctance of decision-makers actually to implement policy packages in their most effective form as this often means demand management and limitations on the use of the car. These issues relating to intervention and the appropriate institutional and organizational structures are taken up in the next two Chapters.

The second set of conclusions relates to the difficulties of comparative analysis, as data are often not consistent between the EU15 and the US. Apart from the usual definitional problems, there is a different set of travel recorded. In the US all travel within the country is covered, but in the EU15 the data are collected nationally and then assembled by the EU. This means that national data are good, but it is only international air that is included (not road or rail) and even the air travel only relates to that undertaken within the EU. This raises an interesting point, namely that one would expect that travel distances in the US to be longer than those in the EU15 as the US is nearly three times the size of the EU15 (Table 3.3). Yet the differences in transport intensity are not as great, at least when matched with growth in GDP, suggesting that in the US there is consolidation for long distance journeys (in trucking and in rail). However, travel distances in the US are still much higher than those in the EU and so the use of resources in transport is correspondingly high.

At the beginning of the chapter, several different interpretations of sustainability were presented, varying from 'weak' economic arguments to 'strong' ecological arguments. These are consistent with the approach taken in this book, in that weak and strong sustainability are a continuous theme throughout. The interpretation used here is that 'weak' sustainability in the transport sense allows some increase in the use of resources, but less than would be expected under the trend assumptions. This is a relative decoupling of transport growth from economic growth as GDP increases at a faster rate than transport growth. That is already apparent in the US, but not in the EU15 where transport growth is still ahead of GDP growth. This is similar to the economic arguments (Chapter 3.1). 'Strong' sustainability is looking for an absolute reduction in the use of resources in transport, while maintaining economic growth. This is a much tougher objective and requires substantial change in transport policy and in policy in other sectors (Chapter 11). It also questions the exclusive use of GDP as the measure of economic growth, suggesting that broader welfare measures should be used (Chapter 3.4). This approach has more in common with the ecological perspective as the natural capital is seen as being crucial to sustainability. The input of the social sustainability arguments is important to both interpretations as it relates centrally to the processes of implementation and public (and political) acceptance of sustainability, the importance of the moral imperative, and the use of softer measures including education and health to increase social capital.

Notes

1 Vehicles include cars, vans, lorries, motorcycles, buses and coaches.
2 Further disaggregation of the energy consumption data is necessary in order to determine energy efficiency trends in the freight and passenger sectors.
3 Glocal refers to a combination of global and local, where production is still controlled by large multinational companies, but produced locally for local markets under franchising and other arrangements

Chapter 4

Public policy and sustainable transport

4.1 Introduction

Sustainable transport is an elusive goal that seems to dominate much of the recent debate on transport policy. In an absolute sense all transport is unsustainable as it consumes resources. Walking and cycling come nearest to being sustainable, as they consume very little non-renewable energy, but even here other types of resources are used, principally space. The excessive use of space could be seen as being non-sustainable, particularly where it is in short supply. This theme is taken up in Chapter 6, but here the concept of personal space need for both walking and cycling is seen as being sustainable. As one moves down the transport hierarchy, more resources are used both in terms of energy consumption and in the production of externalities. Externalities in the transport context cover the emissions of pollution, accidents, noise and congestion. In addition there is water and soil pollution, the waste from the production and disposal of vehicles, the use of public space for roads and parking, the severance effects, destruction of ecosystems and visual annoyance (Maddison *et al.*, 1996).

All forms of motorized transport use non-renewable energy and create substantial externalities. It is generally accepted that all forms of public transport are more sustainable than private transport, but even here there is much debate over the relative efficiencies as these are dependent upon the assumptions made on occupancy levels, whether the vehicles are actually operating at given levels of efficiency, the speed of the vehicle, and the types of externalities (particularly pollutants) being monitored (Table 4.1). There are no simple relationships or answers, but certain general principles are apparent.

In terms of sustainable transport, both walking and cycling come out top. High-occupancy public transport (including rail, bus, tram and metro) follow, but in some cases only just ahead of clean small efficient cars. The third group includes high-speed rail and many other types of cars. Taxis and lorries form a fourth group, with air transport on its own in a fifth group. Air transport is particularly problematic as it both uses large quantities of fuel and the distances travelled are long. It is also a key growth market and options for more sustainable air travel seem to be distant. Most public policy action on

Table 4.1   Primary energy consumption figures by mode for the United Kingdom

Mode		Seats/spaces 1992 (2002)	1992 MJ/vehicle-km	MJ/seat-km	MJ/passenger-km		2002 MJ/vehicle-km	MJ/seat-km	MJ/passenger-km	
Air	long > 1500km	255	344	1.35	2.08		332	1.30	1.73	
	short < 500km	100	185	1.85	3.08		178	1.80	2.57	
Rail	long = TGV/Eurostar	377	170	0.45	1.18		170	0.45	0.92	
	short = local/national	313	91	0.29	1.04		91	0.29	0.81	
Metro	London underground	555	141	0.25	1.00	1.67	141	0.25	0.75	1.00
Light rail and tram		265	79.8	0.30	0.91	1.20	79.8	0.30	0.75	0.91
Bus		48 (40)	14.7	0.34	1.03	1.70	12.0	0.30	1.00	1.78
Lorry					2.94				3.12	
Taxi		4	3.3	0.83	2.94		2.7	0.67	2.41	
Car		4	3.7	0.92	2.08		3.02	0.77	1.87	
Motorcycle		2	1.9	0.95	1.73		1.9	0.95	1.74	
Bicycle		1	0.06	0.06	0.06		0.06	0.06	0.06	
Walk		1	0.16	0.16	0.16		0.16	0.16	0.16	

Notes and assumptions

1992

The 1992 modal primary energy consumption figures are measured in mega joules (MJ) and include energy use in maintenance. Average figures for cars and motorcycles/mopeds weighted according to national (GB) fleet sizes (Department of Transport, 1993). Occupancy figures are as follows air = 60 per cent for short and 65 per cent for long, rail = 28 per cent for local/international and 38 per cent for TGV, metro = 25 per cent and 15 per cent, light rail = 33 per cent and 25 per cent, and Bus = 33 per cent and 20 per cent. Lorry occupancy is more subjective – a figure of 2.3 has been used. Car occupancy figures are a weighted average of 1.76 (work = 1.2 and non-work = 1.85). Occupancy for motorcycle is 1.11 and for taxi is 1.13. The figure for air is a low estimate as Scholl *et al.* give a 3.33 MJ/passenger-km estimate.

2002

For 2002, the figures have been updated to take account of changes in the vehicle stock, efficiencies and occupancy rates. Air occupancy is 70 per cent for short and 75 per cent for long distance, rail is 36 per cent for local/ international and 49 per cent for TGV/Eurostar,. Metro is 25 per cent and 33 per cent, light rail is 40 per cent and 33 per cent. Lorry occupancy is the same, bus has declined slightly to 30 per cent and 17 per cent (as has bus size), car is 1.62, motorcycle is 1.09, and taxi is 1.11. Where there are two figures in the final column, this gives energy consumption for each of the occupancy rates given above. Note that the passenger-km figures are very dependent on the occupancy levels used.

Source: Based on Banister (1997*a*), Hughes (1993), Stead (2000*b*), CEC (1992), Scholl, Schipper and Kiang (1994) and update to 2002 from ONS (2003*c*), Van Essen *et al.* (2003) and EC (2003).

sustainable transport has been directed at the car rather than other forms of transport.

Over the 10-year period (1992–2002) some interesting changes have taken place with the car becoming more efficient, despite a lowering of the occupancy rate. Car passenger-kilometres have increased by 12.2 per cent, and vehicle-kilometres have gone up by 16.1 per cent, but fuel consumption has only increased by 5.4 per cent. Part of the explanation is that there has been a switch to diesel, which is more efficient, with cars (2004) accounting for 25 per cent of all diesel fuel (as compared with about 10 per cent in 1992).

There seems to have been an increase in the energy efficiency of the car stock, which has increased from 30 miles per gallon (1992 – or 9.4 litres per 100 km) to 35 miles per gallon (2002 – or 8.0 litres per 100 km) for all new vehicles. The overall efficiency of the stock is now 32 miles per gallon (8.9 litres per 100 km). Each car is being used less, perhaps due to the acquisition of second or third cars in households (27 per cent of households now have two or more cars). But the car stock has increased by 22 per cent over this period (to 24.5 million cars – ONS, 2003c), and this relates to the reduction in the costs of purchasing cars (Table 3.7). In terms of sustainable transport, the picture is complex and mixed, with some improvements in efficiency, but these benefits must be offset by the net increase in energy consumption and the decline in vehicle occupancy levels.

There are three important reasons why transport should reduce its dependence on non-renewable oil sources and become more sustainable (OECD/IEA, 1997):

1   Energy security. Although there are significant long-term possibilities for substitution, transport is almost entirely oil dependent. There are potential security threats to many highly motorized economies, as well as those at the start of their mobility transition, which are dependent on imports. The energy security and climate change challenge is to use oil more productively and to develop alternative fuels.

2   Environmental protection. Transport's share of global and local pollutants continues to grow. Political barriers to reduce emissions are also high (particularly in air transport), but measures need to be taken to ensure transport makes a significant contribution to the achievement of international (Kyoto) obligations through national and local actions.

3   Economic competitiveness and globalization. Economies are critically dependent on transport and transport has been a key facilitator of the globalization process. Much of the development of globalization and long supply chains is contingent upon high quality and cheap transport. Hence it is important to maintain its quality and strength, but also to charge appropriately for its use.

In this Chapter, the focus is on the role that public policy can and should have in achieving sustainable transport. To a great extent the options available to move policy towards greater sustainability are well known, yet real progress has been disappointingly slow. The argument developed here is that most effort has been directed at reducing the need to travel through a range of technological, economic and planning interventions. Substantial barriers to implementation have been raised and policy-makers seem increasingly to rely upon technological solutions to achieve sustainable transport.

The options are presented, together with the barriers and the means by which they can be overcome. But even where successful implementation has taken place, there is a substantial difference between policy intentions and policy outcomes. Even where identifiable change has taken place, the scale is modest. In the conclusions, it is argued that real change can only be achieved through changing the priorities and actions of individuals and through debates on the types of cities and urban areas that people want to live in. When attitudes and visions coincide it is possible to determine the appropriate contribution of transport to that vision.

4.2   Global perspectives on public policy

Worldwide, there has been a significant change in priorities with the general acceptance of the need to reduce emissions of CO_2 and the five other greenhouse gases (see Fact Box 2.1). The Intergovernmental Panel on Climate Change (IPCC) has estimated that significant reductions are needed in each of these greenhouse gases if stabilization targets are to be reached – 60 per cent for carbon dioxide, 20 per cent for methane, 50 per cent for hydrochloro-fluorocarbons, over 75 per cent for nitrous oxide, and over 75 per cent for chlorofluorocarbons 11 and 12 (Houghton *et al.*, 1990).

As already mentioned in Chapter 2.5, this was first recognized at the 1992 Rio Summit where voluntary stabilization targets were agreed, but more importantly in the 1997 Kyoto Protocol where the thirty-nine developed countries agreed (subject to ratification) to set a series of mandatory targets. These range from a reduction of 8 per cent in CO_2 emissions in the EU and Switzerland to a 7 per cent reduction in the United States, and a 6 per cent reduction in Canada and Japan, but with increases in other countries (Iceland +10 per cent, Australia +8 per cent and Norway +1 per cent – see Table 2.3). The overall reduction was 5.2 per cent between 1990 and 2010. Such a breakthrough in global public policy is encouraging as the targets set are both realistic and mandatory. Some countries (e.g. the UK and the Netherlands) are setting even more challenging targets of up to a 20 per cent reduction, but are still a long way short of the levels demanded by the IPCC.

There is an acceptance that even though the science of global warming and greenhouse gas emissions is not well understood, there is sufficient evidence available to adopt the precautionary principle and take policy action. Transport is a major contributor to global warming, principally through the emissions of CO_2 from all carbon-based fuels (Royal Commission on Environmental Pollution, 1994 and 1997). In most developed economies, transport accounts for more than 25 per cent of the total CO_2 emissions, and it is the only major sector where the absolute amount continues to increase (Table 4.2). It is a direct result of the growth in income levels and affluence, the dispersal of urban activities and the growing dependence on the car (and lorry) and more recently air transport. Over the last 20 years, car ownership levels and travel have doubled in many developed countries, and this increase is expected to continue over the next 20 years by a further 70 per cent (OECD, 1995 and Table 2.2).

Table 4.2 Carbon dioxide emissions globally and from transport, 1990–2000

Globally – million tonnes of CO_2

Country	1990	2000	Increase	Transport 1998	% of total CO_2 emissions
EU15	3115	3161	+1.5%	872	27.8%
USA	4826	5665	+17.4%	1771	32.2%
Japan	1019	1155	+13.4%	278	24.7%
Russia	1284	1506	+17.3%	219	14.9%
China	2290	3036	+32.6%	137	4.5%
India	583	937	+60.7%	n.a.	n.a.
Total	20721	23422	+13.0%		

Transport – million tonnes of CO_2

EU15	Rail	Road	Air	Inland navigation	Total	% of all emissions from transport
1990	8.9	625.0	82.2	19.6	735.7	23.9%
1995	8.4	675.6	96.2	20.5	800.7	26.2%
2000	7.0	762.3	126.0	15.1	910.5	28.7%

Source: EC (2003)

Globally, carbon dioxide emissions have increased by 13 per cent over the period 1990–2000, but even in developed countries that increase has been substantial. The EU15, the US and Japan have had a steady 43 per cent of the total, with the newly emerging economies also showing a rapid rate of increase, but the gap is not yet closing. In the transport sector, the absence of any reduction means that as a percentage of the total emissions, it is increasing towards 30 per cent. Most of the emissions relate to road transport (84 per cent) and air transport (14 per cent).

There is a series of important questions here if the global dimension of sustainable transport is to be achieved, with strong implications for public policy:

1   The developed countries should be taking a strong lead in reducing their

levels of energy consumption and emissions levels through challenging targets, so that other countries at lower levels of development or in transition can increase their levels of consumption and emissions at least in the short term.

2   The use of tradable permits is likely to have a central role in the achievement of all targets. Investment could take place in developing countries where the opportunities for major savings in energy consumption are possible. The question then becomes who actually claims the savings, the country where the investment took place, or the country which made the investment.

3   The responsibility for effective action lies initially in a few major countries – the US, Canada, Japan, Russia and the EU. Unless these countries make a serious contribution through domestic policy programmes and investments in clean technologies, no progress will be made towards the achievement of the Kyoto targets (Table 4.2).

4   At present there is no technological means to reduce the emissions of CO_2. All carbon-based fuels produce CO_2, so reductions can only take place through travelling less, through improved efficiency of travel (more efficient engines, better design, or higher occupancy/load levels), through the use of alternative or renewable fuels (solar power or fuel cells), through switching to non-motorized transport modes, through switching to collective forms of transport (e.g. public transport), and through the substitution of transport activities with other services (e.g. telecommuting and teleshopping). Other emissions, such as carbon monoxide (CO), volatile organic compounds (VOCs), nitrogen oxides (NO_x), nitrous oxide (N_2O), hydrocarbons (HC), particulates (PM_{10}), and methane (CH_4), can all be controlled through catalytic converters and other add on technologies.

The most serious unresolved question for public policy lies in the debate over whether the means to achieve the Kyoto (1997) targets are more important than the ends. If it is agreed that the overall reduction of 5.2 per cent in CO_2 emissions is the main target, then it is possible. But it will not be achieved by reductions in emissions levels in the thirty-nine developed countries. It will only be achieved through giving the United States unlimited rights to trade internationally in carbon credits. The US will buy its way out of its domestic obligations through planting forests, by buying credits from countries that have exceeded their savings targets, and through investments in third countries in clean technology. In the US, CO_2 emissions have increased by 17 per cent (1990–2000, Table 4.2) and there has been no progress towards the reduction target of 7 per cent agreed at Kyoto. Emissions would now have to be 30 per cent below the projected level by 2010 to achieve the Kyoto target and that is impossible (Frank Loy – the US Under Secretary for Global Affairs – July 2000).

This issue was the main topic for discussion at the Hague Climate Change convention meeting (2000). Europe wanted to limit the US ability to buy carbon credits from third countries (e.g. Russia) to 50 per cent of its required savings, otherwise the United States would have 'escaped' from making any direct contribution to CO_2 target reductions. If there were no limits on carbon trading, it would have significantly increased its share from 37 per cent to about 45 per cent of the total global CO_2 emissions in the transport sector. Even within the US, there are now clear signals that the people want action, with industry now supporting change. No agreement was reached at the Hague, and governments are trying to resolve the impasse of carbon trading and the Kyoto ratification at Bonn (2001), but with little expectation of progress, particularly as President Bush has said that he will not ratify the Kyoto agreement.

At the global level, there is considerable doubt over whether the targets set at Kyoto can be achieved, particularly in the transport sector. Although transport may not take an equal share in the CO_2 reduction targets, it still has an important role to play. It seems that only if the US is given unlimited scope to achieve its 'domestic' target through investment in 'other' countries will the targets be achieved through tradable permits. However, the moral responsibility of each country to make a positive contribution to the target achievement will not have been addressed. There will be even less incentive for the highly mobile affluent car drivers to pressure government to implement sustainable transport policies.

The only alternative to the Kyoto targets seems to be the possibility of contraction and convergence (see Section 2.5.4). This is a three-stage process where initially agreement is sought on the upper limits for CO_2 emissions. Once the overall limit has been agreed, there has to be further agreement of the proportion of the gas released, which remains in the atmosphere, so that the rate of reduction in emissions to reach the overall target can be estimated. The third stage is the allocation of maximum consumption targets for each nation (Meyer, 2001). This allocation process is still the centre of dispute as a fair level should be an equal allocation to each person. The means to get round this potential impasse would be to have a transition period for the convergence, with the higher consuming countries trading permits with those who were more efficient in their use of fossil fuels. Such an agreement would allow the flow of capital from the rich to the poorer countries, and there would be a strong incentive to reduce reliance on fossil fuels and to maintain efficiency in all energy use. However, making such a proposition is only the first step in the process, which is likely to be long and difficult. As we have already seen in the last 10 years (from Rio to Kyoto, via the Hague and Bonn), it is extremely difficult to make global agreements on the environment, and progress towards even converging on an approach has been painfully slow. Perhaps it is at the local level that public policy can have a greater impact on the quest for sustainable transport.

4.3 Local perspectives on public policy

It is at the local level that most action has been seen on pushing public policies towards sustainable transport, but even here there are many barriers to successful implementation. To a great extent, the options are well known and there is agreement among policy-makers (at least in principle) about what needs to be done to make transport more sustainable. There are three broad groups of overlapping policy options available: technological policies; economic and fiscal policies; and physical land-use and development policies. In addition to these three basic categories, there is the legislative context within which all decisions must be placed. In each case the intentions are the same – to make the most efficient use of the available transport infrastructure and to use the most appropriate technology available to minimize resource consumption. These are discussed in greater detail in Part 2 of the book, but here their public policy implications are introduced.

The role of technology policy

Technology and transport are integrally linked, as technology has a key role to play in replacing physical movement, in controlling movement on existing infrastructure, in ensuring vehicles are operating efficiently, and in providing real time information. Already, over 30 per cent of the costs of any new vehicle are related to technology and this will increase, particularly for engine management systems and in diagnostics for maintenance, but also in the new generation of route guidance systems (Banister, 2000c). In each case technology has made travel easier and this has probably encouraged more travel.

In the future, the role of technology needs to be directed not only towards increasing the reliability and efficiency of transport systems, but also in minimizing the need for transport. Innovative thinking is required to reduce the transport element in the production process through changes such as the regionalization of distribution networks. Rather than produce globally for global markets, firms can transfer the knowledge to local or regional production units, so that local production is for local markets. Similarly, as employment moves towards more service and knowledge-based industries, the physical requirements for transport can be reduced as products (e.g. computers) have a much higher value to weight component. This is the dematerialization process that may have a significant impact on the demand for freight transport.

The second fundamental technological change is the continuing search for new clean fuels. Technology offers tremendous opportunities for novel forms of transport, mainly based on new fuel sources and designed to reduce the dependence on oil (non-renewable fossil fuel). Included here are:

♦   Electric vehicles – calculations on the total energy chain must be made as the pollution may just be transferred from the vehicle to the power station.
♦   Methanol and ethanol – created from biomass and other renewable sources (e.g. sugar beet and rape oil seed). Conventional engines can run on these with minor adjustments.
♦   Hydrogen fuel cells – based on water, so entirely 'clean' but problems with the storage and generation processes.

It is likely that by 2020 most vehicles will be clean (in terms of fuels), with fleet vehicles, delivery vehicles and public transport vehicles being the first to switch. A much harder problem to resolve is the role of the diesel engine in the city as it has high emissions levels of nitrogen oxides and particulates. In other ways (e.g. fuel consumption) diesel is the preferred fuel, but the technology is not yet available to clean up diesel vehicle emissions. This technology may become available by 2020, but in the meantime, it is necessary to develop hybrid vehicles, which are battery powered in cities and diesel (or petrol) powered outside the city, with the use of regenerative power to recharge the batteries. Some manufacturers, such as Toyota (with the Prius), are already making a small impact in the market with such vehicles.

It would seem that there is no ideal vehicle for the future and that a series of 'niche vehicles' will emerge. Small city-based cars, which are about half the size of conventional cars and customized to individual requirements are already becoming common (e.g. the Daimler-Benz and Swatch joint venture to produce the Smart car). But in the US, a contrary trend is occurring with the growth in the large and high energy consuming sport utility vehicle, sometimes known as the urban assault vehicle.

Whatever future path is chosen, action is required now on which technologies should be adopted. In terms of public policy, clear signals need to be given to industry together with the incentives to invest in the new technology. For example, targets could be given for the proportion of new vehicles in the city, which are zero emission. In California, a target of 10 per cent (150,000 vehicles) was set for all new cars to be zero emission (i.e. electric or methanol) before 2004. This target was originally postponed after intense pressure from the car manufacturers, but has been reinstated with a longer time horizon (now set for 2008). The new California mandate also gives credits for vehicles that are substantially cleaner (e.g. hybrids), but are not zero emission vehicles. In Europe, there is a voluntary agreement between the EU and the car manufacturers to reduce emissions levels of CO_2 for new cars from 185 g per km (1995) to 140 g per km (2008). Both examples illustrate the need for clear policy directives and the possible creation of markets for tradable emissions credits between manufacturers. The transition phase is likely to be about 10 years, even with strong central direction, as this lead time is necessary to set up new vehicle production processes and for market penetration to take place.

In addition to policy actions by governments, there are actions that should be taken by companies and individuals willing to demonstrate best practice. For example, promotion of technological change through adopting best practice in their own businesses so that the transport component in production processes is reduced, or through the adoption of the best available technology for the company vehicle policy, including the use of electric and hybrid vehicles, as well as the emerging fuel cell technology. It is also necessary to promote the necessary supporting infrastructure in cities and at company sites to allow refuelling and priority measures for clean vehicles. Contributions could be made to innovation funds that would promote clean technology in public transport vehicles (including taxis). As in all sectors, transport users could maximize the use of the Internet, E-commerce and other forms of communications to minimize travel requirements. This would include travel minimization as a key element in productivity improvements within the company.

Even if the eco-car powered by hydrogen fuel cells were a reality, we would still not have sustainable transport. Non-renewable resources would be used in the construction of the vehicle, as not all parts can be recycled, and as the hydrogen reformers use rare metals. In addition, the process by which the hydrogen fuel is produced can have substantial emissions costs. The vehicles also need space and the supporting infrastructure would create some of the same problems as existing roads do for the environment. Technology can make vehicles cleaner but this is only part of the sustainable transport solution, as there are many other externalities.

The role of economic and fiscal policies

The problems of congestion cause substantial externalities, principally through congestion where demand exceeds supply. It is often said that transport is too cheap and that this is the reason why demand has increased. All that needs to be done is to increase the costs of travel and demand will be reduced. The economic arguments are clear as the social costs of transport (principally relating to congestion and the environment) can be internalized through the pricing mechanism. Most governments raise substantial amounts of revenue from tax on fuels (Table 4.3), typically between 63 per cent and 74 per cent of the pump price for petrol and slightly less for diesel.

The UK government has already been doing this through increasing the fuel duty by at least 5 per cent in real terms each year. In the transport sector, this is the main policy being pursued to meet the stabilization target for CO_2 emissions. Over the past 6 years, this has increased the price of a litre of fuel from 45 pence to 85 pence (1994–2000), of which 70 pence is tax and duty. Without the fuel price escalator, the pump price would only be about 60 pence and there is now considerable public resentment, particularly from industry, that petrol prices in the UK are uncompetitive. They are the most expensive in Europe and over 4 times as high as prices in the United States (Table 4.3). The escalator has now been removed after pressure from industry and other interests, particularly those in rural areas.

Acutt and Dodgson (1998) have suggested that increases in fuel duty of this level will not stabilize CO_2 emissions in 2000 at their 1990 levels (the Rio targets). Even if the more draconian measures proposed by the Royal Commission on Environmental pollution (1994) are introduced in which fuel prices are doubled in real terms by 2005 (equivalent to a 9 per cent annual increase in real fuel duty), the stabilization target would only be reached in

Table 4.3   **Retail fuel prices in the EU and tax levels (2002)**

Country	Unleaded petrol		Diesel	
Austria	82	(64%)	68	(57%)
Belgium	92	(69%)	68	(59%)
Denmark	104	(70%)	86	(60%)
Germany	99	(73%)	79	(66%)
Finland	101	(70%)	74	(57%)
France	96	(74%)	73	(66%)
Greece	69	(56%)	59	(55%)
Ireland	81	(64%)	73	(57%)
Italy	99	(68%)	81	(64%)
Luxembourg	73	(59%)	60	(53%)
Netherlands	113	(68%)	74	(59%)
Portugal	83	(69%)	61	(57%)
Spain	77	(62%)	65	(56%)
Sweden	96	(70%)	86	(57%)
United Kingdom	110	(77%)	113	(76%)

Note: Prices given in US dollars per 100 litres and percentage tax levels in brackets.
Source: ONS (2003c).

2004. Doubling real fuel prices reduces distances travelled by all forms of transport by 16 per cent and car distances by 20 per cent. The time necessary for stabilization depends on the assumed rate of increase in road traffic, the turnover of the vehicle stock, and the sensitivity of demand with respect to real increases in fuel prices. It seems that pricing strategies at the national level have only a limited impact as elasticities of demand with respect to price are low and because expected levels of increase in demand quickly outweigh reductions in use. There always seem to be problems with setting targets without actually considering the costs involved in actually reaching them.

At the urban level, *road pricing* has been advocated as the best means to tackle both the congestion and the environmental problems, after the original concept had remained dormant for 40 years since the Smeed Report (1964). Apart from Singapore and some limited forms of cordon pricing in Norwegian cities, many of the larger cities in all parts of the world are considering the possibilities. The levels of interest were given an enormous boost as a result of the implementation of congestion charging in Central London in February 2003 (Chapters 7 and 8). Both fuel price increases and road pricing may lead to rebound effects where capacity released by some users not prepared to pay the increased costs of travel is replaced by other users who are now prepared to pay a higher price. Demand management can discourage some car users, but indirectly encourage others.

The role of physical land-use and development policies

It is in this third group of public policy measures that most action has taken place with cities adopting a range of strategies most appropriate to their particular situation. Table 4.4 summarizes some of the main measures that have been used under three headings – land-use policy, technology policy and transport policy. Many of the measures have overlaps with the technological and economic policies, but a clear flavour of the opportunities available at the city and local levels is given.

In terms of achieving sustainable transport, several policy objectives are being addressed. Some policies are directed at increasing cycle and public transport use, whilst others are intended to reduce car use. Other policies increase sustainable accessibility, so that by the location of land uses and activities, new travel patterns can emerge, whilst a further group looks towards improving mobility efficiency so that intensity of use is increased. The role of technology is ambivalent as it enhances sustainable transport if trip patterns are modified or even reduced, but it may also encourage new activities. The policies operate at different levels and often work best when packaged together, rather than being left as stand alone policies. There is

Table 4.4   The public policy options for more sustainable transport

Policy context	Policy measure	Policy objective – to increase	Scope of implementation
1. Land-use policy	Car free development	Sustainable accessibility	Site
	Design of new development	Sustainable accessibility	Site
	Development at public transport nodes	Sustainable accessibility	District
	Mixed use developments	Sustainable accessibility	Site
	Urban concentration	Sustainable accessibility	Region
2. Technology policy	Demand responsive transport	Public transport use	Route
	Home delivery of goods and services	Reduce car use	Region
	Informatics	Mobility efficiency	Region
	Teleactivities	Electronic substitution	Aspatial
	Teleworking	Electronic substitution	Aspatial
	Transport optimization	Mobility efficiency	Region
3. Transport policy	Area access control	Reduce car use	District
	Peak congestion avoidance	Mobility efficiency	Region
	Car pooling	Reduce car use	Region
	Car sharing	Reduce car use	Region
	Company work hours policy	Mobility efficiency	Region
	Cycle priority and roadspace	Cycle use	Route
	HOV priority and roadspace	Public transport use	Route
	Public transport priority and roadspace	Public transport use	Route
	Media campaigns	Reduce car use	Aspatial
	Commuted payments	Public transport use	Region
	Park and ride	Public transport use	Region
	Parking charges	Reduce car use	District
	Parking restrictions and capacity reduction	Reduce car use	District
	Road capacity restraint and reductions	Reduce car use	Route
	Road pricing	Reduce car use	Region
	Traffic calming	Reduce car use	District
	Cycle subsidy	Cycle use	Region
	Public transport capacity investment	Public transport use	Region
	Public transport subsidy	Public transport use	Region

Notes: Policy objectives: each policy measure has been allocated to a main objective category, but some can appear in more than one. For example car pooling reduces car use and increases mobility efficiency; commuted payments, HOV priority and park and ride all reduce car use and increase public transport use; car free development reduces car use and increases sustainable accessibility.
Scope of implementation: Route = along a transport corridor; Site = a specific location or nodal point; District = local level; Region = city or rural level; Aspatial = coverage is flexible.
HOV = High occupancy vehicles.
Source: Based on Banister and Marshall (2000).

substantial potential for implementing sustainable transport policies, but progress has been slow.

4.4   Barriers to implementation

At one level, public policy-making on sustainable transport is straightforward, as it is more or less taken for granted that once a policy decision has been made the policy will be implemented, and the people will respond with the expected changes in behaviour. When the results of a policy fall short of their expectation, the people are blamed. Individuals regularly refuse to behave in ways that the policy-makers would prefer. This gap between the assumptions underlying policy measures on the one hand, and the behavioural responses by individuals on the other, is normally referred to as the policy behaviour gap. In reference to the gap between policy measures and behavioural responses to congestion, Salomon and Mokhtarian (1997) point to the large set of alternative strategies that individuals have at their disposal to avoid the expected behaviour.

But 'non-rational' behaviour by the public may also be reinforced by poor implementation where a measure does not accomplish what was intended. During policy-making, there are not only expectations about the behaviour of the public, but also about the way a measure can be implemented. According to Smith (1973, p. 199) 'problems of policy implementation may be more widespread than commonly acknowledged'. If the programmes are of a new, non-incremental nature, difficulties with implementation may occur. One can imagine that this is the case with measures that try to introduce a sustainable transport policy. The normal way to respond to increased car use has been through providing more infrastructure, but this in turn results in increased accessibility and capacity with higher levels of traffic demand.

There are several forces that prevent a measure from being implemented in its most ideal form. They could either reduce the potential of a measure once implemented, or even make implementation impossible. Barriers can be divided into six main categories:

1   Resource barriers are in essence very simple. To implement a measure, an adequate amount of financial and physical resources has to be available. If these resources are not available in time and in the right amount, implementation will be delayed. Lack of money for implementation is closely linked to institutional barriers, as local, regional and national governmental authorities are unlikely to provide money for schemes that do not concur with policy.

2   Institutional and policy barriers relate to problems with coordinated actions between different organizations or levels of government, and to conflicts with other policies. A large number of public and private bodies are involved in transport provision and this means it is often difficult to achieve coordinated action by the implementing agency. Sometimes, this is due to differences in cultures between departments (e.g. bureaucratic versus market orientated). In other cases, the differences in legal powers between governmental bodies affects the implementation of measures

and schemes. Also the implementing organization itself has to be well equipped to accomplish the implementation job properly. An unstable administrative organization and unqualified personnel may reduce the capacity to implement (Smith, 1973).

3   Social and cultural barriers concern the public acceptability of measures. While some measures may theoretically be effective at promoting sustainable transport, their effectiveness is minimal if people do not accept their introduction or implementation. Social acceptability may often depend on whether the proposed strategy compromises 'push' or 'pull' measures (i.e. whether it is a strategy of discouragement or encouragement). On the whole, pull measures tend to be popular, and may encourage, for example, an increase in the use of more sustainable modes of transport. On the other hand, many people are reluctant to give up the perceived freedom associated with owning and using a car and these push policies tend to be unpopular. Social acceptability involves both the travelling public and local businesses and other organizations that will be affected by the implementation of a new measure.

4   Legal barriers. Many transport policies and measures need adjustment of laws and regulations, within or outside the realm of transport. If implementation is complicated by legal requirements or even made impossible by law, legal barriers are raised. They can occur at several levels. For example, the design and sign-posting of transport schemes in almost all countries is circumscribed by government regulations and directives. While many of these are beneficial in ensuring reasonable standards, others can impose restraints on innovative solutions. When good implementation requires changes in rules or regulations outside the transport domain, one can expect that more effort has to be put into facilitate these changes.

5   Side effects. Almost every measure has one or more side effects. If implementation of a measure has serious side effects, this may hinder other activities to such an extent that implementation becomes too complicated, even though these side effects may only have limited effects on the success of the measure itself. For instance, traffic calming does not only reduce the speed of cars, but also causes inconvenience to public transport, and it may bring about a change in the nature of traffic accidents. It is often difficult to anticipate both the positive and negative side effects, for example, of road pricing. But these side effects and the demonstration effects play a crucial role in promoting widespread implementation of policies.

6   Other (physical) barriers could take the form of space restrictions or are related to the topography of an area. For example, there may not be adequate space on the outskirts of an urban area for the introduction of park and ride facilities, and the large parking areas they require. Hilly terrain may be impractical in the case of promoting travelling by bicycle.

An empirical investigation of a wide range of policy measures has been undertaken (Banister and Marshall, 2000) to assess the scale of the barriers to implementation for public policies aimed at making transport more sustainable. Barriers, which occurred during policy-making and prevented measures from being implemented, are excluded from this analysis. Information was gathered by interviews with decision-makers and implementing agents. In a few cases, studies about the implementation process were available. Either these studies where pilot projects implemented to gather information about how the measures were implemented and their results, or they were successful measures which can be demonstrated as examples of good practice to other cities.

It was found that only one of the sixty-one measures reviewed was implemented without any form of a barrier (Figure 4.1). This is the handicapped bus stops measure in Aalborg (Denmark) – a good example of a

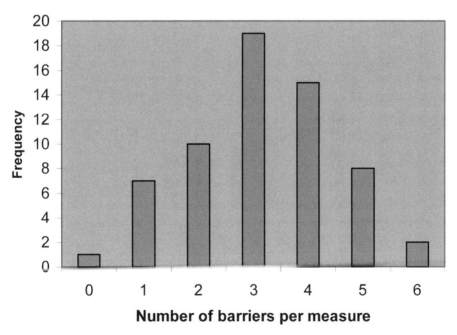

Figure 4.1 Frequency of the number of barrier types per measure
Source: Banister and Marshall (2000).

very cheap 'pull' measure. The other measures had to cope with one or more barriers. There are two measures that encountered all barrier types. These were the development at public transport nodes in Bucharest (Romania) and traffic calming in Zürich (Switzerland).

Barriers may occur in various forms. Sometimes they are of limited importance, but in other situations they can seriously hinder implementation. For each measure and barrier type, the influence of the barriers on the implementation process was assessed as to whether barriers had occurred or not, and if so why (Figure 4.2). The histogram presents the frequencies by the level of seriousness for each barrier type. This kind of visualizing shows us the seriousness of barriers to implementation.

The results show that resource barriers occurred most frequently, followed by institutional/policy and social/cultural barriers. Side effects and physical/other barriers were the categories with the fewest entries. Looking at the seriousness of the barriers, it appears that most of them are real but were overcome. Within the resource category, in 18 per cent of the measures the seriousness of the barrier hindered good implementation. Side effects hardly affected the implementation process.

It is easy to make an extensive list of barriers that occurred during implementation, but politicians have to balance various interests and spend money in the 'public interest'. A scheme is part of a wider policy or a

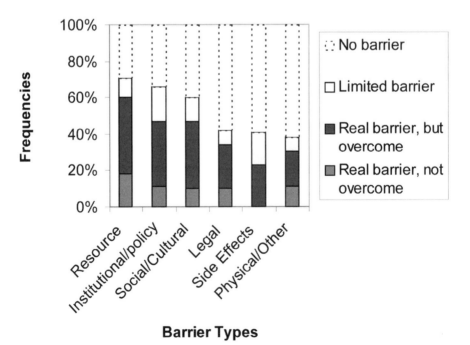

Barrier Types

Figure 4.2 Level of barrier seriousness per barrier type. *Source*: Banister and Marshall (2000).

package of measures, which is aimed at a particular goal, such as sustainable development, and transport is only one element in that policy. To achieve sustainable development, methods of analysis have to be extended beyond single sector analysis to include explicitly the effects of policy decisions. This lack of interaction between sectors is seen by Banister (1998*b*) as one of the main barriers to achieving urban sustainability. A second set of barriers mentioned relates to the responsibilities of the decision-makers themselves. They do not seem to have a real political commitment to introducing measures to address the key issues in a comprehensive and consistent approach.

The points raised above can be illustrated with the case of Edinburgh (Scotland). Edinburgh City Council has a commitment to travel reduction and pursues this goal by promoting a modal shift away from the car. By the year 2000, the number of car journeys was to be reduced from 48 per cent in 1991 to 46 per cent, with a further reduction to 34 per cent by 2010. The share of sustainable transport modes, meanwhile, is to be increased. Cycling is to account for 10 per cent of all journeys by 2010 and public transport is to account for 39 per cent. To turn these targets into reality a number of concrete measures were implemented, ranging from bus lanes and car free housing to car sharing schemes. Some of these measures delivered considerable improvements but according to Mittler (1999) on the whole they are too piecemeal. The measures are too small in their impact because they are rather small in scale or can deliver only local improvements. Also, many projects are too slow in their implementation to reverse the trend.

Mittler also points out that the City Council committed itself to a sustainable transport policy, but at the same time it has a commitment to economic growth. The current planning policy still encourages further traffic growth. Large out-of-town shopping and housing development are still being planned and built. In Edinburgh, this dichotomy of commitments is a key barrier to a wide scale implementation of a travel reduction policy. According to Mittler (1998), as long as there is a commitment to economic growth 'pronouncements on sustainable development will inevitably be mere rhetoric. Talk will not be matched by action . . . To remove this barrier a paradigm shift to a pre analytic vision that acknowledges limits to growth is necessary'.

However, removing this political dichotomy barrier is not a sufficient condition on its own for not achieving a sustainable transport system. In Edinburgh four other barriers are identified (Mittler, 1998):

1   Lack of knowledge and awareness among the population. Opinion polls show that only some 10 per cent of the population knows anything about sustainable development at all. This barrier can be seen as a social barrier in the sense of the expression – 'unknown makes unloved'.

2   Financial constraints and funding arrangements. This resource barrier

does not apply to the amount of money that is available, but to its distribution among those agencies responsible for implementing sustainable policies.

3   The Council remains stuck in an institutional framework that does not allow for holistic policy-making. This is an example of an institutional barrier in which different departments have different agendas and in the end do not support each other's goals.

4   Existing regulations and legislation are in favour of unsustainable practices.

These four barriers show that obstacles to a sustainable transport policy are in fact institutionalized into the economic and social system. This makes them hard to overcome, but in terms of implementation, there are various ways to do things better. One suggestion often made is to raise the awareness of all parties to gain acceptance for policies that are perceived as negative.

A clear example is the implementation of car restricting measures in the city centre of Enschede (the Netherlands). At the beginning of the 1980s, the main shopping streets were transformed into a pedestrian area. By 1989, it became clear that the number of cars entering the city centre was not reduced and that the police were unable to enforce the traffic regulations. A plan was made by the Municipality for a (partial) closure of the city centre to cars. Because of fierce resistance by local entrepreneurs this plan was withdrawn. However it was also clear that something had to be done. Therefore in 1990 the municipality established a study group with the task of producing proposals to reduce car traffic in the city centre. In this group various parties were represented: shopkeepers, the police, local residents, cultural agencies, disabled persons and the economic department of the municipality.

In 1991, the study group came up with its initial proposal, which was discussed during a public hearing. After some adjustments of the plan, it was presented to the City Council, which agreed to a half-year trial period. During this period, a survey was conducted and another public hearing was held. The survey showed favourable results (a reduction in the number of cars) and both city centre residents and entrepreneurs were positive about the measure. By the end of 1992 the City Council decided to make the measure permanent. The most interesting aspect of this approach was that the measure in its final stage restricted the car access to the city centre more than the original plan, which was withdrawn because of public resistance. The area and time-window in which no cars are allowed were increased after the trial period (Louw and Maat, 1999).

In the Netherlands, this method of implementation is called interactive planning, while in the UK it is called community participation (Hathway, 1997). In fact, interactive planning is not just implementation, but decision-making and implementation together. Both the politicians and the general public are involved in decision-making and implementation. This is done not by a formal public inquiry procedure, but by creating awareness and debate with all parties involved. The goal of interactive planning is to bridge the gap between politics and citizens, to democratize decision-making and to create public support.

This makes the success of a policy highly dependent on its implementation. If a potentially high success measure is badly implemented, it is unlikely that the measure will have its desired effect. Unforeseen effects may occur which are counter-productive and have impacts on unrelated areas of policy. Policy-makers therefore need to pay attention to the feasibility of a policy alternative at both strategic and operational levels. But even if the measure is successfully implemented and there is a favourable response by the public, the measure may be too limited in scale to have a measurable impact.

Policy-makers should take account of the various barriers to implementation. When the barriers are not possible to overcome, it may be preferable to abandon a particular policy, rather than to press on with a poorly thought through partial implementation. This is especially true where there are substantial institutional, policy, legal and resource barriers. In most cases, these barriers can be foreseen and addressed. If a measure is innovative, then it is advisable to implement a pilot measure first, so that positive demonstration effects are seen. Experiences are gathered through learning-by-doing, and the measure takes shape during its implementation and through subsequent adaptation.

Another way to avoid bad implementation is to create awareness before introducing a measure. Even better is to get the people involved in the decision-making itself to increase public acceptability. This approach may be most worthwhile for individual measures, and less effective for the implementation of a policy as a whole. For a major change in implementing a sustainable transport policy in a wider context of spatial and economic development, a general political commitment is essential. Only then can the institutional barriers be overcome.

4.5 Conclusions

When discussing sustainable transport and public policy, it is easy to become pessimistic about the outcomes. Even if successful and strong implementation takes place, would it really achieve a sustainable transport system? In essence, the issue being tackled has been presented the wrong way round. As stated earlier in this Chapter, we should be concerned about developing high quality, environmentally attractive and safe cities in which people want to live – this is the vision of the sustainable city. We should then see the role that transport can play in achieving that vision. If we only concentrate on transport solutions to the problems of cities, we are not tackling the causes of the problems, only the manifestations of the problems. There are many opportunities for sustainable cities, and several European cities have succeeded in offering the vision with a sustainable transport system to support it. Zürich (Switzerland) is one example where people are now giving up the ownership of their cars in the city, as they do not need it because levels of accessibility are high and public transport is excellent (Mägerle and Maggi, 1999). But this solution is expensive and not appropriate to all situations. The options for sustainable transport in the suburbs and the rural areas, even in Switzerland are more limited.

Underlying this pessimism are two fundamental questions that need to be addressed and resolved if sustainable transport is to become a reality. The nature and scale of action required is substantially greater than has been admitted. To actually achieve sustainable transport requires people and goods to travel less. There is no way that the global CO_2 targets can be achieved (at least in the transport sector) without a reduction in travel, particularly by those living in the affluent countries. All the measures would only allow travel to stabilize if they were introduced as part of a strong and coherent package of measures. Even in those countries and cities where there are strong commitments to the environment and sustainable transport, it is impossible to detect a situation of non-growth in travel and less non-renewable resources being used in transport. But transport is crucial to the operation of businesses, the global economy and the increases in affluence and leisure. This is the problem to be resolved. Even if substantial investment is made in more sustainable technology, the growth in demand, particularly for long distance travel, will outweigh the environmental benefits. There are many other externalities that also need to be addressed (Section 4.1).

Implicit in much of this discussion is the notion of political will, which underlies all the barriers mentioned here. There is an inherent difficulty in implementing any radical policy as there are so many special interest groups that campaign against change, and this is often compounded by the complexity and length of the necessary legislative processes required to facilitate change. The first fundamental question for public policy is – are we serious about sustainable transport? Should we accept the premise that sustainable transport is not a realistic policy objective and that transport will continue to be unsustainable? Strong actions can be introduced in other sectors to achieve global CO_2 targets, but should transport be exempt from this debate? These issues are taken up again with respect to available measures and packaging in Chapters 7 and 11.

The second, more optimistic fundamental question relates to the willingness to change. Public policy should enhance the reasoning ability of the population through enlarging the scope of public discourse. This in turn will enhance and reinforce democratic processes. All through this Chapter we have emphasized the importance of the involvement and commitment of all actors to raise their awareness, to gain their support, and to empower them to take action. Within transport, there is an acceptance that not all decisions are market-based, and that even if the market did operate efficiently in transport, it would not be democratic. Markets operate best in certain well-specified situations, but they are subject to many distortions from powerful corporate and governmental institutions. Institutional approaches to public policy-making encourage community and corporate involvement and empowerment.

Overcoming barriers to effective implementation requires interactive and participatory processes, so that intentions and outcomes of policy interventions to achieve sustainable transport coincide. This means that individualism needs to be moderated and there must be an increased acceptance of collective responsibility in decisions related to transport. This would result in modal shifts to public transport and green modes, less use of the car, higher vehicle occupancy levels, targeted programmes for companies, shops and schools, car free areas in cities, and strong media and governmental support.

As part of the change in values and attitudes, there should be a clear and open debate on the issues, linked with positive actions to create choices. The broader issues related to sustainability and the environment need to be linked to individual travel decisions and lifestyles. There must be an awareness of the benefits and a willingness to change. If these vital elements are not present, then it is very difficult in a democratic society to pursue a policy of sustainable transport, and decision-makers should recognize what is possible and what is not possible to achieve. It is naïve to pretend that there has been any significant move towards sustainable transport over the recent past, and there are at present few signs that this will change in the near future.

Chapter 5

Institutional and organisational aspects

5.1 Policy perspectives

Throughout the discussion in the previous chapters, it is clear that different combinations of factors are perceived as important in different situations. There is not one solution that will fit all situations. Added to this, there are different cultural contexts within which policy decisions are made. These differences are highlighted in the following table, which demonstrates some of the contrasting priorities between Europe and the US (Table 5.1).

Yet it is clear that all actors need to be involved in achieving sustainable transport. At the international level, there are the global conventions and these have already been covered in Chapters 2 and 4. The motor manufacturers are also key players and they are now taking an active role. In the US, the Partnership for a New Generation of Vehicles (US-PNGV) is a co-operative venture between the federal government, three car manufacturers (GM, Ford and Chrysler) and their suppliers. This venture will produce affordable and attractive cars, which are three times as fuel-efficient (35 mpg – 12.4 kilometres per litre). Such a change would bring the new car fleet to comparable efficiency levels of the current stock in Europe. In the EU, there is an intention to cut CO_2 emissions from new cars by 25 per cent in 2008. This is equivalent to increasing fuel efficiency from 35 mpg to 50 mpg (12.4 kilometres per litre to 17.7 kilometres per litre). Alliances are also taking place between car manufacturers, battery technology developers and power companies. For example, the nuclear power industry is funding some of the electrical vehicle research and development programme.

Table 5.1 Differences in institutional priorities between Europe and the United States

	Europe	USA
Use of taxation to address sustainability problems	Intensive	Not intensive
Stimulation of public transport	High	Low
Role of rail for passenger transport	Large	Small
Deregulation of transport markets	Slow	Fast
Emphasis on equity versus efficiency in policy-making	Equity	Efficiency
Land-use policies	Strong	Weak

Source: Rietveld and Stough (2005).

The oil industry also sees itself as an important player in the development of cleaner and alternative fuels, and in developing renewable energy. There are substantial advantages in being active in seeking ways to diversify company strategies so that there is less dependence on carbon-based fuels. In all cases there are potentially huge new markets to open up for the development of new technology that can increase vehicle efficiency and move towards the goal of the 'clean car'. Such a strategy maintains and expands existing markets in line with the desires of consumers to make some 'contribution' to a cleaner environment.

At the global level, it would seem that reductions have to start modestly as there is so much capital stock tied up in the global energy system. Policy should be encouraged to switch to a low carbon technology and it is here that a carbon tax could be used to give the necessary stimulus to investment in developing the appropriate technologies (Chapter 2.5.5). Industry really holds the key to major change and there are now promising signs that some of the global players (e.g. BP and Shell) are taking the lead.

Such actions at the international level are complemented by governments and local authorities at the national level with taxation policies, new regulations and the setting of a development framework that ensures a greater priority is given to sustainable development. Here it seems that command-and-control actions need to be combined with market instruments. At the local level, there is less optimism about the role of technology. Equally, there is a growing concern over the use of ambitious targets that are not achievable or have a high cost of compliance. More faith seems to have been placed in tradable permits, where economic levers can be used to set the levels, allocate credits and encourage trading (e.g. sulphur dioxide reduction from power stations in the United States and particulate reduction in Chile). The key has been the introduction of tradable rights and heavy fines for non-compliance (Chapter 2.3.6).

Similarly, by switching taxes from labour (production) to consumption, clear signals can be given to industry. This has been successfully used in Sweden, where a tax on the sulphur content of fuel has resulted in a 50 per cent reduction and stimulated power plant to invest in abatement technology. Norway's carbon tax (1991) lowered emissions from power stations by 21 per cent (*The Economist*, 29 September, 2001, p. 104).

Throughout national economies, there needs to be transparency over the levels of subsidies to environmentally harmful activities. Ideally, there should be no subsidies for energy and travel so that the costs of consumption reflect the full costs of production. But, there are social issues that also need to be considered, as markets themselves do not operate efficiently and not everyone can compete equally in that market. There are also possibilities for new markets to be created through advocating local consumption and through eco-labelling of products to allow consumers greater choice and information about products.

5.2 Opportunities for change

There are many options and opportunities for change. These can be divided into three basic groups: technological options (Table 5.5); land-use planning options (Tables 5.3 and 5.4); and transport options (Tables 5.3 and 5.4). In each case, changes can be facilitated by regulation, economic interventions and information, and decisions on each of these can be taken at all levels. In addition to the clear list of policy options, governments are now also agreeing on voluntary and mandatory targets for the achievement of reductions in resource consumption and pollution levels. Much of this information is well known, and can be obtained from a wide range of sources (e.g. Banister and Button, 1993; OECD/ECMT, 1995; Geerlings, 1997; Transportation Research Board, 1997; UNDP, 1997).

5.2.1 Organizational structures

In this Section, some information is summarized through a series of tables, with a commentary to link the main observations with the underlying theme of transport and sustainable development. The basic argument being made is that new approaches are required if serious action is to be taken towards sustainable development. Some of the constraints have already been discussed, but here the focus is on the limitations of the present organizational structures and the policy measures in current use (Tables 5.2, 5.3 and 5.4). Two important conclusions arise out of Table 5.2.

Firstly, as has been observed (Chapter 2), the growth markets are now in the non-OECD countries, principally in the Far East and South America in the short term and in India in the medium term. Responsibility for action should involve government and the motor vehicle manufacturers as the two principal agents. But it also includes the oil industry, as they should be providing clean alternative fuels based on renewable energy sources, and the necessary infrastructure to allow for the distribution and use of that energy. The supply chains in the transport industry are varied and extended, so that

Table 5.2 Traditional roles and responsibilities

National government	Makes national policy, sets standards, makes regulations, provides policy guidance, sets fiscal and financial policy and incentives, provides policy framework for local implementation.
Local authority	Responsible for detailed implementation within the national policy framework, raising local taxes, enforcement of standards and regulations, decisions on development priorities and detailed planning applications.

at each stage the environmental costs and consequences need to be balanced against the economic gains. Other actors include the various interest groups for the transport industry, the operators, the environmental and other pressure groups, and others (e.g. developers, financial institutions). All have different vested interests in transport, as do the general public who are the direct beneficiaries of the available transport system (as users) and as the indirect beneficiaries (as consumers of transported goods), but who may also suffer the consequences. To achieve effective action in sustainable transport, responsibility must be attached to all interested parties and each must be prepared to take action.

Secondly, many of the actions implemented relate to a single sector rather than to more general policy objectives or to cross sector implementation. Actions taken individually have less impact than those that have been packaged together (Marshall and Banister, 2000), but it is also necessary to ensure complementarity in actions. Counterintuitive outcomes may result from the implementation of actions, as users of the system find creative means to continue to do what they have done in the past. This involves the close links between transport and city planning authorities, as well as the new links with other actors. Local Agenda 21 attempts to forge this more comprehensive approach involving all actors, but it has not achieved success, as institutional barriers and the lack of appropriate powers has made effective implementation difficult. However, having more localized powers does not necessarily mean that action will follow. The noble objective of consensus and partnership, central to the UK government's transport policy (2000), may not exist as individuals and organizations have conflicts of interest, objectives, time-scales and do not even communicate effectively with each other (Tables 4.4 and 5.3).

For example, park and ride is seen as a policy to reduce city centre congestion as cars are left at peripheral car parks and public transport is used to get people to the centre. On its own, this policy may simply release more traffic space for other road users so that there is little net benefit, and it may also result in longer journeys as car users (and public transport users) are attracted to the park and ride site (Goodwin, 1998). If the policy objective is to reduce the use of the car in the city centre, the park and ride scheme should be combined with priority to public transport on the routes into the city (reallocation of road space) and strict city centre parking control (to reduce the attractiveness of the city centre for car users). Imaginative schemes could be developed along the corridor to encourage developments that generate/attract high levels of activity – similar to the Dutch ABC policy, but on a corridor basis (Haq, 1997). Information could also be given to drivers about the conditions (e.g. congestion and air quality) in the city centre to convince them of the social and environmental benefits of leaving the car at the peripheral site. Such a holistic approach would give choices to drivers and allocate responsibilities for positive actions at the appropriate level (true subsidiarity). It is only when individuals make 'sustainable choices' that real progress is made.

Action in the land-use and transport sectors has traditionally been seen as the prime responsibility of the public sector. The new agenda suggests that it is necessary to involve all actors in the public and private sectors in achieving policy objectives related to sustainability. At the international level, that is now taking place through the current series of global conventions (e.g. at Rio (1992), Kyoto (1997) and Buenos Aires (1998)). However, the motor manufacturers have not yet been fully involved in developing a global strategy that matches up the economic and financial interests of the car industry with the broader environmental concerns of society. Technology is still being cascaded from the rich to the poor countries. Enormous potential exists for producing more efficient vehicles and recycling the current vehicle stock.

5.2.2   Policies and measures

There are many options and opportunities for change in the land-use and transport sectors. As has already been noted, most measures are well tried. The debate is not really about what needs doing or even the range of measures available. It is more about how to facilitate implementation. Table 5.3 summarizes the range of measures in current use, while Table 5.4 lists the popularity of the measures. An important element here is the public understanding and acceptance of many of the policies.

In the OECD/ECMT study (1995), there were twelve case study cities surveyed in detail[1] and popularity was gauged by the frequency of implementation and discussions with decision-makers in a wider range of cities (132 in all – Dasgupta, 1993).

On the planning side:

1   Strategic land-use/transport planning consisted mainly of linking new developments to the provision of good quality public transport facilities.
2   Regional policy, concerning policy packages, which encouraged a shift of development from one part of the country to another, was an important issue in large metropolitan regions only. It was usually accompanied by restraint measures on the growth of the principal city centre and complementary measures designed to encourage relocation.
3   Policies to encourage a multicentre structure within the metropolitan region were particularly popular in all metropolitan areas and very large cities. These policies were also accompanied by measures to restrain

Table 5.3   Policies and measures in current use

Planning Measures
1   Strategic policy for land-use and transport planning
2   Regional policy affecting economic development in different areas of the country
3   Restraint on economic growth of principle city centres
4   Designated cities or areas for growth/control over the pattern of development
5   Relocation of particular employment groups/sectors
6   Use of preferred locations for travel-generating activities (e.g. town centres)
7   Fiscal inducements to relocate in designated areas
8   Zoning regulations (single use, mixed use, densities etc.)
9   Green belts
10 Regeneration of decaying areas (city centres, inner-city areas)
11 Improvements to housing and neighbourhood quality/facilities
12 Parking standards for new developments

Transport Supply Measures
1   Road construction
2   Rail investment/construction
3   Improved public transport service, fares, ticketing and information
4   Traffic management, driver information
5   Park and ride
6   Pedestrian areas, cycle and walk ways

Transport Demand Management
7   Car restraint/road pricing
8   Toll charges
9   Parking controls
10 Entry prohibitions
11 Goods traffic restraint
12 Pedestrian priority
13 Cycle priority
14 Bus/tram priority
15 Traffic calming
16 Car pooling/sharing

Targets and Standards
1   Targets for improving road safety, reduction of noise and air pollution levels
2   Targets for reduced traffic levels, certain types of traffic (e.g. heavy goods vehicles) and car park supply
3   Targets for reduced fuel consumption and CO_2 emissions
4   Targets for increased car pooling, public transport use, cycling and walking
5   Standards for vehicle noise, emissions control and safety

Source: Based on OECD/ECMT (1995), Table 4.12.

growth of the central city, the setting up of new towns and specially designated growth areas, and included the use of financial and other types of inducements.

On the transport side:

1   Rail construction was one of the most popular measures taken, particularly in metropolitan areas and very large cities, while improving

public transport by other means (including bus priority) became the more dominant policy in the smaller cities. In the middle range of cities, both new construction and improvements by other means were equally popular.

2   Road construction does not feature strongly in any of the cities, with one or two exceptions: Tokyo and Hiroshima – to increase road capacity, and Stockholm for environmental reasons as part of the much heralded, but eventually doomed, Dennis Package.

3   Parking controls were the most common type of restraint used in all the cities studied.

Table 5.4   Popularity of measures in the 12 case study cities

Policy measure	Metropolises (10–30 million)	Large cities (1.5–5 million)	Medium cities (0.5–1.5 million)
Planning			
1 Strategic policy for land-use/transport planning	◆◆	◆◆◆	◆◆
2 Regional policy	◆◆	◆	
3 Restraint on city centre growth	◆◆	◆	
4 Designated growth areas and new towns	◆◆◆	◆	◆
5 Relocation of employment groups	◆		
7 Fiscal inducements to relocate	◆◆		
8 Zoning regulations	◆		
9 Green belts	◆		◆
10 Regeneration of city centre/inner areas			◆
Transport			
1 Road construction	◆	◆	◆
2 Rail construction	◆◆◆	◆◆	◆◆
3 Improved public transport service/lower fares	◆	◆◆	◆◆◆
4 Traffic management and information	◆◆	◆◆	◆◆
5 Park and ride	◆	◆	◆
6 + 12 Pedestrian priority		◆	◆
7 Car restraint		◆	
7 + 8 Toll charges/road pricing			
9 Parking controls	◆◆	◆◆	◆◆
13 Cycle priority		◆	◆
14 Bus/tram priority	◆	◆◆	◆◆
15 Traffic calming		◆	◆
16 Car pooling			
17 Standards for noise/air pollution	◆		

Notes: The 12 case study cities are listed in the note at the end of the Chapter and the numbers refer to those in Table 5.3. Note that some of the measures listed in Table 5.3 are omitted from the study of the 12 cities: in the Planning group, they include use of preferred locations for travel generating activities, improvements to housing and neighbourhood quality/facilities, parking standards; in the Transport group, they include entry prohibitions and goods traffic restraint; in the Targets and Standards group, they include safety targets, traffic reductions, fuel consumption and CO_2, noise and air pollution, car pooling, cycling and walking.
◆ to ◆◆◆ denotes the increasing degree of popularity of measures tried.
Source: Based on OECD/ECMT (1995), Table 4.2.

4   Pedestrian priority, traffic calming and the provision of cycleways featured very little in the policies of the large metropolises, and with one or two exceptions, not a great deal in the other cities. (Abbreviated from OECD/ECMT, 1995, pp 77–78).

In a follow-up study, the ECMT/OECD (2002) carried out a survey of 167 cities in thirty-two countries to see what progress had been made. They investigated the trends that were taking place and the actions that had been introduced to move towards sustainable urban development (Fact Box 5.1). The main conclusions from this report focused on the implementation barriers to be overcome. It seemed that there was still a lack of a national policy framework within which a sustainable urban travel strategy could be embedded, together with the appropriate linkages with other national objectives on transport, the environment and health. It was at the policy integration and coordination levels that most difficulties emerged, as there seemed to be an inability or reluctance to view the problems (and solutions) holistically, rather than by sector. This was in part attributed to inefficient institutional roles and procedures, with a lack of cooperation between agencies and ministries, and no consistency in policy direction. The lack of cooperation between organizations and the lack of consistency in policy objectives was augmented by the diversity of interests in public views on sustainable transport and an often hostile press. It was also found that there were unsupportive legal and regulatory frameworks, weaknesses in the pricing and fiscal regimes, and misguided financing and investment flows. It seems surprising then that any progress has been made, and these types of criticisms do not only refer to a sustainable transport strategy, but to transport policy implementation more generally. In short, the basic problem identified in the ECMT/OECD survey (2002) is a lack of political commitment to tackling the issue of transport in general and a sustainable transport system in particular, as any commitment requires substantial long term funding and a clear set of objectives. These requirements are often outside the short term political agenda, particularly when confronted with a sceptical public, business interests and a hostile press.

5.2.3   Reducing emissions

If the primary concern is over the reduction in emissions levels from transport, there is again a wide range of options available (Table 5.5). The type of action has been grouped by whether it is regulatory, economic or information based. The existing standards within the OECD countries can be tightened and new standards can be introduced in the non-OECD countries where at present there is little control. However, it should be realized that there are costs involved,

Fact Box 5.1   Trends and actions in cities

Trends

1 *Urban development* – continuing suburbanization of the urban population. Urban density is weakening in large urban areas, stabilizing in medium sized urban areas, and dropping in small towns and cities. Percentage of jobs in the CBD is generally stable.

2 *Car ownership* – is increasing (1990–2000), with the average rate among EU cities at 0.41 cars per person. This ranges from 0.60 cars per person in Geneva, Odense and Weimar, to 0.30 cars per person in Athens, Seville, Dublin and Amsterdam. Accession countries increased car ownership by 30 per cent, and Denver had the highest level of 1.07 cars per person.

3 *Overall mobility* – is stable, but car use is up, walking and public transport use down, with cycling stable. Overall trips per person per day are 3.55. Pusan and Atlanta were the only two cities reporting a fall in private car trips. Cycle trips accounted for 0.43 trips per person per day, walking for 0.77 trips, with car accounting for 1.66 trips and public transport for 0.69 trips. Trip lengths by car have increased by about 20 per cent.

4 *Congestion* – seems to be increasing in most cities, but it is difficult to measure.

5 *Ozone* – was the most serious local air pollution issue raised, as there has been considerable improvement in the emissions of SO_2, NO_2, PM_{10}, and HC. Little was said on CO_2.

Actions

1 *Sustainable Urban Travel Policies* – included a range of actions:
   (a) decentralization of responsibilities for actions from the centre to local levels, but sometimes without the necessary resources or revenue raising powers – more negotiation rather than guidance;
   (b) integration of land use and transport to try and balance the forces of dispersal with those of redeveloping the central city area;
   (c) consultation and involvement of partnerships for effective action;
   (d) quality of public transport improved through the use of local revenue raising powers and through the maintenance of low public transport fares;
   (e) traffic management – principally parking controls and priority to public transport on roads and at intersections;
   (f) road and congestion pricing – not yet implemented, except as cordon pricing in Central London, Oslo, Bergen, Trondheim, Rome, Bologna and on some motorways;
   (g) climate change policies – fuel duty escalator, but a lack of focus on reduction of CO_2 emissions at the local level.

Main measures designed to address congestion, urban sprawl and local environmental problems. Questions raised over what is an acceptable level of congestion and how hard policy-makers can 'squeeze' car use in and around cities.

2 *Sustainable Urban Transport Strategy* – would consist of a package of measures to cover
   (a) maximum use of public transport;
   (b) limiting the use of the car through traffic and mobility management;

continued on page 89

continued from page 88

(c) minimizing sprawl through the integration ofland use and transport;
(d) producing a betterenvironment through improvements in air quality, less fuel use, less CO_2 emissions and lower levels of noise.

Strategy to be proactive and consistent, well managed and involving all actors.

Note that 328 ECMT/OECD cities were originally targeted (167 responses) and the quality of data is variable. Also the geographical distribution is distorted – Canada 1 response from 12 cities, United States 6 responses from 22 cities, but Japan has 25 responses from 25 cities and Turkey 10 responses from 10 cities.

Source: Based on ECMT/OECD (2002).

and that successful implementation (and enforcement) takes time to set up the necessary infrastructure (e.g. vehicle testing stations) and institutions (e.g. legal and regulatory authorities). Many governments have now made commitments to the achievement of stringent air quality control targets in urban areas. Such action means that the market mechanisms (pricing) can be used to achieve the targets within a clear regulatory framework. However, the two unknowns are the rate of technological innovation and the trends in vehicle use, and these two factors will always result in some uncertainty.

5.2.4 Combining policies and packages

New institutional and organizational structures are required to bring together the range of policy measures available (Table 5.3), in conjunction with firm action to reduce the levels of emissions (Table 5.5). Four sets of constraints need to be overcome, namely, the organizational/institutional constraints; the absence of a clear policy statement and achievable objectives; the linking of policies to promote public transport with a clearly identified role for the car; and the visions of the sustainable city of the future.

This means that the government must introduce packages of policies that are mutually reinforcing, and combine both land-use and transport elements. Such packaging can both reduce car travel through physical restraint and pricing, and provide improved mode choice and accessibility for those without cars. It also has a direct impact on improving the qualitative factors of the city. However, most important, policy packaging is the means by which sustainable development policies can actually be implemented.

In their comprehensive report on urban travel and sustainable development, the OECD/ECMT (1995) proposed a three-strand approach to policy packaging:

1   To make the best use of available measures (best practice) through

Table 5.5 Overview of policy instruments relevant to a comprehensive emissions control programme

Control issue	Regulation	Economic	Information
Tailpipe emissions	• Maximum emissions standards for conventional emissions (CO, HC, NO_x, PM), for toxic emissions (Lead, 1,3-butadiene, halogenated organics, PAH, benzine/aromatics). • Certification and assembly line testing • Mandatory I/M, anti tampering and enforcement programmes • Diesel smoke control programmes • Durability standards	• Tax differentials favouring abatement technology • Vehicle taxes scaled for emissions levels • Incentives/disincentives • Fiscal incentives for retiring old vehicles	• Driver awareness programmes • Annual publication of emissions rates by fuel and vehicle type • Service industry training
Fuel composition	• Fuel quality standards for petrol (lead, volatility, benzene, aromatics) and for diesel fuel (volatility, sulphur, aromatics, cetane no, PAH) • Limitations on fuel additives	• Differential fuel pricing favouring clean fuels	
Evaporative emissions	• Evaporative emissions standards (SHED testing) and refuelling controls • Fuel volatility standards		• Education of service personnel
Fuel efficiency improvements	• Fuel efficiency standards for vehicle fleets • Maximum power/weight ratios • Speed limits • Traffic management measures to increase share of optimal drive-cycle (anti congestion measures)	• Broad-based carbon tax on fuels/ emissions charges • Marketable fuel economy credits • Fuel-economy-based vehicle taxes • R&D incentives (direct funding, tax credits, emissions test exemptions)	• Annual publication of fuel efficiency ratings • Education programme for high-efficiency driving • Government sponsored R&D conferences
Market penetration of alternative transport fuels	• Tighter emissions standards • Production mandates • Mandated installation of refuelling/distribution infrastructure	• Tax differentiations favouring low CO_2 fuels • Marketable emissions credits • Tax differentiations for alternative fuel vehicles • R&D incentives • Fiscal incentives for developing refuelling distribution infrastructure	• Publicity campaigns for new vehicles/fuels • Government sponsored R&D conferences
Management of transport demand – mode shift – increase load factors – peak demand shift – reduce travel demand	• Parking control measures • Individual ownership limitations • Pedestrian only zones in cities • Car use restrictions • Relative decrease in provision of infrastructure for private transport • Improvement in public transport		

Table 5.5 Overview of policy instruments relevant to a comprehensive emissions control programme – *continued*

Control issue	Regulation	Economic	Information
	(comfort, frequency, cost, security) • Privileges (e.g. restricted highway lanes) for high occupancy vehicles • Improvements of biking/walking conditions • Park and ride programmes • Limitations and restrictions on freight transport	• Broad based carbon tax on fuel • Emission related vehicle tax • Road pricing or kilometrage charges • Parking charges • Fiscal incentives for carpool programmes • Insurance adjustment for kilometrage • Land-use and physical planning instruments to reduce elective and commuter travel and redistribute urban activities • Redistribution mechanisms for financing more efficient transport modes	• Signage indicating efficient routes • Public information campaigns on route planning and alternatives to mobility (i.e. telecommunications) • Public campaigns to promote public transport • Mode cost comparisons between cars and public transport, bicycles, carpools etc.
General	• Regular air quality monitoring • Inventory of air pollution sources • International coordination of air quality goals and policy measures	• Other mechanisms to internalize social costs of transport	• Environmental awareness programmes • Interdepartmental consultation between environment, transport, energy and economic agencies of government • Public reporting of trends and progress • Full costing of environmental effects

Notes: SHED - Sealed Housing for Evaporative Determinations – testing for evaporative emissions as part of the assembly line testing of new vehicles.
PAH – Polycyclic Aromatic Hydrocarbons – unburnt hydrocarbons.
I/M – Inspection and Maintenance programmes.
Cetane number – used in diesel fuel and relates to the ignition quality.
Source: OECD (1995), Table 13.

a combination of land-use management, road traffic management, environmental protection and pricing mechanisms. The conclusion reached in the OECD/ECMT report was that the best use of these measures on their own or in combination will not achieve sustainable development. Accessibility in city centres would improve, but the process of car-based decentralization and suburbanization would continue. Even though public transport and green modes would gain patronage, this increase would still be outweighed by growth in car ownership and use.

Emissions of local pollutants would decrease with stricter standards, but CO_2 emissions would continue to increase. Gradually, the reductions would again turn to increases as the growth in traffic volumes outweighs the gains from exhaust catalysts.

2   Innovative policies in land-use, transport and travel management would be used to supplement the best practice above. Measures here relate to mixed-use policies, new tramways, transit oriented developments, car free zones, a greater use of telecommunications technology, commuter plans, promotion of new vehicle technologies, road pricing, and smart card technology. Many of these elements form parts of the visions of the sustainable city (Chapter 11). Such policy packages would encourage local activities and a greater use of green modes. There may be a greater use of the car for leisure travel, but in cities congestion would be substantially reduced and the qualitative elements improved.

3   Sustainable urban development forms the third strand and directly tackles the CO_2 reduction target. It is designed to influence lifestyles, vehicle design, location decisions, driver behaviour, choice of travel mode and the length of car journeys. Its aim is to reduce car use, fuel consumption and emissions. This final stage combines all three strands with a change in the taxation system to tax all fossil fuels (a carbon tax). It is suggested that a four times real increase in fuel prices (1995–2020 or a 7 per cent per annum increase in real fuel prices) would reach the CO_2 emissions targets (OECD/ECMT, 1995, p. 155). The impact would be to produce fuel-efficient vehicles, to reduce car usage, and to bring about greater efficiency in freight. Again, the quality impacts on cities in terms of congestion, environment, clean air and peace and quiet would all be substantial. The market processes would in turn bring about higher densities, more mixed land uses and more local activities.

This utopian vision from the OECD/ECMT is dependent upon sustainable development being combined with innovative and best practice options. In the visions proposed here (Chapter 11), a more sophisticated approach is developed through scenario building, which explores the sustainable city through a series of sustainability targets, images of the future and feasible policy paths.

5.3 Conclusions

Increasingly, many agencies are now concentrating not just on the measures that should be implemented, but also on the means by which effective implementation can take place. It seems that certain components are necessary conditions for effective implementation of sustainable urban transport policies. The checklist provided by the ECMT (2001) for national governments includes:

1   A supportive national framework that is internally coherent with integrated policies on investment, traffic and demand management, that is externally coherent with consistent cross sectional policies.
2   Improvements in institutional coordination and cooperation so that effective decision-making can take place vertically (between all levels of government) and horizontally (between sectors).
3   Decentralize responsibilities and resources where possible, centralize where necessary. This means the provision of a consistent and integrated framework for the finance and investment issues, and a consideration of all modes of travel and land-use priorities.
4   Encourage effective public participation, partnerships and communication with early involvement and continued activity throughout implementation.
5   Provision of a supportive legal and regulatory framework with guidelines for public sector action and the means by which the private sector can be involved.
6   Comprehensive pricing and fiscal structures, which send out the right messages and are consistent, including channelling revenues from pricing incentives and allocating funding fairly.

In addition to this checklist of good practice, there also needs to be the means to translate the practices into reality at the local level. Various mechanisms are available to achieve this:

1   National targets and local objectives to translate the targets into outcomes. The targets are best set for the ends (e.g. air quality), but the means should be left to the implementing authority.
2   The financial constraints should be recognized and the means to raise the necessary funds should be set in place.
3   There should be transparency and consistency in the policy messages so that informed choices are made.
4   Wherever possible, there should be flexibility, but this should not be seen as an excuse for weak action or inaction.

The role of institutions is crucial to the effective implementation of challenging actions on sustainable urban development, and it is essential that there is real coordination between the responsible authorities (Table 5.6).

Such an allocation of responsibilities begins to bridge the gap between politicians and citizens, so that decision-making can be democratized and

Table 5.6   Responsibilities of central and local government in Implementation

Central government	Regional and city government
1 Set the policy framework – standards and supporting context.	1 Proper coordination between regional and city agencies.
2 Define public service responsibilities.	2 Single agency for public transport.
3 Coordination between all departments (transport, housing, environment, etc.).	3 Manage mobility for the whole region and city.
4 Democratization at the centre to avoid the tendency to pass difficult decisions to the local level.	4 Provision for monitoring.
5 Provide the necessary incentives, including finance.	5 Consultation and agreement, so that local support and involvement can be established – this includes consultation with opposition groups.
6 Decentralize wherever possible, but centralize where necessary.	6 Partnerships (public and private) and joint marketing of schemes and greater use of NGO skills.

public support is created. It is important for awareness creation to take place and for people to understand the reasons why sustainable urban development and transport are desirable objectives. Good demonstration effects lead to support, and from modest beginnings, scale effects take over. Conversely, poor demonstration effects have the reverse effect, hence the importance of successful implementation.

The nature and scale of change necessary to achieve sustainable urban development is substantially greater than has been admitted, and most examples have been small in scale. The real question for public policy is whether we are really serious about sustainable transport? Crucial here is the willingness to change the way in which we think about travel and how we carry out our everyday activities. The scope of the public discourse needs to be enlarged so that a wider involvement and commitment takes place. Not all decisions are market-based and institutional approaches to public policy offer the means by which greater community and corporate involvement can take place.

Planning theorists have developed concepts of communicative planning, which involve a more proactive planning process with and by all stakeholders (Healey, 1997). The interest here is that communicative planning takes an explicitly social and institutional perspective on problem solving, as it totally rejects the systems approach. Policy discourses are developed to cover the different policy communities (stakeholders), policy networks (linkages between stakeholders), and policy arenas (institutions where policies are discussed). These elements relate both to the hard infrastructure (e.g. formal organizational structures, laws, subsidies and taxation) and the soft infrastructure (e.g. social relations, informal networks and professional cultures). It is through combining these two elements that effective change can take place. If only the organizational structures are changed without attention to professional culture and informal routines, little real change will take place (Flyvbjerg, 1998).

Such thinking may be important with respect to transport planning, as innovative thinking needs to focus on the soft infrastructure. However, as Voogd (2001) points out, there may also be a paradox in communicative planning, as individual interests have to be reconciled with collective interests. The question here is whether a consensus can ever be reached (Innes, 1995 and 1999), or whether conflict is an integral part of planning processes. Some of these concepts are now being introduced to transport planning (Vigar, 2001; Willson, 2001), but not really in the context of sustainable urban development.

Perhaps there is a need for partnership between the different interests so that a common understanding can be achieved. Communicative rationality breaks down the barriers so that all parties can bring their skills and knowledge to the discussion. Thus no one party leads the debate or assumes responsibility, as all parties need to have ownership of sustainable urban development. Such an approach would attempt to get around the current compartmentalization and segmentation of powers and responsibilities between the different agencies and stakeholders. To some extent this is what LA21 (set up after Rio to achieve local involvement on sustainable development) tried to achieve, as it was successful in getting many of the key stakeholders together to focus on sustainable urban development, but it lacked the necessary powers and resources to bring about effective implementation.

The outstanding and unresolved problem is that all parties have different agendas and priorities, but the issue of sustainable urban development is not seen as being of sufficient importance for effective action. No single party is prepared to commit itself to that leadership role, and many of the innovative alliances and initiatives that have been taken have not produced positive results. Perhaps the emphasis on 'making things happen' through voluntary partnerships is too simplistic and progress can only be made through strong government action and regulation. This would suggest that the planning system should be the key actor, rather than letting the voluntary and private sectors take the lead. But even here governments do not really seem committed to effective action, as this might result in a political backlash.

As developed in the conclusions (Chapter 12), effective implementation requires a strategic framework within which long term objectives can be pursued at all levels of decision-making by all actors with the necessary powers and resources. This requires innovative packaging of mutually supportive policy measures that bring together the best practice from several sectors (transport, housing, retail, leisure, commercial etc) to be implemented under a variety of situations. The demonstration effects would encourage other cities to look at similar packages in their own situation, and the 'dynamics of success' would allow continuous improvement. A further necessary condition seems to be the cooperation and support of the people living in the city. They need to understand and accept the rationale for implementation, as the quality of life in the city would improve and the overall benefits would far outweigh any individual loss. It is only through evolutionary processes that one can match up the radical intentions of sustainable urban development with the realities of institutional and organizational inertia.

Note

1 Tokyo (32 million), Seoul (18 million), London (12 million), Paris (11 million), Berlin (4.3 million), Milan (4 million), Hiroshima (1.6 million), Stockholm (1.6 million), Portland (1.4 million), Helsinki (0.8 million), Zurich (0.8 million), Grenoble (0.6 million).

Chapter 6

Transport and urban form

6.1 Introduction

The second part of his book explores the policy strategies that can be promoted in order to move towards sustainable development from a transport perspective. Traditionally, there are three broad means by which policy intervention can take place – technological, fiscal, and regulatory. All three have been widely used within transport, some with the intention to improve the sustainability of transport, and more recently as we have seen (Chapter 3) new approaches are being adopted to create liveable cities. Here, it is emphasized that there is no single solution that can be adopted in all cities, but equally important it is necessary to mix measures creatively from all three categories to produce mutually supporting packages (Chapter 11). A crucial element in that process is the need to involve all stakeholders in a continuous process of discussion so that they are part of the proposals and have social capital invested in seeing a successful outcome. Essentially, one is trying to give ownership of the sustainable urban development and transport strategy to those who are affected by it, so that they have a vested interest in seeing it being effectively implemented.

There are strong economic arguments for firms to improve the efficiency of their resource base, normally through capital substitution. Often it is environmental regulations that act as the trigger for change, and these in turn are affected by wider social values and concerns. For example, the Factor Four argument (Von Weizsacker *et al.*, 1997) suggests that wealth can be doubled with half the resource inputs. Technological innovation should be encouraged so that substantial savings in eco-efficiency can be achieved. It might be argued that further gains could be achieved and with harder technological pushes (Factor 10), but care has to be exercised as improved efficiency could lead to rebound effects caused by falling prices and increases in demand. This is why it is necessary to have public support and understanding about why sustainable development is important, so that real long-term savings are made.

More pessimistic views might suggest that firms already operate efficiently as cost minimizers and that additional regulations will act to raise costs and reduce competitiveness (Jaffe *et al.*, 1995). If firms' behaviour becomes more strategic, they might invest in new technology or methods to reduce their environmental impact and give them an advantage through a higher market share. This means that they anticipate both the regulations and the consumer requirements to give them a competitive advantage. Alternatively, they could do nothing until the regulations require them to change – a passive rather than an active role. They could also consider moving production to lower-cost locations (overseas), where environmental conditions are less onerous. The 'Porter Hypothesis' suggests that properly designed environmental regulations can encourage innovation that may partially or fully cover the costs of complying with them (Porter and Van der Linde, 1995). The commonly used counter-arguments about the loss of business efficiency and employment loss have not been demonstrated in reality. Indeed it could be argued that there are new opportunities created in the pollution control technologies, and these may have export potential.

One of the most recent 'hot topics' for debate has been over the relationships (if any) between transport and urban form. The protagonists have often been categorized into those that favour the compact city and those that do not (Breheny, 2001). Much of the discussion has been concentrated on the link between density and travel – the basic argument being that higher densities would result in the maximum use of land, reduced travel distances, and a greater intensity and diversity of activity. It is at the heart of the urban renaissance (Urban Task Force, 1999).

In this chapter, we try to move away from the polarization that has taken place in the debate, suggesting that the situation is very much more complex than is often argued. Much of the analysis has been very simplistic in its approach (Crane, 2000), with the data being open to several interpretations, the analysis inconclusive, and the possible causalities unproven. The complexity being argued here revolves around six separate themes, each of which will be discussed in turn. By exploring each of the different dimensions of the transport and urban form debate, it will become apparent that there may not be clear relationships. To go deeper into these relationships, it is necessary to have detailed longitudinal data that allow the dynamic processes to be explored (not the net effects) by following individual household's and firm's decisions. Much of the available evidence is at the cross section, which helps give a view at one point in time. Repeated cross-sectional data allow some inference about net effects, but the interest is really in the deeper understanding gained through following households (and firms) and their decisions continuously over time.

However, as the 'ideal' data are only rarely available, the role of careful data analysis and interpretation remains important, so that different views can be debated. Many of these debates are not new and issues relating to urban size, density and design have a history of over 100 years (Fact Box 6.1 and

Hall, 2001). It should also be noted that in the twenty-first century there are 'no' compact cities and 'no' dispersed cities. They are both notional urban forms, as all cities are in a continuous state of development. In essence, they are mixtures of high- and low-density, but urban form generally is moving from monocentric structures to polycentric structures. The debates presented in this chapter should therefore be seen against this background of realism.

6.2   The key relationships between transport and urban form

A number of land-use characteristics can affect travel patterns and influence the environmental impacts of transport, and in turn can promote more sustainable transport. At the national level, planning policies can influence the location of new development in relation to existing towns, cities and other infrastructure. Regional policies can influence the size and shape of new development and the type of land use; whether, for example, it is used for housing, commercial and industrial purposes, or a mixture of these purposes. At the city or urban level, planning policies can influence the level and scale of land-use mixing, and the extent to which development is clustered or concentrated. At the local and neighbourhood level, planning policies can be used to influence the density and layout of development.

The focus in this chapter is on empirical rather than modelling studies (see Owens, 1986 or Wegener, 1994 for a review of the vast literature on land-use and transport modelling studies). It must be recognized in all forms of analysis that causality is difficult to establish and that socio-economic characteristics (in particular income and car ownership) are also crucial influencing factors in determining travel patterns. A synthesis of the material is presented here, using a matrix approach, in which land-use and urban form characteristics are placed along one axis and the travel characteristics form the other axis (Table 6.1). Using this approach, it is possible to identify where research has been concentrated and to examine where findings are similar and where they differ. Possible explanations are suggested for the differences of opinion between research findings in the next sections.

Land-use characteristics are divided into six main categories: the size of settlements (measured both in terms of population size and the distance from home to the urban centre); the intensity of land use and activities (subdivided into population density and employment density); the mixing of land uses (measured in terms of the job ratio, the ratio of jobs in the area to workers resident in that area); the decentralization of activities (location); local accessibility to transport infrastructure; and parking provision (Table 6.1). Travel patterns are divided into five main categories – travel distance, journey frequency, mode of travel, travel time, and energy consumption used in transport (Banister *et al.*, 1997). Transport energy consumption is a

Table 6.1 Studies classified according to land-use characteristics and travel patterns

Measures of travel ⇨ / Land-use characteristics ⇩	Settlement size Section 6.2.1	Intensity of land use Section 6.2.2	Mixed use Section 6.2.3	Location Section 6.2.4	Local accessibility Section 6.2.5	Parking supply Section 6.2.6
(measures)	Population size; Distance from home to urban centre	Population and employment density	Job ratio	Location and local employment, facilities and services	Local access to public transport	Availability of residential parking
Distance — Average journey distance	Banister et al, 1997; Stead, 1996; Spence and Frost, 1995; Gordon et al., 1989a	ECOTEC, 1993; Gordon and Richardson, 1997; Breheny, 1997; Banister, 1996; Fouchier, 1997; Cervero, 1989	CMHC, 1993	Cervero and Landis, 1992; Hanson, 1982; Winter and Farthing, 1997		
Average journey distance by car	Johnston-Anumonwo, 1992	ECOTEC, 1993; Hillman and Whalley, 1983; Levinson and Kumar, 1997		Cervero and Landis, 1992; Farthing et al, 1997		
Total travel distance (all modes)	Naess et al., 1995; Curtis, 1995; Headicar and Curtis, 1998	ECOTEC, 1993; Hillman and Whalley, 1983; Breheny, 2001; Richardson and Gordon, 2001		Ewing, 1997; Banister, 1997b; Headicar and Curtis, 1998		
Frequency — Journey frequency	Curtis, 1995; Prevedouros and Schofer, 1991	ECOTEC, 1993; Ewing et al., 1996; Boarnet & Crane, 2001a b; Handy & Clifton, 2001	Ewing et al., 1996	Hanson, 1982; ECOTEC, 1993		

continued on page 101

Table 6.1 Studies classified according to land-use characteristics and travel patterns – *continued from page 100*

Land-use characteristics	Settlement size Section 6.2.1	Intensity of land use Section 6.2.2	Mixed use Section 6.2.3	Location Section 6.2.4	Local accessibility Section 6.2.5	Parking supply Section 6.2.6
Mode						
Proportion of car journeys	Curtis, 1995; Naess and Sandberg, 1996	ECOTEC, 1993; Newman and Kenworthy, 1989a, b, 1999; Gordon et al., 1989a; Banister, 1997b; Ewing, 1995		Cervero & Landis, 1992; Headicar and Curtis, 1998	Kitamura et al., 1997	Kitamura et al., 1997
Proportion of public transport journeys		ECOTEC, 1993; Frank and Pivo, 1994; Wood, 1994		Cervero and Landis, 1992	Cervero, 1994	
Proportion of walk/bike journeys	Headicar and Curtis, 1998	ECOTEC, 1993; Kitamura et al., 1997; Frank and Pivo, 1994		Winter and Farthing, 1997		
Time						
Travel time	Gordon et al., 1989a, b	Gordon et al., 1989a; Gordon et al., 1991	Giuliano and Small, 1993	Cervero and Landis, 1992		
Energy						
Transport energy consumption	Naess et al., 1995; Mogridge, 1985; Newman and Kenworthy, 1988; Banister, 1992; Banister et al., 1997	Naess, 1993; Newman and Kenworthy, 1989a, b; Gordon, 1997; Breheny 1995a, b; Banister et al., 1997		Banister, 1997a; Banister et al., 1997	Banister and Banister, 1995	

Note: This classification shows the range of empirical studies, but many of the entries could be placed in more than one box. The allocation is based on the main focus of each piece of research and some do not explicitly link development to transport. This Table is discussed in more detail by Stead and Marshall (1998). The evidence is mainly from the OECD countries – very little evidence is available from non-OECD countries (UNDP, 1997).

composite measure of the other four indicators of travel as it is dependent on trip distance, time (speed), frequency and mode. This is one means by which the empirical studies can be linked to modelling analysis as the transport energy consumption measures are used with spatial databases (e.g. GIS) to estimate patterns of energy use.

6.2.1 Settlement size

The size of settlements affects the range of local jobs and services that can be supported, and influences the range of public transport services, which can be provided. Diseconomies of scale may occur with very large settlements where travel distances again increase between homes and the urban centre. These centres have large labour market catchments (and leisure, shopping and other functions) and so they also attract people living long distances away to travel to them. These factors may all influence travel patterns and it is unlikely that there is a simple relationship between settlement size and travel patterns (Owens, 1986; ECOTEC, 1993; Banister *et al.*, 1997).

Two measures of settlement size are reviewed here – population size and the distance from home to the urban centre. According to analysis of data from the various National Travel Surveys of Great Britain (DETR, 1997*a*), total travel distance is highest in the smallest category of settlements (containing fewer than 3,000 residents), and total travel distance is lowest in large metropolitan areas (excluding London). Residents of London, the largest metropolitan area in Great Britain, travel longer distances on average than the residents of the six next largest metropolitan areas (West Midlands, Greater Manchester, West Yorkshire, Glasgow, Liverpool and Tyneside). The average journey distance by car is also lowest in conurbations and highest in rural areas, even if the variations in car ownership are controlled for (Banister, 1997*b*).

Research by Gordon *et al.* (1989*a*) shows no easily identifiable relationship between urban population size and modal choice. In a study of commuting patterns in the ten largest urbanized areas in the United States, the proportion of car journeys was found to be least in New York (which has the largest population of the areas studied) and highest in Detroit (which has the sixth largest population of the areas studied). But public transport has never accounted for a very substantial proportion of travel in the US, so one would not expect a great variation.

Several researchers have calculated specific energy consumption by mode from the National Travel Surveys of Great Britain by population size (Banister, 1992; Breheny, 1995*a,b*; Stead, 1996). Transport energy consumption is lowest in metropolitan areas (excluding London) and highest in the smallest category of settlements (containing fewer than 3,000 residents). Transport energy consumption is one-third lower than average in the metropolitan areas (excluding London) and more than one-third higher than average in the smallest settlements. Calculations of transport energy consumption match the figures for total travel distance energy consumption extremely closely, despite significant variations in modal choice by urban size.

Spence and Frost (1995) describe the changes in commuting distance between 1971 and 1981 in the three largest cities in Great Britain, London, Manchester and Birmingham, and show how commuting distance changes with increasing distance between home and the urban centre. In London, commuting distance increases almost linearly with distance between home and urban centre. At a distance of 20 km from the centre of London, commuting distance continues to increase with increasing distance from the centre of the city. In Manchester and Birmingham, however, the relationship is different. Commuting distance in Birmingham first increases with increasing distance between home and the urban centre, but at a distance of around 7 km from the urban centre, commuting distance reaches a plateau. At a distance of around 9 km from the centre, commuting distance begins to decrease as distance from the urban centre increases. Commuting distance in Manchester first increases with increasing distance from the urban centre. At a distance of around 5 km from the centre, commuting distance reaches a plateau and does not increase much thereafter. The trends in commuting distance by distance from home to the urban centre in the three cities between 1971 and 1981 appear similar. Gordon *et al.* (1989*a*) describe the changes in average travel distance in the United States between 1977 and 1983 of people residing inside and outside cities. In various sizes of city, journey distances for both work and non-work journeys in 1977 and 1983 were almost always lower for residents inside cities, than for residents outside cities.

Substantial research has also been carried out by Naess and his colleagues in Norway on transport and energy use in Scandinavian towns and regions. Three separate studies have been completed. In the first, ninety-seven towns with populations over 10,000 and fifteen commuting regions in Sweden were investigated (Naess, 1993). At the individual town level, a dense pattern of urban development gives the lowest levels of per capita energy consumption. As the amount of urban area per capita increases, so does the annual energy consumption per capita (MJ): the relationship is positive, and the correlation is reasonably high ($R = 0.47$). At the regional level (defined as being within 36 km of the regional centre), a more decentralized pattern (measured by a 'concentration index') gives the lowest levels of energy consumption provided that certain density thresholds are exceeded. The explanatory variable used is the actual consumption of energy per capita within the urban area or region – there is no information on travel patterns. The 'concentration index' is the ratio of the average distance from home to the regional centre over the geographical average distance to the centre of the region. A value of 1.0 demonstrates even distribution of population, whilst a ratio of zero indicates that all the population is in the centre.

The second study (Naess, Roe and Larsen, 1995) examines in greater detail the use of the private car and public transport in 30 residential areas in Greater Oslo (329 households). The urban planning variables used are distance to central Oslo, density of population, distance to different daily services, parking conditions, distance to public transport, and the departure frequency for different kinds of public transport. The dependent variables were energy use in transport and frequency of public transport travel. Low energy use for transport is a function of low car ownership, high use of public transport, a short distance to central Oslo, high residential density and high population density. As distance increases from 4 km to 12 km from central Oslo, energy use for transport increases by 41 per cent. Similarly, as area per capita increases from 200 m^2 to 600 m^2, energy use increases by 49 per cent. The other variables tested were not significant.

The final part of the Norwegian team's study (Naess, Larsen and Roe, 1995) examines energy use in transport in twenty-two Nordic towns. Again, the significant variables were high population density in the inner and central areas of the towns, and the low level of employment in manufacturing, building and transport activities, together with low commuting frequencies. These four variables (plus low income levels) explained 72 per cent of the variation between energy consumption per capita in transport in these towns.

In all these studies, the difficulties of calculating the primary energy consumption have been avoided as energy use data are based on information about quantities of petrol and diesel sold at petrol stations, supplemented with data on the fuel and electricity used in public transport. This type of approach may be suitable in countries where the urban areas are discrete and most travel takes place within the local catchment area. But in the UK and most other European countries with dense development and close proximity of neighbouring towns, the assumption made about the use of fuel in the local city would be difficult to support.

In a study of travel patterns in five new housing locations in and around Oxford, Curtis (1995) shows that the distance between home and urban centre may be linked to average work journey distance. A link between average non-work journey distance and the distance from home to urban centre is much less apparent. Local planning authorities can exert a major influence on the amount of car based travel. The average figure of 43 km travelled per adult each weekday varies by location (±15 to 20 per cent), but this variation is not affected by accessibility or by socio-economic attributes. Only just over 1 per cent of households had no car. Headicar and Curtis (1998) conclude the income differences between the new housing locations are not the primary source of the variations in work related car travel between the five locations. Variations in travel have traditionally been based on the differences in household characteristics (principally income), but the importance of location for travel patterns must be understood if sustainable mobility objectives are to be strengthened.

Mogridge (1985) demonstrates a near linear relationship between distance from home to the centre and transport energy consumption. The relationship is shown to be very similar in both London and Paris. On average, residents living at a distance of 15 km from the urban centre consume more than twice the transport energy consumed by residents living 5 km from the urban centre. Similarly, Newman and Kenworthy (1988) identify the relationship between transport energy consumption and the distance from the central business district in Perth. Like Mogridge (1985), Newman and Kenworthy demonstrate a linear relationship, although the regression line for Perth is not as steep. It is reported that residents living at a distance of 15 km from the central business district consume approximately 20 per cent more transport energy than residents living 5 km from the central business district.

Another piece in the jigsaw is the growth in long distance journeys, particularly for commuting, which seems to be on the increase. Most trips do not use much energy as they are locally based, and perhaps carried out on public transport or by walk and cycle. From a limited data source, Banister *et al.* (1997) estimated that 84 per cent of car trips used less than the average amount of energy per trip (15.1 MJ per trip). About 24 per cent of motorized trips use 78 per cent of the total energy. Such evidence again suggests that sustainable transport strategies ought to be placed within the wider regional context, or at least cover journey to work areas.

In summary, a relatively large amount of research has investigated the links between settlement size and travel patterns, but the relationship is unlikely to be simple, due to the interplay of competing factors. Evidence from Great Britain shows that large metropolitan settlements are associated with low travel distance and transport energy consumption. Evidence from the ten largest urban areas in the United States shows no easily identifiable relationship between urban population size and modal choice. In many studies, increasing distance from home to the urban centre is associated with increasing travel distance, an increasing proportion of car journeys and increasing transport energy consumption. The only exception is trip frequency, which does not appear to vary significantly according to the distance between home and the urban centre.

6.2.2 The intensity of land use

The intensity of land use is commonly measured in terms of population density and, to a lesser extent, employment density. ECOTEC (1993) put forward four reasons why population density may be linked to travel patterns. First, higher population densities widen the range of opportunities for the development of local personal contacts and activities that can be maintained without resort to motorized travel. Secondly, higher population densities widen the range of services that can be supported in the local area, reducing the need to travel long distances. Thirdly, higher density patterns of development tend to reduce average distances between homes, services, employment and other opportunities, which in turn reduces travel distance. Fourthly, high densities may be more amenable to public transport operation and use and less amenable to car ownership and use, and this has implications for modal choice. Average journey distance by car, bus and rail decreases with increasing population density, whilst the average journey distance by foot is more or less constant, regardless of population density (ECOTEC, 1993; Hillman and Whalley, 1983). These findings are supported by more recent data from National Travel Surveys (Stead, 1996).

Total journey frequency (1985–1986) does not show a clear gradation with population density, and there is little variation in trip frequency according to population density. The average journey frequency is reported to be close to 14 journeys per person per week. The highest trip frequency is 14.81 journeys per person per week (6 per cent higher than average) in areas where population density is between 1 and 5 persons per hectare. The lowest trip frequency is 12.99 journeys per person per week (7 per cent lower than average) in areas where population density is more than 50 persons per hectare (ECOTEC, 1993). Ewing et al. (1996) report that there is no significant statistical link between trip frequency and population density. There is a potential problem if short trips are not being measured, as these are more likely to be found in the denser urban areas than in the more sparsely populated rural areas. In addition, there are linked trips where more than one activity is undertaken during a trip tour. Again, such trips are more likely to be found in densely populated urban areas where services and facilities are in close proximity to each other.

With increasing population density, the proportion of trips by car decreases, whilst the proportion of trips by public transport and foot both increase (ECOTEC, 1993). Car trips account for 72 per cent of journeys in low density areas (less than 1 person per hectare) but only 51 per cent of trips in high density areas (more than 50 persons per hectare). There is a fourfold difference in public transport trips and almost a twofold difference in walk trips between very low density areas and very high density areas (data from 1989/1991 – Banister, 1997b). As density increases, so does the number of trips by public transport and walk, even after controlling for socio-economic variables (Banister, 1999). Similar findings have been reported in the United

Fact Box 6.1   A brief historical perspective on the density debate

Typical US residential densities are 18 dwellings per hectare, but in New York they are up to 60 dwellings per hectare.

In the UK the Georgians built to high densities of 100–200 dwellings per hectare (London, Edinburgh and Bath), the Victorians to lower densities of 40–80 dwellings per hectare, and current averages are only 23 dwellings per hectare.

The Tudor Walters Report (1918) recommended 30 dwellings per hectare, Howard's Garden City (1898) about 45 dwellings per hectare, and the Friends of the Earth's sustainable urban density is 69 dwellings per hectare (1999).

Current UK government directives are designed to build to higher densities in urban areas – around 35–40 dwellings per hectare, and 50 dwellings per hectare are being sought in some locations – but not much higher than those of over 100 years ago.

Note that much of the potential savings from building at higher densities are obtained from increasing density from low levels to medium levels – 75 per cent of the land savings are obtained by net densities of 40 dwellings per hectare or gross densities (with facilities etc) of 50 dwellings per hectare. There is a need to avoid very low densities (under 20 dwellings per hectare) and to target in the range of 40–50 dwellings per hectare.

Wachs (2002) suggests a doubling of urban residential density would lead to a reduction of about 15 per cent in trips, but an increase in trip density so total travel increases. He also states that the US 'spends more public money on transit per rider served than any country in the world' (p. 24).

Some cities have densities that are much higher, but others are very low – dwellings per hectare – Beijing 146, Tokyo 130, New York City 90, Los Angeles 40, Dallas 2.

Land needed to accommodate 400 dwellings

Density (dwellings per hectare)	Land needed	Net Land saved	% total saving	Area required with local facilities			
				Land needed	Land saved	% total saving	% cumulative
10	40.0			46.3			
20	20.0	20.0	50.0	25.3	21.0	45.4	45.4
30	13.3	6.7	16.7	17.9	7.4	15.9	61.3
40	10.0	3.3	8.3	14.3	3.6	7.8	69.1
50	8.0	2.0	5.0	12.1	2.2	4.8	73.9
60	6.6	1.4	3.5	10.6	1.5	3.2	77.1

All measures in hectares

'Density has little to do with overcrowding or town cramming. It has everything to do with design of the environment – the balance of massing, light and space. By controlling the way buildings are arranged around public spaces, by ensuring that privacy is guaranteed and noise levels contained, it is possible to create attractive living environments, and to develop stronger and more vibrant communities.' Rogers and Burdett (2001), p 12.

Sources: Haughton and Hunter (1994); Wachs (2002); Hall (2001); DETR (1998a); Rogers and Burdett (2001).

States, where the proportion of shopping trips by public transport and the proportion of commuting trips by foot are both positively linked with population density (Frank and Pivo, 1994), again after accounting for socio-economic differences (Kitamura *et al.*, 1997).

Breheny (2001) has identified a link between residential density and travel, only at the metropolitan scale. For smaller scale cities, as size and density decreases the links become weaker. This weakening relationship has been linked to the decentralization process and the decline in household size over time with more housing units for the same population. There would need to be substantial increases in population density to make any real differences as the counter factors of smaller households would diminish the effectiveness of density increases (Fact Box 6.2).

Fact Box 6.2   The compact city debate

Compaction or higher building densities help cut the volume of traffic in urban areas. This concept has been strongly promoted in the EU (CEC, 1992) as the main means to provide cities with environmental and quality of life benefits. Breheny (1992) identifies four main areas where doubts remain:

1   Difference between the need to travel and the demand for travel. Individual's choices about travel are complex and location of facilities near to housing does not mean that they will be used. But equally, it does not negate these arguments, as there may be strong accessibility reasons for co-location of services/facilities and homes.
2   Economic issues such as incomes and fuel prices are much stronger influences on travel patterns than urban form.
3   Planning decisions are seen as difficult and expensive ways to influence travel behaviour. Market pressures for decentralization out of cities are always likely to be stronger influences on city development.
4   The influence of changes in land use on transport has been questioned. This issue is now seen in the UK to be of fundamental importance, as it is recognized that much of the increase in travel is a result of decisions taken in other sectors. The location of new housing and retail centres generate new transport pressures (ODPM, 2003).

Source: Based on Breheny *et al.* (1998).

Evidence from the United States (Gordon *et al.*, 1989*a*) suggests that there is no clear relationship between the proportion of car trips for work journeys and population density, but this may be explained by their definition of population density in terms of workplace locations rather than the conventional residential location. The correlation between urban population density and transport energy consumption has been demonstrated by Newman and Kenworthy (1989*a*,*b*) in their study of thirty-two cities from around the world. Research by Naess (1993) in Sweden also identifies a link between population density and transport energy consumption (Chapter 6.2.1).

As argued by Newman and Kenworthy (1989*a,b*) in their world survey of energy use in cities, it is population density, job density, and city centre dominance, which control petroleum use. There is a strong increase in petroleum consumption when population density falls below 29 persons per hectare, and they argue for cities with strong centres and intensively used suburbs. An essential prerequisite to improved energy efficiency is a substantial commitment to investment in public transport and better facilities for walking and cycling. Their more recent research updates the 1980 data to 1990 to establish at the aggregate level changes in petroleum use over a decade in the thirty-two world cities. In all cities, it seems that there has been an increase in the use of the car over the decade as measured by vehicle-kilometres of travel per person. There has also been an increase in the use of public transport, but only in certain cities (e.g. Zurich and Singapore), and even there the increase has been modest. It is not clear whether this increase in public transport use has come from car users or from existing users of public transport or from walking and cycling. Even in cities where public transport investment has been substantial and where reductions in the use of the car might be expected, this has not taken place. Action has to be more comprehensive than merely the promotion of public transport.

The strong emphasis on control of development, high urban densities and substantial investment in public transport advocated by Newman and Kenworthy (1989*a*) is in marked contrast to those who argue that the market is the only means to determine urban structure (Gordon, Kumar and Richardson, 1989*a*). Large single-centre cities may be more energy intensive, but even here the evidence is mixed (Newman and Kenworthy, 1989*a*). Conversely, the polynucleated cities with a hierarchical structure may minimize travel distances and times (and energy use), as people travel to local facilities wherever possible, and only travel to the city centre for specific reasons. The question here is whether the higher use of energy for the longer (but occasional) trips to the city centre outweighs the gains made on the shorter trips to the polynuclear centres. This issue is raised in a slightly different context in Chapter 9 when the impact of ICT on transport is discussed in terms of whether telecommuting for 2 or 3 days a week actually reduces overall travel to work distance, if it allows people to locate even further away from their workplaces.

Gordon, Kumar and Richardson (1989*a*) argue that co-location of firms and households can reduce journey times, and decentralization can reduce city centre congestion. A comparison of auto commuting trip times from the 1985 American Housing Survey to data from the 1980 Census for the twenty largest metropolitan areas in the US suggests that average trip times either fell by a statistically significant amount or remained the same (Gordon, Richardson and Jun, 1991; Newman and Kenworthy, 1999). Their explanation is simply that the market operates spontaneously through the relocation of firms and households to achieve the balance of keeping commuting times within tolerable limits.

The difficulty with this type of analysis is that it is based on limited data (journey to work) and travel time. It also assumes that there are no adaptive changes from drivers (e.g. flexible working hours), no change in the supply side (e.g. new roads), that both households' and firms' locations decisions can react spontaneously (i.e. that 5 years is a sufficient time to identify location changes), and that commuting times are a sufficient reason for co-location. It would have been interesting to have seen data on the actual number of households and firm movers over this 5-year period (longitudinal analysis), but the cross sectional data do not allow such comparisons to take place.

Travel time is not crucial as the key determinants of energy consumption are the travel mode, trip distance and the frequency of the trip. Travel time is of secondary importance as it relates to travel speed, which in turn influences fuel consumption. More recent research from the Richardson and Gordon group (Bae and Richardson, 1994) is more intriguing. Here it is argued that reversing suburbanization and decentralization will not reduce energy consumption or air pollution levels. Longer journeys are a temporary disequilibrium problem as polycentric metropolitan areas develop with subcentres that compete with the central business district. Even if trip lengths are reduced through increases in urban density, more trips would be created so that there would be no net savings. Their conclusion is that the planning system has little to offer, and that improvements in energy consumption and air pollution levels can be achieved through newer vehicles, pre-warming of catalytic converters, more efficient engines and a shift to improving emissions from stationary sources – a technological fix.

In their updated analysis, Newman and Kenworthy (1999) have maintained their view that urban density is still dominant in revitalizing the city, and they now suggest development should take place around existing rail systems (Section 6.2.4), and public transport systems should be extended. They also advocate measures to discourage urban sprawl, and propose a new generation of urban villages to be built in the suburbs. Richardson and Gordon (2001) are still advocating individual preferences for low densities, not constrained by high land prices, pointing out that only 5 per cent of land in the United States (excluding Alaska) is under urban development. There has been a modest decline in average commuting times in the US over the last 30 years (from 22 minutes to 20.7 minutes). Other commentators in the US (e.g. Handy, 2002) are calling for smart growth to take place through infill development and making cities more attractive to the pedestrian as well as the car.

There is much less evidence concerning the relationship between travel patterns and employment density. Employment density, like population density, is connected to the proportion of public transport trips for both shopping and work journeys, even when socio-economic variations are controlled (Frank and Pivo, 1994).

In summary, there is a substantial body of research that on balance demonstrates a link between population density and many measures of travel patterns – mode, distance, and travel time. The only exception is that there is little variation in journey frequency by population density. Conversely, there has been little recent research concerning the relationships between employment density and travel patterns. The debate is really moving on towards the new urbanism, where the concern is not over density alone, but over the quality of the urban environment as a whole. Within that urban environment, density has an important role to play, but in combination with other factors such as mixed uses, safe and secure places, community, open space, green space, and quality of development.

6.2.3   The mixing of land uses

The mixing of land uses affects the physical separation of activities and is a determinant of travel demand. Some evidence suggests that the mixing of land-uses is not as important as density in influencing travel demand (Owens, 1986; Departments of Environment and Transport, 1994, 1995). Nevertheless, the level of mixed use may contribute to travel demand, particularly through the decentralization of less specialized employment and it is commonly measured using the job ratio. This is the ratio of jobs in the area to workers resident in that area. In the UK (Banister et al., 1997), a significant relationship between job ratio and energy use per trip was established in one of six case studies (Oxford), but not in the other case study cities (Liverpool, Milton Keynes, Leicester, Almere in the Netherlands, and Banbury). If mixed use is linked with density, then this may be reinforcing as denser neighbourhoods have more small shops and other facilities.

Evidence from the United States finds only weak evidence of links between job ratio and travel. Ewing et al. (1996) investigate the effect of the various land-use characteristics, including the balance of homes and jobs, on trip generation. They report that there is no statistically significant relationship between the balance of homes and jobs and journey frequency. In a study of commuting patterns in San Francisco Bay Area, Cervero (1989) reports a weak negative relationship between job ratio and the proportion of journeys undertaken by foot and cycle – where there are many more jobs than houses, the proportion of journeys by foot or cycle falls. Policy could balance housing and jobs so that walking and cycling are encouraged. Giuliano and Small (1993) question the importance of job ratio on travel patterns and present the results of a commuting study in the Los Angeles region to show that job ratio has a statistically significant, but relatively small, influence on commuting time. They conclude that attempts to alter the metropolitan structure of land use are likely to have small impacts on commuting patterns, even if jobs and housing became more balanced.

6.2.4   The location and decentralization of activities

New development should be of a substantial size and located near (or within) existing urban areas so that critical size thresholds (at least 25,000 population and preferably over 50,000) can be achieved (Banister, 1997b). The provision of local facilities and services clearly reduce the need to travel long distances and increase the probability of journeys being made by non-motorized modes. Little evidence has been collected on this subject, and the precise impact of local facilities and services on travel patterns is unknown. Winter and Farthing (1997) report that the provision of local facilities in new residential developments reduces average trip distances but does not significantly affect the proportion of journeys by foot. Evidence from the same study reported elsewhere indicates that the provision of local facilities reduces the average journey distance by car (Farthing et al., 1997). ECOTEC (1993) report from neighbourhood case studies that a clear relationship emerges between the distance from a local centre, the frequency of its use and average journey distance. Hanson (1982) reports similar findings, showing that the proximity to local facilities is positively associated with average distance, after taking into account the effects of various socio-economic differences of the areas studied. Hanson also shows that the provision of local facilities is associated with increased journey frequency, although the effect of increasing journey frequency is not as strong as the effect of reducing trip length. A limited amount of empirical research on threshold analysis has tried to quantify within the UK the levels of population required to support different local facilities (Farthing et al., 1997; Williams, 2001; and Table 6.2).

Table 6.2   Threshold analysis of services and facilities against population

Service or Facility	Farthing et al., 1997	Williams, 2001
Primary school	2500–4000	2000
Doctor	2500–3000	–
Corner shop	2000–5000	4000
Public house	5000–7000	1100
Group of shops	5000–10000	–
Post office	5000–10000	–
Clinic	–	8000
Bank	–	18000
Supermarket	–	10000

The location of new development is a major function for local planning authorities, which has strong implications for the generation and attraction of traffic. Location policy primarily relates to the location of all types of new development, but increasingly important is the refurbishment and conversion of existing buildings (including change of use). The emphasis has clearly moved towards a plan-led system with peripheral development only being allowed if there are no suitable development sites in the town centres. The sequential approach (PPG6) requires developers to search for suitable sites in the town centre. Only if there are no options here will edge of town and then out of town alternatives be considered, and even then these sites will have to be accessible to those with no car available (Department of the Environment, 1993).

The best documented examples are in the decisions about location of new superstores (>2500 m^2 gross trading area in size) in town centres, at the edge of centre, or out of centre locations. All of the major supermarket chains have a range of superstores in these three locations (Table 6.3), with each generating and attracting large numbers of movements by shoppers and delivery vehicles. There are no parking standards; a figure of 12 spaces per 100 m^2 of net floorspace (10 per 100 m^2 of gross floorspace) has been used, but this varies from town centres (lower) to peripheral locations (higher). For example, the Sainsbury's at Witney (Oxfordshire, UK), which is edge of centre, has 494 spaces for a gross trading area of 2617 m^2 (18 spaces per 100 m^2 of gross floorspace). The availability of free and easily accessible parking space is a major attraction of large shopping centres.

Table 6.3   Location of superstores

	Number	Centre (%)	Edge of centre (%)	Out of centre (%)
Tesco	348	32	18	50
Sainsbury	362	42	16	42
Somerfield	600	69	19 [*]	12

Note: * Neighbourhood centre.
Source: Hillier Parker (1997).

Four main variables have been used to explain the changes in travel brought about by new superstores:

1   Trip frequency increases marginally, perhaps by 3–4 per cent, as people take advantage of the new opportunity.

2   Trip mode remains heavily car oriented for both out of town and edge of town development (over 90 per cent by car). It is only in the town centre

that the modal split reduces to about 60 per cent by car, but even here the figures can be much higher in small market towns or where parking is free.

3   The key variable is trip distance and the evidence here suggests that travel distance is reducing. Tesco's research concludes (for eleven free-standing towns) the average miles travelled to the supermarket was 'better than halved after the new superstore was opened'. This meant an average reduction per store of 60,000 miles per week. Other research for the food sector makes more modest claims with a 9.3 per cent reduction in travel distance being countered by a 3.5 per cent increase in frequency, giving a net reduction of 6.2 per cent. The Witney study (edge of centre) gave a figure of 41 per cent reduction in travel distance, countered by a 7 per cent increase in frequency, giving a net reduction of 37 per cent (Sutcliffe, 1996). One explanation is that, within a mature area of food shopping with several alternatives available within relatively easy driving distance, any new superstore will overlap its catchment area with the existing stores resulting in shorter journey lengths and a redistribution of market share.

4   There is an increase in trip chaining or linking activities, which again will reduce overall distance travelled. Location of new superstores near to existing complementary facilities allows this to take place. In the town centre, the level of trip chaining can be as high as 80 per cent of trips, whilst at edge of town this figure declines to about 60 per cent. The opportunities at out of town centres are lower (about 20 per cent).

New patterns of retailing are developing, and there is a clear opportunity for planners to allow development that will ensure accessibility to all, but at the same time allow multipurpose trips to take place and travel distances to be reduced. This is a clear example of where planning decisions can influence travel patterns directly, and similar arguments could be made for the location of business centres, technology parks, leisure facilities (including multiplex cinemas), and industrial estates.

It is not just in retailing that new ideas are being developed. In the Netherlands, the ABC location policy sets the conditions on where businesses can locate in order to control mobility. The mobility characteristics of the business have to match the accessibility characteristics of the area where it wishes to locate. Locations have been categorized as follows:

◆   A: highly accessible by public transport and tight restrictions on parking (10 spaces per 100 employees in Randstad, 20 elsewhere); the target group involves labour or visitor intensive companies such as offices or public facilities;

- B: good accessibility by both car (fewer parking restrictions, namely 20 spaces per 100 employees in the Randstad and 40 elsewhere) and public transport;

- C: highly accessible by car and less reachable by public transport, no parking restrictions; the target group are companies that need to be accessible by car or truck.

All new or amended local plans must grade development sites according to the above categories, while the mobility effects of new developments must reflect their location. Municipalities have a range of objectives, and often attach considerable importance to the economic advantages that companies can provide, such as employment, revenues from land development and local taxes. As a consequence, they often grade development sites using the most flexible 'B' type to maximize the opportunity for development, trading off the mobility effects (Priemus and Maat, 1998).

These ideas have been taken up elsewhere, principally in the US and the UK. Transit oriented developments in the US aim to create development densities around stations to raise patronage levels. Homes, shops and social services would be clustered around these stations so that residential densities rise to 30 dwellings per hectare. But these locations have proved to be more attractive to existing public transit users rather than car users (Crane, 1996). There is some debate in the US as to whether such schemes will ever influence travel behaviour. For example, Richardson and Gordon (2001) state that 'there are no plausible policies to shift car users to public transport in significant numbers at reasonable cost' (p. 60). In the UK, the view is more optimistic with the current interest in Transport Development Areas (TDAs), where sustainability is encouraged through well designed, higher density and mixed developments in and around existing centres, close to public transport (Symonds Group, 2002). The interest here is that TDAs and the other schemes work at the interface between density, design, accessibility and integration to focus development on key locations where there is good quality public transport. Rather than thinking in terms of single solutions to complex problems, a more holistic perspective has been taken, with the initiative coming from the development process so that it might have positive implications in terms of use of more sustainable modes of transport.

The local design issues provide a classic example of the dilemmas that need to be addressed to reconcile transport concerns with those of sustainable urban development. There seem to be substantial benefits in terms of land use by switching away from grid transport networks in cities to loops and culs-de-sac, as the amount of usable land increases from 64 per cent with a grid system to 76 per cent in a cul-de-sac system (Grammenos and Tasker Brown, 2000). This possibility is attractive from the developers' perspective. From the transport planning perspective, it reduces the problems of 'rat runs' or shortcuts through residential areas and it succeeds in reducing traffic speeds through design. But there are disadvantages. Southworth and Ben-Joseph (1997, pp. 120–121) conclude that the cul-de-sac is an 'isolated, insular, private enclave, set in a formless sprawl, separated socially and physically from the larger world and dependent on the automobile for survival'. In contrast, a grid network provides greater accessibility, and a wider choice of routes and better potential for public transport.

The dilemma is the reconciliation of the needs of the pedestrian for short, direct routes, including access to public transport, and the needs of the car driver, which are also for short direct routes. The difference is one of scale and speed, with the pedestrian wanting a memorable experience, pleasure (sociability and walkability) and safety with separation from cars. The car driver also wants separation from pedestrians, but is more interested in ease of navigation around towns (signposting), low levels of congestion and availability of parking. It is where these two sets of different requirements coincide that accidents are likely to take place, as best illustrated at road junctions where pedestrians may want to cross and car drivers may want to turn.

Berman (1996) lists eleven aspects of neo-traditional development that are important considerations in the determination of behavioural change and in determining the quality of the environment:

1   mixed use core within walking distance for residents;
2   local employment and civic centres;
3   a range of housing types for different income levels;.
4   higher housing densities and smaller lots than those found in suburbs;
5   district architecture based on the local vernacular;
6   creation of a sense of community;
7   creation of a sense of tradition;
8   common open spaces;
9   streets that are social spaces as well as a transport facility;
10   narrow streets with side walks and alleys running behind homes;
11   grid street patterns that provide multiple paths for drivers and pedestrians.

Such a local environment is designed to encourage people to get out and walk to local facilities, to take local jobs, and to become part of their own community. This in turn may lead to less car use. There is no clear cut solution to this dilemma, as neo-traditional developments seem to be favoured by planners and urban designers (Calthorpe, 1993), as this promotes walking, mixed land use and a range of housing types. But residents, particularly those with families, still favour culs-de-sac, as it provides greater safety and a more enjoyable living environment.

6.2.5 Local accessibility to transport infrastructure

The proximity to transport networks also influences travel patterns, and consequently transport energy consumption. Better access to major transport networks, particularly road and rail networks, increases travel speeds and extends the distance which can be covered in a fixed time. Major transport networks can be a powerful influence on the dispersal of development – both residential and employment development. The proximity to major transport networks may lead to travel patterns characterized by long travel distances and high transport energy consumption.

Distance from home to the nearest bus stop and railway station affects the modal share (Kitamura *et al.*, 1997). The proportion of car journeys increases and the proportion of non-motorized journeys decreases with increasing distance from the nearest bus stop. Cervero (1994) shows how the proportion of rail journeys decreases with increasing distance from the railway station. Residents living within 500 feet (approximately 150 metres) of a railway station in California typically use rail for approximately 30 per cent of all journeys. The further the distance from the railway station, the lower the proportion of rail journeys made. Residents living at a distance of around 3,000 feet (approximately 900 metres) from the nearest railway station, are likely to make only about half the number of rail journeys than residents living within 500 feet of a railway station. Cervero shows how this pattern of rail use is similar in Washington, Toronto, Edmonton and California, but rail only accounts for a small proportion of all travel.

6.2.6 Parking provision

Current planning policies can have particular impacts on transport demand. In the short term, parking policies have a direct impact on modal choice, whilst in the longer term location policies have a continuing effect on transport demand, in terms of the numbers of trips, mode choice and trip lengths (Section 6.2.4). Trip frequency and modal choice are both influenced by parking availability. As the availability of residential car parking increases, the average number of trips per person decreases (Kitamura *et al.*, 1997). It is suggested that residents with more parking spaces make fewer, longer car based journeys, whilst residents with fewer parking spaces make more journeys but these tend to be short and less car-based. However, as with much of the empirical evidence, the issue of causality is not proven.

Parking restraints form the single most important control that local authorities can exert on travel demand within their area. Parking provision and standards vary from city to city, as indicated in Table 6.4. There is a range of controls available to local authorities including the number of spaces available, the prices charged and the time limitations. They also control the location of parking and have the enforcement responsibility. The limitations on parking control relate primarily to the substantial amount of private non-residential parking (PNR). Parking control can be seen as a particularly powerful element in a city-wide transport strategy, including park and ride, priority to public transport and pedestrianization.

Maximum parking standards have been set (DTLR, 2001) rather than minimum levels so that there is no basis for commuted payments for on-site parking provision, but such payments can still be sought for park and ride or on-street parking controls. The maximum levels for food retailing are now one space per 14 m^2 (above a threshold of 1000 m^2), and one space per 20 m^2 for non-food retail above the same threshold. For B1 uses (the UK use class order in development control that includes offices) the standard is one space per 30 m^2 (above a threshold of 1500 m^2) and 1.5 spaces per dwelling for residential parking. Work Place Parking Levies (WPPL – see Fact Box 7.5) are being considered by some local authorities (e.g. Nottingham) as a means of raising revenues for public transport investment (e.g. trams), but they are also being resisted by businesses which see WPPL as a tax that is not related to congestion (Banister, 2002b).

Car parking is enormously important to local authorities as it is a major source of revenue and as it determines the attractiveness (for some) of the town centre. There does not seem to have been a definitive study that demonstrates whether or not a strong parking policy applied over a period of time with appropriate accompanying measures (e.g. on public transport priority) enhances the economy and environment of the town centre or reduces it. There are arguments in both directions.

Table 6.4 Parking standards in 16 UK cities

	%	Standards	
		Employee	Residential
Private non-residential	43	35	17
Public off street	45	37	18
Public on street	12	10	5
		81	40

Note: Employee = spaces per 1000 employees; Residential = spaces per 1000 district residents.
Source: TecnEcon (1996).

Complementary measures are also important. Complementary is defined in a broad sense to include individual measures that reinforce existing measures and those that are used in combination and involve actions in both transport and planning. In addition to traditional packages of measures in the transport sector (e.g. pedestrian and cycling priorities; traffic management and demand management; public transport priority and park and ride), there is a range of alternatives to promote sustainable development through complementary actions:

◆ company transport plans (some local authorities and businesses have been in the lead in introducing these as part of their sustainable urban development strategy);

◆ travel awareness campaigns and provision of quality information;

◆ school travel provision and accessibility to other facilities (e.g. hospitals and day care centres), particularly for those with no car available;

◆ corporate policies which have an effect on travel decisions – just in time deliveries and the length of freight supply chains, specialization with high consequent levels of transport intensity, rationalization and closure of local facilities with increased travel distances, and company relocation policies for central to peripheral locations.

Park and ride is an interesting example of a transport and planning solution to a city centre problem, namely congestion and a deterioration of environmental quality. On its own, it may have a limited value, but this value is greatly enhanced if it is seen as part of a traffic reduction strategy to limit car parking and give priority to public transport in the town centre – the reallocation of space in town centres (Chapter 5.2.1).

There are many examples of where transport and land-use policies can be used in combination to achieve stated policy objectives, particularly at the city level. The necessary conditions include a clear statement of policy objectives embedded within the concept of sustainable development. The development plan then takes on an instrumental role in implementing those policies through a combination of direct actions in the transport sector (e.g. parking, pricing, priority to public transport), matched by land-use actions (e.g. on mixed land use, location, density). The new dimension underlying this process must be that it is based on debate and discussion with all actors so that the quality of the urban environment is improved. This is where true complementarity takes place through the involvement of firms (commuter transport plans), schools and shops (transport plans), general involvement and awareness of the public, and raising sustainable transport issues within the corporate strategy priorities of all employers.

6.2.7 The role of socio-economic and other behavioural factors

In this extensive description, the individual elements have been identified and evidence cited on each of them (Table 6.1). However, it has not been easy to place all research in clear compartments, and some of the evidence cuts across the divisions. Here, the role of other factors, not related to the built environment, are considered, principally socio-economic factors. In understanding travel behaviour and the role that planning and other interventions can have, one must be aware of their limitations. In democratic societies, there are many factors that affect decisions on location and behaviour. In the most extensive UK study, Stead (2001*b*) concluded that socio-economic factors are more important than land-use factors, explaining more than 50 per cent of the variation in the amount of travel by wards (there are some 8400 wards in England). The most important socio-economic factors are car ownership, socio-economic group and employment. Land-use characteristics explain up to a third of the variation in trip making. There may also be two-way and three-way interactions between these elements. But he also concluded that land-use characteristics such as mixed use developments, settlement size and the provision of local facilities also have a role to play in promoting sustainable development.

Ewing and Cervero (2002) have reviewed the US evidence through a meta analysis of available studies. They have come to a slightly different conclusion in that the built environment is seen to be more important than socio-economic factors in predicting trip lengths, but that socio-economic characteristics are more important in predicting trip frequencies and modal choice. When looking at vehicle distance travelled (a combination of trip lengths, frequencies and modes), the built environment again comes out as being the key determinant. Land-use strategies have the potential to reduce vehicle travel by bringing activities closer to the home location and thereby reducing the length of trips. It should be noted that even though there may be decreases in trip lengths, there may also be a tendency to increase frequency of trips, thereby reducing the net effects (Handy, 2002). The third dimension is the preferences and attitudes of people. Kitamura *et al.* (1997) conclude that these factors were more important than both the built environment and socio-economic factors in predicting travel behaviour. The characteristics of the built environment do not determine travel patterns, rather individuals choose to live in particular locations because they want to adopt a particular lifestyle – a sort of reverse causality. There is some evidence of this in Europe, where people are beginning to choose where to live on the basis of the lifestyle they want, which in turn is partly dependent on their travel patterns and mode preferences, for example in car free communities.

6.3 Case studies

To try and bring the elements covered in the previous section together, a small set of case studies are presented as examples of three cities where different types of actions have taken place. The purpose of the case studies is purely illustrative and they do not represent best practice, but they do help to show how important it is to have complementary measures implemented with a clear overall strategy that is pursued over a period of time in a consistent way.

Oxford, UK (Population 134,000 and situated 100 km north-west of London with a density of 2940 persons per km²)

1993

Oxford Transport Strategy 'to achieve significant environmental improvements in the city centre, whilst allowing continued growth of the city centre economy' (OCC, 2000, p. 1).

Since then, some ninety individual schemes have been packaged together, including bus priority at signals and on radial routes, increased cycling and walking provision, park and ride enhancement with 700 more parking spaces, townscape improvements, and low emissions public transport.

There are more restrictions on cars in the city centre, including alterations on the ring roads, and management in the city centre with restrictions on through traffic. Parking controls in the city centre tightened.

The intention is to reduce car use in the city and improve environmental quality.

2002

Reduction in traffic flows in the city centre (−19 per cent) with reductions in some streets as much as 60 per cent.

Cars and taxis across cordon down from 54 per cent in 1991 to 39 per cent in 2001.

Bus use across cordon increased from 27 per cent in 1991 to 44 per cent in 2001.

Modal share in terms of vehicles shows little change across inner cordon.

%	1991	1998	2002
Cars and taxis	65	61	58
Public transport	5	6	6
Cycle	18	19	22
Other	12	14	14
Outside the centre cars = 80 per cent of vehicles.			

www.oxfordshire.gov.uk/oxford/

Freiburg, Germany (Population 230,000 and situated in south of country with a population density of 1540 persons per km^2)

1950s Decided not to accommodate the car but to maintain the historic city centre.

1969 Kept and developed the tram system.

1973 Old town in the city (50 ha) closed to traffic.

1985 Tramline (7 km) built and another (1994) built to link a 12,000 population new development to the public transport system – further recent investment in trams.

1989 *Gesamtverkehrskonzeption* – the city-wide transport concept set up to reduce the use of the car and increase use of public transport, park and ride, bike and ride and walk. Vehicle traffic restricted to main roads, non-local traffic kept out of residential areas, and speed limits reduced.

Cycle paths increased from 29 km (1972) to 150 km (2002), and these are fully integrated with opportunities to bike and ride – there are some 8600 bicycle parking spaces in Freiburg.

Parking restricted to residents with high fees for long term parking – park and ride is encouraged.

Residential areas have 30 km/h speed limits with reduced space for cars.

New roads also being built (B31 East – October 2002). Part is in a tunnel, but it also goes through residential areas and open space.

Modal split in Inner City (%)

	1982	1989	1999
Walk	35	24	24
Bike	15	21	28
Public transport	11	18	18
Car drivers	30	30	24
Passengers	9	7	6

Bike trips per day in 1976 = 69,000, 1989 = 132,000, 1999 = 210,000.

Car ownership (1999) in Freiburg is 446 cars per 1000 population, lower than the German average of 494 cars per 1000 population.

The *Umwelticket* allows travel by public transport in all sixteen regional transit companies that form the Verkehrsgemeinschaft Freiburg (the Freiburg Region). These monthly passes have reduced car use and those with these passes use public transport for 43 per cent of all their trips.

www.freiburg.de
continued on page 123

continued from page 122

Vauban is a former French army site close to Freiburg and it is being developed as a high density mixed use residential area. There will be 5,000 people living on the 42 ha site at a density of 119 people/ha. It promotes living without the car and the only parking space is available at the periphery of the site. There is good public transport and car sharing is encouraged. Some 300 households have given up their cars – that is about half those living in Vauban. The development will be complete in 2006.

www.forum-vauban.de and Senft (2003)

Hong Kong (Population 6,946,000 in 1099 km^2 and a density of 6320 persons per km^2 and 11 million passenger journeys a day, with 90 per cent by public transport)

Territorial Development Strategy to coordinate land-use and transport development.

Comprehensive Transport study to improve Hong Kong's public transport and road management – CTS-3 (1997).

◆ Integrated land-use and transport and environmental planning, mainly through further development of new towns on high density transport routes.

◆ Priority to rail investment which will carry 50 per cent of public transport passengers (2016).

◆ Coordination and enhancement of public transport services, focusing on interchanges between rail and minibus, taxis and city buses. Integration through use of Smartcards (Octopus).

◆ Some road construction on strategic corridors on reclaimed land.

◆ Use of Intelligent Transport Systems to provide information to public transport users and car drivers, control of traffic, electronic payment and automatic trading.

◆ Promote pedestrian needs, separating pedestrians from other traffic.

◆ Reduce environmental impact of transport to an 'acceptable' level through emissions control, noise barriers, low noise surfaces and alternative fuels.

Hong Kong provides an interesting case of almost having by necessity to adopt sustainable transport strategies, both to protect available open space (about 40 per cent of the land area) and to accommodate its population. The environmental imperative has had to be compatible with the primary concern over continued economic growth. This is illustrated by the mega projects that have been constructed, including extensive land reclamation in the harbour area, the new international airport at Chep Lap Kok (with 45 million passengers and a capacity of 80 million passengers), the Tsing Ma bridge, and new interchanges in Kowloon and at the airport. The single level of planning control facilitates action, but there is little consultation or debate over priorities. Its future lies in maintaining its key position in the Pearl River Delta growth area.

Based on Ng (2004) and Cullinane and Cullinane (2003).

6.4 Conclusions

Underlying much of this debate and the empirical evidence is a lack of detailed analysis. Much of the thinking has been constrained by convention with protagonists being seen as favouring intervention through planning and other controls, or favouring technological fixes, or allowing much greater freedom for the market to operate. As usual, reality is more complex and requires a combination of approaches, not just one. Also, the approaches used may not be compatible and lead to counter intuitive results (Table 6.5). The different researchers have examined the issue of energy use in transport at a variety of levels. Some favour regional and city-wide approaches, others more detailed studies which examine commuting movements and patterns of suburbanization. It should however be remembered that commuting only accounts for about 20 per cent of all trips and that the growth in travel demand is now taking place in non-work based activities, in particular for social, shopping and recreational purposes.

Many of the studies have been severely limited by the amount and the quality of available data. Much of the research effort has been involved in setting up appropriate databases and making as few key assumptions as possible. The results achieved are not necessarily precise but indicative. This in turn has made comparison of results difficult. Even the measure of energy use in transport has not been agreed with some using primary energy consumption (MJ – by mode, distance and passengers), others using gasoline consumption per capita, and others petrol sales within the urban area. This again is a result of data limitations. It would seem that primary energy consumption in MJ should be the preferred unit.

Nevertheless, it is possible to come to some conclusions. In terms of the particular influences that transport has on land use and urban form, it is clear that there are influences on the trip length, speed and mode choice. There is less impact on the frequency of travel. There are six main conclusions[1] in terms of moving towards sustainable urban development. Firstly, location of new development, particularly housing, should be of a substantial size and located near to or within existing settlements so that the total population is at least 25,000 and probably nearer to 50,000. The provision of local facilities and services should be phased so as to encourage the development of local travel patterns.

Secondly, journey lengths by car are relatively constant (12 km) at densities over 15 persons per hectare, but at lower densities car journey lengths increase by up to 35 per cent. Similarly, as density increases, the number of trips by car decreases from 72 per cent of all journeys to 51 per cent. Car use in the high density locations is half that in the lowest density locations.

Thirdly, the larger the settlement size, the shorter the trips and the greater

Table 6.5   Summary of differences in research findings

Resident population size: dispute as to whether population size impacts on modal choice, travel distance and energy consumption.

- No correlation between urban population size and modal choice in the US (Gordon *et al.*, 1989*a*).

- The largest settlements (>250,000 population) display lower travel distances and less by car (ECOTEC, 1993).

- The most energy efficient settlement in terms of transport is one with a resident population size of 25–100k or 250k plus (Banister, 1997*a*).

Resident population density: dispute as to whether increasing densities impacts on modal choice, travel distance and energy consumption. Various conclusions as to the optimum urban form in reducing car travel; ranging from compact cities to 'decentralized concentration' and even low density suburban spread.

- Increasing densities reduces energy consumption by transport (Newman and Kenworthy, 1989*a*).

- There is no clear relationship between the proportion of car trips and population density in the US (Gordon *et al.*, 1989*a*).

- As densities increase, modal split moves towards greater use of rail and bus (Banister *et al.*, 1997).

- Compact cities may not necessarily be the answer to reducing energy consumption, due to effects of congestion, also decentralization may reduce trip length (Breheny, 1997, 2001; Gordon and Richardson, 1997).

- 'Decentralized concentration' is the most efficient urban form in reducing car travel (Jenks *et al.*, 1996).

- Density is the most important physical variable in determining transport energy consumption (Banister *et al*, 1997).

- Higher densities may provide a necessary, but not sufficient condition for less travel (Owens, 1986).

- As people move from big dense cities to small less dense towns they travel more by car, but the distances may be shorter (Hall, 1998).

Provision and mix of services: dispute as to whether local provision of services and facilities impacts on modal choice, travel distance and energy consumption.

- Local provision does not determine modal choice. Personal and household characteristics are the main determinants (Farthing *et al.*, 1997).

- Diversity of services and facilities in close proximity reduces distance travelled, alters modal split and people are prepared to travel further for higher order services and facilities (Banister, 1996).

Location: dispute as to impact of location – in terms of distance from urban centre, strategic transport network and influence of green belt – on modal choice, travel distance and energy consumption.

- Location of new housing development outside existing urban areas, or close to strategic transport network, or as free-standing development increases travel and influences mode split (Headicar and Curtis, 1998).

- Location is an important determinant of energy consumption and car dependency (Banister *et al.*, 1997).

continued on page 126

Table 6.5 – *continued from page 123*

◆   Development close to existing urban areas reduces self-containment and access to non-car owners (Headicar, 1996).
◆   Urban design quality: some anecdotal evidence in the US showing the differential impact of the new urbanist versus cul-de-sac route networks on travel behaviour. Some initial evidence in the UK from Marshall (2001).

Socio-economic characteristics: dispute as to impact of personal and household characteristics on modal choice, travel distance and energy consumption. Also as to whether personal and household characteristics are more important determinants of travel than land-use characteristics.

- ◆   Trip frequency increases with household size, income and car ownership (Hanson, 1982).
- ◆   Travel distance, proportion of car journeys and transport energy consumption increases with car ownership (Naess and Sandberg, 1996; Naess *et al.*, 1995).
- ◆   Dual-income households: assessment of how the choice of new housing location is influenced by the location of two workplaces, extent of 'excess travel' and reasons behind it, role of travel factor in choice of location of new home. No research known.
- ◆   Surrounding mobility levels: impact of the surrounding level of mobility on travel behaviour in terms of mode choice, journey to work length and energy consumption. Some anecdotal evidence in the US. No known assessment in the UK.
- ◆   Attitude: some research in California as to the impact on travel behaviour. No known assessment in the UK.

Source: Based on Hickman and Banister (2002).

the proportion of trips by public transport. Diseconomies of size appear for the largest conurbations as trip lengths increase to accommodate the complex structures of these cities.

Fourthly, and linked with the reasons above, is that mixed use developments should reduce trip lengths and car dependence. Although research here is limited and concentrates on the work journey, there is considerable potential for enhancing the proximity of housing to all types of facilities and services.

Fifthly, development should be located near to public transport interchanges and corridors so that high levels of accessibility for all can be provided. But this may also encourage long distance commuting. Finally, the availability of parking is a key determinant of whether a car is used or not.

Overall, the availability of the car and other socio-economic variables are the two most important factors in determining travel demand and mode choice, explaining about 70–80 per cent of the variation. Land-use factors explain the remaining 20–30 per cent of the variation and provide the main means by which policy interventions can succeed in influencing sustainable development, particularly when combined with actions in the transport sector.

Further analysis required at the urban level includes:

1   The impact of transport measures on the broader economy and environment within cities and regions needs further investigation. It is suggested that many restrictions (e.g. parking) may disadvantage traders

within the city and result in falling turnover, rental levels, and lead to city centre decline. The logic of this argument is clear, but little is known about the short or longer term impacts of transport measures on city vitality and viability, and counter arguments about increases in quality and turnover may be equally valid.

2   Quality neighbourhoods and clear zones are planning solutions to make city living attractive by raising the quality of the environment. Cities must attract people back to them as they form the basis for sustainable living because of the proximity of facilities, the range of opportunities available, and for the possibility of short journeys by public transport, walk and cycle.

3   The reallocation of road space to green modes of transport and people offers real opportunity for change. The traditional transport approach has been to squeeze more capacity out of the road network through traffic management and demand management methods. The interface between planning and transport would allow more radical solutions by allocating space to priority users. This would be carried out in conjunction with parking policy and priority for public transport, and would include bus only streets and shared spaces for cyclists and pedestrians. Reallocation could take place not only in town and city centres, but also in residential locations or near schools and hospitals. More radically, the concept could even be extended to the main radial routes into the city or town.

4   Interchange development would promote the 'seamless' transport system from the start point to the end point. High quality interchanges would allow the smooth transfer of people, and would also provide shops and other facilities so that they become places that people want to be in. Development and transport are explicitly linked together as there would be demand for office, retail and service functions at these attractive and accessible interchange points. Freight transfer facilities can be established in the same way to minimize costs and maximize efficiency – some already operate in this way.

5   In town and city centres (and in residential locations), traffic calming and pedestrianization schemes should not just involve discussion on road safety and reduction in traffic speeds. They are part of a planning strategy to make local areas more attractive to residents, shoppers and others. This means that design and neighbourhood issues need to be considered alongside the transport issues to produce high quality solutions.

The basic argument being presented here is that the role that planning can and should play in avoiding the need to travel has been underestimated. To reduce levels of car dependence and trip lengths, planning decisions must have an instrumental role through establishing and implementing clear development principles based on sustainability. Although transport is only one of the major elements in sustainability, it is the one for which we have substantial information and where positive action can take place. In addition, there is a series of more strategic issues that must be addressed if sustainable land use and transport are to be achieved nationally and regionally.

Note

1   The data used in this final section are from the UK National Travel Survey (1989/91) – Department of Transport (1994), special tabulations (Banister, 1997*b*; and Stead, 1996), and Banister *et al.* (1997).

Chapter 7

Fiscal and regulatory measures

7.1 Introduction

The previous chapter concentrated on many of the positive measures that can be used to bring about sustainable urban development. They can be seen mainly as accessibility enhancing strategies designed to shorten trip lengths (Handy, 2002). Here, we turn to the mobility limiting strategies, which are intended to reduce the amount of travel through shorter trips, less frequent trips, or through mode switching to high occupancy forms of transport (e.g. public transport). Within the sustainability debate, the basic arguments are well known, namely that travellers do not pay the full costs of their travel. These full costs not only cover the direct costs to the users, but the external costs (including the environmental costs) imposed on others (Maddison *et al.*, 1996). The principle of marginal cost pricing is widely accepted, at least in theory, but it is enormously difficult to implement, both technically and politically.

To measure the external costs accurately each vehicle in the system has to be continuously monitored for its individual emissions profile and its contribution to congestion. At present, there are virtually no incentives for car drivers to reduce the environmental costs of their travel. The two main taxes used relate to an annual charge for the vehicle (Vehicle Excise Duty) and the tax element in the price of fuel. In the UK, the VED has been restructured to give some benefits to lower polluting vehicles (Table 7.1).

The taxation element on the price of fuel has been reduced since the fuel duty escalator[1] was removed in 2000. In addition, incentives have been given to the use of alternative fuels, such as sulphur free fuel, biofuels, gases and electricity (VAT at 5 per cent rather than 17.5 per cent). For example, petrol costs 60 per cent more than LPG (£6.89 versus £4.28 per 100 km at 2003 prices). Most of the measures taken recently are likely to reduce exchequer revenues, as car users switch to less polluting vehicles and alternative fuels that have a lower tax element. A new tax regime is required to maintain and increase exchequer revenues, and this is one reason why road pricing and motorway tolls may provide such an alternative.

In this chapter we briefly present some of the major economic arguments and actions for achieving sustainable urban development in transport. As

Table 7.1   New Vehicle Excise Duty rates in the UK (£)

Band	CO₂ (g/km)	Diesel	Petrol	Alternative
AAA	<100	75	65	55
AA	101–120	85	75	65
A	121–150	115	105	95
B	151–165	135	125	115
C	166–185	155	145	135
D	>185	165	160	155

Notes: The old maximum difference was £70, but this has now been increased to £110.
UK diesel car registrations increased by 38 per cent in 2002, with lower CO_2 emissions (but higher emissions of other pollutants). Diesel (2002) accounts for 23.5 per cent of all new registrations, up from 5 per cent in 1990.
Company car taxation (the personal tax on the private use of company cars) has also shifted to a graduated CO_2 linked basis (2002). Tax is payable on the proportion of a car's list price ranging from 15–35 per cent for higher emission cars.

noted before, it is essential that all appropriate measures are used in mutually supporting ways to reduce the amount of travel by energy consuming (and polluting) forms of transport. Pricing strategies obviously have a major role to play in this process, particularly when coupled with complementary actions on land use and development, and technological innovation. The discussion in this chapter revolves principally around pricing and taxation, together with the opportunities for tradable permits so that some of the distributional concerns can be addressed. In addition, there is a shorter review of the ways in which regulations have been successfully used to restrict access and more controversially to reduce capacity.

7.2   Pricing

Although at one level, everyone is in support of marginal cost pricing for all commodities, including transport, the reality is very different. The technology is not yet available to monitor the use of the transport system, the congestion caused and the resources used by each individual traveller (including the pollution caused). Nor is there a clear consensus that road pricing is publicly acceptable as the costs are well known, but the benefits are less clear. It seems that effective implementation is conditional upon the revenues being 'earmarked' as additional monies for transport related investments. This was a necessary condition for implementation in the Norwegian cities (Oslo, Bergen, Trondheim) and in London.

However, such a constraint does not negate the primary justification for marginal cost pricing, namely that all travellers should be aware of the full costs of travel by all modes and that they should pay for it. In the extreme, this means that there should be no subsidy for any form of transport. In reality, this position is not tenable as there are also strong social and spatial constraints as well as economic ones, which result in subsidy being allocated to individual users of transport, and to those living in particular locations that are inaccessible. At present, as noted above, the marginal costs of using the car are low and the fixed costs are higher, but they are often discounted or even ignored in the decision to use the car. In fact, they may be used as a justification for car use, as they have already been paid. It could be argued that there are no costs in using the car (to the user), as it is ready to go at all times and no payment is made for each individual trip.

The most common form of road pricing is through toll lanes, roads and bridges. In most cases, these charges are collected to pay for the costs of construction and maintenance of the roads, rather than to restrict demand. The objective of the owner of the road is to maximize revenue so that the loans and bonds taken out to finance the project can be repaid, as early as possible, so that further revenues can then contribute to profits or to the financing of new toll road schemes. So these measures are primarily targeted at the means to raise finance for investment (and maintenance), with environmental issues being of little importance. Indeed, if the environment is a key concern, these projects may be counterproductive as they bring forward funding and build schemes not in the public investment programme. This means that the net effect is to increase mobility and the use of resources rather than seeking to reduce them.

In the US, the Transportation Equity Act for the 21st Century (1998) has promoted a \$55m programme to fund the development of a series of value pricing projects on bridges that have already been tolled (in New York, New Jersey and Florida), and on high occupancy toll (HOT) lanes in Texas and Southern California (Handy, 2002). A series of schemes has been set up and monitoring is continuing to assess whether there is value added for charging for use (Federal Highway Adminstration, 2002*a*).

In Europe, there are many examples of bridges and tunnels having charges on them, and for the use of tolls on motorways. There seems to be an acceptance that charges are legitimate for new infrastructure, but less support where the road has already been available 'free' at the point of use. Nevertheless, at the urban level, road pricing has been advocated by many influential organizations (e.g. CEC, 2001*a*; ECMT, 1999) as the best means to tackle both the congestion and the environmental problems.

7.2.1 The London congestion charging scheme

London has provided the first real example of cordon pricing in a major European city (February 2003). Each vehicle is charged a fixed amount for crossing the cordon into the city centre. Prior to congestion charging, it was estimated that about 15 per cent of commuters to Central London came by

Table 7.2 Estimated traffic impacts and economic benefits of a £5 area licence for Central London

Impact	Central London		Inner London	
Change in traffic levels	Base vehicle km		Base vehicle km	
am peak (07.00–10.00)	– 0.8m	(–10%)	– 5.9m	(–3%)
14-hour (06.00– 20.00)	– 3.6m	(–12%)	– 25.5m	(–3%)
Change in average traffic speeds	Including junction delays		Including junction delays	
am peak (07.00–10.00)	from 15 to 18 km/h		from 21 to 22 km/h	
14-hour (06.00-20.00)	from 16 to18 km/h		from 22 to 23 km/h	
Economic benefits per year	£125m to £210m; mid point £170m			
Area licensing annual operating cost	£30m to £50m; mid point £40m			
Overall annual benefit	£95m to £160m; mid point £130m			

Source: ROCOL (2000) and www.open.gov.uk/glondon/transport/rocol.htm.

car (about 50,000 vehicles in the peak hour), and these vehicles spent about half their time in queues (stationary or slow moving) with an average speed of about 15 km per hour. The Road Charging Options for London Report (ROCOL, 2000) estimated that a £5 per car charge would reduce traffic by 12 per cent, raise speeds by 3 km/h, and give a net annual benefit of about £130m (Table 7.2).

The cordon pricing scheme provides a major source of funding for the Mayor of London. It is one of the few possibilities for the Mayor to supplement the Greater London Authority's revenue base. There does seem to be public support, provided that the revenues are invested in transport improvements (prior to implementation, 67 per cent of Londoners supported this option, but only 45 per cent of car drivers). These transport improvements would include upgrading underground and surface rail services, improving bus services and lowering bus fares, and in building a series of new links across the River Thames to the east of the city centre (Fact Box 7.1).

Since its introduction in February 2003, congestion charging in London has exceeded expectations. It shows the value of a radical approach to policy and the power of demonstration effects from actual implementation. Although it is too early to judge its full impacts, the broader effects of the scheme also appear beneficial. About 50,000 fewer cars are entering the charging zone, with many people switching to alternative public transport and other modes that are exempt (taxi, cycle, motorcycle), or diverting from the zone. Some 15,000 extra bus passengers are now travelling into the congestion charging zone during the morning peak, with faster journey times (excess waiting time at stops has reduced by 30 per cent) and lost kilometres due to traffic delays reduced by 60 per cent. Only 4,000 fewer people are entering the zone (TfL, 2003).

The wider effects on the local economy are harder to quantify, but from the retail 'footfall index'[2] it seems that 7 per cent less shoppers are coming

Fact Box 7.1 Congestion charging in London

The congestion charging scheme is designed to target transport priorities in Central London – reducing congestion, improving bus services, improving journey time reliability, and to increase the reliability and efficiency of freight distribution. It also raises funding for investment in transport in London. The boundary is formed by the area within the Inner Ring Road of Central London, covering 21 km^2 or 1.3 per cent of the total area of London. There are 174 entry and exit points, with a daily charge of £5 for each registered vehicle – the penalty for non-compliance is £80, reduced to £40 if paid within two weeks and raised to £120 if not paid after 4 weeks. The total budget was about £200 million, including £100 million for complementary traffic management measurements. The operating costs are about £80 million per annum and a £12 million budget for communication and marketing (London Assembly, 2002)

Impact of congestion charging six months on (February to August 2003)

- Congestion in the charging area has reduced by 30 per cent. It is lower than at any time since the mid 1980s. But taxi journeys have increased by 20 per cent, and van and lorry movements have decreased by 10 per cent. Cycling has increased by 30 per cent.

- The number of motor vehicles entering the area during the charging hours (07.00 to 18.30 on Mondays to Fridays) has dropped by 16 per cent – note that buses, taxis, residents (10 per cent charge), and 13 other categories of vehicles are exempt or have discounts.

- Car journeys to and from the charging zone are quicker and more reliable, with travel times reduced by 14 per cent and reliability increased by 30 per cent.

- Public transport is coping with the increase in passengers.

- Bus services are more reliable as a result of less congestion.

- No significant traffic displacement around the zone has been observed.

- Provisional data show a 20 per cent reduction in accidents in the zone.

- The various payment schemes seem to be working, with a reduction in call centre enquiries from 167,000 to 70,000 per week.

- Penalty notice charges have averaged at 106,200 per month, and payments for 60 per cent of these are made within a month – a current proposal (February 2004) will substantially raise the penalty and enforcement charges.

- The public remain supportive of the scheme – 50 per cent of London residents support it and 30 per cent oppose it.

- Average net revenues will be £68m in 2003/2004 and about £90m in 2004/2005.

Source: http://www.tfl.gov.uk/tfl/cc_intro.shtml.

to Central London. For all purposes, this means that 70,000 less people have come into Central London out of a total of 1.6m, but as the vast majority of these already use public transport (85–90 per cent), the contribution of congestion charging is likely to be less than 1 per cent of the total fall. Other benefits from more reliable transport and more efficient deliveries should more than compensate for this loss. There is no doubt that road pricing has raised substantial amounts of revenue, but even here the estimates of some £130m were well above the actual levels (£68m). This is because the success of the scheme is greater than expected with less car drivers paying the charge, and due to higher than expected costs of enforcement. Little has been said about the improvements in environmental quality resulting from less traffic, but the increase in numbers of taxis and buses may have resulted in more diesel emissions.

There are also substantial problems with the implementation of road pricing. The question of public acceptability of road pricing has not been fully addressed, particularly if the revenues raised are not reinvested (at least in a major part) in the transport system. Similarly, the impact on the attractiveness or quality of life in the city is unclear, and its effect on business confidence, rents and land prices will only be understood after a period of 3 to 5 years. Although society as a whole will be better off, low-income car owning households will be faced with a substantial increase in the costs of using the car (see Chapter 7.3). These are all public policy issues that will only be understood when road pricing is widely implemented over a period of time. The London scheme has two main objectives, to reduce levels of car use within the cordon area and to raise revenue for investment in public transport. This differs to the Norwegian experience where tolls have been used to raise revenue for investment in new road construction (and some public transport) (Larsen, 2000). There do not seem to have been schemes that have been introduced for environmental reasons. Such schemes would cover a much wider area with differential charges to reflect the environmental costs imposed. Public transport, taxis, residents' vehicles and motorcycles would all be treated in the same way, where these modes did not address their full environmental costs.

7.2.2 Pricing alternatives – theory and practice

The pricing methods outlined so far relate simply to the right to enter an area or to use a road or a bridge. The charge does not reflect the marginal costs imposed, it is more of an additional cost to the user. The theoretical case for marginal social cost pricing is clear, with users paying both their direct costs of travel and their externalities. But in its pure form where a charge is levied on the difference between marginal social costs and marginal private costs, several strong assumptions are made (Emmerink *et al.*, 1995):

- behaviour is rational in that drivers are utility maximizers or cost minimizers;
- full information on all costs for the road user are available;

- time is a normal economic good and has a positive value;
- congestion pricing is applied to all relevant segments of the network;
- transaction costs are low, so that the welfare gains exceed the costs of implementation.

Even if these assumptions are accepted, there are many other problems with determining the correct prices to be charged. The system described is a static one, but the reality is continuously changing and affected by random circumstances. So it is very difficult to set appropriate prices, and there are no empirical data available to solve this problem. Even if that information was available, should prices be based on current (or immediately preceding) levels of congestion or on predicted levels – probably the latter? It is then important to inform the driver of the price in advance so that a decision can be made before the trip is made. This requires high quality information systems, which car drivers would access prior to a journey. That information system would also give details of alternative modes, timings, destinations and routes.

The valuation problem also needs to be addressed as it covers congestion, pollution and safety. Some of these issues can be measured, at least in part, but road pricing does not necessarily help all these at the same time. For example, higher speeds often result in higher accidents. Congestion is a widely used concept that is difficult to define. It has often been measured as the difference between average free-flow speed and actual average speed. This set of assumptions is unrealistic as we are not expecting to travel under free-flow conditions at the speed limit, so this definition should be seen as a maximum measure of congestion. It also takes no account of length of queues, time spent stationary, uncertainty in travel time, or frequency of gridlock. There are even greater complications when environmental factors are being measured and then attributed to individual vehicles. The measurement of concentrations of pollutants is difficult and their dispersion rates depend on other traffic, street layout, canyon effects, and weather conditions. Different vehicles have different pollution profiles according to their engine type and size, their age, their speed and whether the engine is in the warm up cycle. In short, it is impossible to price according to first best principles, so it is necessary to look at second (and third) best alternatives. As Emmerink *et al.* (1995) concluded 'some kind of weighted average of the costs caused by the external factors' should be used. This is a classic example of reconciling theory and practice.

In conclusion, on the arguments for and against the different forms of pricing in theory and practice, there is a useful summary given in Maddison *et al.* (1996), which has been adapted here as a Fact Box 7.2.

There are two types of charge that relate more explicitly to the conditions under which the area or route actually operate. One is the full-scale electronic road pricing (ERP) scheme, such as that now implemented in Singapore

Fact Box 7.2   Pricing measures recommended for a sustainable transport system

1	Uniform tax on carbon emissions throughout the economy so that the marginal costs of abatement are equalized across all sectors of the economy.
2	Fuel prices to be based on the environmental damage caused. This pricing regime should apply to non-conventional fuels so that their emergence and penetration in the market is enhanced.
3	Purchase or ownership taxes need to be differentiated to reflect the emissions characteristics of the vehicle.
4	Monitoring systems need to be established to check on gross polluters and to check on the air quality in real time so that remedial action can take place.
5	Similar systems would monitor noise pollution and check on particular violations.
6	Extensive road pricing schemes should be introduced into urban areas to control for congestion and pollution effects of vehicles.
7	Any charging system should be distance related, particularly for heavy goods vehicles, where road damage is weight, axle and distance related.
8	The external costs of accidents can be charged through a distance fee representing the additional costs they impose on others. These charges will be different for the various classes of road users and situations where accidents take place.
9	Speed limits need to be 'revisited' to balance the advantages from the savings with the lower numbers of accidents and fuel savings.
10	Accidents can be reduced by significantly increasing the value of life. This will also switch priorities for investment away from schemes that save time and relieve congestion to those intended to save life.

Source: Based on Maddison *et al.* (1996), Box 8.7.

where the charges relate to the level of congestion within the central city and according to distance travelled. The use of pricing in Singapore has evolved over nearly 30 years, and it must be seen as part of the transport strategy that is based on heavy investment in public transport and demand management (Fact Box 7.3). In addition to road pricing, vehicle ownership is constrained through the restriction on the numbers of cars registered each year (each buyer needs a Certificate of Entitlement), and the high entry costs into ownership (Keong, 2002).

As can be seen from Fact Box 7.3, Singapore has been in the lead both for testing the different technologies and in placing road pricing at the centre of its transport strategy. It provides one example of sustainable urban development in that it combines pricing with other elements including heavy investment in public transport and the mass rapid transit system. Two main

Fact Box 7.3   The evolution of the Singapore road pricing schemes

1972   *Additional Registration Fee* – raised the customs fees and introduced a new tax on all new motor vehicles.

1975   *Area Licensing Scheme* – this covered parts of the Central Business District (called the Restricted Zone – RZ), and required prior purchase of a licence. It operated for 2¾hrs during each weekday (07.30–10.15) to June 1989. Then extended to cover the evening peak as well (16.30–19.00). In January 1994, the restrictions covered the whole day. Exemptions have gradually been reduced, with only public transport and emergency vehicles now exempt. Cars, car poolers, taxis, goods vehicles and motorcycles all pay. The fees charged were S$3 for the whole day and S$2 for part of the day. Demand fell initially by 44 per cent, but then rose to a 31 per cent reduction, and this needs to be set against a growing economy, rising incomes and a 77 per cent increase in the vehicle fleet.

1995   *Road Pricing Scheme* – to operate at four points on three congested expressways outside the Restricted Zone.

1998   *Electronic Road Pricing* – The technology was tested from 1996–1997, including a Smartcard and an In-vehicle unit. Charges introduced in 1998, with rates related to time and levels of congestion. Traffic volumes in the CBD have fallen by a further 10–15 per cent, despite the charges now being lower at S$0.50–S$2.50. This is due in part to the differences between the old and new charging systems – the old system charged for a day or part of a day, and the new system charged for each trip. So the additional reductions were due to those making multiple trips in the RZ (about 23 per cent of all trips).

See also Chapter 9, Table 9.8.

---

lines intersect in the CBD giving a network of 83 km, joining the new towns to the centre. A more recent 20 km line (2002) has opened (in part) running from the World Trade Centre in the south of the Island, bypassing the CBD, to the new towns of Hougang, Senkang and Pungol. In addition to the investments in transport, there has been a planned decentralization of government offices and private businesses to suburban centres, initially to a ring of new towns around the centre (in the 1970s), and more recently to four regional centres (Tampines, Jurong East, Woodlands and Beletar), all of which are served by the mass rapid transit. This polycentric development conforms to many of the principles of sustainable urban development (Chapters 6 and 9), and it has allowed urban densities to be maintained (Hall and Pfeiffer, 2000).

The second type of charge is fuel tax, which is paid on the costs of each litre of petrol or diesel. Taxes on fuel in the US have always been low, and there is continuous pressure to reduce them further from the sales tax of $0.41 on the $1.18 cost of fuel per US gallon (€0.30 of the €0.90 per litre price – 2004 prices). This figure is made up of a Federal contribution of $0.184 per gallon and a local tax of $0.226 per gallon (Congressional Budget Office, 2004). Fuel taxes in the US account for about a third of the total costs, but in the EU the figure is much higher, ranging from 56 per cent in Greece to 77 per cent in the UK (Table 4.3). The advantage of such schemes is that those who travel further pay more, but this has to be balanced against the possibility of using more fuel efficient vehicles and the fact that once the fuel is bought, it is there to be used. Fuel taxes are an important source of government revenues and it is here that there is a dilemma for finance ministries, which are keen to be seen as environmentally oriented, but at the same time need to maintain flows of revenues to fund investment. The ideal situation occurs where both the environmental benefits and the revenues are maximized, but more often, it is the economic imperative that is stronger than the environmental aspirations. This means that maintenance of revenues is more important than having the maximum environmental impact.

The possibilities of making car insurance distance-based is attractive, rather than having a fixed amount based on your driving record and where you live (Paul, 2002). Progressive Auto Insurance in the US has a pilot programme for 1200 drivers in Texas that charges them by the amount of time, time of day and where they drive (Handy, 2002). The Netherlands seems to be most advanced in terms of a national system of road user charging, where most costs are switched to use of the car (or lorry), and the fixed (ownership) charges are reduced. The scheme is intended to be revenue neutral (Fact Box 7.4).

Parking charges are often even less popular than raising fuel taxes, particularly when the driver has been used to free parking, as is the case for 99 per cent of vehicle trips in the US (Shoup, 2002). But in Europe, there is less free parking and more of a tradition of paying for parking. The costs of parking have often been used in cities to deter commuters and others, but many seem prepared to pay for parking, at least for short term space. They seem to be most effective when combined with other measures to reduce space available to motorists, and they provide local authorities with an important revenue stream.

In recent years the number of free parking spaces in Zürich has been reduced from around 75 per cent of the total to zero, and parking charges have been more than doubled. Roadside parking spaces in the city are equipped with parking meters, permitting a maximum parking time of between 30 minutes to 2 hours. The aim of this measure has been to reduce the number of car commuters and to encourage people to travel to work by other means. As a result, there has been a shift from long term parking to short term parking, with a concomitant purpose shift to shopping and leisure purposes. By increasing short term demand for parking, there is a greater use of spaces because of the higher turnover of parked cars. In effect, an increase in parking capacity has taken place, leading to a growth in traffic. Research suggests that parking charges would have to be significantly higher in Zürich to discourage

Fact Box 7.4   Road user charging in the Netherlands

The proposal from the Ministry of Transport in the Netherlands is to reduce the costs of vehicle ownership and to place more emphasis on raising the costs of use. The kilometre charge is seen to be progressive in that users are more aware of their costs and fairer in that charges are related to use. The overall levels of revenue raised will not change. In time (after 2006), the charge will relate to the time and location of use of the vehicle. It will apply to all Dutch motor vehicles for their use in the Netherlands.

Initially, the existing system of motor vehicle taxation, the *eurovignette* for lorries, some of the purchase tax on vehicles (25 per cent), and a proportion of duties (18 per cent) will be replaced – at present this accounts for €4.5b of revenue. Initially, the same charge will be made for all vehicles, but this will change, as the charge will relate to vehicle type, weight, fuel and emissions, and a provincial surcharge.

Car-kilometres and emissions will be reduced by about 10 per cent and the number of hours of traffic congestion per 24 hour period will fall by 25 per cent, as compared with the situation in 2020 if no kilometre charges were introduced. Anyone driving their car less than 18,000 km a year will be better off – this covers more than half of all drivers. The total monthly cost will be about €100 per car.

All vehicles will have to install mobimeters to register the number of kilometres driven and then automatic payment is made. The mobimeter could also be used to give information on parking availability, dynamic route planning and breakdown assistance.

Source: Ministry of Transport the Netherlands (2002) and RAC Foundation (2002).

additional car parking, even though higher parking charges are prohibited by federal law, so in this case there is a legal barrier. The authorities in Zürich have therefore focused their efforts on reducing the number of parking spaces and improving public transport to achieve travel reductions (Mäder and Schleiniger, 1995).

In the UK, it is now possible for local authorities to introduce work place parking levies (WPPL), where a charge is made for all private workplace parking in the city. It was seen as an alternative to congestion charging to make employers more aware of the costs imposed on society by having 'free' parking available to their employees. The costs could be passed on to the employees, or paid by the employers. Implementation would be cheaper and quicker than congestion charging, and the revenues raised would again be used for transport investment. The start-up costs and operating costs would be substantially less than those required for a comparable congestion charging scheme. This possibility has raised more concern among businesses than the congestion charging alternative, as it is seen as not being related to levels of congestion, and as it does not discriminate between the different types of employments and where they are located. This can be illustrated with respect to Nottingham (Fact Box 7.5).

Fact Box 7.5   Work place parking levies in Nottingham (WPPL)

Business is concerned that WPPL will reduce inward investment in the City and that
there are other fairer ways to raise revenue for investment in public transport. The
WPPL does not address the congestion in the city centre, but is a tax on all business
in the city. The City sees WPPL as a means to reduce car use and to raise revenues for
investment in the tram system and other public transport schemes. The intention is to
introduce WPPL in 2005 after a public inquiry in 2003 at a rate of £150 per space, and
this rate would rise over seven years to £450.

This single issue has provoked the most serious challenge to the Greater Nottingham
Transport Partnership, with confrontation over how it emerged as a policy and how
it is going to be introduced. There is considerable political support for WPPL. A
Stop Taxation On Parking (STOP) campaign has been initiated by the Chamber of
Commerce, with many of the larger employers in Nottingham involved – Boots, CBI,
Imperial Tobacco, IBM, Raleigh, Carlton TV and the two hospitals.

Source: Banister (2002*b*).

Freight transport has also come under review for possible charging
schemes, which are again distance-based and revenue neutral. The system
will use satellite technology so that distance can be monitored and then
charged accordingly. Although no figures have been produced for the UK, in
Switzerland the charge would be about 20p per kilometre and in Germany
about 10p per kilometre for lorries over 12 tonnes (Fact Box 7.6). After a
suitable period of time, the system could cover both distance and congestion
to give a combined charge.

The EU is debating a EU15 wide scheme that would cover all lorries over
3.5 tonnes on 60,000 km of the strategic road network, as compared with the
existing scheme that only applies to lorries over 12 tonnes. The new system
would be introduced in 2008, and vary between Member States by time,
duration, location and distance travelled, and the revenues raised can now
be used for road investment (new roads and maintenance) and limited rail
investment. Environmental costs and accidents costs can also be included in
the charges. This marks a substantial step towards beginning to charge users
directly for their full costs of road use, and it has been strongly supported by
those countries with large amounts of transit traffic (Germany and Austria),
but opposed by the poorer countries (Spain and Portugal) where higher
charges are seen as a threat to exports.

7.3   Distributional effects of congestion charging in London

Pricing strategies are unpopular and perhaps this is a good reason to see them
as having a major role to play in any sustainable urban development strategy,
as they get individuals and firms to think more carefully about their travel

Fact Box 7.6 Lorry road user charging in the UK

Two complementary schemes are being considered:

1 *Time-based scheme* – this gives a lorry an entitlement to use the UK roads for a specified length of time. This charge is varied according to the weight of the lorry and the axle arrangement.

2 *Distance-based scheme* – this uses GPS to track vehicles and charge them for the use of the UK roads by time and location. This scheme will be introduced in 2005 or 2006 to apply to: all lorry operators, regardless of nationality; all UK roads. It will vary according to the characteristics of the lorry; vary according to the characteristics of the road; and vary according to time of day.

Over the next 2 years, the legislative authority will be sought to permit charging and to enable the government to invest in preparing for its implementation. Consultation with the industry will take place on operational and administrative aspects, together with the procurement of the support systems. Design and letting of supply contracts will be made, together with the testing and supply of equipment prior to going live in the spring of 2006.

However, problems with a similar scheme in Germany could mean that the full scheme will not be introduced until 2011. The scheme would ensure that all foreign truckers paid for using British roads, with domestic truckers being reimbursed through lower diesel charges.

Source: www.cfit.gov.uk/congestioncharging/factsheets/lorry.

decisions. Although elasticities are low, raising prices does have an effect on demand, both in the short term and through changing consumption patterns in the longer term. The difficulties with effective implementation of pricing strategies lie outside the basic economic arguments. It is over the question of public and hence political acceptability of substantially raising travel costs that is at the heart of the reluctance for effective action. Governments have tended to devolve the difficult issues of implementation to the local level, by supporting the necessary enabling legislation, but at the same time keeping well clear of any potential political fallout. Ironically, in Central London, where congestion charging has been successfully introduced, the government was an observer in the process and it was only after it was seen to be a 'success' that they have given the scheme their support. The political process is not in the business of taking risks, and the necessary commitment to radical policy changes on pricing is not present at the national level, and even if it were, there is not sufficient motivation to promote action within the political time scales, typically over 5 years (Banister, 2003).

A second key issue is that of the distributional effects of pricing measures, both spatially and socially. If road pricing is imposed, there is likely to be boundary effects on both people and businesses, as additional costs are imposed on those within the area. In London, there has been a fall of about

7 per cent in retail sales within the congestion charging zone in the first six months of implementation (since February 2003 – Bell *et al.*, 2004). Although congestion charging may have been a contributing factor to this decline, there were also less tourists in London, the effects of the Iraq war and terrorism more generally, the downturn in the economy, the temporary closure of the Central Line (this key link through Central London on the underground network was closed from 25 January 2003 to 2 June 2003), and changes in parking charges both inside and outside the charging zone. There is also a concern that the 7 per cent fall may in part be due to the high levels of retail activity in 2002, when there were many events related to the Queen's Jubilee. The best estimate is that about 1 per cent of that 7 per cent decline (i.e. 14 per cent of the total decline) is due to the congestion charging scheme, and the marginal impact in terms of total retail expenditure is quite small. It should be remembered that only 6 per cent of shoppers actually come to Central London by car, and some of these also use other modes. Nevertheless, it is important and it seems to have affected small business in food and corner shops more than the larger stores or those selling luxury goods.

The income effects are also important as all pricing changes affect the marginal user. It is clear that marginal car users from lower income households spend more (in percentage terms) of their disposable income on transport than middle income groups (Blow and Crawford, 1997; Crawford, 2000; Chapter 2.5.4). The impact of congestion charging on all travellers is progressive overall, but the impact on low-income car drivers is regressive[3] (Banister, 1994). The conclusions from the Institute for Fiscal Studies report (Crawford, 2000) demonstrate the regressive impacts at the lowest income levels (but car ownership levels are also very low here), then progressive across income levels to about the 50 per cent level (about average income levels), and then flat (meaning that the average charge rate is about the same proportion – 0.3 to 0.4 per cent – of income).[4] The propensity to own a car in London is also lower than in than the UK average (Table 7.3). Many of the standard analyses of road pricing ignore the distributional effects by concentrating average welfare gains. The £5 daily charge for entry into Central London has achieved a 16 per cent reduction in peak demand (Transport for London, 2002). But

Table 7.3   Car ownership by income (1997)

Income	UK	London
Top 10%	98%	94%
Bottom 10%	25%	18%
Overall	70%	60%

Source: Blow and Crawford (1997).

these charges have a substantial impact on household budgets, across the whole range of incomes (up to £1,200 per annum).

One argument would be to take compensating measures to ensure that the net effect was fiscally neutral, but this in turn might reduce the effectiveness of the measures. To overcome equity concerns, the revenues should be reinvested in transport projects that benefit all Londoners, particularly low-income car owners. The agreement with the Treasury that all revenues from the scheme can be reinvested in transport for a period of 10 years (to January 2013) was a crucial determinant of acceptability. The congestion charging scheme would not have been implemented without this guarantee that there would be additional monies available for transport investment. The draft TfL (Transport for London) budget for 2003 to 2004 indicates that 65 per cent of the anticipated net revenue (originally estimated to be £130m, now substantially less at about £68m) will be spent on improving bus services, 28 per cent on road safety measures, 3 per cent on closed-circuit television on buses, and the remaining 4 per cent in developing safer routes for children to take to school (House of Commons, 2003, para 67).

Those who pay the charge will be net losers as the financial cost (£5) is unlikely to be offset by the gains from the faster or more reliable travel times. The reduction in traffic levels is likely to lead to improvements of 20 to 25 per cent in travel speeds by car across the congestion charging zone (House of Commons, 2003). This means that speeds will increase to an average of about 22 km per hour. The maximum journey length across the zone is about 5 km and this will now mean that the journey will take six minutes less. Most journey time savings within the congestion charging area will be less than this figure of six minutes for a 5 km journey. At the aggregate level, it is estimated that the revenues from the car users paying the standard charge will be £110m per annum (Transport for London, 2002 – since reduced in reality to £68m), with the travel time savings amounting to an additional £75m. There are also further savings from reliability increases (£35m) and vehicle operating cost savings (£8m). This last figure includes all car users (not just those paying the standard charge), and the estimates for reliability include all road users (Transport for London, 2002).

There have been improvements in the speed and reliability of bus services meaning that existing bus users benefit from the congestion charging scheme, even though the buses are more crowded. Additional buses have been provided and existing buses have been rescheduled to provide extra capacity through more frequent running. Car switchers to buses have benefited from the improved services, but they are now taking a 'non preferred mode', so they could also be seen as losers.

The real gainers are those who benefit from the discounts and exemptions, including bus and coach operators, taxis, minicabs and private hire cars. They should benefit from lower levels of congestion, with faster and more reliable journey times, but at the same time not paying any more. Users of taxis may be major beneficiaries, as their fares should be lower with a reduction in travel time, where the fare is based on both distance and time taken. There are similar benefits for motorcycle and pedal cycle users.

There has been considerable debate during the consultation period and immediately before implementation over low-income car drivers. Although the poor are least likely to own a car, the additional charge is likely to be a major deterrent to using that car in Central London. It could also be argued that there are key low-income workers that need their car to get to work, because they work unsocial hours. But these drivers should not be affected by the charge if they come into London outside the operating time of the congestion charging scheme (07.00–18.30). Some public service employees (and others such as those in the voluntary sector) are on low incomes and the additional charge may affect recruitment and retention of staff.

The question here is whether transport is different from any other economic good in that demand relates to price and any pricing mechanism discriminates on the basis of ability and willingness to pay. There should be no subsidies in transport, particularly if there is a real concern over sustainable transport, and compensation mechanisms should be sought through the taxation and benefits system if particular groups are seen to be disadvantaged. These individuals could then choose whether to spend any additional income on the congestion charge or on any other economic good.

Overall though, the charge is progressive as 90 per cent of those driving into Central London come from the wealthiest 50 per cent of society (Transport and Environment, 2003), and the revenues are being used for socially progressive transport schemes. Where it may be argued that the system is unfair is over the extent and levels of discounts. It seems that there is no clear logic as to why certain groups of vehicles or users have no charge or a reduced charge.

If the charge relates to the level of congestion caused, then motorcycles should have no charge and vans and lorries should have a much higher charge than the standard rate (as was originally proposed). If the charge relates to the level of pollution caused, then again there should be a similar rate for most petrol cars and motorcycles, but a higher rate for diesel-engined vehicles (including taxis minicabs, and private hire cars). Alternative fuelled vehicles still pollute and so should be subject to a charge. If the charge is to deter commuters and to benefit residents, then there may be a case for a reduced rate for residents. But why that reduced rate should be set at 90 per cent is not clear. Residents may be one of the main beneficiaries of the congestion charging scheme, as they benefit from less traffic and pollution. These are the real beneficiaries of a double dividend, as they are paying much less as well. If it can be demonstrated that the estimated 21,000 residents inside the cordon area with cars (Transport for London, 2002) are from higher income groups (very likely), then in this respect at least, the scheme is not equitable.

The difficulty faced by the Mayor was that to gain support for the congestion charging scheme from a wide range of affected parties, he had to accommodate their requirements (at least in part) through the discount scheme. But having granted reduced rates and exemptions to over half the vehicles entering Central London, the effectiveness of the scheme is reduced and it is difficult to recapture those concessions (Banister, 2003).

Overall, it would seem that the scheme does not discriminate against low-income car users and that the main beneficiaries are those who continue to use the buses, as their service quality has improved and will continue to do so through the additional investments from the congestion charge revenues. Where this is inequitable is in the granting of discounts and exemptions to particular types of vehicles or to particular users. But even here it is difficult to estimate the scale of the inequity, as the objectives of the congestion charging scheme are not clear. Depending on those objectives, it must be concluded that these discounts and exemptions should be reassessed as soon as possible.

7.4 Regulatory incentives

Complementary to the pricing methods are the restrictions placed on access to certain areas, together with the means by which the best use of resources can be made. This regulatory group of public policy measures provides the context within which most action has taken place, with cities adopting a range of strategies most appropriate to their particular situation. Some of the main measures can be summarized under three headings – land-use policy, technology policy and transport policy (Table 4.4). However, the discussion is now moving on in two important respects. Firstly, policy interventions have traditionally been seen as the prime responsibility of the public sector. The new agenda suggests that it is necessary to involve all actors in the public and private sectors in achieving policy objectives related to sustainability. At the international level, that is now taking place through the current series of Global Conventions (e.g. at Rio (1992), Kyoto (1997), Buenos Aires (1998) and Johannesburg (2002)). However, the motor manufacturers have not yet been fully involved in developing a global strategy that matches the economic and financial interests of the car industry with the broader environmental concerns of society.

Responsibility involves government and the motor vehicle manufacturers as the two principal agents. But it also includes the oil industry to provide clean alternative fuels based on renewable energy sources, and the necessary infrastructure to allow for the distribution and use of that energy. The supply chains in the transport industry are varied and extended, so that at each stage the environmental costs and consequences need to be balanced against the economic gains. Other actors include the various interest groups for the transport industry, the operators, the environmental and other pressure groups, and others (e.g. developers, financial institutions). All have different vested interests in transport, as do the general public who are the direct beneficiaries of the available transport system (as users) and as the indirect beneficiaries (as consumers of transported goods), but who may also suffer the consequences. To achieve effective action in sustainable transport, responsibility must be attached to all interested parties and each must be prepared to take action.

Secondly, many of the actions implemented relate to a single sector rather than to more general policy objectives or to cross sector implementation. Actions taken individually have much less impact than those measures that are packaged together (Marshall and Banister, 2000), but it is also necessary to ensure complementarity in actions. Counterintuitive outcomes may result from the implementation of actions as users of the system find creative means to continue to do what they have done in the past. This involves the close links between transport and city planning authorities, as well as the new links with other actors. Local Agenda 21 attempts to forge this more comprehensive approach involving all actors, but it has not achieved success as institutional barriers and the lack of appropriate powers have made effective implementation difficult. But having more localized powers does not necessarily mean that action will follow, as has been found in Germany. The noble objective of consensus and partnership, central to the UK government's Integrated Transport Policy White Paper (DETR, 1998c), may not exist as individuals and organizations have conflicts of interest, objectives, time-scales and do not even communicate effectively with each other.

In terms of achieving sustainable transport, a range of policy objectives is being addressed in Table 4.4 (Column 3). Some policies are directed at increasing cycle and public transport use, whilst others are intended to reduce car use. Other policies increase sustainable accessibility, so that by the location of land uses and activities, new travel patterns can emerge, whilst a further group look towards improving mobility efficiency so that intensity of use is increased. The role of technology is ambivalent as it enhances sustainable transport if trip patterns are modified or even reduced, but it may also encourage new activities. There is substantial potential for implementing sustainable transport policies, but progress has been slow, although there are now signs that change is happening. Switzerland is often taken as a location where good practice is evident (Fact Box 7.7), but interestingly out of the 398 annual car trips taken by the average person in Zürich some 209 are without constraints (53 per cent). This means that they could have been taken by another mode of transport – 60 had a potential for replacement by walk, 166 by public transport and 83 by cycling (Socialdata, 1993).

Fact Box 7.7 The new mobility culture in Switzerland

Some 600,000 people in Switzerland (9 per cent of the population) are interested in car sharing, and the present (2000) car sharing population amounts to 33,000 people. Those involved in car sharing make use of public transport and tickets are now available in Zürich to combine public transport and car sharing (Züri mobil). A national scheme was set up by Swiss Railways and the Hertz car rental firm in 1998 called 'Mobility Car Sharing Switzerland'. By 1999, there were more than 700 stations served. Car shares make less use of the car, and it may be one step towards not owning a car.

Car free households 1999

Zürich	city	45%	urban	18%
Berne	city	47%	urban	21%
Basle	city	54%	urban	23%

Note that these proportions fall by 7 per cent (city) and 4 per cent (urban) if the elderly are excluded.

Misperceptions	Green transport oriented	Car oriented
People state that they are	91%	9%
Opinion leaders state that they are	94%	6%
Opinion leaders think people are	56%	44%
People think that opinion leaders are	49%	51%

Source: Muheim and Reinhardt (2000) and Socialdata (1993).

7.5 Carbon taxes

Much of the earlier part of this chapter has concentrated on pricing at the micro level to make the user more aware of the actual costs of travel. There also seem to be strong macroeconomic arguments for a change towards a more environmental tax regime where the onus is on taxing consumption rather than production. It has always seemed to be anomalous that taxes have historically been related to labour and income, making it less attractive to work.[5] A shift in taxation towards pollution taxes could both improve the quality of the environment and enhance taxation efficiency. This is the double dividend hypothesis (Pearce, 1991), which has raised considerable debate amongst economists as to whether the quality of the natural environment can be improved at the same time as the non-environmental components of the economy (employment and economic welfare). Although there is no clear resolution to the debate, it does seem that there may be adverse income distribution effects as lower income groups will pay more in taxation than at present. This leads to the conclusion that rather than concentrate on the non-environmental dividends from environmental tax reform, there should be a greater emphasis on the welfare improvements resulting from a cleaner environment (de Mooij, 1999).

7.6 Air travel

Although air travel is not strictly within the scope of this book, it is important
not to forget this large source of emissions. It is not as important as the car as
a source of concern, but it is the main growth sector with expansion taking
place in the UK at about 3.5 per cent per annum. This figure is less than
the recent levels of growth (about 6 per cent per annum), but still sufficient
to double demand every 20 years. More important though is the fact that
emissions from air travel are outside any international agreement and they
were explicitly excluded from the Kyoto Accord. In the UK, the current (2002)
level of emissions from air transport is 8 MtC per annum (9 MtC including
domestic air – the corresponding figure for road transport is 35 MtC), and
this is expected to increase to between 14 and 16 MtC by 2020 (DfT, 2003).
By 2050, aviation carbon emissions in the UK will exceed those from road
transport, and will account for 40 per cent of all UK carbon emissions.

The exact effects of pollution from air transport are not well known.
Emissions of CO_2 and NO_x (results in ozone formation) both contribute to
global warming, and these can be valued provided that the cost per tonne
of carbon released is accurately known. Current international research
values carbon at £70 per tonne (2000 prices with equity weightings to take
account of differences in income between geographical regions of the world
– Government Economic Service, 2002). This figure should be raised by £1
per tonne of carbon in real terms for each subsequent year. The secondary
effects are also important, as there are increased levels of tropospheric ozone,
contrail formation (water vapour[6]) and stratospheric ozone depletion. The
total impact of all aviation emissions on climate change is obtained by
multiplying CO_2 released by 2.7 to take account of 'radiative forcing' (HM
Treasury and DfT, 2003). The costs of global warming attributed to UK
aviation in 2000 was £1.4b, rising to £3.6b in 2020 assuming unconstrained
demand increases.

In addition to the global warming effects, there are two other major
environmental costs from aviation. Aircraft noise causes disturbance to those
living and working close to airports. At take off, the noise levels reach 140
dB(A), and at 300 metres from the aircraft the levels are still at between
80 and 100 dB(A). Noise is particularly disturbing at night time, but even
during the day, many households (around London Heathrow) are subject to a
continuous daytime sound level of over 57 dB(A) Leq.[7] The total costs for all
airports in the UK are estimated to be £25m for 2000 (HM Treasury and DfT,
2003). The second set of costs relates to the loss of local air quality resulting
from emissions during take-off and landing, together with the other related
ground-based movements. The two main ground level pollutants are NO_2
and PM_{10}, both of which come under new mandatory EU limits in 2010 and

2005/2010 respectively. The estimates of the costs here are about £180m for all UK passengers (HM Treasury and DfT, 2003).

The science of air pollution, particularly in the upper atmosphere, is not well understood, but it is sufficiently important to adopt the precautionary principle to look at ways to internalize some of the costs (RCEP, 2002a). Aviation has always been in a privileged position in terms of taxation, as international airports and airlines benefit from tax free shopping facilities. More important though is the ability to offer cheap tickets and the fact that excise duties on kerosene for international flights are zero-rated. These benefits come to about £10b a year in the UK, made up of £5.7b loss from no tax on aviation fuel, £4.0b loss of VAT on aviation fuel and tickets, and a £0.4b loss from no excise duty on consumer goods (Fact Box 7.8). The tax from passengers (Air Passenger Duty) brings in £0.9b, leaving a shortfall of £9.2b. At present, there are no financial incentives to correct for air travel externalities. Only a few countries charge VAT on domestic airline tickets and even then it is set at a reduced rate (e.g. Germany at 19 per cent and France at 5.5 per cent).

These anomalies are in direct contrast with other sectors of the transport industry that have traditionally been subject to heavy taxation. The airline industry is price sensitive, yet the forecasts have been made as if there are no constraints on demand. Indeed, it is assumed that real prices will come down. In the UK, air passenger numbers are expected to increase from 180m (2000) to 500m (2050) (DfT, 2002). Unless aviation is included within the picture, it will not be possible to even reach the modest Kyoto targets for CO_2

Fact Box 7.8   Summary of some air travel pricing anomalies

UK Forecasts for air travel 2030 are 500m passengers, and an increase of 275 per cent from 2000 (180m passengers). There are some £10b tax exemptions, as there is no tax or VAT on international fuel and only VAT on national fuel. Airlines pay about 18 pence a litre for fuel. If this were taxed at the same rate as petrol, then it would raise £5.7b in revenue. There is no VAT on tickets, aircraft purchase and maintenance, meals or baggage handling – this accounts for a further £4.0b in lost revenue. Duty free prices on goods taken outside the EU account for a further £0.4b in lost revenue. The British Airports Authority receive £412m from duty free and £690m from landing charges per annum (DfT, 2002).

Air travel was not included in the Kyoto Accord. Air passenger duty was introduced in 1993 and raises £0.9b in revenues. Air's anomalous position is a result of the Chicago Convention, which set out to help develop the industry immediately after World War 2 (1945).

It is estimated that 4.5 per cent of the UK population earning over £30,000 a year make 44 per cent of all flights, and that there are 10 'rich' flights to each 'poor' flight (Bishop and Grayling, 2003).

reductions, let alone the 60 per cent target for 2050 agreed recently by the UK government (DTI, 2003).

The report from the Environmental Audit Committee (EAC) of the House of Commons (2003) was damning in its criticism of current aviation policy, and it raised serious concerns about the consistency of government policy on the environment and the underlying rationale for the proposed massive expansion of airport capacity in the UK. The six main conclusions of that report were:

1   Consultation assumes passenger numbers will rise by 3.5 per cent per annum for 30 years, and fares will decrease by 40 per cent over the same period.

2   The government seems to be against any pricing strategy for aviation. The EAC strongly argues for a decoupling of air traffic growth from economic growth through the use of fiscal and other policy instruments.

3   There is no systematic strategic integrated appraisal of airport proposals so that the overall benefits of the different degrees of expansion can be assessed.

4   The economic benefits of aviation are not supported by the evidence. For example, there is a substantial negative balance of £15b on the tourism account as many more people from the UK travel overseas by air for holidays than come to the UK. Much of the growth in passengers is from interlining at UK hub airports and this brings minimal benefits to the UK economy.

5   'The net present value associated with the increase in the costs of aviation emissions amounts to minus £18b. Including this amount would entirely wipe out the economic case for an expansion in runways and result in substantial net deficits for almost all options the Department for Transport has put forward (para 49).

6   Environmentalists argue that aviation is receiving subsidies of more than £9b through the absence of fuel tax and VAT on tickets.

The main recommendation from the EAC is that the current Air Passengers Duty is replaced by an emissions charge levied on all flights. The total level of that charge should be £1.5b per year initially, rising at an agreed rate each year (effectively an escalator). In addition, the introduction of VAT on tickets for domestic flights should be considered. Such a recommendation would mean that on average tickets would increase in cost by about £9 plus any VAT. This seems a very modest change and unlikely to have much effect on demand. Crucial here is the acceptance that the £70 per tonne of carbon charge is a fair valuation of the costs (equivalent to £19 per tonne of CO_2[8]). This means that to equalize the taxation treatment between the different forms of transport would have major cost implications. Bishop and Grayling (2003) estimate that the tax exemptions enjoyed by the aviation industry amount to about £35 per single ticket. A carbon tax can be justified on the basis of the environmental costs and the need to create a sound basis for sustainable development.

7.7   Pricing and the United States

Whatever the political acceptability of various sustainable transport policies may turn out to be in the EU, it is certain that most of them will be less acceptable in the United States. As observed in recent years, the US has lagged far behind other OECD countries in adopting measures that would save energy and reduce global warming. Under the Clinton Administration, the US Congress refused to sign the Kyoto Accords, and under the Bush Administration, they are being ignored completely (National Energy Policy Development Group, 2001). Transport emissions contributing to global warming are now rising in the US by about 3 per cent per year, and emissions from residential and commercial sources are rising even faster (Oak Ridge National Laboratory, 2002).

So it is difficult to end this chapter on pricing and regulation without reference to the US situation, where the total volume of greenhouse gas emissions (GHG) from transport is now second only to electricity generation, and its growth is also as fast (Greene and Schafer, 2003). The current 33 per cent share of transport will increase to 36 per cent by 2020. As a major producer of pollution, it must take a leading role in implementing reduction strategies, and much is now being done in terms of increasing energy efficiency, exploring the potential for new fuels, improving system efficiency, and even reducing transport activity.

To date, all advances in energy efficiency and pollution control in the United States have come as the result of technological improvements whose cost is largely hidden to consumers and which can result in direct benefits to motorists, such as reduced petrol bills for more fuel-efficient cars. Even those technological advances have stagnated in recent years. While the average fuel efficiency of new cars doubled between 1975 and 1990, it has barely increased at all since then (Oak Ridge National Laboratory, 2002). Federal EPA fuel efficiency standards for passenger cars in the US (the CAFE standards – Corporate Average Fuel Economy) have remained constant since 1990, and they have increased only 4 per cent for light trucks. Similarly, enormous progress was made in reducing tailpipe emissions from cars from 1975 to 1995, but progress since then has been much slower and the overall average has declined since 1998, due to the increase in SUV (Sports Utility Vehicle) sales. Moreover, the Bush Administration recently (2003) relaxed and delayed the Clean Air Act standards and regulations enforcing motor vehicle inspection programs at the state level.

With vehicle-kilometre of travel in the United States continuing to rise rapidly, total energy use and emissions of greenhouse gases have also burgeoned (Oak Ridge National Laboratory, 2002; Wilson, 2002; Federal Highway Administration, 2002b). Air quality in most American metropolitan areas improved significantly from 1980 to 2000, but technology-induced reductions in pollution per kilometre have levelled off and may soon be offset by the rapid growth in kilometres driven (US Environmental Protection Agency, 2002).

Yet, the use of the pricing mechanism as a key element in that strategy is minimal. As already noted, the price of fuel in the US is about a third of that in the EU, and the efficiency of vehicles is also lower (about 60 per cent of the car fleet in the EU). Even though new taxes on 'gas guzzlers' have been introduced for new cars with less than 22.5 mpg ($1000) and 12.5 mpg ($7000), light trucks escape this requirement, and these vehicles now account for over 50 per cent of new purchases (2001) in the US (Pucher and Renne, 2003).

There are also welcome incentives for the use of alternative fuels (including ethanol), electric vehicles and hybrid vehicles. Similarly, the experiments of adding insurance costs to the distance travelled again help relate costs to actual use. The discussion over the use of feebates also shows promise. Here, taxes are raised for low efficiency vehicles to help reduce the costs of those using higher efficiency vehicles. Such policy initiatives give clear incentives to manufacturers to make the best use of fuel efficiency technologies to reduce levels of tax liability and to acquire rebates. To the consumer, there would be clear pricing messages. Feebates, as with other forms of taxation, can be made revenue neutral as their main objective is to change the purchase patterns of consumers.

The conclusion from the influential Pew Center on Global Climate Change (Greene and Schafer, 2003) was that US transport related carbon emissions 'could be cut by 20–25 per cent by 2015 and by 45–50 per cent by 2030, in comparison to a continuation of current trends in energy efficiency, petroleum dependence and traffic growth' (p. 55). They add that policies need to cover a range of possibilities and that technological progress is a key element. But this modest level of reduction is not an absolute one, only a relative one in terms of the expected growth in demand. If strong action, including clear pricing signals, is not taken, there is even less likelihood of achieving even a relative reduction.

The authors of the Pew Center report are more optimistic in their conclusions, and see strong actions emerging in the use of the best available technology, so that energy efficiency of vehicles is increased, and oil dependency can be reduced. But the US accounts for 25 per cent of global GHG emissions, and it has the largest transport system, which is the fastest growing source of GHG emissions in the US economy. It is the sheer scale of the problem to be addressed that is frightening, and proposals to raise prices even slightly meet with furious political opposition and public outrage (Transportation Research Board, 2001). Restrictions on auto use such as auto-free zones, traffic calming, and limitations on parking are rare in American cities. The Clean Air Act of 1990 instituted requirements that firms somehow convince increasing percentages of their employees to carpool, walk, bicycle, or take public transport. The programme was so unpopular with both firms and employees that it was at first not enforced and then completely rescinded by the Federal government. Similarly, proposals to reduce existing subsidies to free parking at the workplace were explored by the Clinton Administration but then dropped. Virtually any measure that would force changes in travel behaviour among Americans is politically taboo and sure suicide for the career of any politician.

If it is impossible to raise substantially the costs of transport in the US, then the technological alternatives with heavy investment in efficient vehicles, new fuels and the hydrogen or hybrid car must be high on the agenda (Chapter 8). The 'new mobility' concept (Salon *et al.*, 1999) takes these technologies to provide travel options that generate less environmental impacts, through packaging for individual companies and users. Included here are company car sharing schemes, neighbourhood electric vehicles, and 'smart' paratransit (Handy, 2002). The new urbanism debate emphasizes the importance of community through targeting a more individual-based service for those members of the population that do not have cars (CTA, 2001). Perhaps these schemes need to be extended to all members of the community?

The main reason why Americans oppose most sustainable transport policies is that cities in the US are extremely car-dependent. Sprawling suburban developments feature long distances between residences and virtually every other type of land use, making the car a virtual necessity. Since the vast majority of Americans perceive no good alternative to their cars, and have become used to the high level of mobility, comfort, and convenience of their cars, they vehemently reject any policies that would force them out of their cars or even curtail their usage in any way. Free roads, free parking, cheap petrol, and universal, cheap driver licensing are viewed as a natural right.

Any sustainable transport policy, that would restrict driving or make it more expensive, is a non-starter in the United States. Only in the event that an immediate crisis is perceived in the US itself would Americans be willing to sacrifice their use of the car for virtually all travel. Energy use is not viewed as a crisis at all, and both air pollution and congestion are concentrated in a few especially problematic metropolitan areas. Thus, the only sustainable transport policies that are currently feasible in the US are those that could be achieved through technological measures without affecting the travel behaviour or lifestyle of Americans. That makes the range of candidate policies far narrower than in the EU, with its history of much higher prices of auto ownership and use, as well as many restrictions on car use in cities.

7.8 Comments on fiscal and regulatory measures

There are strong arguments within the economics literature to make sure that all travellers are fully aware of their external costs. Ideally, these costs should be internalized and form a substantial part of the total costs of travel. They should vary according to the exact situation and type of transport used, thus reflecting the congestion conditions, the environmental characteristics of the mode used and other factors (such as occupancy levels and load factors). This is the ideal world, but there are also important social, distributional and moral issues to be addressed. Not all costs can be valued and internalized.

Some environmental economists (e.g. Daly and Cobb, 1989) maintain the argument that irreplaceable environmental systems cannot be viewed as tradable commodities (Chapter 3.1). Although it may be possible to estimate costs, at least indirectly, this does not mean that the valuation system developed is appropriate for actual use. It should be used to guide policy, not only on pricing, but on what can or cannot be consumed. Climate stability is one such system that is hard to quantify and even if it can be quantified, then it should not be traded. Other systems include health, air quality, water quality and peace and quiet. Hence, the selection of a value of £70 per tonne of carbon in the air sector is useful as a guide to the scale of the problem, but it should not be used as a determining factor as to what price individuals should pay for air travel (Clarkson and Deyes, 2002). Apart from the arguments relating to social justice, this figure does not include long-term uncertainty, the imprecision of the science, and the different impacts on different countries. This is the narrow pathway that needs to be followed, namely to balance the convenience of generating values so that the costs can be internalized, with the broader policy objectives of a consistent and fair strategy on seeking sustainable development.

Yet it is seen by many that pricing is the only way to make sure that decisions are made rationally, even though the levels of charging necessary to achieve full internalization of externalities is too high (at least politically). Recent evidence from London suggests that price elasticities are high, at least in dense urban areas where there are alternative forms of public transport. It is remarkable that the centre of a city can be transformed in such a short space of time by a relatively 'crude' form of pricing. Many other examples of pricing exist, but in all cases there are alternatives. This is where solutions in the US are so hard to find as there is no tradition of public transport, only a strong cultural commitment to the car. Hence this fundamental difference exists between the US and the EU where on the one hand there is a steady (but slow) promotion of technological innovation, whilst on the other hand more direct action has been taken (again slowly) to charge the user for the congestion and pollution caused. It would seem that in the EU there is a real opportunity to combine planning measures (Chapter 6) with pricing and regulation (Chapter 7) and technological excellence (Chapter 8) to achieve sustainable urban development. But in the US, there is only the technological option available, and even here there seems to be enormous difficulty in effective implementation. This suggests that pricing is a key component in the EU that is supported by action from the EU and national and local governments. This is not yet the case in the US, but serious consideration needs to be given to raising the costs of transport, even if it is seen to be politically difficult to introduce.

In addition to the differences of views on either side of the Atlantic, there is the potential problem posed by the emergence of China as a new global force, with high levels of growth and little priority given to sustainable development. Progress requires all the major economic centres in the world to work together towards the same sustainability goals, albeit from different starting points and through different means, and over different periods of time. Sustainable urban development cannot rely wholly on technological futures or on pricing, but on a combination of these two, supported by the active involvement of governments and other stakeholders in the development process. It is to the technological futures that we now turn.

Notes

1   The fuel duty escalator was first introduced by the Conservative government in 1993 at 3 per cent and subsequently raised in 1994 to 4 per cent. It was continued by the Labour government and again raised in 1997 to 6 per cent. It was abolished in 2000 after a series of fuel duty protests. The fuel duty escalator raised duty on fuel (about a half of the pump price) by 3,4 or 6 per cent in real terms each year. It was the main means by which the UK government was seeking to achieve the Kyoto targets in the transport sector.

2   Footfall indices estimates the amount of shopper activity through credit card transactions, and can be used to compare locations, identify where customers come from, and summarize the types of goods being purchased – www.caci.co.uk/retailfootprint.htm.

3   A flat rate charge is regressive, as it does not relate to the ability to pay.

4   Note that this relates to the average and not individuals, and to liabilities rather than choices that are actually made.

5   Pigou in his classic 1947 book demonstrated that pollution taxes can internalise the adverse externalities associated with polluting activities. At the optimum, the pollution tax is equal to the marginal environmental damage from pollution – this is the Pigouvian tax.

6 Water vapour returns as rain and snow in a week or two, but if it is emitted in the troposphere it takes much longer to return, and CO_2 can remain in the upper atmosphere for 100 years. Sulphates and soot aerosols (airborne particles) are also thought to encourage cloud formation.

7 L_{eq} is the equivalent continuous sound level. This is the notional steady noise level over a stated period giving the same energy as the actual intermittent noise. $57L_{eq}$ is some disturbance, $69L_{eq}$ is high disturbance and $72L_{eq}$ is considerable disturbance. dB(A) is the measurement of noise expressed in decibels, which is a measure of acoustic pressure on a logarithmic scale and proportional to the square of energy. An increase of 3dB is equivalent to a doubling of energy or twice the sound generating activity. A is a weighting scale reflecting the different frequencies in the noise spectrum (Carpenter, 1994).

8 There is a conversion factor of 3.67 between CO_2 emissions and the carbon value per tonne of emissions.

Chapter 8

Technology and transport

8.1 Introduction

Technology has a major role to play in moving towards sustainable urban development, and there is considerable interest from governments and the motor industry in switching to clean low carbon transport. This is seen by many to be the principal means by which transport can help meet greenhouse gas emission targets, as it requires no change in the way activities are carried out. It does not tackle the congestion problem. Indeed, it may even encourage more travel, as the concern that many have over the environmental consequences of transport will have been met, at least to some extent. Changing technologies is also politically attractive as it helps diversify fuel sources and reduces dependence on imported oil.

In the short term though, the use of light-duty vehicles with improved energy economy provides the most cost effective means of reducing oil consumption (IEA, 2001). Average fuel consumption could be reduced by between 25–30 per cent by 2010 by using the best available current petrol and diesel technologies, and even in the US where fuel prices are low, a 20 per cent target is achievable.

In addition, there are good opportunities in all countries to use the best available technology to tackle other emissions, principally with add on technology of catalytic converters. Provided that these are working, the potential for substantial reductions in CO, NO_x, VOC and PM will be obtained and maintained until 2030 (OECD, 2002*a*). The real problem still remains, namely that of CO_2 emissions for which there is (at present) no technological fix. The expected increases in emissions of CO_2 from transport are frightening, both in the OECD countries (a 60 per cent increase) and also in the non-OECD countries (a 3½ times increase). Such an increase requires transport not only to decouple from economic growth (GDP), but also more importantly to decouple transport growth from energy consumption (Chapter 3).

Such an argument places considerable expectations on the development and take up of far more efficient technologies to push the current engine design to its limits, so that the maximum distance output is obtained from a given energy input. It also must focus attention on the development of alternative fuels to replace oil dependence in the transport sector (Table 8.1).

Table 8.1   Producers and consumers of oil – December 2001

Country	Producers		Consumers	
	Reserves (billion barrels)	Production (million barrels per day)	Country	Consumption (million barrels per day)
Saudi Arabia	261.8	8.768	US	19.633 (26%)
Iraq	112.5	2.414	Japan	5.427 (7.2%)
UAE	97.8		China	5.041 (6.7%)
Kuwait	96.5		Germany	2.804 (3.7%)
Iran	89.7	3.688	Russia	2.456 (3.2%)
Venezuela	77.7	3.418	S. Korea	2.072 (2.9%)
Russia	48.6	7.056	India	2.072 (2.7%)
US	30.4	7.171	France	2.032 (2.7%)
Libya	29.5		Italy	1.946 (2.6%)
Mexico	26.9	3.560	Canada	1.941 (2.6%)
Other	178.71	28.167	Other	30.192 (40%)
Total	1050.11	76.230		75.779

Notes: Other producers include Norway = 3.414, China = 3.308, Canada = 2.763 and UK = 2.503 million barrels per day.
Sourced from the statistical review of world energy, June 2002.

The pessimism of the OECD Report (2002*a*) is not only addressed at the alarming rates of increase in demand for car-based mobility, but also the slow turnover rate of the stock and the possible cascading of existing inefficient technologies to developing countries. The typical 10-year turnover cycle of the vehicle stock means that those vehicles being produced on current production lines or new models are likely to be in use until 2015 or even 2020. To make matters worse, this prognosis does not include air travel, which at present accounts for about 12 per cent of energy use in the transport sector, but it is the main area of continuous growth.

8.2   The technology

Considerable interest and investment in alternative fuels is now taking place to reduce the oil dependence of the transport sector and to reduce the levels of emissions. The goal of the technologists and car manufacturers is the hydrogen powered vehicle, but as can be seen from Fact Box 8.1, this technology is at present costly and creates new problems with respect to storage and the high costs of materials. The supporting infrastructure to store and distribute the fuel safely may also be costly. The possibility of generating hydrogen for use in cars from renewable sources may be the ultimate aim, but at present that commercial possibility is some way away.

In the meantime, it may be necessary to produce hydrogen from methanol, using an on-board reformer. Alternatively, hybrid vehicles are commercially viable today, and mandating tough fuel economy standards seems to be the only means to achieve the targets set, at least in the short term. Hybrid vehicles are cleaner than petrol, but not as clean as hydrogen from renewables. One advantage is that the use of an intermediate technology would encourage the development and mass production of fuel cell cars so that a later transition would be easier. For example, the NECAR5 car (Daimler/Benz) has a methanol reformer that powers a 50 kilowatt fuel cell stack. Much of the debate on technology is about the future some ten years ahead, rather than on what can be achieved relatively easily now.

Fact Box 8.1 Fuel cells and cars

Toyota + General Motors (25 per cent of world car production) have decided to make hybrid vehicles (petrol + electric) and fuel cell vehicles.

DaimlerBenz/Chrysler + Ford (25 per cent of world car production) and Ballard Power Systems (Canadian Firm) have decided to produce fuel cell vehicles – tested in Sacramento.

Limitations

1   Take time to 'warm up' and produce power.

2   Compressors to transform methanol to hydrogen are noisy.

3   Infrastructure for refuelling. Hydrogen is explosive, so likely to be distributed as methanol, which is liquid at room temperature. Shell, Texaco and Arco are participating in the Sacramento tests and will make methanol available at petrol stations.

A fuel cell works by chemically combining hydrogen with oxygen from the air. Energy is produced which can then power an electric motor. Water is the principal waste product. Fuel cell vehicles seem to offer the best opportunity to reach the 10 per cent target for 'zero emission vehicles' in California. If methanol is used, then CO and CO_2 are also produced. The total energy efficiency is 27 per cent compared with 17 per cent in a petrol engine. A methanol powered fuel cell vehicle is worth 0.6 of a true zero emission vehicle for legal purposes.

4   Costs about $4000 per kilowatt to make a fuel cell engine, compared with $40 per kilowatt for an internal combustion engine. Mass production will reduce the costs, but the price will still be at a premium compared with conventional cars.

Ballard fuel cells have a polymer membrane coated on either side with platinum electrodes (act as a catalyst). Hydrogen is decomposed into electrons and protons on one side of the membrane. The electrons disappear into the electrode, while the protons pass through the membrane. The electrons return via the second electrode having passed through the coil of an electric motor that drives the wheels of the car. They recombine with the protons and oxygen atoms to form water.

continued on page 160

continued from page 159

5   High cost of materials, particularly platinum. The amount is being reduced. The grooved graphite plates used to direct the flow of hydrogen and oxygen are also costly, but new carbon composites are now being used. Costs per kilowatt hour can potentially be reduced to $20 with cheaper materials and mass production (250,000 units).

6   The methanol needs a chemical reactor (reformer) to release the hydrogen. It also needs an efficient and cheap electric motor. The reformers are bulky and expensive, with the smaller ones producing more CO, which in turn 'poisons' the platinum plates. The electric motor has magnets made of molybdenum and titanium (both expensive), and it needs complex thyristor control systems to work it. The electronic control systems need simplification.

The tests being carried out in Sacramento are designed to test the system for reliability on 45 cars and buses. Fuel cell buses are also operating in Vancouver, Stuttgart, Chicago and London, and Fedex and UPS have fuel cell delivery vehicles.

To get round the infrastructure problem, it is proposed to link fuel stations to the natural gas network. On-site reformers (being developed by United Technologies and others) would extract the hydrogen from the gas, so allowing for little change in the way in which motorists use fuel stations. Honda and Plus Power (a US fuel cell firm) have developed such an 'energy station' that makes hydrogen from natural gas and also produces heating and water for domestic use – a new form of combined heat and power.

Source: Economist, 24 April 1999 and 6 December 2003.

To make any real impact requires zero-emissions mandates such as that used in California. The expectation that a new technology will be sufficient to encourage the necessary supporting investment is very unlikely, as there is substantial capital tied up in the existing technologies. Over a 20-year period, it may be possible to switch from a carbon-based fuel to a non-carbon-based fuel provided that clear directions are given to the motor industry and the fuel technologists. There also needs to be a major publicity campaign to persuade consumers that there are important welfare benefits from the new technology, even if it may cost more (at least initially). Even in California, the early optimism has not been met in practice, as zero emissions regulations have been delayed, in response to pressure from the motor manufacturers and the costs of developing a viable electric car. There is also the question of whether the regulators should support a particular technology (e.g. electric vehicles), rather than just setting the targets that can then be met by the manufacturers through a variety of measures.

In the UK, the Foresight Vehicle programme involves over 400 companies and organizations in a range of projects. About a third of them are researching low carbon vehicle technologies, including new power-trains, advanced electronics and advanced materials and structures (DTI, 2003, p. 65). The Low Carbon Vehicle Partnership (LowCVP) is an action and advisory group, set up to promote the UK's shift in policy to all stakeholders, and then to get them to participate in promoting change. It is trying to encourage innovation and dissemination of best practice. There is also a commitment to getting at least 10 per cent of new cars with an emission level of less than 100 g/km of CO_2 by 2012, and more than 20 per cent of new buses will also be low emission (DfT *et al.*, 2002). This is equivalent to 75 miles per gallon of diesel (26 km per litre of diesel). These objectives go further than the EU voluntary agreements on fuel efficiency with manufacturers (in Europe, Japan and Korea), which set out a long-term framework within which to improve emissions. Rather than promoting particular technologies, the approach sets the target levels of carbon emissions and allows the manufacturers the flexibility to develop the most appropriate mixture of cost effective technologies, as has been seen with the Toyota Prius. Average new car emissions will reduce from 190 g/km of CO_2 (1995) to 140 g/km by 2008, a reduction of about 25 per cent (DTI, 2003). It is estimated that carbon efficiency in transport in the UK will increase by 10 per cent to 2020 (DTI, 2003, p. 70). There was a similar programme in the US in the 1990s called 'Car Talk'. In the end it turned out to be mostly talk, as many saw it merely as a form of corporate welfare. Again, as with the zero emissions vehicles, there has to be a balance between setting the standards and then letting the private sector get on with meeting those requirements in the best way possible.

Technology and transport are integrally linked, as technology has a key role in replacing physical movement, in controlling movement on existing infrastructure, in ensuring that vehicles are operating efficiently, and in providing real time information. Already, over 30 per cent of the costs of any new vehicle is related to technology and this will increase, particularly in engine management systems and in diagnostics for maintenance, but also in the new generation of route guidance systems. In each case technology has made travel easier and this has probably encouraged more travel.

In the future, the role of technology needs to be oriented not only towards increasing the reliability and efficiency of transport systems, but in minimizing the need for transport. Innovative thinking is required to reduce the transport element in the production process through changes such as the regionalization of distribution networks. Rather than produce globally for global markets, firms can transfer the knowledge to local or regional production units, so that local production is for local markets. Similarly, as employment moves towards more service and knowledge-based industries, the physical requirements for transport can be reduced as products (e.g. computers) have a much higher value to weight component. This is the dematerialization process that may have a significant impact on the demand for freight transport (Chapter 11).

Conversely, the rise of consumerism has been accelerated through increases in global gross product, particularly in countries such as China, and these increases may overwhelm any savings resulting from dematerialization.

The second fundamental technological change is the continuing search for new clean fuels (see Fact Box 8.1). Technology offers tremendous opportunities for novel forms of transport, mainly based on new fuel sources (see Fact Box 8.2) and designed to reduce the dependence on oil (non-renewable fossil fuel). Included here are:

- Electric and hybrid vehicles – must be aware of the total energy chain as this may merely transfer the pollution from the vehicle to the power station.

- Methanol and ethanol – created from biomass and other renewable sources (e.g. sugar beet and rape oil seed). Conventional engines can run on these with minor adjustments.

- LPG and natural gas – now available at over 1000 filling stations and there are tax advantages in using gas.

- Hydrogen fuel cells – based on water, so entirely 'clean' but problems with storage and generation process (Fact Box 8.1).

With each of these new fuels, there are vehicles available and it is likely that by 2020 most vehicles will be clean (in terms of fuels), with fleet vehicles, delivery vehicles and public transport vehicles being the first to switch. A much harder problem to resolve is the role of the diesel engine in the city as it has high emissions levels of nitrogen oxides and particulates. In other ways (e.g. fuel consumption) diesel is the preferred fuel, but the technology is not available to clean up diesel vehicle emissions (see Fact Box 8.3). This technology may become available by 2020, but in the meantime, it may be necessary to develop hybrid vehicles, which are battery powered in cities and diesel powered outside the city, with the use of regenerative power to recharge the batteries.

It would seem that there is no ideal vehicle for the future and that a series of 'niche vehicles' will emerge. Small city-based cars, which are about half the size of conventional cars and customized to individual requirements, are already becoming common (e.g. the Daimler-Benz and Swatch joint venture to produce the Smart car). But in the United States, a contrary trend is occurring with the growth in the large, high energy consuming sport utility vehicle, sometimes known as the urban assault vehicle.

Whatever future path is chosen, clear action is required now about which

Fact Box 8.2   Alternative fuels – the UK situation

Hybrid Vehicles – use conventional engines in conjunction with electric battery power. They incorporate energy recovery from braking systems and eliminate engine idling in static traffic. Can switch to zero emissions in towns – high efficiency, lower fuel consumption and CO_2 emissions.

£1000 grants under the TransportEnergy programme and lower VED.

Three hybrid cars are available in the UK – Toyota Prius – family car with CO_2 emissions of 120 g/km. Honda Insight – two seater with CO_2 emissions of 80 g/km. Honda Civic hybrid – family car with CO_2 emissions of 116 g/km.

UK-based Ricardo Engineering Consultants have produced the i-MoGen – a demonstration hybrid diesel car.

The New Vehicle Technology Fund is being used to develop innovative ideas for other hybrid vehicles. The electric traction and control systems in hybrid cars are likely to be key components in fuel cell cars.

Biofuels for Transport – are mainly made from biomass with reductions in the fuel duty – for example, biodiesel has duty at 20 pence per litre below that for standard diesel. It can be blended with diesel (5 per cent). Biofuels could account for 5 per cent of all fuel sales in the UK by 2020.

The same reductions in duty will be available for bioethanol, which can be used in blends up to 85 per cent in cars.

The biomass is mainly food crops, but there is considerable potential for fuel to be made from farm waste, forestry residues, coppice crops and domestic waste. Recent research (Delucchi, 2004) indicates nitrogen fixing in soils may suggest that biofuels increase overall greenhouse gas emissions.

LPG and Natural Gas – there are now some 75,000 LPG cars in the UK, and LPG is now widely available at over 1000 filling stations. Models are available from eight manufacturers.

Grants are available from TransportEnergy for conversion and purchase of gas cars, and there are lower rates of fuel duty.

Natural gas is mainly used in heavy vehicles, where there are lower emissions and a two-thirds reduction in noise levels. TransportEnergy grants are available for the conversion of lorries, buses and utility vehicles.

Strong support for the EU policy of promoting a greater diversity in fuel sources so that the energy security in the transport sector can be maintained.

Hydrogen – this is the energy carrier of the future. There will be zero emissions from the tailpipe, emitting only water vapour and minimal noise.

The first vehicles are likely to be buses, utility vehicles and depot-based fleets, as they have a larger scope for storage of fuel and can be refilled at the depot. Hydrogen buses are being tested in London.

The US has given itself 10 years to produce a hydrogen powered vehicle, together with the supporting production, distribution and storage technology. But this objective seems to be becoming increasingly ambitious.

Note: TransportEnergy has been set up by government as part of the Energy Saving Trust to administer the grants.
Source: Based on DTI (2003).

Fact Box 8.3   The diesel problem

Diesel engines use less fuel than petrol engines, but have higher emissions levels than petrol engines for carbon monoxide (CO), hydrocarbons (HC), nitrogen oxides (NO_x) and particulates (PM_{10}).

Two way oxidization catalysts can be used to reduce the emissions of carbon monoxide and hydrocarbons. To meet the more stringent new EU standards (Stage III), particulate traps will have to be fitted to exhausts, but present designs are too bulky to fit in small vehicles. In addition, the engine is often not working sufficiently hard to keep the exhaust hot enough to burn off the collected particulates. Conversely, for those engines that do burn at higher temperatures (e.g. buses and lorries), the amount of particulates (and hydrocarbons) are minimized but the nitrogen oxides produced are increased. This is a classic example of the trade offs that have to be made.

One solution is being developed by the PSA group (Peugeot and Citroen) where additional fuel is burnt in the exhaust system so that the particulate burning temperature can be reached. The required temperature is 550°C, but this can be reduced to 450°C through the addition of cerium oxide to the fuel. The oxidizing catalyst achieves the 250°C threshold and extra fuel is injected to raise the exhaust temperature to the 450°C level. The PSA experimental system requires a sophisticated control system to operate and monitor the diesel injection system

technologies should be adopted. Signals need to be given to industry together with the incentives to invest in the new technology. For example, targets could be given for the proportion of new vehicles in the city, which are zero emission. In California, a target of 10 per cent (150,000 vehicles) was set for all new cars to be zero emission (i.e. electric or methanol – see Fact Box 8.1) before 2004. This target was originally postponed after intense pressure from the car manufacturers, but has been reinstated with a longer time horizon. It does illustrate the need for clear policy directives and the possible creation of markets for tradable emissions credits between manufacturers (Chapter 2). The transition phase is likely to be about 10 years, even with strong central direction, as this lead time is necessary to set up new vehicle production processes and for market penetration to take place.

In addition to policy actions by governments, there are actions that should be taken by companies and individuals willing to demonstrate best practice:

♦   Promote technological change through adopting best practice in their own businesses so that the transport component in production processes is reduced.

♦   Adopt the best available technology for the company vehicle policy, including the use of electric and hybrid vehicles, as well as the emerging fuel cell technology.

- Promote the necessary supporting infrastructure in cities and at company sites to allow refuelling and priority measures for clean vehicles.

- Contributions to innovation funds that would promote clean technology in public transport vehicles (including taxis).

- Maximize the use of the Internet, E-commerce and other forms of communications to minimize travel requirements. This would include travel minimization as a key element in productivity improvements within the company.

- Make sure that employees are aware of the environmental costs of transport – through promotion of cycling, provision of bicycles and safe storage, paying for employees to use public transport, implementation of company transport plans to reduce the use of single occupancy cars, and to charge for parking at the work place or to compensate those choosing not to use their cars for the journey to work.

8.3 Freight

Much of the distribution of goods is by road transport and trends similar to the passenger sector are apparent in that the weight of goods is relatively constant (like the number of trips), but the average haul length is increasing (as with trip distance). For example, in Great Britain, 82 per cent of goods are transported by road, and although tonnage has remained relatively constant (1970–2002), average distance has doubled to nearly 100 km (Table 8.2).

As illustrated in Chapter 3 (Tables 3.4, 3.5 and 3.6), freight intensity as measured against GDP is likely to decline in future in the EU if the transport policy is effectively implemented. The historic evidence in the UK is that in the period from 1965 to 1985 freight traffic (both HGV and LGV) grew at a lower rate than the economy, but this situation reversed in the 1985–1995 period, particularly for LGV (Table 3.6).

Freight growth is dependent on a mix of factors, each of which can have a positive or a negative effect (RAC Foundation, 2002). Freight growth is dependent on:

1 value density of the product (product weight to value);
2 modal split, including the price and service quality by each mode;
3 handling factors, including the number of transfers in the production process from its primary state to its final consumption;
4 average length of haul, including the physical patterns of production and consumption, logistics, and the different types of supply chains from the global to the local;

Table 8.2   Domestic freight transport 2002 in Great Britain

	Million tonnes lifted	Billion tonne-kilometres	Average haul length (km)
Road	1708	15	92
Rail	87	20	223
Water/pipeline	278	70	252
Total	2073	247	119

Source: ONS (2003*a*), based on Table 9.5.

5   load factors, affected by the bulk and size of vehicles, and their
     scheduling efficiency;
6   empty running, including balanced flows and specialization of vehicles.

The two main influencing factors are the costs of transport and the way
in which industrial organization has been implemented. In the past transport
has been cheap and so location decisions really only considered the firm's
requirements in terms of suppliers, markets, labour force, government
incentives, site availability and other factors. As transport costs have risen
and as competition increases, the transport-related cost factors become a
more important consideration, and the length and reliability of supply chains
are now an integral part of the production process. There is pressure to fill
lorries and reduce empty running and make sure that the vehicle fleet is used
efficiently. Innovations include the development of online freight exchanges
and Internet trading of vehicle capacity (Fact Box 9.3). These issues are
discussed further in Chapter 9, where the impacts of ICT (Information and
Telecommunications Technologies) on production are considered.

8.4   The limits of technology

As consistently stated, technology has an important and crucial role to play in
moving towards sustainable transport, yet it is not a solution in itself. It has to
be seen as part of a larger picture and combined with other strategies outlined
in this part of the book (Chapters 6 and 7). For many, the technological fix
is real as it allows a continuation of all the current activities with little or no
change in behaviour. That in itself is not necessarily bad, but the technology
should really be seen as an opportunity to give us a little more time to develop
alternative means by which at least some of our activities can be undertaken.
One problem is that if technology is seen as the only solution, decision-makers
in government and industry will not push so hard in other directions.

Selling the notion of a 'clean car' may result in high levels of public
acceptance and a realization that no other actions need to be taken. It is
important to get the message across that there is no clean form of transport

(except walking and cycling) and that all transport uses resources in terms of its use, manufacturing, scrapping and recycling, infrastructure and maintenance. The levels of resource consumption and pollution can be reduced but not eliminated. It is important to look at the whole lifecycle of a vehicle from its manufacture, through its use to the scrapping and recycling processes, in terms of the resource consumption and its emissions profile, and its use of the supporting infrastructure. That does not seem to have been done in any systematic study. It would also help in the debate over whether it is better to use the best available technology with a short lifecycle, or a longer lifecycle and perhaps continue with a more dated technology for longer. The rate of technological innovation is increasing, but this should result in the average life of a car being reduced from about 12 years to say half that length?

Even if it were possible to produce a pollution free vehicle, would this be desirable? This is the hypermobility argument (Adams, 2001), where the technological fix is taken to its logical conclusion through the invention of a totally pollution free car, even though the laws of physics dictate that this can never exist. In conjunction with this vehicle, it is possible to develop Intelligent Transport Systems (ITS) that enormously increase the capacity of all forms of transport systems, and it is also assumed that the Internet is universally available and free.

The net results of such a set of assumptions would be that mobility will increase hugely, as there would be no constraints on travel as it is cheap and pollution free. The additional capacity would be used and travel supplemented by electronic mobility. Location constraints would cease and migration out of towns could take place as cheap motoring over long distances replaces shorter distances by a wider range of transport means.

In hypermobile societies, old fashioned geographical communities are replaced by aspatial communities of interest. One set of logical arguments (Adams, 2001), leads to the conclusion that society would become more dispersed geographically and more polarized socially, with greater disparity between the rich and the poor, and those living with and without access to the car. Society would be more anonymous and less convivial with less socializing with neighbours, and it would be less child-friendly and less culturally varied. It would be more dangerous for those not in a car, people would take less exercise and social cohesion might break down as crime rates increased. Communities become gated with CCTV surveillance and huge information databases are built up to collect data on all movements. It may even lead to the collapse of democracy as individuals have less control over the decisions, with power becoming centralized higher up the political hierarchy or in unaccountable institutions.

In the US, doubts are now being expressed over whether a switch to hydrogen is possible before 2030, as fuel cells will not prove as effective as gasoline-electric hybrid vehicles. Two main limitations have been highlighted. One is the cost of the technology, where it is estimated (Fact Box 8.1) that even in the foreseeable future, the cost of hydrogen energy will be at least four times that of petrol, and that a technological breakthrough is required to solve the energy storage problem. It has been concluded that by 2030, a 5 per cent market share might be achieved (Romm, 2004). The second concern is over whether hydrogen is necessarily clean, as this depends on what sources of energy are used. The cheapest hydrogen comes from gas, which has a carbon element to it, and it is only when renewable sources are used that the fuel becomes cleaner. Both arguments suggest that progress needs to be made in improving the efficiency and cleanliness of existing technologies rather than switching to an expensive and untested new technology. There are severe limits to technology, particularly where it is untried and expensive.

Chapter 9

The impact of ICT on transport

9.1 Introduction

The late twentieth century witnessed the second great economic transformation (Castells, 1990). The first was the switch from agrarian to an industrial mode of production, which led to the development of transport and the high mobility, car-based society. The second has been the transition from an industrial mode of production to an information mode where the fundamental inputs are knowledge-based. Such dramatic changes have resulted in an increase in the spatial division of labour, the decentralization of particular production processes, flexibility in location, and the generation of information 'hotspots'. For certain activities, space has become increasingly irrelevant as cities have spread and as many routine information functions have centred on peripheral, low-cost and low-density locations; some have dispersed overseas. New centres of high technology activities form the magnets for economic growth and dynamism (Hall, 1988). It is here that the global shifts in power have taken place, and it is through the control of technology that power will be maintained (Toffler, 1991).

These 'mega trends' form the new global framework within which capitalist economies will operate, and this process will involve all the major trading nations of the world. There will be a transition from centrally controlled and planned economies to market-based economies. It is here that a clear understanding is required of both the links between economic growth and transport demand and between the operation of the monetary economy and transport markets (Banister and Berechman, 2000).

Technological change will fundamentally influence the location of economic development, and the function and form of cities. Convergence of computing and communications will allow a user-friendly interface for many transactions, for information, and for business and social activities. But equally, information and technology may cause divergence as the knowledge and ability to use the system is not universal, as costs of access to the high-quality broad-band communications systems will initially be expensive, and as control of these systems may reside in the hands of a few multinational companies. Power may be concentrated in existing centres of information exchange at accessible points on the network or in the few world cities where rapid innovation and high-level service competition can take place. Second-order cities and those in peripheral locations will continue to be centres of low demand and low innovation.

Similar developments can be seen in transport where key centres in Europe are likely to be located on the high speed rail network and at international airports, particularly at interchanges between road and rail, and between road, rail and air. The international nodal points will be located where the global airlines have their hub operations, and where good quality transport links are available to the local and national centres of population and activity – technopoles. Increasingly, these nodal points will also be centres of the international information networks – the logistics platforms.

As history has demonstrated with respect to the industrial revolution, the technological revolution is likely to promote concentration, but at an international rather than national level. Traditional arguments based on scale economies and decreasing returns to scale are being replaced by new debates on increasing returns to scale (Krugman, 1994). In addition to the economic factors of production, two new dimensions have entered the theoretical debates. Human capital in terms of the skills and learning capacity of the workforce, and the role that innovation can have in production have both suggested that the most dynamic locations will be created where these three positive factors coincide (i.e. economics, human capital and innovation). It seems that the demand for transport will increase in scale, in range and in quality as these changes take place. Much of this revolution has been predicated on globalization of the economy, the move towards market economics and the dismantling of trade barriers. It is also dependent on maintaining the capacity and quality of the ICT[1] (information and communications technologies) networks and crucially upon the availability of 'cheap' and reliable transport.

With the breaking down of trade and technological barriers, the differences between the rich and poor nations may be reduced, as nationally based activities are outsourced to cheaper locations around the world, and as migration takes place between countries. There is even some evidence (e.g. in the United States) of developed countries considering protectionism by restricting the outsourcing of employment to low-wage economies. Although this new entrepreneurship is taking place in some countries, it may again act as a barrier to those countries that are not technologically rich. Financial wealth may be important, but technological knowledge and the ability to innovate are equally important. At the individual level, the increased polarization, between those who are financially secure and technologically rich and those that are not, may lead to political and social instability. This trend is already taking place through the job market that has become more demanding in terms of skills requirements and less protective of its workforce, as work itself becomes increasingly casualized.

Technology in a variety of forms has been a central concern in much of the debate over solutions to transport problems (Banister, 2002*a*). Three basic arguments have been used to categorize the possible impacts of ICT on transport:

1 stimulation of more travel as new opportunities become available;
2 substitution for travel as activities can now be carried out remotely rather than by travel;
3 modification of travel, as the two elements combine to change the ways in which activities are carried out.

This rather simplistic conceptualization has been widely criticized in the literature (e.g. HOP Associates, 2002), as it does not attempt to understand how technology develops and shapes society (Table 9.1). These early studies all seemed to suggest a huge potential for change, but in reality the changes made seem to be far less obvious and much more subtle. Realization depends on the quality of the technology (including its reliability), its ease of use and its cost. It also needs to be embedded in the wider changes taking place in society, both in transport and more generally. Even if there are reductions in one set of transport related activities (e.g. the journey to work), there may be compensating increases elsewhere as the car is now available during the day for other uses (e.g. for shopping and social activities) or for other users. The net effects of change may conceal quite large variations in individual behaviour (Lyons, 2002).

More generally, cities are spreading as decentralization takes place. ICT innovation, like transport, may be one (important) factor in facilitating this process. The net effect may be that fewer journeys to work take place each week, but these journeys may be much longer and so the total distance has increased. This is an example of substitution and stimulation effects taking place simultaneously (see also Mokhtarian, 2003).

During the 1990s, there was huge optimism about technological futures and expectations of high take-up and acceptance rates of the technologies. Now it seems that for every successful technology, there were at least ten unsuccessful ones. The dot.com revolution marked the pinnacle of the 'bubble', and the subsequent demise of both the optimism and the confidence in the new technology reflected the new realism. Nevertheless, technology has been (and still is) enormously influential *in* transport, and perhaps this is its main role, namely to influence the operation of transport systems, to provide in-vehicle monitoring and control systems, and to provide information to users of all transport systems. This role may be more important than that *on* transport.

Towards the end of the 1990s, it was realized that the linkages between

Table 9.1 Key features that shape the future role of new technologies

Contemporary concerns and hopes	Perceptions of the future are shaped and coloured by current problems and aspirations resulting in optimistic rather than plausible scenarios.
New technological trajectories	The pathway of technological innovation and product development may significantly change, introducing new possibilities and expectations concerning the role in and impacts on society of the technology.
New for old substitution	The role of a new technology is often phased in terms of replacing or substituting the old technology, whilst in reality old and new technologies often co-exist, serving different markets, circumstances or purposes.
Social practices neutral	It is often wrongly assumed that the pool of social practices and needs remains unchanged, thereby implying that new technology will (only) substitute certain social practices. In reality, the pool of social practices can increase.
Narrow functional thinking	Through only functional thinking, new technologies can be judged capable of enabling the purpose of an activity to be fulfilled. This neglects the consideration of other social and psychological aspects of an activity.
Societal embedding	The process of societal embedding of new technologies can be viewed as unproblematic, when in practice many social and institutional adjustment processes have to take place, which may not be straightforward and can take some time to achieve.
Hopeful monstrosities	Promoters of an emerging technology can voice unrealistically high expectations. This may create a 'breathing space' for investment and development to continue. It may also be a consequence of neglecting the co-evolution of technology and society, and the understanding of the practical difficulties and resulting slowness in the processes of societal embedding of technology.

Source: Lyons (2002) and adapted from Geels and Smit (2000).

ICT and transport are much more subtle and the opportunities created were being used in different ways, thus making analysis much harder. For example, the logic that teleconferencing is a substitute for business travel was based on the assumption of a fixed number of social contacts. 'The possibility that teleconferencing might add an extra mode of social contact, that would increase the total number of contacts was not considered' (Geels and Smit, 2000, p. 873). Similar examples can be given of all expected changes brought about through ICT innovations.

Current thinking has moved away from simple cause and effect type relationships towards co-existence and complementarity between the old and new technologies. Internet shopping provides a good example of this new complementarity and a break with the conventional approach that treats shopping solely as a functional activity. While much can be purchased via the Internet from home, there are still various fresh goods customers may wish to see before purchase. Other aspects of shopping include its social function as a place to meet people and to satisfy the need to get out of the home.

There is evidence of this in the United States and elsewhere (e.g. Bluewater, Milton Keynes and Thurrock in the UK, City Centre in Dubai, UAE) where visiting shopping malls has a social as well as functional rationale. All of these processes take time to have an impact as new patterns of activities establish themselves. Apart from the problems with the system being established, for example whether Internet shopping is done through the local supermarket outlet or through the regional distribution centre, there is the user interface and the delivery window problem, and the acceptance of the basic concept. There is a need to move away from a primary concern over the technologically led futures to one that places a much greater emphasis on the social and cultural context within which change takes place (Geels and Smit, 2000).

As can be seen from this summary of both the general trends and the more traditional interpretations of the impacts of ICT on transport, the actual impacts are varied and complex. They require an understanding of the context within which change can be placed (Table 9.2). These general trends towards globalization mean that more and longer distance travel is required for goods, services and meetings. Changes in the nature of work (from manufacturing to service and information), and the labour force (more women and part-time labour) may act to reduce travel frequency, but again encourage longer distances

Table 9.2 General trends

Trend	Role of ICT	Impacts on transport
Global markets	Improves communication, assists global marketing	More long distance transport for goods and services, and also for business meetings, unless the business meeting is held electronically
Changes in nature of work – manufacturing to service and information. Greater female participation	Higher levels of skills and access to ICT at work, home and local centres	Reductions in travel frequency, but possibly longer distances and some substitution
Flexibility of the labour market	Technology for flexible and remote working	Reduction in travel frequency, but perhaps longer distance travel (when individuals move further from work) and also substitution of work travel with other travel (with time saved by not travelling to work)
Footloose industry	Technology for industries to be located far from clients	Increases travel distance for business client journeys, unless done through telecommunications
24-hour economy	Improves ability to carry out transactions automatically and in real time	Reduces the need to travel for many transactions, but requires more people to work outside 'regular' work hours – implications for transport modes

Source: Banister and Stead (2004).

and some substitution effects. The traditional arguments for centralization of production have been replaced by more flexible location patterns, some where labour is cheap and others where agglomeration and short supply chains are important. Again, the implications for travel are varied with some increases in distance, some remote working, but also the need for face-to-face contact. Such changes have been reinforced by the 24-hour economy where activity is continuous within countries (through shift working), but also on a global scale, where markets are open all the time in at least one of the key financial centres of London, Tokyo and New York. Global commerce requires servicing and support at all hours, and this in turn has implications for transport modes and supply chains.

It is against this background that the effects of ICT on transport must be placed. It is not a matter of simple cause and effect, but part of a much richer background of change that creates different responses under different conditions. Much of the development of ICT has been paralleled by substantial increases in travel as levels of affluence have increased, as trade barriers have been dismantled, and as leisure time has increased. As the costs of travel have been maintained at low levels, the opportunities for travel have increased substantially. In this chapter the impacts have been divided into three 'types' – production, living and working – to help structure the argument. This holistic approach allows both the direct and indirect effects to be investigated, but the division into the three 'types' has the weakness that the same ICT solutions may affect more than one area (e.g. teleshopping affects all three areas), but this again underlines the complexity of ICT innovation.

There is also a social dimension to the debate. In 2003, 41 per cent of those over 14 years old in the UK were non-users of the Internet, but this should be seen as a lifestyle choice rather than a form of social deprivation. Some non-users (22 per cent) get others to use the Internet for them, and a further 44 per cent are informed about the Internet, but are indifferent to it. It is the remaining 34 per cent that are really non-users, as half of these are not bothered about the Internet and the other half are anti-technology.[2] The conclusion from this pattern of Internet use is that the lack of interest in its potential is a greater barrier to use in the UK than costs, skills or knowledge. As expected, it is the higher income groups that have most access, with age and education also being important determinants of use (see Fact Box 9.5). The availability and use of the Internet is related to the increased flexibility and potential for new forms of activity, often involving greater complexity – this is the complementarity that ICT offers to transport.

9.2 Production

There are three main sets of implications ranging from e-commerce and just-

Table 9.3 ICT and production: implications for transport

Application	Role of ICT	Impacts on transport
e-commerce and e-everything	Internet, sms, email etc	May reduce the need for the movement of goods in certain cases – for example, music is downloaded from the web, and orders are transmitted electronically
Just-in-time production	Technology for stock control, ordering and tailored production	More frequent deliveries; smaller loads –faster delivery – more air movements
Logistics and freight distribution	Real-time route guidance, track and trace technology – optimizing delivery vehicles and routes	Savings in reliability and travel time, but may add to journey distance. Possibilities for trip chaining and load matching. Also savings in terms of vehicles and route choice
e-marketing and publicity	Internet, email, sms, etc	Could potentially reduce the amount of other sorts of marketing/publicity material produced. More likely that e-marketing will be an additional source of information rather than a substitute

Note: Spam mail can also reduce the efficiency of ITC and hence reduce its usage.
Source: Banister and Stead (2004).

in-time production (manufacturing systems), through logistics and freight distribution to e-marketing and publicity (Table 9.3).

Manufacturing systems have been restructured to give a substantial cost saving to companies by reducing product lifecycles and increasing value added. There are two main aspects affecting manufacturing systems. One relates to the direct selling of goods and services over the Internet (e-commerce – Fact Box 9.1, which can be business to business or business to customer), and the other relates to changes in the production processes themselves (mainly business to business, such as just in time production – Fact Box 9.2). The main advantages of ICT are that it provides the potential to cut costs and increase efficiency (some 20–30 per cent) through electronic transactions that allow the use of computer-aided manufacturing and electronic data interchange. Nearly all aspects of the manufacturing process are now interconnected with ICT (Saxena and Sahay, 2000), and even virtual fabrication (Hsieh *et al.*, 2002).

Production schedules can be changed weekly according to the variability in demand patterns, and suppliers are increasingly acting as retailers. Such developments have led to a reduction in the transport requirements as orders are now processed electronically from the supply of goods to the invoicing of customers. But as requirements become more demanding there may be an increase in the number of deliveries required to meet production deadlines with smaller loads. As customer demands have become more individualized, production lines are being converted to individual requirements (as is

Fact Box 9.1   e-commerce

UK businesses sold £23.3 billion over the Internet in 2002, an increase of 39 per cent over the previous year (£16.8 billion) – this represents 1.2 per cent of total sales. Some £6.4 billion (27 per cent) was sold to households, an increase of 58 per cent on the 2001 figure of £4.0 billion.

Goods represented the largest share (66 per cent) of Internet sales by UK businesses (£15.4 billion in 2002), and the sale of services online accounted for a further £6.8 billion (29 per cent in 2002) – the majority of online sales were in the wholesale, the retail, the catering, and the travel and telecommunications sectors.

In addition, UK businesses (excluding financial services) bought £22.9 billion online in 2002, an increase of 14 per cent on 2001 (£20.1 billion).

The value of orders received over non-Internet ICTs (EDI, email, PC-based fax and automated telephone entry) was £169 billion in 2002, a decrease of 6 per cent on 2001.

Source: ONS (2003*a*).
Note that e-commerce is the method by which the order is placed, not the payment or delivery channel.

Source: Banister and Stead (2004).

happening with computers and cars). Supply chains may become more extended as sourcing is international, but it may also lead to clusters and strong agglomeration economies as suppliers seek to reduce their risk and locate around the assembly plants (Banister and Berechman, 2000).

Fact Box 9.2   Just-in-time production

Disk-drive manufacturer, Maxtor, supplies companies such as Dell, Compaq and HP in Asia and America, often within 48 hours. The supply chain is managed and optimized by Exel, one of the world's leading firms of pure logistics (formed from a merger of a shipping line and a road haulier). Increasingly specialist companies like Exel are taking over from more traditional supply chain management to provide customized services and effectively manage production (*The Economist*, 7 December 2002, p. 94).

In the *automobile industry*, where it used to take 10 business days to assemble a car, firms are now aiming to respond to specific vehicle orders within 5 or even 3 days. With the support of ICT, customers will be in a position to customize their new car online to their preferences but without having to wait many weeks for delivery. This requires massive changes in the way manufacturers (and also suppliers) approach the entire process of ordering supplies, producing and delivering parts. The need to sequence the delivery of parts to the vehicle assembly line on time, and in the proper order, is leading to the formation of supplier villages around each vehicle assembly plant. This means short distances for the transport of supplies and which could lead to a reduction in traffic. Efficient enterprise resource planning systems as well as customer management systems are a prerequisite for achieving the goal of short assembly times.

Source: Banister and Stead (2004).

Logistics and freight distribution has been revolutionized by the increased use of ICT. This is perhaps the area in which the impact of ICT on transport is greatest. The structure of the supply chains has changed as the location and size of production, processing and warehousing sites have adapted to the new technology. This has affected the spatial concentration of production and inventory activities, the development of new break/bulk locations and transhipment systems, and hub satellite networks. The alignment of supply chains has also been altered with the concentration of international trade on hub ports and airports, the rationalization of the supply base, the vertical disintegration of production, the wider geographical sourcing of supplies, customization and the increase in direct delivery. Many of these trends have already been noted, but other changes are also taking place. The product flow scheduling has been reorganized through the use of time compression principles, the increased control by retailers over the supply-chain, and the creative use of time scheduling for deliveries.

Such changes have been reflected in the increased use of road freight vehicles, as these can be more easily adapted to the new logistics. Transport costs have been further reduced through improved design, the use of containers and the increase in the freight capacity of ships and aircraft. New automated handling for freight at distribution centres, airports and ports, together with greater modularity and reductions in packaging have all helped to revolutionize freight systems. ICT has played an instrumental role here in information exchange, tracking and tracing, in enabling new concepts for production and services to be introduced, in cutting turnaround time, and in determining shipment size (Fact Boxes 9.3 and 9.4).

e-marketing and e-publicity provide a new set of opportunities for businesses to direct market their products to their customers or through a third party as part of their website (e.g. Amazon and Google). In principle, this development

Fact Box 9.3   Logistics

Trucking supply is being optimized through Online Freight Exchanges (OFE). In order to prevent trucks making empty return journeys, these exchange portals aim to connect available loads to available trucking space on a dynamic basis. Overall, this could lead to fewer trips and it might affect the role of intermediaries and the reduction of shipment costs along the supply chain. The future of OFEs is nevertheless unclear. Some studies are optimistic, but others remark that most of the OFEs do not make profits, and that in the case of successful sites only one dominant player controls the exchange (Visser and Nemoto, 2002; Peters and Wilkinson, 2000).

28 per cent of lorry distance in the UK involves empty running, and this has been reduced by 20 per cent through freight exchanges (Mansell, 2001).

Source: Banister and Stead (2004).

Fact Box 9.4   Freight distribution

Manufacturers need custom designed delivery systems. This is being achieved through the Third Party Logistics Market, where the right goods are delivered to the right place on time. Consolidation is taking place in the fragmented freight industry, with international companies acting as 'consolidators' or 'integrators' – FedEx, UPS and DPWN (Deutsche Post World Net).

The services provided ensure the three parallel flows of physical goods, information and financing coexist and complement each other. The total US logistics market is worth about $1 trillion a year and it is expanding by 4 per cent each year. The Third Party Market is worth $50 billion a year, but is expanding by over 15 per cent annually.

The businesses that make most use of this level of logistics are in electronic components, consumer electronics, pharmaceuticals, fashion and cars. With over 10,000 components in each car and sourcing from all parts of the globe, it is important to use evermore sophisticated logistics. For example, TPG (a major transport integrator) organizes 800 deliveries from 300 suppliers to the Ford factory in Toronto to produce 1500 Windstar minivans a day. Loads are timed to arrive at 12 different points along the assembly line within a 10 minute time slot. All the loads are in a particular order in the trucks to ensure a continuous flow of components. The vehicles involved are owner operated, but under contract to TPG, and the 7-year contract with Ford means that TPG have to lower costs by 2 per cent each year (*The Economist*, 7 December, 2002, pp. 93–94).

Source: Banister and Stead (2004).

could substitute for the more traditional forms of marketing through advertisements in papers or direct mailing, but it is more likely to provide a complementary form of marketing. As it is a relatively cost-free means of promotion, the returns do not need to be high, but the aim is to increase the market penetration of products and market share. The transport implications are likely to be small, with some additional deliveries.

In conclusion, changes within production processes are in most cases made for commercial reasons and the necessity to improve productivity over time. Investment in ICT is one of the main means by which productivity has been improved and it has also resulted in substantial cost savings for transport. There are often conflicting forces at work with the increased flexibility and innovative production processes within the company, and as outsourcing and the vertical disintegration of companies takes place with more of the production taking place outside the company. However, appropriate control mechanisms still need to be made in maintaining quality and cost targets. In transport terms, this has led to long supply chains for sourcing, but also arguments for agglomeration to maintain reliability in that sourcing. Companies tend to account only for the direct (private) cost, not the broader social costs or the costs transferred to users. For example, with the electronic transfer of books, magazines and newspapers, the costs of printing are passed onto the final user. However, the total costs may be reduced for the electronic version as against the printed version if all costs (including transport costs) are included. Transport costs have traditionally only provided a small proportion of total costs, particularly in the new service economy where goods have a high-value to weight ratio. The development of hub and satellite networks allows larger units to be transported along the main routes at a higher frequency, but distances are increased.

9.3 Living (and travelling)

Again, the main impacts on 'living' can be divided into three main groups. *Public transport and private transport planning* relate to the impacts for transport rather than on transport. In both cases, the intention is to increase the reliability of the system and thus to maintain or increase modal share. For public transport this is particularly important, as the system needs to be seen as an integrated set of multi-modal alternatives with easy transfer between the different forms of transport. This requirement covers not just the services provided, but information, timetables and ticketing. Technology permits the provision of a 'seamless' transport system provided that the user interface covered here is combined with other actions to give public transport priority within the system.

For the car, there are now many optional systems available to give the driver information about recommended routes to minimize delay and advanced warning about 'hazards' on the road system. Again, these systems are used to provide direct benefits to the driver with privileged information that is paid for so that his or her journey times can be reduced. But there may be increases in travel distances, as second best routes are likely to be longer in both time and distance terms than the preferred route. The two major impacts covered here include e-everything and the ability to use the Internet to make spontaneous decisions about travel and other activities (Table 9.4).

e-everything requires the home to have access to the Internet. This is taking place with over half the households in the EU now having a home computer and some 70 per cent of these with Internet access. Even though most traffic on the Internet is business-related, there is a growing increase in 'home' use. Shopping has a much wider role than the purely functional one, as it is one of the main means by which social and family activities take place (Fact Boxes 9.5 and 9.6). Shopping often provides the pretext for a wide range of activities, hence the growing importance of leisure shopping (shopping whilst the shops are closed – window-shopping).

In addition to shopping, there are many other opportunities for e-activities, particularly in locations that are relatively inaccessible. These include e-

Table 9.4   ICT and living – implications for transport

Application	Role of ICT	Impacts on transport
Public transport planning	Integrated public transport planning information	Modal shift in favour of public transport and shorter wait times – improved quality of services
Private transport planning	Real-time route guidance and hazard warning	Savings in congestion and travel time – but may add to journey distance
e-everything: shopping, medicine, education, banking, entertainment, chat rooms, network games etc	Internet, sms, email, iDTV etc	Reduces the need for individuals to travel for many transactions, but the existence of these services requires more people to work outside 'regular' work hours – with implications for transport modes. May also lead to 'new' journeys to replace the ones that would have been necessary in the absence of the e-Activity or to completely new demand resulting from social networking
'Last minute' deals: flights, hotels, holidays etc	Internet, sms, email, etc	Assist companies to increase capacity and revenues – create additional travel

medicine, e-education, e-banking, and e-entertainment. For example, there have been dramatic business losses to music retailers and film studios with respect to e-entertainment, as individuals 'download' music and films from the Internet. The losses may be substantial and reflect on those industries that do not react to the changing environment for product and service delivery. Alternatively, there is a potential substitution effect for existing activities, but the intention is to allow 'low-level' activities to be carried out remotely (e.g. self-diagnosis of minor illnesses or primary-school education). Higher order activities would still have to be carried out through face-to-face contact, involving travel. The intention is also to encourage greater participation in activities and so generate new customers and revenues. Initially, this should not result in more travel, but there would be increases as new people become involved, and the need for face-to-face contact increases.

The direct effects on transport may be some replacement of existing travel, but in the longer term new patterns of longer distance travel may take place as the ICT becomes embedded in lifestyles. It should be noted that not all individuals have equal access to the technology or the ability (or inclination) to use it. As with the advent of the car (another ICT technology that revolutionized lifestyles), the ICT impacts initially on the affluent with the necessary skills to use it. All the user interfaces have now become far more 'friendly', but there are still many barriers that need to be overcome. Within a few years, most of them will be, and the technology will also be affordable.

The indirect effects are likely to be far more fundamental as the new activity

Fact Box 9.5   e-shopping

US sales of goods over the Internet during the Thanksgiving to New Year period in 2003 were expected to grow by 20 per cent to $16.9 billion, as 63.6 million shop online (up from 53.7 million in 2002) – average spend per buyer is about $265.

Source: http://news.zdnet.co.uk/internet/ecommercial/0,39020372,39117661,00.htm

UK Internet access has increased from 10 per cent in 1998/1999 to 40 per cent in 2001/2002 to 45 per cent in October 2002. Some 67 per cent of adults (over 15 years) had accessed the Internet at least once by February 2003 and 12.2 per cent are now buying online. There is a huge potential here for changes in travel patterns as shopping accounts for 20 per cent of all trips (2002) and some 13 per cent of travel distance, with 80 per cent of trips being made by car.

From a MORI survey in 2002, it was found that 26 per cent had bought goods or services on the Internet. The four most important categories were books (34 per cent of Internet users), hotels and travel (34 per cent), tickets for events (30 per cent) and music or CDs (30 per cent). The users of the Internet were from the higher social classes (67 per cent of classes A and B – the professions), the higher income groups (75 per cent of those earning over £30,000 and 54 per cent of those earning between £17,500 and £30,000), and in the younger age groups (56 per cent of 15–24 year olds, 63 per cent of 25–34 year olds, 58 per cent of 35–44 year olds, and 50 per cent of 45–54 year olds).

Sources: ONS (2003*b*) and DTI (2002)

Source: Banister and Stead (2004).

and location patterns emerge. It may allow people to live in remote parts of the EU and to develop local based travel patterns with occasional longer distance journeys to the city. Other activities will be carried out remotely, and so the traditional problems of rural inaccessibility or isolation may be overcome. However, such futures still leave many questions open about the importance of social interaction. Travel is not only undertaken for functional reasons (e.g. shopping and work), but it is also instrumental in establishing social networks (Putnam, 2000).

In the city, the need to own a car may be reduced as the quality of public transport is so high and as there will be severe restrictions on pollution emissions. Car-sharing and innovative forms of leasing may result in less city car ownership. Online booking and debiting systems can be combined with personal digital assistants with embedded intelligence to ensure that high quality options are presented to allow customized mobility (Hoogma *et al.*, 2002). The reduction in city car ownership will have a substantial impact on the efficiency of transport systems, as parked cars would consume less space (often on the streets), and the quality of life in cities will improve, as accessibility is enhanced.

Fact Box 9.6 e-business

<table>
<tr><td>

The trends that the study identifies in the B2C-sector are the following:

Business-to-Customers (B2C) will result in the increase of small-part dispatches to an increased number of end-customers with individual delivery-places and delivery-times.
B2C-traffic will concentrate on suburban areas.
B2C induces more courier, express and packet deliveries.
B2C will lead to homogenous transport in urban locations, and at the same time to a better consolidation of long-distance traffic.

Storage concepts, distribution and collecting traffic have to be adapted.
Comeback tours of delivery vehicles will produce additional traffic.
Some shopping trips will be replaced by deliveries.
Applying logistic concepts can result in package effects (less single traffic).
In-time deliveries are always price sensitive and will almost always lead to street traffic.

The following trends are expected in courier, express and packet (cep) deliveries (ongoing trends but supported by increased Online-shopping):
Cep-services will require more small vehicles;
the total number of tours will increase;
Cep-traffic will mainly affect suburban areas (housing areas);
delivery drop-offs (pick-up stations) will be asked for in suburban living areas;
because of the increasing transport of small-parts, other transport will be substituted;
speciality transport like grocery deliveries will remain a niche market.

</td></tr>
</table>

Source: BMVBW (2001), p. 28.

Last-minute deals have become increasingly important, as the flexibility of the Internet has been used to sell excess capacity, particularly for flights, hotels and holidays. More generally, the Internet has provided a means for companies to reduce their marketing costs through a direct interface between the customer and the supplier. Apart from the cost savings, companies can build up a profile of that market and can adapt their products to meet the perceived requirements of the customer. The databases built up by railway companies and airlines, supermarkets and holiday package firms are now being used in direct marketing of new products to customers.

The direct effects have been higher occupancy rates on airlines, railways and hotels, as space is sold at costs that are slightly above the margin. In the longer term, new markets are being created and services provided that better match expectations. The potential increase in travel is immense, as people take more overseas holidays and cheap trips to see friends, sights or other destinations. It has facilitated new ownership patterns of second homes in the Sunbelt of Europe and the ability to reach them regularly for long weekends.

In conclusion, many of the living opportunities resulting from ICT would initially result in less travel, as there is a potential for substitution effects. But there are two important conditions here. One is that over time, it may encourage greater participation in higher order activities, which still require travel often over longer distances. Secondly, new customers will become engaged in e-activity and this will again lead to greater involvement and encourage travel. There seems to be strong complementarity between many of these activities, and if some are carried out remotely, there may be more travel for other activities. Home-based entertainment systems, for example, may mean less social activities in the evening, but it may encourage greater participation in other related activities and these require travel (e.g. to visit DisneyWorld or Hollywood).

It is in the last-minute deals that the greatest potential for additional travel may arise, as individuals seize upon the bargains being offered by airlines and hotels. At one level, this may just be using up excess capacity and so there is little additional travel, but in the longer term it may result in additional capacity being designed in, as new markets are developed. In this case, the growth in long-distance travel is likely to be substantial. The main indirect effects are the flexibility that technology allows in the location of homes and in the choice of alternative opportunities. ICT permits decentralization and accessibility increase to take place at the same time. Many other traditional concerns over the isolation of rural lifestyles can be overcome with social networks and shopping choices being maintained through ICT. Perhaps surprisingly, there seems to be little quality empirical information about the actual impacts, and much of the evidence on the take-up rate seems to be optimistic. This particularly applies in the context of Internet shopping potential.

9.4 Working

The three applications here relate to the *e-office, e-meeting* and *e-information*. In terms of the *e-office*, much of the debate has concentrated on the potential for working at home and the end of the division between home and work (Table 9.5). The latest data from the UK (ONS, 2002) suggest that in 2001 some 2.2 million people (7.4 per cent of the employed population) were teleworkers. This is an increase of 65 per cent on the 1997 figures. It is really the advent of email that has made the difference as most (82 per cent) need both the telephone and email access to work effectively from home. The figures for the UK quoted here include those who work at home for at least one day a week. The one day a week group probably accounts for about 50 per cent of all teleworkers (ONS, 2002).

As with shopping, there is more to work than its functional aspects. The

Table 9.5 ICT and working – implications for transport

Application	Role of ICT	Impacts on transport
e-office	Internet, email, mobile communications, portable computers etc. Teleservicing	Possibly a reduction in travel frequency but longer distance travel could also result (when individuals move further for work), and/or substitution of work travel with other travel – with the time saved by not travelling to work. May also lead to the use of more on-the-move working options during long distance travel
e-meeting	Videoconferencing	Potential reduction in travel distance but limited in application – many face-to-face meetings may be more useful and productive – telephones have not reduced the need for meetings. There may also be some substitution of meeting travel with other travel – with the time saved by not travelling to a meeting
e-information	email, ftp, extranet etc	May reduce the need for meetings to exchange routine information

Source: Banister and Stead (2004).

social interaction with colleagues at work is a key factor in job satisfaction, and so new forms of work patterns are developing that mix office work with homeworking. Teleworking originated mainly for those who were self-employed, but now over 55 per cent are employees (ONS, 2002). There is a realization that those who work outside the office have a higher level of productivity than those who always come into work. These new patterns of home working increasingly concentrate on skilled workers and more senior staff.

The implications for travel are complex as home working has a substantial potential to reduce the numbers of commuting journeys, which typically are longer than journeys for other purposes. For example, in the UK, the average distance for the journey to work has increased from 11.5 kilometres to 13.4 kilometres (1991 to 2001). Data on the relative lengths of commuting journeys for teleworkers and other workers are difficult to obtain, but figures quoted in Sloman (2003 – from Mitchell and Trodd, 1994) suggest that teleworkers commute 33.6 km compared to an average figure for commuting car journey lengths of 24 km. In the US (1995), teleworkers commuted 25.6 km compared to 20.5 km for non-teleworkers (Tayyaran and Khan, 2003). It should be noted that these figures may merely reflect the travel habits of individuals who are in the socio-economic category that permits teleworking. More general conclusions would require time series data covering those people who have taken on teleworking.

This net reduction in total travel has direct benefits for homeworkers in terms of saved time and indirect benefits for other workers, as roads and public transport are less crowded. Interestingly (Fact Box 9.7), there seems to be a relationship between the average commute time and the proportion of workers teleworking. The main gain is the increase in flexibility, which in turn results in a greater potential for the reorganization of output processes and businesses. There is a new interdependence between global and local working,

Fact Box 9.7 Teleworking

Although the number of teleworkers has increased, the growth is generally much slower than predicted. In 1999, 8 million or 6 per cent of all employees in Europe (EU-11) teleworked in one form or another (regular teleworkers, supplementary (occasional) teleworkers, home-based/mobile teleworkers, etc. (ECaTT, 2000, p. 24)).

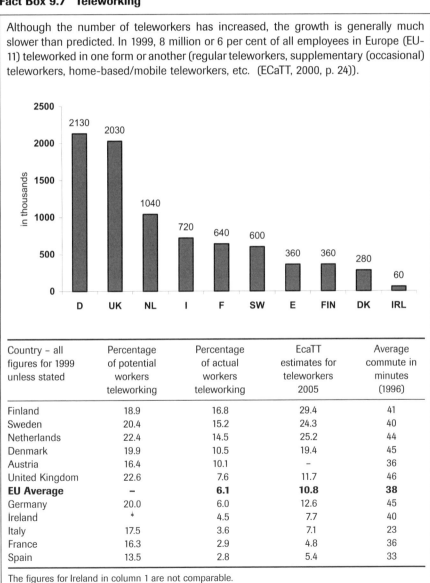

Country – all figures for 1999 unless stated	Percentage of potential workers teleworking	Percentage of actual workers teleworking	EcaTT estimates for teleworkers 2005	Average commute in minutes (1996)
Finland	18.9	16.8	29.4	41
Sweden	20.4	15.2	24.3	40
Netherlands	22.4	14.5	25.2	44
Denmark	19.9	10.5	19.4	45
Austria	16.4	10.1	–	36
United Kingdom	22.6	7.6	11.7	46
EU Average	–	**6.1**	**10.8**	**38**
Germany	20.0	6.0	12.6	45
Ireland	*	4.5	7.7	40
Italy	17.5	3.6	7.1	23
France	16.3	2.9	4.8	36
Spain	13.5	2.8	5.4	33

The figures for Ireland in column 1 are not comparable.

Sources: EcaTT (2000) and CfIT (2001).

as firms disperse their activities and as autonomous market-orientated business units locate in areas closest to their customers (Reichwald *et al.*, 2002).

The same types of linkages can be found in teleservices where routine functions and maintenance can be carried out online or through self-diagnostics, resulting in less travel. More challenging is the opportunity to design products for individual users (e.g. newspapers) where the appropriate mix is made according to their requirements and printed on demand. In a more basic version, similar facilities are available for banking, chemists, and shopping.

e-meetings are another dimension of the conflict between face-to-face and remote contact. Video-conferencing allows visual contact as well as spoken contact, but the need to get a 'feel' for the meeting suggests that face-to-face is still very important. This means that some substitution may take place, but key meetings need face-to-face contact and this in turn may result in longer travel distances, as businesses have become more global. Market penetration for video-conferencing is still relatively low, suggesting that the technology does not 'work' or that the set up costs and skills levels are high. However, routine information can be easily transferred without the need for contact, and this can save on movement, both physical travel and traditional mail (e-information).

Thus there is substantial potential for substitution of travel to work by homeworking, but that potential has not been fully realized. The increased flexibility has resulted in many self-employed and other workers spending more time working from home, typically one to two days a week. The social dimensions of real contact with colleagues are important, and this is also reflected in the need for face-to-face meetings. New dispersed patterns of work may develop as people continue to live further from their workplace and as firms also disperse their activities (internationally and locally). The net result will be fewer journeys to work, but each one is likely to be longer. Again, much of the evidence is limited and there needs to be a more systematic collection of standard information across Europe, both at key points in time and over time. Longitudinal data allow the new complexity and flexibility to be identified, and permits actual changes as well as net changes to be recorded.

9.5 Conclusions

In the new world of high technology, society might only be just beginning to understand the tremendous potential that it has to offer. Much of the evidence cited here is based on current best knowledge, but even here there are the optimists and the pessimists. The optimists anticipate rapid take-up of the new technologies in every aspect of producing, living and working, and that access will be available to all at a low (or even zero) cost. The pessimists suggest a much more cautious take up, with only limited interest in using the new technology, and a strong social division between those that have the knowledge and the resources to take full advantage of it and those that do not. Here we try to take a realist position somewhere in between, really to raise some important new issues as they relate to the impacts of ICT on transport.

Three key questions are raised concerning transport demand:

1   The limits to travel. Taking an historical perspective, it seems that there are no limits to the relentless growth in the demand for travel. Growth rates of 5 to 6 per cent per annum in air travel, means a doubling of demand every 12 years. Even with more modest growth rates, as reported more recently for air travel and other forms of travel, a doubling of demand still takes place every 20 years. In the past, every technological innovation acted to increase that demand rather than reduce it. The question here is whether ICT acts as a brake or an accelerator in this process. The evidence cited in this chapter suggests that there is substantial scope for reducing some types of (less valued) travel demand, like the journey to work, but equally it may encourage other (higher valued) longer distance travel, like leisure travel. Despite the increasing concerns over the environmental and health consequences of the increasing consumption of non-renewable resources, it seems that ICTs on their own cannot change the direction of current trends towards a less sustainable transport system.

2   Not all travel is derived demand. The traditional view that travel is only undertaken because of the benefits derived at the destination being higher than the associated costs is no longer generally applicable (Mokhtarian and Salomon, 2001). Substantial amounts of leisure travel are undertaken for its own sake and the activity of travelling is valued positively. This conclusion has enormous implications for transport analysis as most conventional analysis is based on the premise that travel distances should be short and that travel time should be minimized. As work-related activities become less important in terms of travel, and as the growth takes place in leisure activities, conventional transport 'wisdom' needs to be reassessed. ICT provides access to information about new opportunities and options for leisure trips. Increased social use of ICT may result in much greater networking both on the Internet and through face-to-face contact. New types of travel may be generated or at least facilitated by the technology. The questions that need to be answered are obvious: How are different types of trips valued? What types of trips are regarded as a nuisance, and are thus in principle open

for substitution by ICT applications, and what types are positively valued for their own?

3   The problem of latent demand. The balance between substitutive and complementary effects of ICT use with respect to transport has been one of the main issues of scientific debate over the past decade, and it is based on different assumptions regarding the role of latent demand. If distance working or any other ICT-based activity leads to the substitution of a trip, it is possible that other people may make additional trips. Other road users may take advantage of the 'liberated' road space, family members may make additional trips or the teleworker will use the car for leisure purposes instead. Moreover, the balance of modes may be affected because teleworkers use the car for their remaining trips rather than travelling by public transport as they did before. And in the longer-term, location decisions may change, with people willing to live further from their places of work, thus making fewer but longer trips. Getting answers to these questions will be crucial for assessing the transport impacts of ICT use.

An alternative view is that the Internet increases accessibility and quality of life for the users and that there has been a substitution of additional trips by Internet use. More optimistically, this might also lead to some individuals living without the car, and that this in turn might lead to car free lifestyles. It could also increase the potential for car clubs, as these cater for those who desire the occasional use of the car. Virtual mobility has substituted for the increases in physical mobility (Lyons and Kenyon, 2003), so that more sensitive time use studies over time are necessary to establish the nature and scale of the trade offs.

Three key questions are raised concerning new opportunities for the use of ICT in transport, and to the concept of fixed travel time budgets that have been central to much transport thinking (Banister, 2005):

1   Necessity to take an intermodal perspective on transport. There seems to be considerable opportunity within Europe to exploit the potential for intermodal transport by means of ICT-use. For instance, there is scope to reduce short distance travel by air through the linking of air and rail networks, as has been achieved at Charles de Gaulle and Frankfurt airports. Through innovative hubbing solutions facilitated by ICT, it is possible to optimize the use of air space and rail systems. This applies both to passenger travel and high value freight movements, but it is important that the potential role of ICT is not over emphasized, as the basic driving force for change would be the economics of integration.

2   Sustainable supply chains. There is an increasing awareness worldwide of the transport costs entailed in providing goods to the final user. One of the main growth sectors in air travel has been the freight sector where high value goods are carried long distances to give year round availability. If transport activities pay for their full environmental costs, transport costs would be a more decisive factor and the need to optimize them would arise. The internalization of external costs can thus turn into one of the key drivers of ICT-use in transport because of its efficiency-enhancing potential along the supply chain, so that sustainability can be combined with efficiency.

3   Impact of technology and flexibility. ICT provides tremendous opportunity and choice to carry out the full range of desired activities in a variety of ways. It also provides firms with important new challenges with respect to their production processes. The knowledge base is extended and this may result in more travel, but more important is the transfer of power from the producer to the customer. Users are increasingly controlling their own lives and what they want (at a price), and so the production processes have to react to those new requirements. This flexibility in turn requires the extensive use of ICT throughout the supply chain, but we are far from understanding the multitude of consequences this is likely to have, or their collective impact on transport demand.

Any research work aiming to underpin these key questions and opportunities needs to be based on a sound empirical basis. The analysis of available literature and evidence has shown that the empirical base on the interdependencies between new types of ICT applications and the implications they have for transport is still in its infancy. Even where there is better information (e.g. distance working and e-commerce), most studies concentrate on the direct impacts on trip frequency and distance, whereas second-order effects are hardly taken into account. There is a definitive need for additional empirical research work, broken down for the distinct ICT applications, and their sub-dimensions.

Finally, some ideas and situations are given to reflect the complexity of the links between ICT and transport. The impact of information exchange and use of information means that there is likely to be a coexistence between old and new products, as paper products are matched by electronic products. Although there may be some substitution, new markets will also develop (e.g. in publishing). Shopping is an example of information exchange, where customers view, compare, select, purchase, and then have the item delivered. Some or all of these actions can be carried out remotely, some may require additional travel, whilst others may require less travel.

There is also the impact of virtual mobility and the new accessibility that this brings through the increased use of email and Internet, either at home or at work or increasingly on the move. This reflects co-evolution of technology and society, as evidenced through teleactivities of all types (work and leisure-based), and this again will lead to both generation and substitution effects. The importance of real time information is another situation that will allow greater flexibility in travel and activity participation through the use of the mobile technologies. The functional requirements of being able to carry out daily activities and for business to run efficiently need to be balanced against the social needs of individuals and employers. The different requirements are reflected in the complexity of response and speed of take up of innovation, as expectations are often higher than actual use.

New perspectives are required on the nature of accessibility as the physical and social constraints normally used are matched by virtual constraints. This, in turn, needs to be reflected in transport analysis that replaces the notion of a single activity (travel) being carried out at a particular point of time by a more flexible notion of virtual travel and of multitasking when travelling.

Notes

1   Information and communications technology includes the Internet, electronic data interchange, email, personal computer-based fax, and automatic telephone entry (e.g. voicemail).
2   This information comes from a survey carried out by ICM of over 2000 people (over 14 years of age) for Oxford University Internet Institute – accessed through www.oii.ox.ac.uk.

Chapter 10

Learning from cities with low levels of motorization

10.1 Introduction

This chapter may seem a slight digression, but it is not. It examines the lessons that can be learned from experience in developing countries, and in particular in the burgeoning cities that are growing in population by at least 2–3 per cent a year, with some growing by 6 per cent per annum. Although, in resource terms these cities are consuming far less than those in developed countries, it is here that the growth in demand is increasing exponentially. As we have seen in the introductory part of this book, car ownership levels are increasing, with the same effects as has been seen in the past in Western cities. Road space is being allocated to the car in preference to the multitude of other potential uses to which it has been traditionally put. Streets in these cities were used by people, for walking, for trading, and for living in, but this is now changing. Cars and other motorized forms of transport are beginning to dominate, and people and cyclists find it harder and less safe to get around. This is not to say that it is bad but, in the context of sustainable urban development, these challenges need to be addressed.

Cities in developing countries strongly promote economic growth, often at the expense of poverty reduction and improvement in environmental quality. The economic imperative is much stronger than imperatives relating to social and environmental issues. That is not surprising, but within the constraints of sustainable urban development, the balance must be sought. However, as the World Bank (2001) has stated, the position of urban transport seems to present a fundamental paradox – 'urban transport *can* contribute to poverty reduction both indirectly through its impact on the city economy and hence on economic growth, and directly through its impact on the daily needs of poor people' (p. viii). The evidence is somewhat different, as economies of agglomeration concentrate both people and activity in the cities. This leads to further growth of income levels and the higher levels of consumption being concentrated in the cities. These changes are taking place at a much faster rate than the availability of space for movement about the city, and this has resulted in gridlock on the streets and poor levels of environmental quality. In addition, as land values rise, the central areas have become too expensive for the poor, who have to relocate to the peripheral areas, often with much longer journeys to work. Motorization, which is made possible by the growth process, may also make many people poorer in terms of their environment and safety. The overall picture is captured in the quote given below.

> Urban population continues to expand at more than 6 per cent in many developing countries. The number of mega cities with over 10 million inhabitants is expected to double within a generation. More than half of the developing world's population, and half of its poor, will then live in cities. Per capita motor vehicle ownership and use continues to grow by up to 15 to 20 per cent per year in some countries. Traffic congestion and air pollution continues to increase. Increased use of private vehicles has resulted in falling public transport demand and a consequential decline in service levels. Sprawling cities are making the journey to work excessively long and costly for some of the very poor. Safety and security of urban travellers is an emerging problem, particularly in South America. (World Bank, 2001, p. vii)

Gwilliam (2003) summarizes the problem as consisting of four elements: premature congestion where average speeds in some cities are less than 10 km/h; a deteriorating environment with high levels of particulates and carbon monoxide; concerns over safety and security with some 1,200,000 road fatalities in developing countries (2002); and declining transport options for the poor.

It is worth pausing for a moment to consider the sheer scale of the potential growth of vehicles in developing countries, even though it does repeat some of the information presented in Chapter 2 (Table 10.1).

Table 10.1 Growth in car and vehicle ownership

Thousands	1995		2020		2030	
	Cars	Vehicles	Cars	Vehicles	Cars	Vehicles
OECD	383,329	536,174	574,241	782,361	621,091	842,257
Rest of the world	111,255	340,357	283,349	580,288	391,755	781,130
Total	494,584	776,531	857,590	1,362,649	1,012,846	1,623,387

Source: OECD (1995).

♦ In 1995, there were about 500m cars, 77 per cent of which were in OECD countries, and some 750m vehicles, 69 per cent of which were in the OECD countries.

♦ By 2030, there will be over 1,000m cars, 62 per cent of which will be in the OECD countries, and some 1,600m vehicles of which 51 per cent will be in the OECD countries.

♦ This amounts to a doubling over the 35-year period or a 2 per cent annual growth rate overall, but in the non-OECD countries the growth rate for both cars and other vehicles is 3.5 per cent per annum.

♦　By 2005, there will be 1,000m vehicles in the World.

♦　In China and India, growth rate in two and four wheel vehicle ownership has now exceeded 10 per cent per annum.

In this chapter, the focus is on three of the key aspects of sustainable urban development as it affects cities in developing countries. Transport has important equity implications and it disproportionately affects the urban poor. Air pollution and traffic congestion lead to substantial losses in health, time and economic growth, but the distribution of these costs is not uniform (World Bank, 2001). The second issue is that of innovation, as many novel ideas have been pioneered in these new emerging cities, including road pricing, and the recent reinvention of the bus as a rapid transit mode. There is much that cities more generally can learn from these innovations. Thirdly, there is the institutional and organizational structure within which decisions are made. Many cities do not have a tradition of strong urban governance. The imposition of plans and controls need to be made so that society as a whole benefits, even if some individuals may lose. Sustainable urban development is dependent upon policies and strategies being introduced effectively and in a fair and consistent manner that is acceptable to the population.

10.2　Equity

Much of the debate in developing countries has concentrated on the inequalities created by transport policies, as they tend to favour the middle class and the rich at the expense of the poor (Satterthwaite, 1995 and Vasconcellos, 2001). The important difference here is that sustainable urban development is seen primarily as a social construct in developing countries as opposed to an environmental construct in developed countries – 'the concentration on ecological sustainability, focusing either on sustaining the resource base or limiting human activities that disrupt global cycles, tends to ignore the poverty dimension of the problem' (Mitlin and Satterthwaite, 1996, p. 27). This difference is fundamental, as the concern is not primarily about the use of resources, the levels of local and global pollution, the technological alternatives, or the internalization of costs. It is about the levels of accessibility, the use of non-motorized forms of transport, the location of homes and jobs, and the high level of accidents.

This fundamental difference has been recognized by the World Bank (1975) with their policy statement identifying inaccessibility to basic services within limited resources as the main policy focus. The links between land use and transport and the need to reduce travel distances were both recognized, as were the rational use of transport facilities and the recognition of the coordinating role of institutions and the full involvement of the range of transport operators. That approach marked a clear switch away from capital intensive projects towards making the best use of available facilities. It talked about new forms of charging for the use of road space, but in reality traffic management and public transport were driving the agenda.

It also led in time to a more fundamental review of World Bank transport policy (1996), where sustainability was put at the centre of their agenda. Although economic sustainability was paired with social and environmental sustainability, the impression given was that the economic issues 'influenced by neo-liberal approaches to privatization and deregulation' were seen as being the most important (Vasconcellos, 2001, p. 232). It seems that the World Bank was taking a rather narrow perspective on sustainable development, and that the actual lending practices have not always followed the official stated policies. Apart from the strong emphasis on the use of economic constructs, the use of market mechanisms and the involvement of the private sector, there seems to have been little attempt to integrate the three elements of sustainable development (even though this was stated as being important), and less emphasis was placed on the supporting actions, including institutional change, and novel solutions.

New policies are required to address the issues of poverty, as wealth distribution is very uneven. This situation is compounded by the high levels of inward migration to the cities, and the socio-spatial segregation of the population, as most of the jobs are located in the centre and most of the poor people are located in the periphery. The obvious solution to this problem, which would be both equitable and sustainable, would be to encourage walking and cycling to work. But this solution is not possible as the cities are becoming too large and the distances too great. For example, 20 per cent of workers in Mexico City spend more than 3 hours getting to and from work each day, and 10 per cent take over 5 hours (Schwela and Zali, 1999). In addition, the distribution of public services (schools, hospitals, public transport, etc) is very uneven, and this in turn makes travel distances longer. Decisions seem to have been taken that have compounded the inequality rather than addressing it. Investments in road solutions have led to even longer travel distances and a greater dependence on motorized transport. These structural problems are reflected in the political domain where the power of the lobbies, industry and external agencies seem to dominate in these fragile democracies (Vasconcellos, 2001, p. 212).

The scale of the problem can again be seen with respect to the example of Rio de Janeiro where a limited survey was carried out in 1989 to determine the socio-spatial inequalities, both in terms of travel patterns and in the provision of bus services in the metropolitan area (Fact Box 10.1 and Camara and Banister, 1993).

Fact Box 10.1   Social and spatial inequalities in Rio de Janeiro

Travel patterns

+ Walk times for those living in peripheral areas were 70 per cent higher than for those living in central areas.
+ 75 per cent of those making one transfer and all those making two transfers lived in peripheral areas.
+ Nearly 87 per cent of those who had to travel more than 75 minutes on a one way journey lived in peripheral areas.
+ For those living in the centre, 71 per cent were able to spend the equivalent to only two fares a day, meaning that no interchange was necessary.
+ 65 per cent of those in peripheral areas had to spend at least six fares a day to make the necessary interchanges.

Quality of bus service

+ Wait time at the periphery averaged 19 minutes as compared with 6 minutes in the core.
+ 66 per cent of all travellers from the periphery to the core were able to get a seat for the whole journey, whilst the corresponding figure within the core was 80 per cent.
+ The higher frequency in the core meant that although buses were overcrowded, it was possible to get a seat for at least part of the journey.

Source: Camara and Banister (1993).

The problems of the poor being located at the periphery, often in informal housing with minimal facilities and security, are reinforced by land speculation, disputes over ownership, and a weak planning system. These social clusters are 'highly differentiated by income and social characteristics, with the poorest layers furthest away' (Vasconcellos, 2001, p. 212). The net effect is spatial segregation, which in turn is reinforced by the interests of the more affluent socially mobile population who see a future that is based on individual motorized transport.

The priority for decision-makers should be to invest in the poorer sectors of society to reduce these inequalities. This means that pavements and pedestrian facilities should be made safe and convenient for comfortable walking, and road space should be adapted so that priority can be given to cyclists (and motorcyclists) and public transport (Vasconcellos, 2001, p. 213). But in many developing cities, the priorities are being given to car users. The World Bank's paradox is not being addressed. There is also a question over whether the motorcycle should be seen as part of the solution, as it is a polluting and noisy form of transport. Yet in many developing cities it provides family and freight transport, and it is economic in its use of space. Socially, it provides a solution, but environmentally it does not. The possibilities of subsidizing the poor to use the bus services is another alternative, but as the World Bank (1996) indicates it is difficult to target effectively just the poor, as public transport may still be too expensive for them to use, and as subsidy tends to encourage a loss of efficiency through higher wages and lower operating standards. Direct subsidies could be organized through the tax and benefits system, but many of the poor are not in the formal economy. Direct subsidies to the operators is another alternative, but again this tends to benefit all travellers rather than the poor, and it may exclude the many forms of informal transport. A theme underlying much of this discussion is that change is occurring so rapidly and the responses are not sufficient. Short-term reaction is important, but it is also necessary to include discussion of urban form and the location of services and facilities, ideally to keep them within walking or cycling distance, but also close to corridors where high density public transport routes can be provided. These questions are taken up again in Section 10.3 on innovation and the need for stronger institutions.

Despite all the good intentions, there seem to be more examples of decisions being made that benefit the better off rather than the poor. As in all cities, the poor do not travel as far as the rich, and when they do travel they walk or use the cheapest forms of transport available. The basic problem is to increase the mobility options for the poor, but at the same time limit the more general transport chaos that is inherent in most rapidly urbanizing cities (Fact Box 10.2). For example, many new systems have been introduced, such as the Star and Putra light rail transit systems in Kuala Lumpur, the KLIA (Kuala Lumpur International Airport) airport express and the monorail line (two of these schemes went bankrupt and have had to be nationalized). There is still concern over who are the beneficiaries of such prestige investment schemes.

Fact Box 10.2 Transport in Bangkok

Bangkok has moved from the 8th Transport Plan (1997–2001) to the 9th Transport Plan (2002–2006). The Bangkok Metropolitan Region accounts for 56 per cent of Thailand's GDP and has a population of 14 million. There are some 22 million person trips a day, and some 4 million truck trips. About 57 per cent of travel is private, even with the mass rapid transit. Further investment is planned for 1000 km of roads and 260 km of public transport routes. The car is seen as a symbol of wealth (Rujopakarn, 2003).

The environmental costs of air and water pollution in Bangkok exceed $2 billion a year. Each car in Bangkok is expected to spend an average equivalent of 44 days each year in traffic jams. Traffic-induced delays lose the city about one-third of its estimated gross city product, in one estimate equivalent to $4 million a day. Time savings from a 10 per cent reduction in peak hour journey times would save $400 million annually. Excessive lead levels, chiefly from vehicles, contribute to 200,000–400,000 cases of hypertension and some 400 deaths a year. Rough estimates suggest that excessive lead levels can cause children to lose four or more IQ points by the age of seven.

continued on page 197

continued from page 196

Average speeds in the city are 10 km per hour, falling to 5 km per hour at the peak. The volume/capacity ratio is 0.7 (2001). Congestion-induced delays cost the city $1.5 billion a year, with water and air pollution costs adding $2.0 billion a year to this figure. The emissions of all major transport-related local air pollutants doubled in the period 1991 to 2001 and the proportion of urban space allocated to roads is low (11 per cent compared with 20–25 per cent in European cities). Ownership of motorcycles has risen by 33 per cent per annum and cars by 13 per cent per annum (in the early 1990s and since 2002 again). The local manufacturing of vehicles, together with a reduction of import duties on foreign cars, has encouraged this growth. Congestion is so bad that it is often quicker to walk than to use vehicular transport.

Although public transport accessibility is good in the city centre, elsewhere it is poor and has not been integrated with the 1999 Bangkok Land Use Plan that has promoted a series of self-contained subcentres around the core city. The growth in the economy, together with an active land market and rapidly escalating prices has made it difficult for government to acquire land for construction. Some relief was found in 1997, with the Asian financial crisis, but growth patterns have been re-established.

Privately funded 'megaprojects' have increased road capacity and helped develop a mass rapid transit system (and the Skytrain), but the Hopewell Rail and Road project was cancelled. The complex explanations include:

- The absence of institutional arrangements to provide an appropriate strategic and structural framework is central to the problem.
- The lack of infrastructure planning has accentuated the failure to provide adequate space for transport circulation.
- The diffusion of responsibilities for transport policy among several ministries has paralysed attempts at a comprehensive strategy.
- There is no strong core or tradition of professionals, so that it has been easy for political intervention to take place and it has also reduced the attractiveness for the private sector.
- The Second Stage Expressway was not used after completion because of disputes over toll rates.

The high risks to private sector involvement means that returns have to be obtained in more secure investments – this means low-cost bus-based alternatives may offer better returns.

The urban poor need other forms of transport that are both accessible and affordable. In the formal sector, this includes bus-based systems with exclusive rights of way, supplemented by the multitude of available informal transport systems (Cervero, 1997). The best example of a bus-based system is Curitiba in Brazil (Fact Box 10.3). However, it is in the informal sector that the twin objectives of accessible transport for the poor that is also sustainable can be achieved. Such a package might include rickshaws in Bangladesh (Gallagher, 1992), minibuses and bicycles in Africa (Hook, 1995; World Bank,1994; UNDP, 1997) (Fact Box 10.4). It is important to engage and help improve the informal sector, but cities like Bogotá, Curitiba and Quito have been able to improve their public transport systems radically without the use of the informal sector. There is no single solution, but the costs of the schemes and the needs of the urban poor must form the two central concerns for all cities.

Fact Box 10.3   Transport in Curitiba (Brazil)

Curitiba is a Brazilian city of 1.6 million where 75 per cent of commuters use public transport despite car ownership levels being higher than in São Paulo (there are about 655,000 motor vehicles in Curitiba – 1999). Traffic levels have declined by 30 per cent since 1974, even though the population has doubled. The dedicated bus network cost about $200,000 per kilometre to introduce.

There are 1902 buses on 340 routes. The 270 passenger bi-articulated and 150 passenger articulated red buses operate on the 65 km of dedicated express busways (13 lines) along 5 routes. These are linked to the 340 km of feeder routes (operated by orange buses), which come into the transfer terminals. These 25 transfer terminals and 221 tube stations allow pre-paid boarding, and they in turn are also linked to 185 km of circular interdistrict routes (operated by green buses), that allow access to the express lines without entering the city centre. Several complementary services are operated. These include the silver speedy buses that link the main districts and surrounding municipalities with Curitiba and the bus stations, the yellow buses on the main radial roads (not the busways), and the City Circle Line operated by white minibuses.

Over 90 per cent of the city is accessible to the bus network and the total network length is 1100 km.

The flat fare system allows transfer between services at no cost – Smartcards were being experimented with in 2003. Nearly 2 million passengers are carried each day (2003).

Source: Meirelles (2000) and Horizon International (2003).

The Curitiba Bus System is a financially self-sufficient project that has been achieved through an integrated approach involving changes in the zoning system, a diversified public transport service, the concentration of residential development, the creation of dedicated road facilities, the introduction of innovative 'loading tubes', and the evolution of a special relationship between the public and the private sectors. Its implementation involved local community groups in the planning process.

There are three basic levels to the system. Small buses operate in the low-density areas and these act as feeders to the dedicated busway network which operates along high speed and high capacity corridors. The express bus and feeder network are complimented by the interdistrict routes, which connect the axes of the express lines without passing through the city centre. High-density development is permitted around the express busway corridors, and the allowable densities decline as distance increases from the busway.

continued on page 199

continued from page 198

The 1990 Municipal Housing Act allows developers to pay additional fees to build up to two storeys above the allowable limits on land that was well served by the bus network. The Curitiba Municipal Housing Agency (COHAB) had bought land along the busway route and built 17,000 units of high and moderate density low-income housing, thus increasing the viability of the bus network. Population growth in the busway corridors has been 98 per cent in the first 5 years after the system was implemented, compared with 26 per cent for the city overall. To reduce the time taken for boarding buses, Curitiba introduced 'loading tubes' where passengers paid to enter the tubular waiting area and can then board at all entrances simultaneously to save time.

The public transport system in Curitiba has increased patronage by 2.36 per cent per year for the last 20 years. The system receives no subsidies and the operation has been contracted out to private operators, allowing them to earn profits, and keep fares levels low and quality provision in low income neighbourhoods.

Evolution of Curitiba's Integrated Transit Network (ITN) and passenger load

| Year | Passengers carried per day ('000s) | | | Extent of ITN by route type (km) | | |
	Total	Conventional	ITN	Express	Feeder	Interdistrict
1974	677	623	54	19.9	45	0
1992	1,028	398	630	41.0	266	166
2000	976	276	700	65.0	340	185

Source: Rabinovitch and Hoehn (1995), p. 17; Wright (2001)

The ITN is based on a series of high-speed bus routes (with modern buses) that are supported by lower volume feeder routes. The high volume routes are in the higher density areas where most of the economic activity is located, but the complementary network is equally important in terms of linking the low-density neighbourhoods with the city centre and other neighbourhoods.

In Curitiba, land use and transport complement each other. Land-use controls limit high density growth within the city centre (pedestrianized). New growth is concentrated in the transport corridors (known as structural sectors), which are served by high capacity express and direct buses, using exclusive central lanes on arterial highways. Before developing these corridors, the city acquired adjacent land and built low-income housing. Land-use density controls are related to public transport with densities up to six times the plot ratios along the structural routes.

Sources: Stickland (1993); UNDP (1994); Rabinovitch and Leitman (1996); Gallagher (1992); World Bank (1994 and 1996); Koerner (1998); Hall and Pfeiffer (2000); and Replogle (1992).

The social dimensions of sustainable urban development must not be underestimated, as in all cities it seems that the opportunities for addressing the transport needs of the urban poor are not being given priority. It is not just the supply of transport services that must be considered, but also the location of housing and workplaces, as well as services and facilities. The problem of inaccessibility for the poor is not just a physical one, but also economic as they cannot afford to travel. The mode of transport most suited

Fact Box 10.4   Rickshaws in Bangladesh and bicycles in Africa

There are now more than 4 million hand pulled and cycle rickshaws in the world, mostly in Asia. In Bangladesh, there are probably over 500,000 rickshaws in Dhaka accounting for over 50 per cent of all vehicles and 7 million trips a day or 70 per cent of all passenger movements and 43 per cent of all passenger kilometres – but only 100,000 permits have been issued. More than 1.25 million people are employed in this business, with over 5 million poor people directly dependent on the rickshaw for their livelihood.

Ownership of rickshaws is mainly with the rich who rent them to the poor with high charges to ensure good rates of return. Attempts (in Jaipur and Nagpur) to restrict multiple ownership of rickshaws or cheaper finance to owner-operators have not proved successful. Restrictive licensing has encouraged the replacement of rickshaws with motorized vehicles. In poor countries this has failed to limit the number of rickshaws but it has fostered systematic corruption, transferring income from the operators to the police. Again, this has favoured the larger and richer operators at the expense of the owner operators. Cycle rickshaws provide low cost emissions free services.

Dhaka in conjunction with the World Bank have begun systematically to eliminate cycle rickshaws from major streets, thus making their business increasingly untenable.

In 1992, a bicycle cost an average per capita income of 7 months in Uganda, 10 months in Malawi and Tanzania, and 36 months in Ethiopia. In Asia, the cost of a bicycle is between $25 and $100 or 6 months wages. Some countries (Burkina Faso, India, Zimbabwe) have used government financed integrated rural development programmes to provide the poor with credit to purchase bicycles. Private sector finance (Bangladesh, Sri Lanka) has been used to develop credit schemes for bicycles. Essential elements are the high levels of decentralization, with non-governmental organizations involved in the administration. The role of social or kinship groups is also important so that the formal liability for loan repayments can be established. But theft is a major problem that has to be included in any risk assessment. In Africa only 3.5 per cent of people use bicycles, but in Asia 40 per cent own bicycles – some areas in China have 700 bicycles per 1000 population.

Sources: Stickland (1993); UNDP (1994); Rabinovitch and Leitman (1996); Gallagher (1992); World Bank (1994 and 1996); and Replogle (1992).

to their use (the bicycle) is being restricted in where it can be used, as space is reallocated to motorized forms of transport. The growth in car ownership and the construction of new roads together with the reallocation of existing space all mean that the poor are being 'squeezed out'. In addition, they also suffer from higher accident rates, increased noise and higher levels of pollution. Their quality of life is deteriorating.

Yet it is in these same cities that innovative thinking and leadership have developed, through a commitment to and investment in new forms of bus transport. Informal transport and new high-speed bus services are now reaching out to the suburbs where the poor are located, and this has changed the accessibility map in several cities. It is to these positive innovations that we now turn.

10.3 Innovation

In the richer countries, the use of regulations has been very effective in improving the efficiency of the vehicle stock and in reducing the emissions. But in poorer cities, such an approach is likely to be less effective, particularly if it raises the costs of travel. There is less political will to impose strictly enforced regulations, and even if they are used, there is the related problem of enforcement. The easier path is to encourage the use of the best available technology so that new cars are 'clean'. Often clean technologies such as catalytic converters require higher quality lead free petrol and better maintenance. The vehicles replaced will also create secondary problems, as there will be a strong market for the older dirtier vehicles, which in turn will continue to pollute. It is difficult to speed up the turnover of the vehicle fleet in situations where demand for vehicles is high. This argument presents a rather gloomy picture with little opportunity for short-term improvement, but many innovations are coming from the poorer countries. Sustainable development is a global issue and all parties can learn from each other.

However, it is in public transport innovation that developing countries seem to be taking the lead. Conventional thinking promotes bus-based systems at relatively low levels of demand (up to 25,000 passengers per hour per direction), with rail-based systems (trams, light rapid transit, metros and heavy rail systems) being used for higher demand corridors. But even here there are problems, as trams and light rail transit have capacities of about 12,000 passengers per hour per direction, about half that of the purpose built bus rapid transit (BRT).

A clear hierarchy has evolved and much of the World Bank investment in urban transport systems has followed this pattern (Fouracre *et al.*, 2003 and Table 10.2). The high capital and operating costs of the rail-based systems has raised concerns about servicing debts on these loans and the implications for the urban poor, who are often located some distance from the rail system and cannot afford the fares. New thinking (Wright, 2001 and Cervero, 1998) is promoting the use of more flexible systems of public transport (principally the use of busways and BRT), as these are much cheaper and more flexible in their operations, and they can penetrate the areas where the low-income population live. Capacities can be increased above the thresholds above, for example in Bogotá where over 36,000 passengers per hour per direction are carried on the Avenue Caracas.

The conclusions reached from Allport (2000) and Wright (2001) strongly suggest that the capacity differences between the systems is not as great as

Table 10.2 Examples of mass transit systems in developing countries

City – all data for 2000	Number of mass transit corridors	Passengers carried (millions/year)		Daily passengers per transit corridor (thousands)
		total	per route km	
Metros				
Buenos Aires	6*	242	5.1	112
Bangkok	2	90	3.8	125
Caracas	3	403	8.8	373
Hong Kong	6	792	9.0	367
Mexico DF	11	1433	7.1	362
Santiago	3	208	5.1	192
Singapore	2	296	3.6	411
Light rail transit (LRT)				
Kuala Lumpur	2	61	1.1	85
Manila	2	109	3.5	153
Medellin	3	105	3.2	97
Bus rapid transit (BRT)				
Bogotá	3	184	4.7	174
Curitiba	5	684	1.3	380
Quito	2	83	7.4	115
Sao Paulo	4	273	4.4	190

Notes: * includes a 'pre metro' line. Note that the three LRT schemes cited are all elevated systems. The bus systems in each of these cities carry many more passengers than the rail systems in the Table, and the BRT systems are now carrying (2003) some three times as many passengers as indicated in the table (2000).

Source: Based on Fouracre *et al.* (2003), Table 2.

originally thought, as new high capacity buses on exclusive rights of way can operate much more efficiently than tram and light rail systems, reaching levels of 35,000 passengers carried per hour in each direction. At grade, Light Rail Transit (LRT) systems carry about 4,000–6,000 passengers per hour compared to a busway average of 15,000 passengers per hour at the same operating speed, and there is no known LRT that approaches the passenger carrying capacity of the existing Curitiba, Quito or Bogotá BRT systems (Allport, 2000). Wright (2001) concluded that the maximum capacity of an LRT system operating at 20 km/h is likely to be about 12,000 passengers per hour per direction.

Although public transport systems do not seem to have a great effect on land use, they may be more effective in changing existing land uses through concentration of activities close to accessible transport corridors (Cervero, 1998). In addition, the importance of public transport in getting to the areas where the poor live in these rapidly expanding cities cannot be underestimated, as their viability may depend on job locations being accessible (Schipper, 2001). It may also provide the means by which the process of sprawl can be limited, as higher densities for housing and other land uses can be maintained, and the potential for expanding car-based cities is reduced. This is where rapidly growing cities can learn from the extensive literature on sustainable development, and in turn other cities can learn from their experience of modern public transport based systems.

Before describing some detailed examples of innovative public transport systems in developing countries, we turn briefly to the informal sector, where many niche markets have been identified in the provision of public transport services. Paratransit is the term normally given to innovative services that operate outside the regulated fixed route services, and provide more flexible transport, mainly with minibuses. In most developing countries, these informal transport services coexist with formally organized municipal services in a relationship that is often confrontational (Fact Box 10.5). Investment is needed in new vehicles, so that emission levels can fall and efficiency can rise. But if this change also results in higher fares, then less people can afford to use these new more comfortable vehicles, and so there is a further erosion of the bus market. This is one of the difficult choices facing decision-makers, namely to strike the right balance between control and freedom of operation, and the necessity to provide access for the poor to jobs.

Fact Box 10.5　*Collectivos* in Mexico City

> There are over 30,000 collectivos (minibuses and vans) in Mexico City, which carry about 30 per cent of all travellers. Politically, the collectivos are tolerated, but they represent a chaotic, uninsured and sometimes unsafe mode of transport. Yet they deliver much desired services and their drivers form a strong political force. Little effort has been made to clean up the vehicles or to organize their routes to fit in with the established bus and metro services. The fleet is ageing and polluting, consuming as much fuel as the two established bus companies.

Source: Schipper (2001), p. 8.

Bus rapid transit (BRT) has provided the impetus to reinvent the bus as a new, high speed and environmentally clean form of public transport. Although not exclusively operated in cities in developing countries, it has been seen as starting there since its introduction in Curitiba in the 1970s as part of their integrated land-use and transport strategy (Fact Box 10.3). Since that time, some 30 BRT systems have been opened around the world and a further 35 are under planning or construction. BRT offers high-speed, reliable and cheap transport along the major routes within cities. By using new high capacity buses, pollution levels are reduced at source and there are likely to be second round effects as people switch to the bus in preference to using their own cars or older buses. These systems are innovative in that they reinvent the traditional bus as a new mode with different speed and comfort characteristics,

Fact Box 10.6   Bus rapid transit in Bogotá – the TransMilenio

Bogotá has a population of 6.5 million and covers an area of 28,000 hectares – this gives it a (high) density of 230 persons per hectare. Although the GDP per capita (US$ 2300 in 1999) is 15 per cent higher than the national average, car ownership is lower than average (110 cars per 1000 residents).

In 1999, the average speed in the peak hour on main roads was 12 km/h. BRT was introduced as part of a strategy to address the problems of mobility, to reclaim the streets for pedestrians, and to increase the access of residents to green spaces.

The BRT was opened on two routes in December 2000, with government funding for the infrastructure and the long-term planning, and with private operators running the services. The articulated buses run on exclusive rights of way with off-board fare collection. The system cost US$ 5 million per km to construct, and when the total system is completed (388 km), it will accommodate over 80 per cent of the daily public transport demand in the city.

Fares have been set at 1000 Colombian pesos (US$ 0.36 in 2003), and the revenues are sufficient for the operators to be profitable. In 2003 there were some 800,000 one-way trips each day on the three corridors now open (42.3 km of busways).

The uniqueness of Bogotá's system is the 'transformation of a busway corridor with severe pollution, safety problems and aesthetically displeasing into a new BRT system with significantly lower travel times, lower noise and fewer greenhouse gas emissions' (Rodríguez and Targa, 2004).

with high levels of reliability, with flexible ticketing and interchange, and with advanced technology to give information and priority across the system (Fact Box 10.6).

As happened with the advent of high-speed rail in the 1980s and 1990s, the rail system has been revitalized. The same phenomenon is now occurring with respect to buses, which have been reinvented as innovative transport systems or as high-speed bus routes. As with the high-speed rail, the design of buses has also been transformed, and many of them are 'clean' vehicles powered by alternative fuels (e.g. electricity or natural gas), or have clean diesel engines. Public transport has taken a lead in testing many of the new technologies, and it is in the cities of the developing world that many examples of good practice can be found.

10.4   Institutions and governance

In addition to these options and the various means by which the poor and others get around in developing cities, there is a need for good quality and stable urban governance. The appropriate organizational structures may not be present, while if they are, they lack the political and financial powers to turn ideas into action. It is difficult to introduce policies and measures as comprehensive packages that actually achieve the objectives of sustainable development as in the OECD cities. In non-OECD cities, there are even greater barriers, as there is not the tradition for effective urban governance and the necessary financial or revenue raising institutions. Policy processes are more difficult to implement, so the emphasis here is on more straightforward solutions to urban congestion and pollution. Transport measures can be taken that limit the role of the car through enforceable physical restraint, and clear priority can be given to all forms of public transport, together with informal modes such as rickshaws and bicycles.

In many cities the underlying imperative is economic growth, and all other societal concerns seem to take second place. This means that it is often very difficult to use planning controls on development and transport to implement effectively a sustainable urban development strategy. Even if there is a system in place, it does not receive the funding required for effective implementation, and the best professionals do not see it as an attractive occupation, so that there are inherent weaknesses in the whole process. In addition, enforcement mechanisms to push through policies and measures are often not available, hence the tendency for people to 'occupy' the land. If this is the case, then nothing can be done. But this cannot actually be true, as effective action has been seen in several cities. It is through a process of demonstrating the effects of good implementation and raising levels of public support that successful action can be seen to have taken place. As a result of this, funds have been made available and there does seem to be a new civic pride in terms of outcomes. Gradually, over time, the professionals will see the attractions of being associated with these changes and recognition will ensue.

Planning has moved from being a primarily control and enforcement activity to one that promotes and enables change to take place. In poor cities, it should be used as a means to facilitate self-help and private investment in the infrastructure. Cities in developing countries can become sustainable, as they are already compact and high density, with a strong tradition for self-build housing and strong neighbourhoods (e.g. the Kampungs in Indonesia). There is a huge informal sector that accounts for over 50 per cent of the labour force (Brennan, 1994), and this can be used to promote better quality development at the local level and at the same time work with the urban authorities.

Hall and Pfeiffer (2000, p. 304) in their review of urban futures propose eight universal principles (with local variants) for planning and urban governance:

1   Promotion of the city's wealth creating capacities;
2   Promotion of adequate shelter for all (rich and poor);
3   Maintenance of an adequate and sustainable level of environment in terms of air and water quality, drainage and noise;

4   Efficient use of land to reduce unnecessary journeys and demands on non-renewable resources;
5   Protection of the natural environment both within and around the city – this might involve the transformation of the city into a polycentric urban region of networked cities;
6   Conservation of the quality historic built environment;
7   Protection of the standards of the poorest;
8   Encouragement of people to help themselves and get them to use their own skills and energies.

These principles apply to all cities, not just those in developing countries. They require a combination of vision and strategy at the level of government, and the ability to implement change according to local needs. This is a partnership and a sharing of responsibilities. But it also means an adequate and fair distribution of revenues, so that subsidiarity can take place. Sustainable solutions need to strike the balance between over centralized and over localized systems so that effective cooperation takes place at all levels of decision-making. Examples of best practice take place where cooperation is most effective, and where the electorate is energized into participation in the implementation of the strategy (Chapter 5).

Two examples will be given here of the integrated approach to land-use and transport planning that have been adopted in different situations. Singapore is a good example of how within a small nation state it is possible to implement the most radical policies in land use and transport over a 30-year period (Fact Boxes 7.3 and 10.7). Some of the policies introduced in Singapore are now being tested in cities in the developed world, but the key to success has been the vision for the city, the consistent application of the policies over a considerable period of time, and the linking of development strategies with transport investments in public transport, together with a strong restraint on the ownership and use of the car. Supporting the policies has been stable governance, and it might be said that Singapore is unique in this respect, but this does not reduce the levels of its achievements. It might be called a sustainable urban development.

The second example is Bogotá. The development of the bus rapid transit (BRT) system has already been described (Fact Box 10.6), but that is only part of the strategy now being introduced. Here the situation with respect to urban governance is rather different as the initiative has resulted from a visionary mayor (Enrique Peñalosa, Mayor from 1998 to 2001) being sufficiently motivated to put his own political future at stake to achieve a major improvement in the city (Fact Box 10.8). Ironically, the political system in Bogotá does not allow for re-election, so the mayor has to carry out any reforms within a 3-year term, and this creates enormous problems with implementation as political processes are often not geared to radical change over such a short time period. In Bogotá, there has been success and it is fortunate that Peñalosa's successor (Antanas Mockus[1]) is a close political ally on transport policy in the capital, and this has allowed for continuity and continuation of the strategy. In 2005, Peñalosa can again be elected. The successful implementation of a sustainable urban development strategy, together with radical transport policies, is enormously dependent on leadership and vision. This is one of the main messages from all cities,

Fact Box 10.7   The Singapore approach

Singapore has a population of about 3.2 million and occupies a land area of 646 square kilometres giving it a density of about 50 persons per hectare.

There has been rapid economic growth, and the demand for cars has also been high. From 1975, Singapore has developed a radical transport strategy to restrain car ownership and use, to encourage use of public transport, and to locate land uses and activities around a high quality public transport system.

1   Restraint on car ownership is through a quota system introduced in 1990, when a certificate of entitlement (CoE) was required before a car could be bought. A bidding system was introduced and this substantially raised the price of new cars. There are also high vehicle registration fees, stringent requirements for driving licences and high fuel costs.

2   Restraint on car use was introduced in June 1975 through the Area Licensing Scheme (ALS), when every motorist was required to purchase and display a paper license before entering the restricted zone in the city centre. The scheme operates on each weekday and a half day on Saturday, with the costs of licenses being higher at peak times than at other times. Price also varied according to type of vehicle. The scheme was extended to three expressways during the morning rush hour in 1995 and 1997.

3   The Electronic Road Pricing (ERP) scheme was implemented in 1998 with smartcard technology in each car and the facility to photograph vehicles without a valid card. Charges relate to time and the levels of congestion. Traffic levels have fallen and there has been some diversion of trips to unpriced routes.

4   The mass rapid transit (MRT) system has two main branches and extends some 83 km, intersecting at the city centre and linking the planned new towns. The new 20 km North East line, which opened in 2002, runs from the World Trade Centre around the centre, linking the new towns of Hougang, Sengkang and Punggol.

5   Integrating land use and transport has been central to the plans, with decentralization of government offices and other businesses to suburban centres. Initially these were in a ring around the central area, but in 1991 four new centres were set up in Tampines, Jurong East, Woodlands and Beletar, served by the MRT and light rail transit. Comprehensive planning is helped by the fact that (1994) 87 per cent of the population live in public housing, many in the new towns.

Source: Based on Hall and Pfeiffer (2000), pp. 274–276. See Fact Box 7.3.

Fact Box 10.8 The Bogotá approach

Several schemes have been introduced to reduce car use and these have enhanced the impact of the TransMilenio Bus Rapid Transit system:

1   Tag number systems where 40 per cent of all cars have to be off the street during peak hours for two days a week. This has reduced daily travel times by 58 minutes and lowered pollution levels. Petrol consumption has been reduced by 10.3 per cent.

2   Ciclovia – This is where main roads are closed to motor traffic for 7 hours every Sunday, so that streets can be used by people for walking, cycling, jogging and meeting each other. Some 120 km of main city arteries are now closed to motor vehicles.

3   Car free days – On one Thursday, the city went to work by bus, bicycle and taxi. In the referendum in October 2000, about 64 per cent voted to establish a car free day on the first Thursday of each February, and by 2002 83 per cent supported the idea.

4   Some 300 km of bicycle paths have been built (to 2002).

5   There is a 20 per cent surcharge on all petrol sold in the city, and half of it is used to help finance the TransMilenio infrastructure extensions (US $40 million per annum).

Source: Peñalosa (2003).

whether it is Enrique Peñalosa in Bogotá, Ken Livingstone in London or Pasqual Maragall in Barcelona.

10.5   Conclusions

It does seem that there is a great opportunity for the poorer countries to become much more efficient in their use of transport through the rapid adoption of best practice in terms of appropriate technology and innovative ideas. The success of both Bogotá and Curitiba has been based on simple low-cost solutions that required both vision and political leadership. This requirement is crucially important, as is the necessity for the institutional capacity for change, the legal framework for enforcement, and the financial resources for implementation. Underlying this is the quality of the politicians and their ability and will to bring about a sustainable city vision.

China provides the best example of this challenge, as it is rapidly emerging as a major new economy with growth rates of 12–15 per cent per annum and the consequent problems of lack of capacity within the transport system. It has a fundamental choice to make, namely whether to follow the same path of road construction and car ownership, with the ensuring social and spatial problems of equity and the environmental consequences, or whether to accept the challenge of pioneering a new sustainable development future that does not entail high levels of private ownership of vehicles, but the public provision of transport (Fact Box 10.9). The signs are not promising as Shanghai has banned bicycles from much of its main roads and it has also invested in a hugely expensive maglev connection between Pudong airport and the city.

These huge challenges will determine whether sustainable urban development can ever be a reality, and whether lessons can be learned from one situation and applied elsewhere. One part of the world that seems to be developing new ways of approaching the old problems of public transport in cities is South America, where a new transport paradigm is emerging. Central to this thinking is the busway, a surface metro system that utilizes exclusive rights of way to move large numbers of people, swiftly, efficiently and cost effectively (Wright, 2001). The characteristics of these systems are their low costs, high levels of flexibility and speed, so that people choose to use them in

Fact Box 10.9   The challenge for China

In 2015, there are expected to be 70 million motorcycles, 30 million lorries and 100 million cars in China. At present, transport accounts for 15–20 per cent of the annual total of 6 billion tonnes of carbon emissions. By 2030, there will be 828 million city dwellers in China, principally in Beijing, Shanghai, Guangzhou, Shenzhen, Shenyang, Xiamen, Xi'an and Quinghuangdao.

Overall, the contribution from urban transport to environmental pollution in Chinese cities is estimated to be between 30–50 per cent (Qiu *et al.*, 1996). Individual city levels are much higher.

Percentages		CO	HC	NO_x
Beijing	2000	76.8	78.3	40.0
Shanghai	2000	83.0	96.0	56.0
Guangzhou	2000	83.8	50.0	45.0
Shenyang	1990	27–38	–	45-53

Shanghai has a population of over 20 million, of which about 13.5 million are considered permanent residents – the remainder are migrant workers from the surrounding region. The average annual income is £2900, some nine times the Chinese average – 2 per cent of the population are producing 5 per cent of GDP and attracting 10 per cent of foreign investment. About 20 per cent of the local GDP is in car-related businesses, with major employment implications and high levels of consumer expenditure on cars.

The current Shanghai Master Plan (2000–2005) will reduce density in the city centre, by creating new urban centres and the development of 9 new towns in the periphery. This decentralization will lead to longer trip distances and higher levels of motorized travel. The choice for the Shanghai government is to follow the market approach and accommodate the car with further extensive road construction and decentralization, or to limit the growth in car ownership and use, and invest in public transport and local accessibility (Qi Dong, 2003).

preference to other forms of motorized transport. Innovation also extends to the design of the bus stations (and stops), simplified ticketing systems, service information, the overall quality of the service, and the appearance of the bus itself.

Replogle (1991, p. 7) has commented

> Major changes are needed in priorities for transportation policy in the Third World if development is to meet human needs rather than benefit only the current elite groups. The costs of failing to redirect transport policies today will be paid in the decades to come through a sharply reduced quality of life in the world. As cities grow, one can anticipate increased conflict between the mobile elite and the mobility restricted poor, and reduced capacity to solve the problems of capital shortages, unpayable debt burdens, toxic air pollution, and global climate change.

There seem to be several paradoxes evident when sustainable transport is discussed within the context of developing countries:

1   There is the World Bank paradox, which argues that urban transport can contribute to poverty reduction, but often it does not.

2   There is the paradox that conventional thinking (Section 10.3) still seems to promote rail-based systems where demand levels are high, even though the inflexibility, the capital costs, and the high fares charged would all argue against such investments.

3   There is the paradox or conundrum (Schipper, 2001) that transport, which makes cities viable, is also threatening their viability. As transport allows cities to expand outwards, that expansion also threatens to break the city.

There is a deep symbiosis between city and transport, with each of them affecting the other, and it is in the rapidly growing cities in developing countries that these tensions are most apparent. The choice is clear, namely that there are many innovations in terms of restraint on the use of the car, effective pricing policies, designation of priority users and uses of scarce urban space, the substitution of travel by teleactivities, and a range of exiting new modes of transport. But equally, there is a strong desire to produce and sell cars to new consumer markets and to provide employment in those same cities. The economic imperative has never been greater, but nor have the social and environmental consequences. The balance between the three main pillars of sustainable development and transport has never been more severely tested.

Note

1   Antanas Mockus is not a close political ally of Enrique Peñalosa, but a fierce competitor. They do, however, have similar views about urban redevelopment and transport. Enrique Peñalosa may run for President in 2006, and so may not be available for the Bogotá mayoral election in 2005.

Chapter 11

Visions for the future

11.1 Introduction

Transport planners need to think more imaginatively about the future, rather than being content with current trends just continuing much as they are at present. There are three main reasons why this current paradigm, based on trend extrapolation with minor modifications, should be revisited.

The first is that the external world is changing and that analysis needs to embrace the exciting new challenges that are being presented. Included here is the globalization process with international networks, outsourcing, long supply chains, and the 24-hour society. There is also the switch from a work-based society to one that has more money to spend on leisure activities. Work and business-related activities account for under 20 per cent of all activities (but 29 per cent of travel distance – 2002), yet most analysis still concentrates on these two activities. Then there is the potential that new Information and Communications Technologies (ICT) offer for many transport-related activities including production, living and working (Chapter 9 and Banister and Stead, 2004). We are now in the midst of a new technological revolution, and its impacts are likely to be just as profound as the agricultural and industrial revolutions in changing society and cities, and the ways in which we actually do things.

Secondly, there are the issues relating to the future of the planet and the hugely important concern over sustainable development. Although the science is not clear, there is sufficient evidence available to support the precautionary principle, namely to take action now to reduce the potential effects of global warming through effective management of the use of carbon-based energy and to facilitate the switch to hydrogen. In addition there are the health effects, related to carbon and other emissions at the local level, that also need to be addressed so that the impacts of pollution related illnesses can be reduced. This is the central theme of the book, and much of the first five chapters have outlined the nature and scale of change required to achieve sustainable development.

Thirdly, society is becoming increasingly urbanized. If we are concerned about sustainable development, then it is in the cities and large towns that people must locate as it is here that the full range of jobs, services and facilities can be provided for all people. In the UK, about 90 per cent of the population are classified as urban[1] (EC, 2003), and it is in these urban areas that the principles of sustainable development must be established (Chapters 6 and 10).

Taken together, these three fundamental changes in society are at the heart of sustainable development, as they address the economic, environmental and social dimensions of that concept. They also provide researchers and others with a unique opportunity to challenge existing conventional wisdom based on trend following analysis, with a more radical trend breaking future.

11.2 Visioning and backcasting

Visioning about the future encourages researchers to develop Images of the desirable city some 20 to 30 years ahead. If the characteristics of those cities can be determined in terms of its economic, environmental and social roles, we can think about how to get from where we are now to where we might want to be in the future – this is the essence of backcasting. Within the city context, such a visioning approach starts with a range of desirable futures, which could be technologically based, or lifestyle based, or a combination of both, and then determine the role that transport should play in moving towards that vision. The important point here, not often acknowledged in much transport analysis, is that travel is a product of changes in existing patterns of demand and the travel generated by new activities. Much of the growth in travel is caused by decisions taken outside the transport arena, yet it is often the transport system that has to accommodate to these changes. Simple examples would include location decisions affecting new housing, retailing and leisure activities, but more fundamental are decisions concerning education and health policy with concentration and closure, the Common Agricultural Policy with its promotion of larger holdings and subsidies, and the globalization process with its longer supply chains.

Visioning and backcasting is one form of scenario building, which itself has a history going back some 50 years (Table 11.1).

Two kinds of scenarios can be distinguished (Banister *et al.*, 2000):

- Projective scenarios. These are concerned about probable futures and are based on predictions, including extrapolation, forecasts and use of Delphi groups. They are positive in nature and use quantitative modelling approaches.

- Prospective scenarios. These are concerned about possible or preferable futures. There are two types: the exploratory scenarios are concerned with eventualities and scenario planning, using some quantitative

Table 11.1   A brief history of scenario use in transport and energy research

Originally developed in the US by the Rand Corporation in the 1950s to study how nuclear wars could start.
Used by major oil companies (e.g. Shell) in the 1970s to anticipate the impacts of oil shortages; they needed to be able to predict the unpredictable.
Projective scenarios have been extensively used in energy and transport forecasting by the OECD and other international agencies.
Prospective scenarios were used in the 1970s in Sweden to investigate alternative energy futures, including the switch away from the nuclear option.
In transport, several applications of backcasting have taken place in the Netherlands (1990s) in both the passenger and freight sectors, and in the national Sustainable Economic Development Study.
The 1990s also saw longer term use of backcasting in Sweden for sustainable transport to 2040, in the EU to assess the Common Transport Policy to 2020, and the OECD EST project to assess the potential for reductions of over 80% in non-renewable energy consumption to 2030.

Source: Based on Geurs and Van Wee (2004).

and modelling approaches; the anticipatory scenarios using visioning approaches towards common or desirable futures, and they are more normative in approach and make greater use of qualitative and participatory methods.

The term backcasting was introduced by Robinson (1982) to analyse future (energy) options in terms of how desirable futures could be attained. It is explicitly normative in its approach, working backwards from the desired end point to the present to determine which package of policy measures could be used to reach that vision (Table 11.2 and Dreborg, 1996). In the remaining parts of this Chapter, the process of backcasting is outlined together with an example of its application within the urban context. It is then interpreted within the OECD and non-OECD city context.

11.3   The scenario building process outlined

When considering transport futures, it must be argued that the current trends are unsustainable and that the driving forces for the scenarios should be strongly environmental to establish whether it is possible to maintain economic growth with less transport. Three separate stages to the scenario building process can be identified (Figure 11.1).

1   Tough yet achievable targets for sustainable transport have been

Table 11.2   Differences between forecasting and backcasting studies

	Forecasting	Backcasting
1 Philosophical view	Context of justification Causality and determinism	Context of discovery Causality and intentions
2 Perspective	Dominant trends Likely futures Possible marginal adjustments How to adapt to trends	Societal problem in need of a solution Desirable futures Scope of human choice Strategic decisions Retain freedom of action
3 Approach	Extrapolate trends into the future Sensitivity analysis	Define interesting futures Analyse consequences and conditions for these futures to materialize
4 Methods and techniques	Various econometric models Mathematical algorithms	Partial and conditional extrapolations Normative models, system dynamics models, Delphi methods, expert judgement

Source: Geurs and Van Wee (2004) and adapted from Dreborg (1996)

developed and discussed with experts from the EU and UK government. They cover the three basic elements of sustainable transport (Table 11.3).

2   Visions of the sustainable city are then developed to meet the targets set (Figure 11.1). The statements under each of the three Images concentrate on four main issues: the general scale of change required; the impact on the city; the increasing role that technology[2] should play; and the broader organizational and financial instruments that can be used. The focus is primarily at the urban scale and concentrates on the passenger

Table 11.3   Targets for sustainable transport

Environmental targets:
25 per cent reduction of CO_2 emissions from 2000–2025;
80 per cent reduction of NO_x emissions from 2000–2025;
no degradation of green or protected spaces in cities;
minor (<2 per cent) increase of net infrastructure surface in cities.

Distributional and equity targets:
improve proximity and accessibility within cities and between cities, including the substitution of physical accessibility by telecommunications;
improve the quality of life in cities for all residents.

Economic targets:
full cost coverage (including external costs) of transport under market or equivalent conditions;
reduce public subsidies to all forms of transport to zero. Subsidy only permitted where there are clearly defined social equity objectives.

sector, but many of the measures would apply equally to the freight sector.

3   Policy packages (and paths) are then constructed from the Images back to the present day – this is the essence of the backcasting methodology used here (Dreborg, 1996). The intention here is to explore the various options available and to establish whether there are policy packages that can be applied to achieve the targets and Images set. These alternatives are then discussed with experts to establish the problems with implementation and the necessary conditions for successful action. Policy packages and paths are not developed for the Business as Usual Image as this does not meet the targets for sustainable transport.

It should be made clear that this approach to scenario building covers all three stages – targets, Images and policy packages/paths – together they form the scenarios. This approach differs from that of developing the drivers of change and then visualizing the future. Here, clear targets are set as the

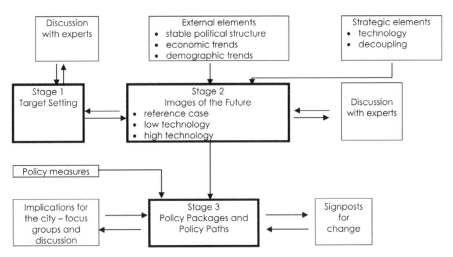

Notes: The scenario building process consists of three stages, the setting of targets for sustainable transport, the development of Images of the future, and the means by which we can move from now to the future Images (2025) through the development of policy packages and paths.

External elements are taken as given and are common to all scenarios

The Images of the Future can be driven by technology in the generic sense (given in note 2 at the end of the chapter), social and economic factors or a combination of these as has been used here – see Tables 11.5 and 11.6.

Figure 11.1 The scenario building process

framework within which the Images of the future can be developed. But more importantly, the alternative paths are thought through in terms of how we can move from the present (now) to the future (2025) and meet the constraints set. This is not prescriptive, but a creative process by which a range of different policy packages can be combined to achieve targets set, and these have been discussed through expert workshops and focus groups.

11.4   Discussion of the visions within cities in OECD countries

The problems of transport and sustainable development have been clearly outlined, together with the key relationships between transport and urban form. The key assumption here is that sustainable living must be based on the city, as high levels of accessibility and proximity can be maintained only within urban areas. This means that people should be living in settlements that are of a sufficient size (over 50,000) so that the full range of facilities can be provided within walking, cycling or public transport distance (less than 5 km). These settlements should be at a medium density (at least 40 persons per hectare), have mixed land uses and high levels of accessibility to the public transport network (for inter-urban travel). It also means that these areas have to provide a high-quality environment within which people wish to live. This includes access to open space, a safe and secure environment, peace and quiet, a wide-range of social and recreational opportunities, as well as the other benefits of urban living. Most services and facilities can be provided locally, but the most difficult to provide is local employment. Even here, in the timescale given, services and technology-based employment can be dispersed to where people live.

These constraints concern the framework within which transport policy options can be placed. Most of them require a strong planning system at the city and regional levels that will direct development to achieve larger, high density, mixed use and accessible cities. Although the planning system is not immediate in its effect, in the medium term it is one of the most important determinants of travel patterns. As a general rule, the shorter the journey, the greater the probability that it will be walk, cycle or public transport based. The planning system should be seeking to ensure proximity between where people live and the services, jobs and facilities that they may wish to access (Table 11.4).

A second constraint is the role that technology (in its widest sense) will have on travel demand. There has been much debate over the potential for substitution of travel through telecommuting, teleconferencing, teleshopping, telebusiness and other forms of teleactivities (Chapter 9; Salomon and Mokhtarian, 1997; NERA, 1997). It is clear that the scale and the nature of change induced by technology will be substantial and complex, with

Table 11.4   Context and constraints

Context	
Transport technology:	• eco-car in mass production by 2010–2015; to include hybrid vehicles • measures to promote rapid replacement of existing vehicle fleet • research funding increased substantially from EU and other sources • industrial support for new energy and environmentally efficient technology • tax incentives to buy eco-cars and scrap old vehicles
Transport demand:	• traffic still increasing as car ownership rises • capacity limited so congestion increases • measures required for demand management • allocation of road space to improve accessibility and proximity
Public, people and transport:	• investment in new buses, better information and ticketing – reinvent the bus • improve the quality of the infrastructure for people and cyclists • integration of all forms of public transport • quality interchanges and spaces in cities
Constraints	
Physical:	• size > 50,000 • density > 40 persons/hectare • mixed land use • proximity to public transport interchanges and corridors
Quality:	• open space • safe and secure environment • peace and quiet • social and recreational opportunities • full range of services and facilities

adaptations to existing patterns of activity. It will not affect all people in the same way, but will provide greater choice and flexibility to many 'computer literate' people. In the visions being put forward here, it is assumed that technology will have an impact, but more at the margins than fundamentally changing the demand for travel in cities. The two visions being presented here will place a different emphasis on the role that technology plays (Table 11.6).

Table 11.5 attempts to summarize in broad terms the changes necessary to achieve the three sets of targets relating to environment, equity and efficiency. There is a difference of emphasis between the two visions, with one having slightly lower ambitions related to the impact of technology and the other placing a greater reliance on technology to reduce travel. In both visions, the continuing development of new technology in transport and the need to reduce travel is crucial to the target achievement. Similarly, actions relating to planning and development decisions are important in supporting those policy actions in the transport sector.

From these visions, there are two different paths, which can be followed,

Table 11.5 Visions of the sustainable city 2025

Targets (2000–2025)	High quality urban living (low technology)	High quality urban living (high technology)
Environmental: Reduce CO_2 emissions by 25 per cent Reduce NO_x emissions by 80 per cent Limited road building	*General:* Total mobility the same as 2000, but lower than reference case (64 per cent RC) Some electric and hybrid vehicles, but technological innovation moderate – 20 per cent of market electric Lower car ownership Niche vehicles, car rental, smart card technology Public transport competitive in price, but not fast – information on home computers, internet etc. Car use for commuting reduced, but increased for leisure	*General:* Total mobility more than 2000, but lower than reference case (80 per cent RC) Methanol and hydrogen the principle alternative fuels – 20 per cent of all fuel, particularly lorries and buses Car ownership increases moderately Battery cars are niche vehicles, but not many sold Public transport commercially organized – information on routes and times through personal communicators Telecommuting widespread
Equity and distribution: Improve proximity and accessibility in cities Improve quality of life in cities for all residents	*Impact on city:* Concentration of development in cities and corridors – invest in cycleways and footways Telecottages and teleshopping Reductions in work and shop travel Shift to public transport and bike – higher occupancies Less space for cars – limited parking Lower speed limits – priority to public transport	*Impact on city:* Urban decentralization continues, but at a slower rate Telecottages and teleshopping, together with high use of teleconferences telebusiness and other teleactivities Local multimedia centres Reductions in travel for all purposes Some shift to public transport Space still allocated to the car Lower speed limits and some priority for public transport
Efficiency: Full internalization of all costs Reduce subsidies to all forms of transport to zero	*Technology:* Cars 15–20 per cent lighter Feebates related to weight and efficiency Diesel vehicles phased out due to emissions problems Limited use of cars in cities – as public transport is so good – increase prices and controls on parking City bus and lorry are hybrid drives with gas turbine and Otto engines *Organization, investment and finance:* Market incentives – limited city road pricing Public transport publicly owned, but independent of government Limited investment in urban rail systems, most in bus priority	*Technology:* Cars 25 per cent lighter Common technical standards agreed internationally Diesel fuel use reduced in all cities All purpose cars – hybrid electric with gas turbines, fuel cell power Fuel cells introduced in buses and lorries *Organization, investment and finance:* Strong market incentives – road pricing on all roads Private sector runs all transport – roads privately managed High speed rail investment in corridors – city development at stations

Note: The Reference Case (RC) is set out in Annex 1.
Source: Based on Banister *et al.* (2000) .

with many different combinations between them. In all cases, the city is seen as being instrumental in achieving sustainable development and the principal goal is to achieve a high quality of urban living.

1 The low technology alternative works from the 'bottom up' with a trend towards more 'local lifestyles' and green values among the general public. People increasingly take responsibility for the common good and attitudes towards collective actions are positive, especially at the local and regional levels:

* People are pushing the politicians to adopt stricter environmental regulations and standards, especially at the local level (urban areas). At the global level no agreement on harmonizing standards is achieved.

* People are willing to pay for greener products as well as for locally produced goods – there are changing patterns of demand.

* Settlement patterns and location of workplace and service functions are also affected. Many urban sub-centres have developed to a higher degree of self-sufficiency and city centres are being re-urbanized.

* There is an increased acceptability for urban public transport, bicycles, and electric or hybrid urban cars.

Production is more local and mainly serves local markets, but it is based on licences and the know-how of the big international firms and networks (glocal production). There is also an increasing share for the service sector, with traditional manufacturing industry showing a declining share of total production. GDP grows at a moderate pace, but green GDP develops faster. Freight transport volumes have actually levelled off.

A tax base reform (in line with a dematerialization strategy) has taken place in the OECD countries, shifting taxation from labour to the use of natural resources and energy, with the aim to stimulate conservation of resources. This tax reform combined with green demand has made producing firms reduce their use of energy, materials and hazardous substances.

General approach to transport policy. The shift in values and lifestyles has led to a higher acceptability for changes in residential and travel patterns, providing an opportunity to bring the growth of transport volumes under control. Therefore the prime political strategy *vis à vis* the environmental goal, is to promote a decoupling of transport growth from GDP growth (Chapter 3). As mentioned above, the shift in demand has in itself led to a considerable degree of decoupling regarding freight. This is complemented by policy measures intended to reduce structurally enforced travel, such as commuting to work and service trips. Here, urban land-use planning and measures to facilitate telecommuting are important.

A *policy for cleaner transport* (pertains to both personal travel and freight) is important:

* measures to promote a *shift in modal split* towards a higher share for cleaner modes (e.g. more public transport, a higher share for freight by rail etc.);
* measures intended to make each mode cleaner, by *spread of cleaner technologies*;
* measures to increase load factors.

Measures affecting modal choice form an important part of the general policy. Cleaner technologies are supported by R&D funding, and niche markets for the introduction of new vehicles, and systems such as car pooling with specialized vehicles are all created. National and international agencies have an important role in coordinating regional and national policies and in harmonizing targets and standards in all OECD countries.

To sum up, the main elements of the transport policy are:

* measures intended to reduce structurally enforced travel, such as land-use planning, the promotion of telecommuting etc. (*decoupling*);
* measures such as standards and pricing, intended to achieve a shift from private cars and lorries to public transport and freight by train and ship (*modal shifts*);
* investment in high quality public transport and in facilities for cyclists and pedestrians so that a real choice is provided (*modal shifts*);
* funding of R&D and promotion of market uptake, e.g. by creation of niche markets for novel systems (*cleaner technologies*);
* measures to ensure that disadvantaged people have access to local facilities and the transport network (*local equity*).

2 The high technology alternative works from the 'top down' with a certain degree of 'green consciousness' and an acceptance of policy measures intended to mitigate the environmental problems related to transport. However, these issues are not pushed by a broad opinion among the public. Rather, it is the politicians that are at the forefront, trying to find solutions at the national and global levels. Politicians are relatively successful in forming opinions and there is an understanding that transport must in principle pay its full costs. But most people are not inclined to accept a major change of travel behaviour. Also, there is some green demand, but of a modest size.

The international lifestyle has gained strength. Many people prioritize the broader international output to the narrow local assortment. Also, there is a trend towards segmentation of society into different lifestyles that go across the world. Many enterprises have specialized on a specific segment of customers and provide their specific brand across the world. An early sign of this trend was in the 1990s when Swatch and Mercedes exploited Swatch's knowledge of a certain market segment to launch the A-class car.

Production is increasingly characterized by 'flexible specialization', and economic development is generally dynamic with a relatively high average GDP growth. Some regions will tend to lag behind. Despite a trend towards dematerialization, transport volumes continue to grow due to increasing distances. A high degree of accord has developed in the relations between the OECD countries as regards international regulations and standards in order to cope with global environmental problems.

General approach to transport policy. The widespread environmental consciousness among leading politicians on the world stage, makes it possible to reach agreements on international standards and norms for cleaner vehicles, reductions of CO_2 emissions and similar levels of taxation of externalities, at least in the OECD area. The accord among world leading politicians motivates the general public and makes it possible to gain popular support for such measures. However, as mentioned above, people will not accept measures that interfere with their habitual ways of living, such as using private cars and living in sparse residential areas.

Consequently, the prime policy regarding the environmental goal in Europe is to *make transport cleaner*. Although some measures are directed towards *raising the share of cleaner modes* (per person-km), the emphasis is on promoting the *development and introduction of cleaner technologies and fuels*. As people adhere to the private car, much of R&D is directed towards improving the technology of the conventional all-purpose car. However, more far-sighted policies exist and are promoted, such as the creation of niche markets for fuel cell vehicles (the eco-car). This is achieved by experiments with environmental zones. As can be seen, there is far less of a push for modal shift, and a greater emphasis on continuing to depend on the (cleaner) car.

Policies to reduce transport intensity and volumes (*decoupling*) are also employed, but mainly by the use of pricing. This strategy has led to a somewhat more uneven distribution of accessibility, which may be one of the major obstacles for realizing this vision.

To sum up, the main elements of the transport policy are:

- international agreements on CO_2 emissions and other regulations (*contraction and convergence*);
- internalizing externalities of transport by means of taxation and feebates. All modes should pay their full costs – road pricing in cities (*pricing*);

- funding of R&D for cleaner technologies (*cleaner technologies*);
- promotion of new markets by the creation of niche status for novel systems (*innovation*);
- operation of transport systems is largely privatized, but funding of new infrastructure is mainly public (*organizational change*).

Within each of these two alternatives it is then possible to describe in detail the range of policy actions necessary to achieve the visions set out here (Table 11.6). It should be noted these policy actions are not prescriptive, but give an indication of the scale and nature of change required.

Table11. 6   Policy actions to 2025

	Vision 1	*Vision 2*
Technology		
Efficiency	Increase real fuel prices by 9% pa	Increase real fuel prices by 6% pa
	Insurance and tax related to efficiency of vehicles and charged on fuel	
	Targets to industry to achieve 19km per litre for all new vehicles	
	Research into fuel cells funded by the EU and industry	
	Targets to industry to produce commercial fuel cell vehicle by 2005	
Weight	*Research on new lighter materials for vehicles*	
Fuel	*Raise diesel fuel prices by 50% in real terms over 5 years*	
	Agreement to phase out diesel in cities	
	Hybrid diesel vehicles for city (electric) and non-city (diesel) use	
	No new car tax on electric vehicles	
Scrapping	*Scrap non-catalytic vehicles – completed by 2005*	
	Research on new add on technology – next generation in use by 2005	
Demand Management		
Financial	New car tax levied at 10% of total cost increasing to 50% by 2025	Road pricing introduced in all cities – to double the real cost of using the car in the city
	Parking charges on all non-residential parking spaces – €1000 pa rising to €2000 pa in 2025	
	Company car benefits eliminated by 2005	
	Elimination of most subsidy to public transport by 2005	
Regulation	*All main routes into the city with HOV lanes*	
	Clear zones and no cars in city	Clear zones, but some clean car centre access to city centre
	Reallocation of road space to public transport and walk/bike	Remote sensing of emissions and efficiency tests with fines
	Bus and cycle networks	Limited bus and cycle networks
	Speed limits – 20km/hr	Speed limits – 30 km/hr
	Extensive traffic calming and green spaces created	Some traffic calming

continued on page 223

continued from page 222

Company transport plans - produced by all shops, employers, schools, hospitals, to reduce use of the car – clear targets for reductions 10% by 2005, 25% by 2025

Concentration of new development – mixed uses and decentralised concentration	Less control over development – some peripheral development, and lower city densities

Technology

High quality real time information available on all public transport in home, local centres and through communicators – better quality public transport in terms of service frequency, ticketing, interchange, facilities on board – priority for pedestrians and cyclists in towns, at interchanges, in shopping areas, with safe and secure parking for bicycles.

Investment in local telecentres, videoconferencing facilities	All banking and other services remote
Smartcards available for all travel transactions	Interactive multimedia for con- erences and distance learning

Lifestyles and Attitudes

Local schemes for car sharing	Personal communicators to
Community based car rental schemes	journey match and link activities
All cities to have park/bike and ride schemes	Market for public transport
Access to cities limited to those with clean vehicles and high occupancy levels	Roads managed privately
Local communities involved in monitoring traffic and pollution levels	

The role of technology in each vision is important. In the longer term, the eco-car will be built, primarily for use in urban areas. Although resources (mainly renewable and recyclable) will still be needed to construct the vehicle, it would be powered by hydrogen fuel cells. This car will probably be available within 10 years, but will not have had a major impact on the total stock of vehicles for a further 10 to 15 years given the current turnover levels. This means that the eco-car would only be in standard use by the end of our time period (2025), but even here there are increasing doubts over whether this time horizon can be achieved (Romm, 2004). One set of policy actions must be to facilitate the research and development of the eco-car and to give clear signals to the motor manufacturing industry to invest in the small city based vehicle:

- to give clear objectives for emissions standards to be achieved by industry over time (EU and government role);
- to increase research and development budgets on the eco-car and associated technologies (EU role);
- to develop the necessary supporting infrastructure so that it can be used when available (industry role);

- to provide tax incentives for companies to invest in the appropriate technology and to take it to the production stage (government role);
- to provide tax disincentives for purchasing large inefficient vehicles for city use (government role);
- to phase out all forms of subsidy to the private car (government role);
- at a later stage to have a scrappage programme to encourage people to purchase the eco-car (industry and local role).

The purpose of these actions will be to speed up the process of innovation, and to give clear signals to industry and people that the eco-car is the replacement technology for the current car stock.

Even if the 'technological solution' is promoted, there still remains the historic problem of transport growth (congestion) and the 'gap' between now (2005) and when the eco-car is in common use (2020–2025). Even then, we may have resolved only part of the environmental issues as the eco-car and the supporting infrastructure will still use non-renewable resources. The problem of traffic congestion and space still remain.

This means that in cities innovative forms of public transport must play a key role. Much of the discussion is concerned with the development of the eco-car and the use of technology in manufacturing, control and information processes. Many of these technologies also apply to public transport, but no radically new form of urban public transport is expected over the next 20 years. Even the high-speed rail technology and the advanced urban transit systems (e.g. Lille VAL system) are really only developments of existing technologies. Magnetic levitation offers a new technology, but it is only suitable for long distance travel and competes directly with air. The main technologies available relate more to generic factors such as control and information systems as they relate to public transport (Table 11.7), and these will be in common use by 2025.

Table 11.7 New technologies and public transport

Urban public transport	Rail
Satellite tracking/GPS	Tilting and improved suspension systems
High-frequency, short distance radio	Transmission-based train control
Spread spectrum communications	Radio signalling
Stored value smart tickets	Widespread use of sensors in automatic monitoring
Fuel cells	and analysis
LPG/CNG fuels	Use of composite and lightweight materials in both
Guided bus automation	structures and vehicles
Tracked and cable-suspended people	Application of modular design to signals, controls
movers	and buildings
Hybrid-powered buses and trams	Automatic train protection
	Satellite tracking

Source: Office of Science and Technology (1998).

11.5   The north-south divide on perceptions of sustainable development

Substantial differences exist between the cities of the North and those of the South. The view from the North is that all cities have to work together to reduce the use of non-renewable resources, improve environmental quality, and create liveable cities. Most governments in the North still see economic growth as the main means to reduce unemployment and increase incomes, which is a contradiction to the more broad-based interpretation given by Brundtland (WCED, 1987) with equal weighting being allocated to the environmental and equity objectives. Even Brundtland is ambiguous on this point as greater integration is called for, but a five-fold increase in global production is also anticipated.

The view from the South is that lack of progress in the North inhibits action in the South. It is here that three-quarters of the World population lives, together with a growing share of the economic activity, consumption, energy use, waste generation and pollution. But the contribution of the South cities to global environmental degradation is still far less than that of the North cities, and they do not have the same levels of historic contributions. Action must come from the North both in terms of good practice and in supporting the achievement of sustainable development goals in the South (Satterthwaite, 1997).

Many of the cities of the North developed settlement patterns and transport systems that were based on cheap oil and high levels of economic growth. This makes change both difficult and costly. The cities of the South have developed institutional and regulatory frameworks, which encourage energy conservation, minimize the need for heating and cooling in buildings, and settlement patterns that are not car dependent.

Sustainable development is not just about the improvement of environmental quality within cities, but also about reducing the transfer of environmental costs to other people, to other locations or ecosystems, and to future generations. These important additional factors suggest that the limits of city boundaries are often drawn too tightly, and that regional structures for governance are necessary so that the wider spatial implications can be assessed, and the impacts on other sectors controlled. Action and monitoring of outcomes have to be carried out over time, with some means for future indemnity.

The notion of sustainable development, particularly from the cities of the South, cannot be drawn solely in terms of ecological and intergenerational responsibilities. Satterthwaite (1997) identifies five components of sustainable development, three of which relate to immediate human needs and are of instrumental importance to the cities of the South (components 1–3):

1   controlling infections and parasitic diseases and the health burden they place on urban populations;

2   reducing chemical and physical hazards within the home, the workplace and wider city. World-wide, more than 1.5 billion urban dwellers are exposed to levels of ambient air pollution that are above the recommended maximum levels and an estimated 400,000 additional deaths each year are attributable to this pollution (WHO, 1997);

3   achieving a high quality urban environment for all urban inhabitants;

4   minimizing the transfer of environmental costs to the inhabitants and ecosystems surrounding the city;

5   ensuring progress towards 'sustainable consumption', including reductions in the transport intensity of goods and services.

The last two components focus on ecological sustainability, examining the longer-term goals and the intergenerational aspects. The question left unanswered is the role that the different actors must take to ensure progress towards these five objectives. Although international leadership and responsibility is crucial, particularly from the cities and nations of the North, most real change must come locally. The uniqueness of place and space make it necessary to use local resources, knowledge, skills and commitment to achieve sustainable development objectives, with a more detailed regional and national framework that sets the broader agenda. There is no clear way forward as the lead needs to come from the cities of the North. Yet the consumption patterns of these cities are locked into high levels of resource use by the physical infrastructure over which there is little control – energy, housing, transport and waste collection systems. Improved environmental performance is not achieved by focusing on sustainable cities, but on how consumers, businesses and governments can contribute to sustainable development.

One topical example is road safety, which was taken as the WHO theme for 2004. Road traffic injuries are a major, but neglected, public health challenge that account for nearly 1.2 million deaths globally, and some 50 million injuries. These injuries make up 2.1 per cent of the global mortality rate and 2.6 per cent of all disability-adjusted life years lost (Peden *et al.*, 2004). But this high level of deaths and injuries is not distributed evenly, as 85 per cent of deaths and 90 per cent of the annual disability adjusted life years lost from road accidents come from low- and middle-income countries. The levels of deaths and injuries are likely to continue to rise in these countries, whilst in the high-income countries they will fall by 30 per cent to 2020. This means that road accidents are predicted to be the third leading contributor to the global burden of disease, ahead of other health problems such as malaria, tuberculosis and HIV/AIDS.

11.6 Discussion of the visions within cities in non-OECD countries

The problem facing cities in non-OECD (South) countries are very different to those in the OECD (North) countries. In fact, it could be argued that they are at opposite ends of the spectrum as they are growing rapidly as mega agglomerations (over 5 per cent per annum), the labour markets are also expanding, levels of car ownership and income levels are higher than those found outside the city, and much travel is still based on the public transport system. For each of these characteristics, the cities of the North have very different trends. The dynamic of city development is fundamental to our understanding of urban sustainability and of the appropriate actions to take (Hall, 1997). It is in these new emerging cities that real growth in traffic and transport related pollution is taking place, but the total levels of emissions are still far lower than those found in the OECD cities. Consequently, the visions of the sustainable city 2025 must be different and the paths to be followed will also be fundamentally different.

Not all non-OECD cities are at the same levels of development, so there is considerable variation within cities. This variation is probably greater than that of the OECD cities. The views of sustainable development from the non-OECD cities also differ very substantially to those of the OECD cities. In the rapidly emerging cities the key concerns relate more to the basic concerns of economic development, a fair distribution of wealth (poverty reduction), and access to basic infrastructure (UNDP, 1997). This is closely related to immediate human needs (Satterthwaite, 1997), whilst the concerns in the OECD cities are related to the environmental quality within cities. Within all cities, the availability of clean water (and sewerage) and clean air should be seen as a right, but in reality there are huge variations as the poor are less likely to have such access. In terms of transport, many of the major cities in developing countries (Chapter 10) are now promoting sustainable development far more actively than many of the major cities in developed countries.

Even when examining the transport dimension, there are clear differences. At given levels of income, there is a greater propensity for individuals to purchase cars in the non-OECD cities than in the OECD cities. In non-OECD cities, the amount of space available for roads (7–11 per cent) is less than that in the OECD cities (20–25 per cent). So for given levels of car ownership, there are substantially higher levels of congestion (World Bank, 1996). Given the different context of the non-OECD cities, there are two basic choices that can be made. In an ideal sense, they should be treated no differently to the cities of the OECD, so the two visions (Table 11.5) would apply equally to all cities in the world.

1   The ideal vision is unrealistic as the starting point is not the same, the

levels of traffic, congestion and pollution are different, and the potential
for the range of measures and the role of technology would also vary.
Yet this must be the ultimate goal as more of the cities of the non-
OECD countries (e.g. Singapore, Hong Kong, Taipei and Seoul) adopt
the characteristics of those in the OECD countries. These cities in the
'Tiger Economies' of the East have flipped from being developing cities
to being developed cities and should be treated in a similar way. The
process of transition is crucial to the long-term convergence on the ideal
vision for all world cities (Chapter 2.5.4).

2   The realistic vision for the non-OECD cities is different. There is limited
road space, high levels of in-migration, increases in car ownership
levels of 10–15 per cent per annum, and few possibilities for major
infrastructure investment. The basic question is whether these cities have
to follow the same path as those in the OECD countries (Tables 11.5
and 11.6), or whether they can (or should) follow a different path. It is
here that innovative forms of public transport have a major role to play
(Chapter 10).

There are four main elements to the alternative path for non-OECD
cities:

1   Physical measures. As road space is limited, it is appropriate to establish
bus networks to make the best use of existing roadspace. These networks
would be available to paratransit, motorcycles (and their derivatives) and
bicycles. The extensive use of green modes (including rickshaws) needs
to be maintained and encouraged. There would be access restrictions
in the city centre and extensive modal interchanges at peripheral sites
to encourage park and ride, bike and ride, and transfer from local rail
to the bus network. Investment would take place in maintenance and
upgrading of existing infrastructure, in exploring the full potential for
non-motorized transport and in the possibility of low speed limits to
enhance quality of life. As well as having substantial congestion benefits,
the levels of traffic-induced pollution would be reduced.

2   Technology. The role that technology plays in the non-OECD cities is
different as the emphasis should be on maintaining the traffic priority
system (traffic management) and communications so that travellers are
fully aware of the options available to them. Cheap communications
technology allows greater efficiency in movement and the possibility
for substitution of travel. The most up-to-date technology, including
the eco-car should be made available to the non-OECD countries so
that the levels of resource use and pollution are reduced. The question
of appropriate technology is important, but the fuel cell car is basically

a simple technology once an efficient (commercial) method has been developed for generating power from hydrogen, together with the means to store it. The main problem is likely to be the cost of the eco-car, as innovations have to recoup development costs, so that initially the new vehicle will be expensive to buy unless it is subsidized by the more polluting vehicles. However, experience has not been positive, as technology transfer has not taken place. Of particular importance is the transfer of appropriate technology – this needs to be discussed within the global arena.

3   Pricing. Price elasticities are much higher in the non-OECD cities so road pricing and other forms of taxation on the car have an instant effect. Several countries (e.g. Hong Kong and Singapore) have had effective pricing policies to restrict car ownership and use. The World Bank (1996) is actively promoting supplementary taxes on fuels so that the user charges can be linked to commercially restructured road administrations (in the private sector) and to the promotion of other modes of transport. In addition, although there is the problem of enforcement, further limitations (and pricing) on existing and new parking provision form powerful restraint measures. Pricing measures, particularly in low-income economies, have important distributional consequences. Hence it is crucial that pricing is linked with positive actions to reallocate road space to public transport and bicycles.

4   Planning systems. The three elements above focus on the adverse impacts of current policies rather than on the more fundamental question of whether the mobility increase is desirable (Gakenheimer, 1997). Cities have to be structured and organized so that transport supports the main wealth creating functions of the city. This means that transport has to be linked with city development, to support the central city functions, and to be part of any new (or changing) development. The vision of the sustainable city in the non-OECD countries is equally important to that in the OECD countries, as this is where three-quarters of the world's urban population lives and this is where growth is now concentrated. The difficulties of introducing effective governance in the non-OECD cities is considerable, but appropriate planning systems, that are perceived to be fair, to have the powers to raise and spend, to have the support of the population and other interest groups, are an essential prerequisite to sustainable development.

11.7 Conclusions

These visions of the sustainable city 2025 are not easy to construct and there are many possible variants, but the intention has been to raise the main issues. As a conclusion, five key unresolved issues are raised:

1   The Car and the city. By reducing the levels of congestion in cities and making cities liveable, the need to own a car may also be reduced. High quality public transport, the use of paratransit and taxis, together with imaginative forms of rental may all lead to a reduction in the levels of car ownership. There is also the need to reduce the use of diesel in cities so that NO_x reduction targets can be achieved. If there is a general reduction in car use, then the potential market for the eco-car may also be reduced, thus making it less attractive for the motor manufacturers and governments to invest heavily in research and development. The role of the car in the city is the key element in all the discussion.

2   Carbon taxes. There may be a general move to switch taxation away from employment-based measures to consumption-based measures. Substantial increases in fuel taxes have taken place in some countries to achieve target reductions in CO_2 emissions, but there are distributional issues that need to be addressed, particularly as they relate to low-income car-owning households. The possibilities of tradable permits have been discussed and action has taken place within the EU with the 2003 Directive (CEC, 2003 and Chapter 2.5.5 and 2.5.6).

3   Selling the visions. The key to successful implementation must be the acceptability of action and the involvement of all parties in that process. Central to the debate here is the use to which revenues from transport related taxes and charges will be put. Whether they will be invested in public transport, in improving the quality of the urban environment, in promoting research and development, in setting up innovation funds to assist particular projects, or merely adding to exchequer revenues.

4   Transferability. The basic thinking here has been to develop city visions of the future to pursue a sustainable transport strategy. Although each city will have a different starting point, there is likely to be a commonality of paths (and individual measures) between cities. At this level, the alternatives available seem both consistent and practical, given the underlying commitment of governments, business, interest groups and individuals. Yet there is still the unresolved question of transferability, as there are many institutional and organizational differences, as city governments have their own agenda, as there are variations in the environmental context, and as the powers and controls available to governments vary. The underlying rationale here is that these differences

are acknowledged, but the aim is to discuss the range of possibilities. In that respect, it is concluded that realistic visions of the transport sustainable city 2025 are desirable, possible and achievable in all contexts.

5   Property and land markets. One of the unresolved questions is the impact that a non-car based urban future would have on the city economy and the property market. One view would be that as movement around the city would be easier, particularly on public transport, and cleaner (with the eco-car), this would lead to the revitalization of the city centre and strong pressures for further development. But the effects on congestion are likely to be negative if the car is still the main form of city transport. The contrary view is that development pressures would move towards the peripheral sites, the edge cities and greenfield locations, which would still be (clean) car accessible. These new locations would become the principal pressure points for development, with the city centres becoming less attractive. At present, the evidence is mixed with many key locations within cities still commanding high rents and property prices, but elsewhere it is the peripheral locations that are becoming the new growth centres.

The possible signposts can be seen in a variety of contexts (Figure 11.1), ranging from the specific introduction of demonstration projects, monitoring systems and the setting of targets, to the promotion of good practice and the levels of well being in our cities, to the levels of public support and acceptance of action. The city has been taken as the main focus here, as it is central to sustainable development. The approach adopted has also been pragmatic with a clear emphasis on the technological and policy interventions, which are already reasonably well known. The possible attractions of opting for more speculative technologies (e.g. freight tunnels or personal helicopters) has been deliberately avoided, as have the more imaginative urban futures (e.g. telecottages, virtual reality centres, and cities as centres of recreation rather than work). This is not to say that the more speculative futures should be ignored, but rather that in the next 20 years such radical changes are unlikely, and that if they were to take place, the consequences would be even harder to envisage.

The city can be made sustainable both in a more general development sense and in transport, through the implementation of a combination of technological innovation and other policy actions, such as those outlined here. As such, people can adopt lifestyles that are consistent with sustainable development and sustainable mobility. All stakeholders, including central and local government, as well as industry, business and the general public, must be committed to change. It is only through concerted action that we will ever get from where we are to where we want to go.

Annex 1   The expected growth in traffic in the UK

The Business as Usual case for growth in travel; (2000–2025) as compared with the two visions

Billion passenger-km	Volume 2000	Volume 2025 Reference Case		Volume 2025 Vision 1	Volume 2025 Vision 2	Growth 1975–2000
Car (fossil)	614	1000	(+63%)	367	535	+185%
(methanol and hydrogen)		0		100		
(electric)		90		0		
Motorcycle	5	8	(+60%)	8	8	−17%
Air	50	130	(+260%)	115	155	+360%
Bus	45	59	(+30%)	115	90	−25%
Rail	47	56	(+20%)	105	112	+130%
Total	761	1250	(+64%)	800	1000	+165%

Notes: These figures are national ones (not cities) for the UK.
  Volumes for 2000 and trends 1975–2000 are based on transport statistics (DfT, 2003) and EC (2003). The car total includes vans and taxis. Air includes all domestic flights and those within the EU.
  The Business as Usual case is a relatively cautious estimate compared to most forecasts and the historic development between 1975 and 2000.
  There are no figures here for walking or cycling. It should also be noted that the figures are in passenger-kilometres, which bias numbers against short trips and non motorized modes – one of the main ways to reduce travel distances is through concentration of facilities and a switch to local destinations (or to carry out trip tours).

Notes

1   Eurostat classifies 89.5 per cent of the UK's population as urban, about the same level as the Netherlands (89.4 per cent). Only Belgium (97.3 per cent) and Luxembourg (91.5 per cent) have higher levels in the EU, where the average was 80.1 per cent in 2002.
2   Note that technology here (and throughout the book) is used in a generic sense to mean different systematic approaches to the problem and its practical implementation – it covers technical issues (Chapter 8), ICT (Chapter 9), but also the broader attitudes of society to change, lifestyles, urban development and the future (Chapters 6 and 7).

Chapter 12

Conclusions

12.1 Sustainable transport planning

> Sustainable mobility is a term that summarizes what is at stake in contemporary attempts to redress the balance of costs and benefits in the transport sector. It marks a shift away from traditional transport planning which conceptualizes transport as a derived demand and as a support infrastructure for economic growth, towards a policy approach that is informed by evidence and risk assessment and which recognizes the pitfalls of unconstrained growth. (Giorgi, 2003, p. 179)

Traditionally, transport planning has developed out of engineering and economics, where the concerns have been to accommodate traffic and to ensure value for money, often interpreted very narrowly (Banister, 2002a). More recently, a wider range of social science perspectives has become influential in transport thinking, and new priorities have gained credence, including demand management, the allocation of priority to certain users of the system, and most recently by creating spaces for people rather than cars in cities. Sustainable urban development, which is now at the heart of planning and many of the requirements placed on local authorities, is the next stage in that process, but it requires a more fundamental rethink on priorities if transport is to be central to that new thinking.

However it should be remembered that the World GDP is expected to grow by 75 per cent between now and 2025, with energy consumption also growing by 57 per cent and vehicle-kilometres by over 80 per cent. Clear and substantial action is required either to accommodate this scale of expected growth or to explore the means by which economic growth is not limited by substantial increases in energy and transport consumption. This is the challenge for sustainable urban development.

Transport, as usual, has been rather reluctant to embrace the new thinking on sustainable urban development, as some of the questions raised are contrary to the conventional transport wisdom. It also seems to be much harder to think of strategies to accommodate transport within sustainable urban development, at least if a real impact is to be made without fundamentally changing the way in which activities are carried out.

The two fundamental dilemmas now being confronted by transport planners are the nature of travel and the importance of time in travel. In the past, transport has been seen as a derived demand or a negatively valued activity that is only undertaken because of the positive outcomes at the destination. This seems to be an example of schizophrenic paths in transport, when it is clear that something is not quite right, but no action is taken to remedy the situation.

Dilemma 1 – Transport as a derived demand or as a valued activity?

Travel patterns are changing, with work related activities accounting for less of the total (about 20 per cent of trips and 30 per cent of distance – 2002). The increase is taking place in leisure activities, and this will become increasingly more important in the future. According to escape theory, leisure mobility is an attempt to compensate for declining quality of life (Heinze, 2000). In part, this is seeking pleasure in a different location, often of great contrast to where the individual actually lives. For example, the destination could be open space or countryside, or it could be in the mountains or by the sea. But it is also a desire to associate with other people or cultures, and to encounter new experiences. A study in Bern (Fuhrer *et al.*, 1993, quoted in Heinze, 2000) identified six deficiency factors in the field of housing which produce compensatory leisure mobility:

- Security effect – people who feel safe and secure at home leave it less, particularly at weekends.

- Traffic effect – people who live on busy roads cover the greatest distance in leisure travel and at weekends (thus creating traffic for others).

- Garden effect – the car replaces small gardens – leisure distances for houses with gardens is 16 km and for those without is 32 km (Knoflacher, 2000).

- Storey effect – high-rise dwellers travel more at weekends and for leisure as it is one way to come down to the ground.

- Rendezvous effect – people who get away in their leisure time principally want to meet others, and this applied to 60 per cent of all activities in the Bern study.

- Car-living room effect – the more the car is able to offer qualities that are missing in the home (e.g. power, control and self esteem), the higher the leisure mobility.

This is an example of FlexiTheory, which is about giving people and firms more choice and opportunity, so giving them control over their lives and businesses. Business and leisure travel will be customer driven and tailored to individual requirements. The package holiday where the provider determines where you go, when you go, and what quality there is at the destination disappears as the customer specifies his or her own requirements for holidays. With the use of the Internet, it is possible to match up the exact requirements or modify destinations to meet the specifications of the user. As those requirements become more demanding, the higher the price (Banister, 2000*b*).

Such explanations are attractive and have a clear logic to them; they can be articulated in terms of urban living, the use of the car for leisure travel, and all forms of transport. There seems to be a basic desire to get away from one's everyday environment, and to break out so that one has the opportunity to do something completely different. The implications of these arguments are profound, as it has been assumed in the past that there is no pleasure or value in the travel activity itself. The underlying premise of all transport modelling is that travellers are cost minimizers, so that all trips should be as short as possible. Many of the pricing strategies used are designed to reduce the attractiveness of more distant destinations so that the volume of travel is reduced.

However, there is increasing evidence that leisure mobility is on the increase, that there is a substantial amount of excess travel,[1] and that some travel is desired (Mokhtarian and Salomon, 2001). Empirical studies in the United States are suggesting that people like to travel, to seek adventure, to look for novel or exciting experiences, to break the monotony of everyday activities. In this way, they can assert their independence and their control over their lives (Schafer and Victor, 1997). This is an even stronger version of escape theory and it is another excellent illustration of the concepts of FlexiTheory.

Mokhtarian and Salomon's conclusions are equally strong as they suggest that it is evident:

> that a great many people enjoy long drives to vacation spots, some even driving very long distances as a major ingredient of their vacations. The popularity of mobile house-trailers and Winnebagos, that permit one to travel while living 'at home', is a telling indicator that sheer travel can serve as a medium for absorbing leisure time and as an integral form of recreational activity. Even when combined with visits to national parks and other en route destinations, the travel per se seems to be an important component of a vacation's activities. To be sure, it would be difficult to separate a subjective evaluation of the time spent in one's car from the time spent hiking or fishing. (Mokhtarian and Salomon, 1999, p. 31).

As leisure time and incomes increase, as the working week decreases, and as more individuals seek early retirement, it is not surprising that leisure-based activities are becoming the largest element of people's weekly activities, accounting for about 30 per cent of activities and 40 per cent of the distance travelled.[2] These figures for Great Britain are lower than those for Austria, where leisure trips account for 41 per cent of trips and 55 per cent of distance, and Germany where the corresponding figures are 40 per cent and 50 per cent (Knoflacher, 2000). In the British figures, personal business and escort trips are not included in the leisure category and these two purposes account for 19 per cent of trips and 13 per cent of distance – this may account for the difference.

Such a line of argument leads to a fundamental dilemma about whether all travel is a derived demand. The traditional view that travel is only undertaken because of the benefits derived at the destination is no longer generally applicable. Substantial amounts of leisure travel are undertaken for its own sake and the activity of travelling is valued. This conclusion has enormous implications for transport analysis as most conventional analysis is based on the premise that travel distances should be short and that travel time should be minimized. A corollary concerns the impact of technology and the new technological flexibility on travel. The new technology provides tremendous opportunity and choice in leisure activities, whether this means time spent in the home at the terminal or out of the home at local or national facilities. The knowledge base is extended and this may result in more travel, but more important is the transfer of power from the producer to the customer. Increasingly, users will control their leisure activities tailored to their own specific requirements (at a price). Consumers will determine what type of leisure activity they participate in, where and when it takes place, and who actually goes with them – and the range of alternatives will also increase substantially. Finally, there is the crucial role of the individual. In all these questions there is an increasing importance attached to city residents as they have the power to make the city sustainable through where they live and work, where they carry out their activities, where they take their holidays, whether they use the car, and whether they try to substitute or reduce car travel. For an accessible sustainable city to become a reality requires active citizen support and new forms of communication between experts and citizens, through new forms of discussion and involvement of all major stakeholders.

Dilemma 2 – Time minimization and reasonable travel time

The second dilemma is the increasing contradiction between the desire to speed up and the desire to slow traffic down. For evaluation purposes, much of the user benefit (often over 80 per cent of total benefits) is derived from savings in travel time, which in turn are based on the desire to travel as fast as possible between two places. This is not the place to enter the debate on how these values of travel time saving are derived, or how they are used by the beneficiaries or in the analysis. But there does seem to be an inconsistency in the travel time-savings argument within cities, where much effort is now going into slowing traffic down for environmental and safety reasons. Although it is not explicitly stated, a certain level of congestion on roads is now seen as 'desirable' and in many locations (e.g. residential streets and around schools), new low speed limits have been introduced, together with appropriate enforcement measures (e.g. speed cameras).

There are the perpetual complaints from industry that the time lost in congestion is costing business money. But there is also a contradictory transport strategy that both tries to speed traffic up (to save time) and slow it down (to increase time). The notion of a transport system with no congestion has never been a reality and much of the recent debate has been over what should be considered as a reasonable level of congestion (Goodwin, 2000). The key policy objective now becomes that of reasonable travel time, rather than travel time minimization. People and businesses are already concerned about knowing how much time it should take to travel to their destination with a reasonable degree of certainty. It is the reliability of the system that is crucial.

These two dilemmas are both important in terms of the rationale behind transport planning, as many of the methods used cannot handle travel as a valued activity or travel time reliability. But they also have important implications for travel planning, if it is to embrace the concepts of sustainable urban development. It strongly argues for the sister disciplines of urban planning and transport to become fully integrated as a subject area. It also means that the focus has switched from the physical dimensions (urban form and traffic) to the social dimensions (people and accessibility). The major differences between the traditional view and the 'new perspective' are highlighted in Table 12.1.

12.2 The achievement of sustainable transport objectives

In the discussion in Chapter 2, seven basic objectives were stated as to the means by which the ten principles of sustainable development could be achieved. The reference to the objectives stated here needs to be linked back to the earlier commentary in Chapter 2 (see pages 15–19).

1 Reducing the need to travel – substitution. In its pure form this means that a trip is no longer made (objectives 1 and 7). It has either been replaced by a non-travel activity or it has been substituted through technology, for example Internet shopping. The impact of ICT on transport is complex and most recent thinking (Chapter 9 and Banister and Stead, 2004) argues

Table 12.1 Contrasting approaches to transport planning

The conventional approach Transport planning and engineering	The new perspective Sustainable urban development and transport
Physical dimensions	Social dimensions
Mobility	Accessibility
Traffic focus, particularly on the car	People focus, either in (or on) a vehicle or on foot
Large in scale	Local in scale
Street as a road	Street as a space
Motorized transport	All modes of transport often in a hierarchy with pedestrian and cyclist at the top and car users at the bottom
Forecasting traffic	Visioning on cities
Modelling approaches	Scenario development and modelling
Economic evaluation	Multicriteria analysis to take account of environmental and social concerns
Travel as a derived demand	Travel as a valued activity as well as a derived demand
Demand-based	Management-based
Speeding up traffic	Slowing movement down
Travel time minimization	Reasonable travel times
Segregation of people and traffic	Integration of people and traffic

Source: Adapted from Marshall (2001), Table 9.2.

for complementarity between transport and ICT. Although there is a large substitution potential, the relationships between transport and ICT seem to be symbiotic with a greater opportunity for flexibility in travel patterns, as some activities are substituted, whilst others are generated, and some replaced by fewer but longer distance journeys. The new flexibility also reflects the congestion within the system and the increasing time spent commuting.

However, underlying much of the potential is the still important argument for agglomeration economies, which are increased by the potential for increasing returns scale (when human capital innovation are added to the conventional economic returns) and the importance of the continued role that face-to-face contact plays in all important interrelationships. If transport has a value in its own right, then reducing the total amount of travel might not be possible, as expendable income levels rise and as leisure time increases. One reduced set of travel needs will only be replaced by other new sets of travel needs. But this situation does not negate the basic argument for reducing existing travel needs, even if new ones are created.

2 Transport policy measures – modal shift. Many of the transport policy measures address seven basic objectives reducing levels of car use and road freight (objective 2), promoting more energy efficient modes (objective 3),

and improving safety for pedestrians and other road users (objective 6). It is through the promotion of green modes of transport (walk and cycle) and the development of the new transport hierarchy that changes in modal split can be made (objective 5). This can be achieved through slowing down urban traffic and reallocating space to public transport, through parking controls and road pricing, and through making it easier to use public transport. Such measures encourage modal shift to green modes and public transport, and also by using demand management to restrict access and reallocate space, more effective use is made of the available capacity. A much wider notion of the street is being created, as it is no longer only being considered as a road but also as a space for people, green modes and public transport. Creative use of that space at different times of the day or day of the week means also that new uses can be encouraged (e.g. street markets or play zones). Measures to encourage modal shift must be combined with strategies to make the best use of the 'released space', so that there is a net reduction in traffic (Banister and Marshall, 2000).

3   Land-use policy measures – distance reduction. These measures address the physical separation of activities and the means by which distance can be reduced. The intention is to build sustainable transport into the patterns of urban form and layouts, which in turn may lead to a switch to green modes of transport. It is one area of public policy were intervention can take place (Chapter 6), through increasing densities and concentration, through mixed use development, through housing location, though the design of buildings, space and route layouts, through public transport oriented development and transport development areas, through car-free development, and through establishing size thresholds for the availability of services and facilities. Often, it has been argued that land-use interventions are long-term. But this is no longer the case as brand new buildings replace other relatively new buildings. The timescale over which sustainable urban development might be realized is similar to the turnover of the building stock (about 2 per cent per annum). Certainly, decisions on the location of new housing will have a single dramatic effect on travel patterns and these effects will impact over the lifetime of that housing. The distance factors again address the seven basic objectives, mainly to reduce car and lorry use (objective 2), to improve safety (objective 6), and to reduce the need to travel (objective 1), as well as to improve the attractiveness of cities for all their residents (objective 7). The impact of land use is more indirect than the transport measures but, as with all measures, there is a complementarity between them that needs to be encouraged, so that there is a mutual reinforcement.

4   Technological innovation – efficiency increase. The role of technology is

important as it impacts on the efficiency of transport and three of the basic objectives (objectives 3, 4 and 5). It is important to promote energy efficient modes, directly by ensuring that the best available technology is being used in terms of engine design, alternative fuels, and the use of renewable energy sources. In addition, standards can be introduced to reduce levels of noise and emissions at source, and measures can be taken to ensure that access to certain parts of the city are restricted to those vehicles that are seen to be environmentally cleaner than other vehicles.

Table 12.2 summarizes the coverage of the seven objectives against the four groups of measures that can be used (See Tables 4.4, 5.3 and 5.5). These measures also relate to the means by which travel can be reduced. As stated in Chapter 3, there were three components of travel, namely the volume of travel, the distance travelled, and the efficiency of travel (in terms of energy used). Positive impacts on any or all of these should reduce energy use and emissions levels.

Table 12.2 Summary of the seven basic objectives against the measure types

	Objective
Reducing the need to travel – substitution	1, 7
Transport policy – modal shift	2, 3, 5, 6
Land-use policy – distance reduction	1, 2, 6, 7
Technological innovation – efficiency increase	3, 4, 5

12.3 Importance of involving the people

12.3.1 The issues

There has been much discussion on delivering environmentally sustainable transport, and the measures available are well known. There is even agreement between the main actors concerned about what should be done. There is also a growing literature on the barriers to implementation and why outcomes never match up with expectations. The commonly used economic arguments of rationality and complete knowledge do not seem to apply in transport.[3] Much of the debate has centred on raising awareness, providing information and education, and the use of the media and advertising as the means to achieve environmental sustainable transport (OECD, 2002a). But there always seems to be a reason for maintaining the *status quo* rather than changing. However good public transport is, there will always be an additional reason for still using the car. The manufacturing business is adept at selling the symbolism and seductiveness of the car.

Ownership of cars as with all other consumer goods will always become cheaper over time, so that more people can afford to own one. The main barriers to entry are not the cost of the vehicle, but the costs of insurance and the need to pass the driving test. Charges to use the car may increase substantially, but political pressures are always present (at least in democracies) to moderate any substantial rises in price so that motoring remains relatively cheap. The advent of low-cost airlines has considerably enhanced the availability and attractiveness of air travel, but there are substantial social and environmental costs that are not paid by the traveller or airline.

It is easy to become pessimistic and much of the literature relates to the difficulty if not the impossibility of achieving environmentally sustainable transport. Hence one can understand the attractiveness of technological solutions with the promise of clean motoring through hybrid and fuel cell vehicles. But there are substantial costs of not doing anything, whether it relates to congestion and time loss, or to the increase in levels of pollution, or to increases in the costs of health and stress levels. The main aim might be to reduce the use of the car for short journeys that can most easily be substituted for by other cleaner modes, such as walk, cycle and public transport.

12.3.2 Community values and healthy transport

Conventional wisdom emphasizes the importance of habits and routinized behaviour, suggesting that only a major change in the system will induce modification in travel patterns. But congestion is now accepted as a major constraint on individuals' quality of life and the efficiency of business. Increasingly, surveys of public opinions are indicating that change is essential and that action is expected. Both the general public and business support priority being given to environmentally friendly modes, and even decision-makers agree (usual levels of support are about 80 per cent). Yet the same people are less positive in their views of others' support for the same policies (typically around 40 per cent) – a Factor 2 argument. This suggests that there is a greater than expected willingness to experiment to reduce trip lengths, to combine trips, to switch modes, or to cancel trips altogether and reduce the need to use the car. This is not an anti-car argument as any such proposal is doomed to failure. It is an argument about individuals and firms reducing vehicle-kilometres travelled, particularly where there is only one person in the vehicle (or empty return trips for freight vehicles).

Small initial change, if sufficiently well supported and publicized (like a Car Free Day – 22 September 2003) can lead to new attitudes to the car. It is through the active involvement of users of transport in a partnership that change can be realized. There are many such events happening in cities through direct action (Reclaim the Streets), through the reallocation of spaces and streets to people (the World Squares initiative, pedestrianization, street closures), through lowering speed limits (Home Zones), through travel plans, and through cycle networks and exclusive bus networks. It must be seen as an active process that is participatory and inclusive. Simple passive advertising and promotion will not work.

One soft means by which such a change can be facilitated is to demonstrate that sustainable transport improves city health (individually and collectively). Increasing evidence is linking transport-induced emissions with declining health, and there are now the new arguments about the links between exercise (or lack of it) and obesity. Walking, cycling and public transport are all more healthy than using the car. Physical activity 'almost halves the risk of cardiovascular disease and also reduces the risk of diabetes, osteoporosis and colon cancer as well as relieving anxiety and depression' (Warren Centre, 2002). Active transport is good for you, but there are still the indirect effects emanating from pollution, which damages health and causes problems relating to asthma, bronchitis, leukaemia and lung disease. There are also the wider effects of increases in CO_2, ozone depletion, acid rain and smog. Environmentally sustainable transport seems to offer individual health improvements and a better quality of environment. Surely this is a message that can and should be easy to sell?

Healthy transport means strong action on separating people from traffic and having exclusive routes for people and cyclists. It also means the promotion of travel plans in all locations that are major generators of traffic. It is often thought that such policies would result in political suicide, but there now seems to be strong support for action and many decision-makers have underestimated the strength of feeling for change. It requires decision-makers with a clear vision, and the power and commitment to make radical decisions.

12.3.3 Demonstration effects

To many people, environmentally sustainable transport requires a radical change in the way in which travel decisions are made. Naturally, people feel nervous about it and they are reluctant to alter their behaviour. High quality implementation of radical policy alternatives will have substantial positive demonstration effects. Congestion charging in Central London is the most radical transport policy implemented in the UK in the last 20 years. It represents a watershed in policy action. The idea has been around for many years, but no politician had the conviction to take it forwards. Even with a new Mayor hugely committed to congestion charging, it was a struggle to get through the legal, planning and political processes within a 30-month period (1 July 2000 to 17 February 2003). This relates strongly to the issue of the conflicts between long- and short-term strategies. The long-term view is that congestion charging is an essential element of a sustainable transport strategy, whilst the short-term view is that it is almost impossible to introduce in a four-year electoral cycle (as exists in the UK). But even if congestion charging is not politically acceptable, some other form of pricing or restraint on car use is an essential element of any sustainable transport strategy.

To achieve implementation, there has been an extensive consultation process with all parties and a substantial amount of compromise. For example, under half (45 per cent) of vehicles actually pay the full charge (£5), with a further 29 per cent having discounts of varying kinds, and the remaining 26 per cent of vehicles are exempt. The large number of discounts and exemptions has reduced the effectiveness of the policy, and this can create problems later if they are to be eliminated. Other changes included the reduction of a proposed charge of £15 for lorries to £5, minor boundary changes, and a slight shortening of the charging period (07.00–18.30 on weekdays). A substantial amount of analysis and monitoring is now being carried out to determine both the transport and the non-transport impacts of congestion charging, both within the cordon area and in the London conurbation as a whole (ROCOL, 2000; TfL, 2002 and 2003).

Such an example raises important policy dilemmas. The demonstration effects of the congestion charging scheme are substantial as many other cities will follow London if it is seen to be successful. But in order to achieve implementation, many concessions have been made, and these may in turn reduce the effectiveness. A balance must be struck between the desired scheme and an acceptable scheme. The potential risk is substantial, but such choices have to be made if radical environmentally sustainable transport polices are to be introduced at all. Conversely, implementation of a scheme could be seen as the first step in a process where incremental changes are then added to the basic scheme until the final goal of a full electronic road pricing scheme in London is achieved.

12.3.4 Principles of advice

To achieve environmentally sustainable transport through soft measures, four concepts need to be considered and resolved. The first is a necessary condition, but the other three also need to be addressed.

1   Acceptability. The measure should not be too controversial as it must be accepted or at least tolerated by the majority. There must be positive outcomes in terms of new money for investment or a measurable improvement in the quality of life. Politics is about reflecting prevailing preferences and also about forming opinions. Acceptability requires the involvement of all actors including residents, businesses, interest groups

and institutions so that each of them can take on responsibilities and give a commitment to change through action. It is only with the support of all (or a substantial majority) of stakeholders that effective action will be implemented. It requires individuals to move away from simple self-interest to accepting the wider societal benefits of change. All parties must buy in to the proposals. It is here that leadership is essential at all levels of decision-making from the EU level to the national and local levels.

2   Long-term perspectives and holistic views. When thinking about measures to achieve sustainable transport, there are some (like pricing) that are common to all futures. Such measures need to be implemented now, even though their impacts might be slow in the initial stages. For example, the UK government has increased the costs of driving through raising fuel duty by at least 5 per cent in real terms each year. In the transport sector, this is the main policy being pursued to meet the stabilization target for CO_2 emissions. Between 1994 and 2000 this increased the price of a litre of fuel from 45 pence to 85 pence, of which 70 pence is tax and duty. Since then, prices have risen with inflation and world energy prices, so the current (2005) price is about 85 pence a litre. Without the fuel price escalator, the pump price would only be about 60 pence per litre. There is considerable public resentment, particularly from industry, that petrol prices in the UK are uncompetitive (see Table 4.3, but note prices there in $, so the £ equivalent is £0.58 – at 2004 exchange rates). UK fuel prices are the most expensive in Europe and over four times as high as prices in the US. The escalator was removed (2000) after pressure from industry and other interests, particularly those in rural areas. So the long-term commitment was terminated, and it seems that only through concerted action at the EU level will a European price escalator be introduced for all carbon-based fuels.

A second element here is that even though the science is not well known, the precautionary principle should be followed, particularly on the global warming effects of transport emissions. Some measures may have unexpected results, and these need to be accommodated. For example, a major change in the built form has an enormous potential to influence travel patterns and mobility, but it will take time to actually happen. Location decisions made now on where to build new houses, schools, hospitals and shops will substantially influence future travel patterns. Many of the problems created for the transport system do not emanate from the transport sector, but from other sectors. So a more holistic perspective is needed that integrates decision-making across sectors and widens the public discourse.

3   Trigger effects and sequencing of implementation. Simple decisions can act as triggers and generate new forms of activities. For example, telecentres can encourage more local patterns of activities as the journey to work is replaced by local movements. If sufficient uptake happens, it would be worthwhile to open local services such as cafes and shops creating self-contained local centres. Alternatively, controversial policies such as road pricing could be introduced in a series of stages, rather than in one action. Initially, road space could be reallocated to public transport services and parking charges in the city raised substantially, but new park and ride facilities would also be provided to give the motorist a choice. In stage two, cars would be allowed in the bus lanes if they pay and gradually more of the road space would be allocated to the paying motorist and public transport. As public transport is now more reliable, patronage would rise and further investments would be initiated to increase capacity further. Eventually parking charges would be reduced, and all the road space would be paid for by those continuing to drive their cars. Such a dynamic facilitates implementation, gains public acceptability and gradually familiarizes users with road pricing, whilst at the same time providing choice through high quality public transport. The disadvantage of such a policy process is that it may be regressive as the more affluent car driver will always be able to 'buy' road space.

4   Adaptability. Decisions today should not unnecessarily restrict the scope for future decisions. When the impact of strong measures is hard to predict, a good strategy may be to make piece-meal changes and to test several solutions in small-scale experiments. As with all of these conditions, there is no prescription or blueprint for the correct procedures to follow. Each situation requires separate analysis and implementation, including flexibility to change policy measures if intentions and outcomes do not match up. Assessment of risk and reversibility are both strong components of environmentally sustainable transport. However, the goal of sustainable mobility must remain with support from all political, business and public decision-makers. But adaptability is not an excuse for inaction or weak action. It is an argument for clear decision-making, leadership supported by analysis and monitoring to check on the effectiveness of policy action.

The messages are clear. There is a strong support for enlarging the scope of public discourse and empowering the key stakeholders through an interactive and participatory process. This is a much more effective active involvement of all parties and it would have much greater influence than conventional passive means of persuasion. There must be a willingness to change and an acceptance of collective responsibility. To achieve environmentally sustainable transport, the arguments must be sufficiently powerful to overcome the dependence on the car and the fact that the costs of delay and congestion have already been internalized by drivers. If the driver still resents paying more for something that has already been discounted in their travel decisions, then the battle has only just begun.

12.4 Sustainable urban development and transport

A clear conclusion is reached, namely that transport can have and must have an instrumental role in achieving sustainable development. The city is the most sustainable urban form and it has to be the location where most (70–80 per cent) of the world's population will live. The key parameters of the city are that it should have over 25,000 population (preferably over 50,000), with medium densities (over 40 persons per hectare), with mixed use developments, and with preference given to developments in public transport accessible corridors and near to highly accessible public transport interchanges. Such developments conform to the requirements of service and information-based economies. Settlements of this scale would also be linked together to form agglomerations of polycentric cities, with clear hierarchies that would allow a close proximity of everyday facilities and accessibility to higher order activities.

Such urban form would keep average trip lengths below the thresholds required for maximum use of the walk and cycle modes. It would also permit high levels of innovative services and public transport priority, so that the need to use the car would be minimized. Through the combination of clear planning strategies, cities would be designed at the personal scale to allow both high quality accessibility and a high quality environment. In transport terms, this is the vision of the sustainable city. The intention is not to prohibit the use of the car as this would be both difficult to achieve and seen as being against notions of freedom and choice. The intention is to design cities of such quality and at a suitable scale that people would not need to have a car and would choose to live in a car free location.

The measures available to bring about such a change are well known, but they have not really been explored to their full potential, either individually or collectively in packages.

1   Technology alone cannot solve the problem as the underlying growth in traffic outweighs the benefits of clean technology. However, it can have a major role in reducing local air pollution levels from transport, but it is the global emissions of CO_2 resulting from the consumption of oil that will remain as the main problem in the next 25 years. The

OECD countries must take the lead and seek to reduce substantially their levels of emissions (particularly of CO_2) so that the rest of the world can increase their emissions levels to achieve global stabilization targets. This is the strong position taken by the developing countries as they argue that the OECD countries have a moral responsibility to take action and as they have the financial and technological means to achieve stabilization and reduction targets.

2   The underlying traffic growth and high levels of car ownership will result in higher congestion, particularly in cities. This reduces efficiency and has substantial environmental costs. Even if technology reduces unit energy consumption and emissions levels, there is still the underlying problem of congestion which in turn influences the levels of energy use and emissions. This means that restraint policies have to be introduced – some 30 per cent improvements can (and have) been achieved through traffic management, but stronger comprehensive policies must also be introduced (World Bank, 1994).

3   Traffic growth can be explained in a substantial part by the growth in income levels and car ownership, but journey lengths have increased at a greater rate as cities have become decentralized and as developments have taken place on peripheral sites. The number of trips is relatively stable between countries, but it is the trip length that varies, particularly between European countries and the United States (+33 per cent), and these trip lengths have increased by over 40 per cent (1972–2002) in many developed countries. For example, in Great Britain average trip distance has increased by 47 per cent from 1972/73 to 2002 (from 7.5 km to 11.04 km).

4   In the longer term, choices have to be made by people and firms within cities about whether a car is needed in the city. Provided proximity and accessibility are maintained and improved, most activities can be carried out locally, and access to higher order activities will be carried out on public transport. It will not be necessary to own a car in the city. Longer distance leisure and recreational activities, and visits to the countryside would be facilitated through imaginative forms of car rental and shared patterns of ownership.

   The logic of this argument is clear, namely that the car's role in the city of 2025 is limited.[4] The service- and knowledge-based society with high values placed on leisure activities can be achieved through sustainable urban living in clean cities. However, the problem is not in the vision, but in the means to achieve it. There are two basic options:

- The value system of individuals and firms needs to change so that the car (even the eco-car) is not seen as the current dream that is promoted in the adverts. The collective benefits of clean cities must be given a higher priority than the individual mobility provided by the car. The cultural link between cars and freedom has to be tackled.

- An ecological disaster would have to occur that is directly related to the problem of the car – some kind of health epidemic that is of a sufficient scale to change values and priorities. But even if such an event occurs, it would also have to result in a fundamental reassessment of values.

Realistically, it is hard to conceptualize such a change, particularly as current lifestyles are so transport dependent. Such a change might occur if there was a technology (the eco-car) that could be seen as a replacement rather than having to adopt a radically different lifestyle. There is enormous capital tied up in cities, in local and national economies, and in the motor industry (not to mention in private cars). One of the unresolved questions is the impact that a non-car-based urban future would have on the city economy and the property market (Chapter 11.7). One view would be that as movement around the city would be easier, particularly on public transport, and cleaner (with the eco-car), this would lead to the revitalization of the city centre and strong pressures for further development. The contrary view is that development pressures would move towards the peripheral sites, the edge cities and greenfield locations which would still be (clean) car accessible. These new locations would become the principal pressure points for development, with the city centres becoming less attractive. At present, the evidence is mixed with many key locations within cities still demanding high rents and property prices, but elsewhere it is the peripheral locations that are becoming the new growth centres.

This suggests that the strong sustainability arguments have a high risk associated with them. Apart from the direct impacts on the vehicle manufacturers and their suppliers, the city would have to alter its structure so that efficient local movement could take place. An instrumental role would have to be placed on technological substitution to replace current activity patterns.

A demonstration or experimental city would be one mechanism to test the concept of a 'car free city', both in terms of the transport related costs and benefits, but also in terms of the wider impacts on density, structure and its economy. It could provide the testbed for new technology (including the eco-car), and help measure the benefits and costs of accelerated technological innovation. However, in addition to the environmental imperative, the city must still remain as a vibrant wealth creating economic unit and be 'socially fair'. The role of the eco-car must be established, and priority allocated through pricing and space allocation. Perhaps, a greater emphasis should be given to a low speed, small eco-car that could be used (through Smartcard technology) by all residents (between 10 and 80 years of age) with advanced guidance technology. Conversely, a priority could be allocated to the development of the eco-bus (and eco-paratransit) and the eco-taxi as the principal vehicles for use in the city. It is unlikely that the traditional taxi would exist in 2025 as they would be driverless with the use of innovative hire and drive systems.

The technological arguments are attractive, as difficult choices can be avoided and the *status quo* maintained. However, it must be recognized that in its true form, the sustainable city has no place for the car. Transport would be by walk and cycle, together with new combinations of eco-public transport. Such a combination minimizes the use of all non-renewable resources, makes the best use of available space, and provides maximum accessibility for all.

The radical conclusion reached above may seem unacceptable, particularly given the current range of megacities in the world, the long travel distances which have developed in the last 20 years, and the existing problems which have to be addressed. The weak sustainability option recognizes that the car will still form an essential element of the transport system, but its role will be reduced as a result of the introduction of new forms of pricing, restraint and regulation. The underlying argument here is that we must look for ways to maintain economic growth with less transport (decoupling) and strong incentives (market and regulatory) should be given to promoting efficient and clean transport by all modes. The weak sustainability option forms an essential link to move from the current situation to the sustainable city. It provides the means to reassess priorities, it begins to revalue space in cities, and it gives some indication of the sustainable city. As such, it will help to change values systems. What then would the essential ingredients of a weak sustainability option be that might achieve sustainable urban development over a 20-year time horizon? Action is required at international and national levels, as well as at the regional and local levels.

12.4.1 The international and national action plan

1   The taxation system should be changed so that taxes are based primarily on consumption, rather than production (labour). A carbon tax in the transport sector would allow the price of petrol and diesel to be substantially raised so that clear incentives would be given to users to drive economically, to purchase fuel-efficient vehicles, to switch modes, and to consider whether a journey is essential or could be carried out locally or as part of a tour.

2   Clear direction would also be given to industry to produce more fuel-

efficient vehicles. Tradable permits for zero emission vehicles would also be included in this package, where targets would be set for manufacturers to produce and sell a certain percentage of particular types of vehicles by certain dates (as in California). The eco-car would form part of this package so that a phased programme could be introduced. Coupled to this would be increases in research and development programmes, and the means to accelerate the transfer from old technology to the new eco-technology.

3   Measures would be taken to ensure the existing fleet is operating efficiently, with testing, emissions regulations, the phasing out of old vehicles (scrappage programmes), the use of feebates to encourage change, efficiency targets for new vehicles, promotion of renewable energy sources and other forms of low carbon fuels.

4   The intention of these macro-economic and regulatory policies would be to encourage change and a more rational use of energy in transport. The impact should not be deflationary, but should be fiscally neutral, with investment taking place in public transport, the research and development costs of the eco-car, and the technological alternatives for traffic management and demand management measures.

12.4.2 The regional and local action plan

1   Priority will be given to the most efficient forms of travel – walk, cycling and public transport – with road space being reallocated to these modes, together with preference in demand management and traffic management.

   ◆ Road pricing would be introduced in cities to internalize fully all the social and environmental costs of using the car.
   ◆ The use of Smartcard technology would allow the charges to relate to the traffic conditions prevailing (i.e. levels of congestion) and the characteristics of the car (e.g. its pollution profile, the number of passengers etc.). Higher vehicle occupancies must be promoted through pricing and preferential allocation of space (roads space and parking space).
   ◆ Speed limits in cities would be lowered, parking would become taxable, clear zones would be established, and all forms of subsidy to the car would be eliminated.
   ◆ Subsidies to public transport should also be eliminated on sustainability grounds, as all travellers should pay the full costs of

travel. However, there may be grounds for subsidy to individual users of public transport for social reasons and for particular services (e.g. in rural areas or at weekends and in the evenings).

- Public transport would be promoted through (public) investment, financed from the tolls raised from road pricing on the car in urban areas and the revenues from parking fees.

2   Actions in the planning and development sectors would ensure new development is located where trip lengths can be reduced, and that existing development is refurbished for reuse along with vacant sites within cities – mixed use and high density developments.

- The availability of parking in the city would be severely limited, and travellers from outside (and inside) would be encouraged to use park and ride (or bike and ride) facilities.
- All decision-makers in the city would be involved in discussing how traffic reduction and pollution targets could be reduced.
- All employers would have to devise commuter plans for their employees, and retailers and others (e.g. leisure centres) would also have to prepare and implement plans to reduce levels of car dependence for their customers.
- Similar strategies would cover schools, educational activities, hospitals and other public (and private) services.
- Sustainability forums would be established to discuss targets, programmes of action and best practice from elsewhere.

3   In the information sector, actions would be taken so that the full advantage of the technologies can be realized. For example, information dissemination would cover targets for the city, whether they are being achieved and hot spots of pollution or congestion.

- Technology would form an essential part of the high quality public transport system with Smartcard ticketing, so that all forms of public transport in the city could be used and information/choices on alternatives in real time can be presented to the user.
- Information would be given to the car driver about the possibility of car sharing, parking and routes to reduce fuel consumption.
- Experimental and high profile demonstration cities to test policy packages.

4   The motor industry has an instrumental role to play in changing attitudes of consumers and in promoting new environmental benign technology.

The industry is beginning to accept the environmental imperative and the more limited role that the car should play in cities. As part of the move towards sustainable development and new technologies, industry should be given a clear set of responsibilities that permit innovation and technological development, so that they participate in the process as equal partners seeking the same goals of more efficient management and use of city road space. With the switch from current technology to the new technology and the replacement of polluting vehicles, there is a tremendous opportunity for the motor industry.

Central to all levels of decision-making is the necessity to have clear and visionary leadership and commitment to change. These leaders must be prepared to make agreements and to argue for change, as well as being instrumental in pushing the agenda forwards. Part of this process is to accept responsibility and to engage all relevant stakeholders in a fully participatory debate about the need for action and the necessity of their involvement.

12.4.3   Cities in developing countries

Many of these measures would be appropriate in both the OECD and the non-OECD cities, but some of the more technologically sophisticated measures may be less suitable in the non-OECD cities. Here the focus would be on physical restraint and the reallocation of road space to public transport and the bicycle, together with high petrol prices, parking controls and new enforcement methods. In the non-OECD cities, there is already a rich choice of informal bus services, and this could be enhanced with shared taxis and cars. Even in the non-OECD countries, the road building option should only be considered as an extreme choice as there remain many simple management options available. Investment should take place in the public transport system (new efficient vehicles), in new flexible operating systems (more demand responsive), in maintenance and upgrading of the existing network (including high occupancy vehicle lanes), in providing space for pedestrians and cyclists (i.e. city-wide cycle routes), and in low-cost information systems for transport users. It is likely that road space will always be scarce in cities, so public transport and other informal services must continue to play the major role in providing accessibility. Permanent differences will continue – there will be no convergence and cities will maintain their individuality.

Underlying much of the discussion relating to all cities is the most efficient form of urban governance. The OECD cities have a tradition for strong local government, which is democratically accountable and has powers to raise local taxation. In promoting new forms of sustainable development, action needs to be consistently applied across all cities, as there may be (perceived) first mover disadvantages. If one city takes a leading role, then other cities may benefit and travel may increase as demand switches to alternative (more distant) locations. Questions also have to be raised about the suitability of current sectoral structures within local authorities and whether these are the most appropriate for dealing with sustainability concerns. In the non-OECD countries, there is much less of a tradition for democratic local government, so new decision structures need to be established that have the powers, the responsibilities and the respect of all parties.

12.4.4   The social implications of policies

In devising a strategy for transport and sustainable development there will be winners and losers. The new focus on policies, which shift the pendulum from the economic imperative more towards the environmental imperative, should not ignore the social imperative. New roads through inner-city areas provide quicker travel for car owning suburban dwellers (high income) and a poorer environment (more noise, pollution and community severance) for inner-city dwellers (lower income). It is only with the acquisition of a car that the new drivers join the polluting class and their travel patterns change dramatically. But with every new car, the environmental costs are increased, and the demand and quality of the alternative services are reduced. Even with car ownership at saturation levels, there will still be 25 per cent of the population without exclusive access to a car. Sustainable cities allow a real opportunity where lifestyles need not be car dependent and where community welfare can be matched with high levels of accessibility through non-car-based transport.

The classic argument here is that at present road space is rationed by time and this is seen as being socially just as all road users have the same amount of time available. But rationing by time is inefficient and pricing is the best available means to allocate a scarce resource, such as space. Even if equity is a high priority, there are fiscal mechanisms (e.g. investment in public transport, reductions in social contributions) that would allow the reallocation of some of those revenues. When the environmental dimension is added to the economic and social dimensions, the arguments are even more emphatic. As noted above, it is the non-car user and the urban resident who is exposed to many of these environmental costs. There is a strong case that any reallocation of revenues raised from pricing in transport should be targeted at improving the quality of life of those city dwellers without access to a car.

The arguments presented here are consistent with the priorities of the United Nations (UNDP, 1997), as clear preference is given to poverty alleviation, environmental sustainability and good governance. Measures have been promoted that will allow the poor to make more efficient use of their time. At present in the non-OECD countries, the rich travel more than the poor, but the poor often spend more time to travel less distance. The poor do not even use public transport, but walk almost everywhere. In some continents (e.g. Africa), cycle ownership is low (3.5 per cent), but elsewhere the levels are much higher (e.g. 40 per cent in Asia). It is important to improve the efficiency of travel, as this will allow more productive use of time for education and other wealth creating activities. As stated above, it is important to invest in the public transport system and non-motorized modes so that the access for the poor can be significantly improved.

12.4.5 The benefits of change

The main benefits of moving towards providing a sustainable transport system is that it is socially inclusive (all parties benefit) and the quality of life in the city improves. However, this conclusion has to be modified in at least two respects. Firstly, the revenues raised from additional fuel costs, parking charges and road pricing systems must be retained in the city and used for investment in the transport system and other socially important priorities (e.g. public services and social housing). If the revenues are retained in large part by government, the benefits are substantially reduced and the city may become a less attractive rather than a more attractive place to live. Secondly, the policies being adopted in the city must have the support and confidence of the people living there and the other major interest groups in the city. This acceptance requires all parties to be involved and empowered by the process. The changes being proposed here will fundamentally change the way in which people get around the city, and such radical changes require political and public support. Otherwise, these changes would be political suicide.

The principal choice that has to be faced is simple. Within a high quality urban environment of the kind outlined here, is a car necessary? If the answer to this question is no, then the strong sustainability argument can be followed. If the answer is yes, then the weak sustainability argument should be followed. The strong sustainability argument allows more innovative policies to be followed and it is clearer how the sustainability objectives can be achieved. However, the visions presented in Chapter 11 follow the weaker sustainability argument, but even here it is possible with the combination of policies to achieve fairly tough environmental targets, without compromising economic and equity objectives. Nevertheless, there does seem to be a basic inconsistency in following the weak sustainability argument, as the car in its present form is completely incompatible with the notion of sustainable development. Even in its eco-form, it is still a net user of resources and it is socially exclusive. So weak sustainability is not the solution, but a compromise and a means to move in the right direction. It may act as a springboard for the growing support for the strong sustainability option.

Inevitably, there is a compromise between the sustainability objectives and other policy objectives, and so the question is then modified to whether there is sufficient commonality of interests to address seriously the problems of transport and sustainable development. From the arguments presented here, the conclusion is that there is a sufficient commonality of interests. The first best solutions of the strong sustainability arguments have been replaced by the more realistic weak sustainability arguments to achieve tractable solutions to transport and sustainable development. The strong sustainability arguments will only become relevant when the benefits of high quality urban areas are achieved in a variety of situations through a range of policies selected from those presented in this book. Now it is time to decide!

Notes

1 Excess travel is unnecessary distance attached to routine trips where the driver deliberately takes a longer route.
2 These figures are based on the UK National Travel Survey for 2002, and include social, recreational and holiday travel trip purposes. They do not include overseas travel and so underestimate the true scale of leisure activities (ONS, 2003c).
3 Note that the Nobel prize for economics was awarded to Daniel Kahneman (November 2002). His research in the 1970s argued against rationality, suggesting that people worry more about losing what they have than about winning a bigger stake. Although his work focused on behavioural finance and the way in which markets sometimes have 'bursts of irrational exuberance', prospect theory still seems relevant to individuals' transport decisions today, as it relates actions to uncertainty and risk.
4 The car and the car free city concept relates to all forms of polluting transport. It does not include the eco-car and its derivatives.

References

Acutt, M. and Dodgson, J. (1998) Transport and global warming: modelling the impacts of alternative policies, in Banister, D. (ed.) *Transport Policy and the Environment*. London: Spon, pp. 20–37.

Adams, J. (2001) The Social Consequences of Hypermobility. Royal Society of the Arts lecture 21 November 2001. Available at http://www.geog.ucl.ac.uk/~jadams/PDFs/hypermobilityforRSA.pdf.

Allport, R. (2000) Urban Mass Transit in Developing Countries. Halcrow Fox with Traffic and Transport Consultants, http://wbln0018.worldbank.org/transport/utsr.nsf.

Anderson, V. (1991) *Alternative Economic Indicators*. London: Routledge.

Apogee Research Inc and Greenhorne and O'Mara (1998) *Research on the Relationship between Economic Development and Transportation Investment*. Report 418. Washington DC: Transportation Research Board.

Bae, C.-H.C. and Richardson, H.W. (1994) *Automobiles, the Environment and Metropolitan Spatial Structure*. Cambridge, MA: Lincoln Institute of Land Policy.

Banister, D. (1989) Congestion: market pricing for parking. *Built Environment*, 15(3/4), pp. 251–256.

Banister, D. (1992) Energy use, transport and settlement patterns, in Breheny, M. (ed.) *Sustainable Development and Urban Form*. London: Pion, pp. 160–181.

Banister, D. (1994) Equity and acceptability questions in internalising the social costs of transport, in European Conference of Ministers of Transport, *Internalising the Social Costs of Transport*. Paris: OECD and ECMT, pp. 153–175.

Banister, D. (1996) Energy, quality of life and the environment: the role of transport. *Transport Reviews*, 16(1), pp. 23–35.

Banister, D. (1997a) Reducing the need to travel. *Environment and Planning B*, 24(3), pp. 437–449.

Banister, D. (1997b) The Theory behind the Integration of Land Use and Transport Planning. Paper presented at the Chartered Institute of

Transport Conference on Integrating Land Use and Transport Planning, Millbank Centre, London, October.

Banister, D. (1998*a*) (ed.) *Transport Policy and the Environment*. London: Spon.

Banister, D. (1998*b*) Barriers to implementation of urban sustainability. *International Journal of Environment and Pollution*, **10**(1), pp. 65–83.

Banister, D. (1999) Planning more to travel less: Land use and transport. *Town Planning Review*, **70**(3), pp. 313–338.

Banister, D. (2000*a*) Sustainable urban development and transport: a Eurovision for 2020. *Transport Reviews*, **20**(1), pp 113–130.

Banister, D. (2000*b*) The tip of the iceberg: leisure and air travel. *Built Environment*, **26**(3), pp. 226–235.

Banister, D (2000*c*) The Future of Transport. Paper prepared for the Royal Institute of Chartered Surveyors' Research Foundation Project on 2020 Visions of the Future, London, January.

Banister, D (2002*a*) *Transport Planning*, 2nd ed. London: Spon.

Banister, D. (2002*b*) Making Transport Work: Business and the Local Transport Plan Process. Paper prepared for the RICS Planning and Development Faculty, October, p. 36.

Banister, D. (2003) Critical pragmatism and congestion charging in London. *International Social Science Journal*, **176**, pp. 249–264.

Banister, D. (2005) Time and travel, in Reggiani, A. and Schintler, L. (eds.) *Methods and Models in Transport and Telecommunications: Cross Atlantic Perspectives*. Berlin: Springer Verlag.

Banister, D. and Banister, C. (1995) Energy consumption in transport in Great Britain – macro level estimates. *Transportation Research*, **29**A(1), pp. 21–32.

Banister, D. and Berechman, J. (2000) *Transport Investment and Economic Development*. London: UCL Press.

Banister, D. and Berechman, J. (2001) Transport investment and the promotion of economic growth. *Journal of Transport Geography*, **9**(3), pp. 209–218.

Banister, D. and Button, K. (eds.) (1993) *Transport, the Environment and Sustainable Development*. London: E and FN Spon.

Banister, D. and Marshall S. (2000) *Encouraging Transport Alternatives: Good Practice in Reducing Travel*. London: The Stationery Office.

Banister, D. and Stead, D. (1997) Sustainable Development and Transport. Paper presented at the Expert Group Meeting of the URBAN 21 Project, Bonn, November.

Banister, D. and Stead, D. (2004) The impact of ICT on transport. *Transport Reviews*, **24**(5), pp. 611–632.

Banister, D., Dreborg, K., Hedberg, L., Hunhammer, S., Steen, P. and

Åkerman, J. (1998) Development of Transport Policy Scenarios for the EU: Images of the Future. Paper presented at the 8th World Conference on Transport Research, Antwerp, July.

Banister, D., Stead, D., Steen, P., Akerman, J., Dreborg, K., Nijkamp, P. and Schleicher-Tappeser, R. (2000) *European Transport Policy and Sustainable Development*. London: Spon.

Banister, D., Watson, S. and Wood, C. (1997) Sustainable cities – transport, energy and urban form. *Environment and Planning B*, **24**(1), pp. 125–143.

Bartelmus, P. (1999) Sustainable development – Paradigm or Paranoia? Wuppertal Institute for Climate, the Environment and Energy, Wuppertal Paper 93, May.

Baumol, W.J. and Oates, W.E. (1988) *The Theory of Environmental Policy*. Cambridge: Cambridge University Press.

Becker, H.A. (1997) *Social Impact Assessment*. London: UCL Press.

Beckerman, W. (1994) Sustainable development: Is it a useful concept? *Environmental Values*, **3**(2), pp. 191–209.

Beckerman, W. (1995) *Small is Stupid: Blowing the Whistle on the Greens*. London: Duckworth.

Bell, M.G.H., Quddus, M.A., Schmoecker, J.D. and Fonzone, A. (2004) The Impact of the Congestion Charge on the John Lewis Retail Sector in London. Imperial College, London, Centre for Transport Studies.

Berman, M. (1996) The transportation effects of neo-traditional development. *Journal of Planning Literature*, **10**(4), pp. 347–363.

Bishop, S. and Grayling, A. (2003) The Sky's the Limit: Policies for Sustainable Aviation. Institute of Public Policy Research (IPPR), May.

Blow, L. and Crawford, I. (1997) The Distributional Effects of Taxes on Private Motoring. Institute of Fiscal Studies, London, December.

Boarnet, M.G. and Crane, R. (2001a) *Travel by Design: The Influence of Urban Form on Travel*. New York: Oxford University Press.

Boarnet, M.G. and Crane, R. (2001b) The influences of land use on travel behaviour: Empirical strategies. *Transportation Research A*, **35**(9), pp. 823–845.

Breheny, M. (ed.) (1992) The Compact City – Special Issue. of *Built Environment*, **18**(4).

Breheny, M. (1995a) The compact city and transport energy consumption. *Transactions of the Institution of British Geographers NS*, **20**, pp. 81–101.

Breheny, M. (1995b) Counterurbanisation and sustainable urban forms, in Brotchie, J., Batty, M., Blakely, E., Hall, P. and Newton, P. (eds.) *Cities in Competition. Productive and Sustainable Cities for the 21st Century*. Melbourne: Longman Australia, pp. 402–429.

Breheny, M. (1997) Urban compaction: Feasible and acceptable? *Cities*, **14**(4), pp. 209–217.

Breheny, M. (2001) Densities and sustainable cities: the UK experience, in Echenique, M. and Saint, A. (eds.) *Cities for the New Millennium*. London: Spon, pp. 39–51.

Breheny, M., Gordon, I. and Archer, S. (1998) Building Densities and Sustainable Cities. EPSRC Sustainable Cities Programme, Project Outline No. 5, June.

Brennan, E. (1994) Mega city management and innovation strategies: regional views, in Fuchs, R.J., Brennan, E., Chamie, J., Lo, F. and Uitto, J.I. (eds.) *Mega City Growth and the Future*. New York: UN University Press, pp. 233–255.

British Medical Association (1997) *Road Transport and Health*. London: BMA Science Department.

Bundesministerium für Verkehr, Bau- und Wohnungswesen (BMVBW) (2001) *Auswirkungen neuer Informations- und Kommunikationstechniken auf Verkehrsaufkommen und innovative Arbeitsplätze im Verkehrsbereich*. Bericht, November 2001, Berlin: BMVBW/BMWi. Available at http://www.bmvbw.de.

Bureau of Industry Economics (BIE) (1993) *Environmental Regulation: The Economics of Tradable Permits – a Survey of Theory and Practice*, Research Report 42. Canberra: BIE Australian Government Publishing Service.

Button, K. and Rietveld, P. (2002) Transport and environment, in Van den Bergh, J. (ed.) *Handbook of Environmental and Resource Economics*. Cheltenham: Edward Elgar, pp. 581–589.

Calthorpe, P. (1993) *The Next American Metropolis – Ecology, Community and the American Dream*. NY: Princeton Architectural Press.

Camara, P. and Banister, D. (1993) Spatial inequalities in the provision of public transport in Latin American cities. *Transport Reviews*, **13**(4), pp. 351–373.

Cannell, M. (1999) Growing species to sequester carbon in the UK – answers to common questions. *Forestry*, **72**(3), pp. 237–247.

Carpenter, T.G. (1994) *The Environmental Impact of Railways*. Chichester: Wiley.

Castells, M. (1990) *The Informational City: Information, Technology, Economic Restructuring and the Urban Regional Process*. Oxford: Blackwell.

CEC (Commission of the European Communities) (1992) *Sustainable Mobility: Impact of Transport on the Environment*, COM 92(46). Brussels: CEC.

CEC (Commission of the European Communities) (1998) On Transport and

CO_2 – Developing a Community Approach, Communication from the Commission to the Council, the European Parliament, the Economic and Social Committee, and the Council for the Regions, Brussels, March, COM(1998) 204 Final.

CEC (Commission of the European Communities) (2001*a*) *European Transport Policy for 2010: Time to Decide, The White Paper on Transport Policy.* Brussels: CEC. Available at http://europa.eu.int/comm/energy_transport/en/lb_en.html.

CEC (Commission of the European Communities) (2001*b*) *A Sustainable Europe for a Better World: A European Union Strategy for Sustainable Development.* Communication of the European Commission, COM(2001)264. Luxembourg: Office for Official Publications of the European Communities. Available at http://www.europa.eu.int/comm/environment/eussd/index.htm.

CEC (Commission of the European Communities) (2003) EU Trading Emissions Directive, COM (2003) 403, Brussels, July.

Cervero, R. (1989) Jobs-housing balancing and regional mobility. *Journal of the American Planning Association,* 55(2), pp 136–150.

Cervero, R. (1994) Transit-based housing in California: evidence on ridership impacts. *Transport Policy,* 1(3), pp. 174–183.

Cervero, R. (1997) *Paratransit in America: Redefining Mass Transit.* Westport, CT: Praeger.

Cervero, R. (1998) *The Transit Metropolis: A Global Inquiry.* Washington DC: Island Press.

Cervero, R. and Landis, J. (1992) Suburbanization of jobs and the journey to work: a submarket analysis of commuting in the San Francisco Bay area. *Journal of Advanced Transportation,* 26(3), pp. 275–297.

CfIT (2001) European Best Practice in the Delivery of Integrated Transport. Report from the Commission for Integrated Transport, London. Available at http://www.cfit.gov.uk.

CMHC (1993) *Urban Travel and Sustainable Development: The Canadian Experience.* Ottawa: Canadian Mortgage and Housing Corporation.

Clarkson, R. and Deyes, K. (2002) Estimating the Social Costs of Carbon Emissions. Government Economic Service Working Paper 14, HM Treasury, London.

Cobb, C., Goodman, G.S. and Wackernagel, M. (1999) Why Bigger Isn't Better: The Genuine Progress Indicator – 1999 Update. Redefining Progress, 1904 Franklin Street, Oakland CA 94612, November. Available at http://www.redefiningprogress.org/publications/gpi1999/gpi1999.html.

Committee on the Medical Effects of Air Pollutants (1998) *The Quantification of the Effects of Air Pollution on Health in the United Kingdom.* London: The Stationery Office.

Community Transportation Association (CTA) (2001) What is Community Transportation? Available at www.ctaa.org.

Congressional Budget Office (2004) *Fuel Economy Standards Versus a Gasoline Tax*. Washington, DC: CBO.

Constanza, R., Perrings, C. and Cleveland, C. (eds.) (1997) *The Development of Ecological Economics*. Cheltenham: Edward Elgar.

Council for the Protection of Rural England (2001) *Running to Stand Still? An Analysis of the 10 Year Plan for Transport*. London: CPRE.

Crane, R. (1996) Cars and drivers in new suburbs: Linking access to travel in neo traditional planning. *Journal of the American Planning Association*, 62(1), pp. 51–65.

Crane, R. (2000) The influence of urban form on travel: An interpretive view. *Journal of Planning Literature*, 15(1), pp. 1–23.

Crawford, I.A. (2000) The Distributional Effects of the Proposed London Congestion Charging Scheme. Institute for Fiscal Studies, Briefing Note 11, October.

Cullinane, S. and Cullinane, K. (2003) City profile: Hong Kong. *Cities*, 20(4), pp. 279–288.

Curtis, C. (1995) Reducing the need to travel: strategic housing location and travel behaviour, in Earp, J.H., Headicar, P., Banister, D. and Curtis, C. (eds.) *Reducing the Need to Travel: Some Thoughts on PPG13*. Oxford Planning Monographs 1(2). Oxford: Oxford Brookes University, Planning Department.

Daly, H. (1972) In defence of a steady-state economy. *American Journal of Agricultural Economics*, 54(4), pp. 945–954.

Daly, H. (1977) *Steady-State Economics*. Washington, DC: Island Press.

Daly, H. (1992) Allocation, distribution and scale: Towards an economics that is efficient, just and sustainable. *Ecological Economics*, 6(3), pp. 185–193.

Daly, H. (1996) *Beyond Growth*. Boston: Beacon Press.

Daly, H. and Cobb, J. (1989) For the Common Good. Redirecting the Economy Toward Community, the Environment and a Sustainable Future. Boston, MA: Beacon Press.

Dantuma, L., Hawkins, R. and Montalvo, C. (2002) State of the Art Review – Production. Paper prepared for the ESTO Study on the Impacts of ICT on Transport and Mobility, November.

Dasgupta, M. (1993) Urban Problems and Urban Policies: OECD/ECMT study of 132 Cities. Paper presented at the International Conference on Travel and the City – Making it Sustainable, Dusseldorf, June, and published by OECD, Paris.

Delucchi, M.A. (2004) *Estimating the Size of Transportation Externalities*. Washington DC: Transportation Research Board.

De Mooij, R.A. (1999) The double dividend of an environmental tax reform, in Van den Bergh, J.C.J.M. (ed.) *Handbook of Environmental and Resource Economics*. Cheltenham: Edward Elgar, pp. 293–306.

Department for Transport (DfT) (2002) *The Future Development of Air Transport in the UK: A National Consultation*. London: The Stationery Office.

Department for Transport (DfT) (2003) *The Future Development of Air Transport in the UK: South East*, Annex E. London: The Stationery Office.

Department for Transport (DfT), DTI, DEFRA and HMT (2002) *Powering Future Vehicles: The Government Strategy*. London: The Stationery Office.

Department of the Environment (1993) *Town Centres and Retail Development, PPG6 (Revised)*. London: HMSO.

Department of the Environment, Transport and the Regions (1997a) *National Travel Survey*. London: The Stationery Office.

Department of the Environment, Transport and the Regions (1997b) *Building Partnerships for Prosperity*, Cm 3814. London: The Stationery Office.

Department of the Environment, Transport and the Regions (1997c) *National Road Traffic Forecasts* (Great Britain). London: The Stationery Office.

Department of the Environment, Transport and the Regions (1997d) *Land Use Change in England* No. 12. London: Department of the Environment, Transport and the Regions.

Department of the Environment, Transport and the Regions (1997e) *Transport Statistics Great Britain 1997*. London: The Stationery Office.

Department of the Environment, Transport and the Regions (1997f) *Digest of Environmental Statistics 1997*. London: The Stationery Office.

Department of the Environment, Transport and the Regions (1997g) Air Quality and Traffic Management [LAQM. G3(97)]. London: The Stationery Office.

Department of the Environment, Transport and the Regions (1998a) *The Use of Density in Urban Planning*, Report for the Planning Research Programme by the Bartlett School of Planning and Llewelyn Davies Planning. London: The Stationery Office.

Department of the Environment, Transport and the Regions (1998b) *The Future of Regional Planning Guidance: Consultation Paper*. London: DETR.

Department of the Environment, Transport and the Regions (1998c) *A New Deal for Transport: Better for Everyone*, White Paper on the Future of Transport. London: The Stationery Office. Available at www.dtlr.gov.uk/itwp.

Department of the Environment, Transport and the Regions (2001) *Transport Statistics – Great Britain 2000*. London: The Stationery Office.

Department of Trade and Industry (DTI) (1997) *Digest of UK Energy Statistics*. London: The Stationery Office.

Department of Trade and Industry (DTI) (2002) *Cross Border Shopping Report*. Research Study Conducted for Department for Trade and Industry. Available at http://www.dti.gov.uk .

Department of Trade and Industry (DTI) (2003) *Our Energy Future: Creating a Low Carbon Economy*. Energy White Paper. London: The Stationery Office. Available at www.dti.gov.uk/energy/whitepaper/ourenergyfuture.pdf.

Department of Transport (1994) *National Travel Survey 1989/91*. Government Statistical Services. London: HMSO.

Department of Transport, Local Government and the Regions (2001) *PPG13 Transport (Revised)*. London: The Stationery Office.

Departments of the Environment and Transport (1994) *PPG13 – Transport*. London: HMSO.

Departments of the Environment and Transport (1995) *PPG13 – Guide to Better Practice: Reducing the Need to Travel through Planning*. London: HMSO.

Dobes, L. (1999) Kyoto: Tradable greenhouse emission permits in the transport sector. *Transport Reviews*, **19**(1), pp. 81–97.

Downey, M.L. (1995) Transportation Trends. Paper presented at the Symposium on Challenges and Opportunities for Global Transportation in the 21st Century, Cambridge MA.

Dreborg, K. (1996) Essence of backcasting. *Futures*, **28**(9), pp. 813–828.

EC (European Commission) (2002) *EU Transport in Figures 2002 – Statistical Pocketbook*. Brussels: Eurostat, DG Energy and Transport, European Commission.

EC (European Commission) (2003) *EU Transport in Figures 2003 – Statistical Pocketbook*. Brussels: Eurostat, DG Energy and Transport, European Commission.

ECaTT (2000) Benchmarking Progress: On New Ways of Working and New Forms of Business across Europe. EcaTT Final Report. IST Programme of the European Commisssion. KAII: New Methods of Work and Electronic Commerce, August. Available at http://www.ecatt.com.

ECMT (European Conference of Ministers of Transport) (1997) *Trends in the Transport Sector*. Paris: ECMT.

ECMT (European Conference of Ministers of Transport) (1999) *Traffic Congestion in Europe*. OECD: Paris.

ECMT (European Conference of Ministers of Transport) (2000) *Assessing the Benefits of Transport*. Report to the Committee of Deputies. Paris: ECMT.

ECMT (European Conference of Ministers of Transport) (2001) Implementing

Sustainable Urban Transport Policies. Background paper CEMT/ CM(2001)13, Paris.

ECMT/OECD (2001) *Survey of Cities 1999–2000*. Paris: ECMT/OECD.

ECMT/OECD (2002) *Implementing Sustainable Urban Travel Policies*. Paris: ECMT/OECD

ECOTEC (1993) *Reducing Transport Emissions Through Land Use Planning*. London: HMSO.

Ehrlich, P.R. and Ehrlich, A. (1989) How the rich can save the poor and themselves. *Pacific and Asian Journal of Energy*, **3**(1), pp. 53–63.

Ehrlich, P.R. and Holdren, J.P. (1971) Impact of population growth. *Science*, **171**, pp. 1212–1217.

Emmerink, R., Nijkamp, P. and Rietveld, P. (1995) Is congestion pricing a first best strategy in transport policy? A critical review of arguments. *Environment and Planning B*, **22**(4), pp. 581–602.

Environmental Audit Committee (EAC) (2003) *Budget 2003 and Aviation*. 9th Report of the Session 2002–03, House of Commons HC 672. London: The Stationery Office.

Esty, D. (2002) Quoted in the World Outlook 2002 Report, World Economic Forum, Boston, Massachusetts, Economist, 6 July 2002.

European Federation for Transport and the Environment (EFTE) (1994) Green Urban Transport: A survey, Preliminary Report 94/2, January, Brussels.

Ewing, R. (1995) Beyond density, mode choice, and single trips. *Transportation Quarterly*, **49**(4), pp. 15–24.

Ewing, R. (1997) Is Los Angeles-style sprawl desirable? *Journal of the American Planning Association*, **63**(1), pp. 107–126.

Ewing, R. and Cervero, R. (2002) Travel and the built environment. *Transportation Research Record*, No. 1780, pp. 87–110.

Ewing, R., DeAnna, M. and Li, S.-C. (1996) Land use impacts on trip generation rates. *Transportation Research Record*, No. 1518, pp. 1–6.

Farthing, S., Winter, J. and Coombes, T. (1997) Travel behaviour and local accessibility to services and facilities, in Jenks, M., Burton, E. and Williams, K. (eds.) *The Compact City. A Sustainable Urban Form?* London: E & FN Spon, pp. 181–189.

Federal Highway Administration (FHWA) (2002*a*) Value pricing pilot program: notice of grant opportunities. US Department of Transportation. Available at www.fhwa.dot.gov/policy/vppp.htm.

Federal Highway Administration (FHWA) (2002*b*) *Highway Statistics 2002*. Washington DC: US Department of Transportation.

Flyberg, B. (1998) *Rationality and Power*. Chicago: University of Chicago Press.

Fouchier, V. (1997) Urban Density and Mobility: What do we know? What can we do? Paper presented at the 2nd Symposium on Urban Planning and the Environment, Groningen.

Fouracre, P., Dunkerley, C. and Gardner, G. (2003) Mass rapid transit systems for cities in the developing world. *Transport Reviews*, **23**(3), pp. 299–310.

Frank, L. and Pivo, G. (1994) Impacts of mixed use and density on utilization of three modes of travel: Single-occupant vehicle, transit, and walking. *Transportation Research Record*, No. 1466, pp. 44–52.

Fuhrer, U., Kaiser, F.G. and Steiner, J. (1993) Automobile Freizeit: Ursachen und Auswege aus der Sicht der Wohnpsychologie, in Fuhrer, U. (ed.) *Wohnen mit dem Auto*. Zurich: Ursachen und Gestaltung Automobiler Freizeit, pp. 77–93.

Gakenheimer, R. (1997) Sustainable transport and economic development. *Journal of Transport Economics and Policy*, **31**(3), pp. 331– 335.

Gallagher, R. (1992) *The Rickshaws of Bangladesh*. Dhaka: University Press.

Geels, F.W. and Smit, W.A. (2000) Failed technology futures: Pitfalls and lessons from a historical survey. *Futures*, **32**(9/10), pp. 867–885.

Geerlings, H. (1997) *Towards Sustainability of Technological Innovations in Transport: The Role of Government in Generating a Window of Technological Opportunity*. Rotterdam: Erasmus University.

Geurs, K. and Van Wee, B. (2004) Backcasting as a tool for sustainable transport policy making: The environmentally sustainable transport study in the Netherlands. *European Journal of Transport Infrastructure Research*, **4**(1), pp. 47–69.

Gilbert, R. (2000) Sustainable Mobility in the City. Paper presented at the Global Conference on the Urban Future URBAN 21, Berlin, July.

Gilbert, R. and Nadeau, K. (2002) Decoupling Economic Growth and Transport Demand: A Requirement for Sustainability. Paper presented at the Conference on Transportation and Economic Development 2001, Transportation Research Board, Portland Oregon, May.

Giorgi, L. (2003) Sustainable mobility. Challenges, opportunities and conflicts – a social science perspective. *International Social Science Journal*, **176**, pp. 179–184.

Giuliano, G. and Small, K. (1993) Is the journey to work explained by urban structure? *Urban Studies*, **30**(9), pp. 1485–1500.

Goodland, R. (2002) The biophysical basis of environmental sustainability, in Van den Bergh, J (ed.) *Handbook of Environmental and Resource Economics*. Cheltenham: Edward Elgar, pp. 709–721.

Goodwin, P. (1998) Unintended effects of transport policies, in Banister, D. (ed.) *Transport Policy and the Environment*. London: E and FN Spon, pp. 114–130.

Goodwin, P. (2000) Transformation of transport policy in Great Britain. *Transportation Research A*, **33**(7/8), pp. 655–229.

Goodwin, P., Dargay, J. and Hanley, M. (2004) Elasticities of road traffic and fuel consumption with respect to price and income: a review. *Transport Reviews*, **24**(3), pp. 275–292.

Gordon, I. (1997) Densities, urban form and travel behaviour. *Town and Country Planning*, **66**(9), pp. 239–241.

Gordon, P. and Richardson, H.W. (1997) Are compact cities a desirable planning goal? *Journal of the American Planning Association*, **63**(1), pp. 95–106.

Gordon, P., Kumar, A. and Richardson, H.W. (1989*a*) Congestion, changing metropolitan structure and city size in the United States. *International Regional Science Review*, **12**(1), pp. 45–56.

Gordon, P., Kumar, A. and Richardson, H.W. (1989*b*) Gender differences in metropolitan travel behaviour. *Regional Studies*, **23**(6), pp. 499–510.

Gordon, P., Richardson, H.W. and Jun, M.-J. (1991) The commuting paradox: evidence from the top twenty. *Journal of the American Planning Association*, **57**(4), pp. 416–420.

Government Economic Service (GES) (2002) Estimating the Social Cost of Carbon Emissions. GES Working Paper 140, London.

Graham, D. and Glaister, S. (2004) A review of road traffic demand elasticities measures. *Transport Reviews*, **24**(3), pp. 261–274.

Grammenos, F. and Tasker Brown, J. (2000) Residential street pattern design for healthy liveable communities. *New Urban Agenda*. Available at www.greenroofs.ca/nua/ip/ip02.html.

Greene, D.L. and Schafer, A. (2003) Reducing the Greenhouse Gas Emissions for US Transportation, Report from the Pew Center on Global Climate Change, Arlington, Virginia, May. Available at www.pewclimate.org.

Gwilliam, K. (2003) Urban transport in developing countries. *Transport Reviews*, **23**(2), pp. 197–216.

Hall, P. (1988) *Cities of Tomorrow: An Intellectual History of Urban Planning and Design in the Twentieth Century*. Oxford: Blackwell.

Hall, P. (1997) Urban change from the Individual Standpoint. Paper presented at the Expert Group Meeting of the URBAN 21 Project, Bonn, November.

Hall, P (1998) Conclusions, in Banister, D. (ed.) *Transport Policy and the Environment*. London: E & FN Spon, pp. 333–336.

Hall, P. (2001) Sustainable cities or town cramming? in Layard, A., Davoudi, S. and Batty, S. (eds.) *Planning for a Sustainable Future*. London: Spon, pp. 101–114.

Hall, P. and Pfeiffer, U. (2000) *Urban Future 21: A Global Agenda for Twenty First Century Cities*. London: Spon.

Handy, S. (2002) Accessibility v Mobility-enhancing Strategies for Addressing Automobile Dependence in the US. Paper presented at the ECMT round table on Transport and Spatial Policies: The Role of Regulatory and Fiscal Incentives, Round Table 124, Paris, November, pp. 101–114.

Handy, S. and Clifton, K.J. (2001) Local shopping as a strategy for reducing automobile travel. *Transportation*, **28**(4), pp. 317–346.

Hanley, N., Moffat, I., Faichney, R. and Wilson, M. (1999) Measuring sustainability: a time series of alternative indicators for Scotland. *Ecological Economics*, **28**(1), pp. 55–73.

Hanson, S. (1982) The determinants of daily travel-activity patterns: relative location and sociodemographic factors. *Urban Geography*, **3**(3), pp. 179–202.

Haq, G. (1997) *Towards Sustainable Transport Planning: A Comparison between Britain and the Netherlands*. Aldershot: Avebury.

Hardin, G. (1968) The tragedy of the commons. *Science*, **162**, pp. 1243–1248.

Hardin, G. (1993) *Living within Limits: Ecology, Economics and Population Taboos*. Oxford: Oxford University Press.

Hathway, T. (1997) Successful community participation in local traffic proposals. *Journal of Advanced Transportation*, **31**(2), pp. 201–213.

Haughton, G. and Hunter, C. (1994) *Sustainable Cities*. London: Jessica Kingsley Publishers.

Headicar, P. (1996) The local development effects of major new roads: M40 case study. *Transportation*, **23**(1), pp. 55–69.

Headicar, P. and Curtis, C. (1998) The location of new residential development: its influence on car-based travel, in Banister, D. (ed.) *Transport Policy and the Environment*. London: Spon, pp. 220–240.

Healey, P. (1997) *Collaborative Planning: Shaping Places in Fragmented Societies*. Basingstoke: Macmillan.

Heinze, G.W. (2000) Transport and Leisure. Paper prepared for presentation at the ECMT Round Table 111 on Transport and Leisure. Paris: OECD, pp. 1–51.

Hickman, R. and Banister, D. (2002) Reducing Travel by Design: What happens over Time? Paper presented at the 5th Symposium of the International Urban Planning and Environment Association, Oxford, September.

Hillier Parker (1997) The Impact of Large Foodstores on Market Towns and District Centres. Draft Report for the Department of the Environment, June.

Hillman, M. and Whalley, A. (1983) *Energy and Personal Travel: Obstacles to Conservation*. London: Policy Studies Institute.

HM Treasury and Department for Transport (2003) *Aviation and the Environment: Using Economic Measures*. London: DfT.

Hommels, A., Kemp, R., Peters, P. and Dunnewijk, T. (2002) State of the Art

Review – Living. Paper prepared for the ESTO Study on the Impacts of ICT on Transport and Mobility, November.

Hoogma, R., Kemp, R., Schot, J. and Truffler, B. (2002) *Experimenting for Sustainable Transport – The Approach of Strategic Niche Management*. London: Spon.

Hook, W. (1995) The economic advantages of non-motorized transport. *Transportation Research Record*, No 1487, pp. 14–21.

HOP Associates (2002) *The Impact of Information and Communications Technologies on Travel and Freight Distribution Patterns: Review and Assessment of Literature*. Report prepared for the UK Department for Transport, Local Government and the Regions by HOP Associates (in association with the Transport Research Group, University of Southampton). Cambridge: HOP Associates. Available at http://www.virtual-mobility.com/report.htm.

Horizon International (2003) Efficient transportation for successful urban planning in Curitiba, From the Horizons Solution Site, info@solutions-site.org. New Haven CT: Yale University, Department of Biology.

Houghton, J., Jenkins, G. and Ephraums, J. (1990) (eds.) *Climate Change: The IPCC Scientific Assessment*. Cambridge: Cambridge University Press.

House of Commons (2003) *Urban Charging Schemes, First Report of the House of Commons Transport Committee 2002–03*, Volume 1. HC 390-1. London: The Stationery Office.

Hsieh, Y., Lin, N. and Chiu, H. (2002) Virtual factory and relationship marketing: a case study of a Taiwan semiconductor manufacturing company. *International Journal of Information Management*, **22**, pp. 109–126.

Hughes, P. (1993) *Personal Transport and the Greenhouse Effect: A Strategy for Sustainability*. London: Earthscan.

Innes, J. (1995) Planning theory's emerging paradigm: communicative action and interactive practice. *Journal of Planning Education and Research*, **14**(3), pp. 183–189.

Innes, J. (1999) Consensus building in complex and adaptive systems: A framework for evaluating collaborative planning. *Journal of the American Planning Association*, **65**(4), pp. 412–423.

International Energy Agency (IEA) (1993*a*) *Cars and Climate Change*. Paris: International Energy Agency.

International Energy Agency (IEA) (1993*b*) *Energy Balances of OECD Countries 1990–1991*. Paris: OECD.

International Energy Agency (IEA) (1997) *Transport, Energy and Climate Chang*. Paris: International Energy Agency.

International Energy Agency (IEA) (2000) *The Road from Kyoto – Current CO_2 and Transport Policies in the IEA*. Paris: IEA.

International Energy Agency (IEA) (2001) *Saving Oil and Reducing CO$_2$ Emissions in Transport: Options and Strategies*. Paris: IEA, September.

International Energy Agency (IEA) (2002) Energy Balances of OECD Countries and Energy Balances for Non-OECD Countries. Paris: OECD. http://data.iea.org/ieastore/default.asp.

Jackson, T. and Marks, N. (1994) Measuring Sustainable Economic Welfare – A Pilot Index: 1950–1990. Stockholm Environment Institute, Stockholm.

Jaffe, A.B., Peterson, S.R., Portney, P.R. and Stavins, R.N. (1995) Environmental regulation and competitiveness of US manufacturing: What does the evidence tell us? *Journal of Economic Literature*, **33**(2), pp. 132–163.

Jenks, M., Burton, E. and Williams, K. (1996) *The Compact City: A Sustainable Urban Form?* London: Spon.

Johnston-Anumonwo, I. (1992) The influence of household type on gender differences in work trip distance. *Professional Geographer*, **44**(2), pp. 161–169.

Keong, C.K. (2002) Road Pricing: Singapore's Experience. Paper presented at the 3rd Imprint Europe Conference on Implementing Reform on Transport Pricing: Constraints and Solutions: Learning from Best Practice, Brussels, October.

Kitamura, R., Mokhtarian, P. and Laidet, L. (1997) A micro-analysis of land use and travel in five neighbourhoods in the San Francisco Bay area. *Transportation*, **24**(2), pp. 125–158.

Knoflacher, H. (2000) Transport and Leisure. Paper prepared for presentation at the ECMT Round Table 111 on Transport and Leisure. Paris: OECD and ECMT, pp. 53–88.

Koerner, B.I. (1998) Cities that work. *US News and World Report*, No. 8, June, pp. 26–36.

Krugman, P. (1994) *Peddling Prosperity*. New York: Norton.

Larsen, O. (2000) Norwegian Urban Road Tolling: What Role for Evaluation? Paper presented at the second TRANS-TALK Workshop, Brussels, November. Available at www.iccr.ac.at/trans-talk/workshops/workshop2.

Levinson, D.M. and Kumar, A. (1997) Density and the journey to work. *Growth and Change*, **28**(2), pp. 147–172.

London Assembly (2002) *Congestion Charging: The Public Concerns behind the Politics. London Assembly Transport Committee*. London: London Assembly.

Louw, E. and Maat, K. (1999) Mind the Gap: pitfalls on measures to control mobility. *Built Environment*, **25**(2), pp. 118–128.

Lyons, G. (2002) Internet: New technology's evolving role, nature and effects on transport. *Transport Policy*, **9**(4), pp. 335–346.

Lyons, G. and Kenyon, S. (2003) *Social Participation, Personal Travel and Internet Use*. Proceedings of the 10th International Conference on Travel Behaviour Research, Lucerne, 10–15 August. Available at http://www.ivt.baug.ethz.ch/allgemein/iatbr2003.html.

Maddison, D., Pearce, D., Johansson, O., Calthorp, E., Litman, T. and Verhoef, E. (1996) *The True Costs of Road Transport*. London: Earthscan.

Mäder, S. and Schleiniger, R. (1995) Kosten Wirksamkeit von Luft-reinhaltemassnahmen. *Schweizerische Zeitschrift für Volkswirtschaft und Statistik*, **131**(2).

Mägerle, J. and Maggi, R. (1999) Zurich Transport Policy: Or the importance of being rich. *Built Environment*, **25**(2), pp. 129–138.

Mansell, G. (2001) The development of online freight markets. *Logistics and Transport Focus*, **3**(7), pp. 2–3.

Marshall, S. (2001) The challenge of sustainable transport, in Layard, A., Davoudi, S. and Batty, S. (eds.) *Planning for a Sustainable Future*. London: Spon, pp. 131–147.

Marshall, S. and Banister, D. (2000) Travel reduction strategies: intentions and outcomes. *Transportation Research A*, **34**(4), pp. 324–328.

Meadows, D.H., Meadows, D.L. and Randers, J. (1992) *Confronting Global Collapse: Envisioning a Sustainable Future*. Post Mills, VT: Chelsea Green.

Meadows, D.H., Meadows, D.L., Randers, J. and Behrens III, W. (1972) *The Limits to Growth*. New York: Universe Books.

Meirelles, A. (2000) A Review of Bus Priority Systems in Brazil: From Bus Lanes to Busway Transit. Paper presented at the Smart Urban Transport Conference, Brisbane, 17–20 October 2000.

Meyer, A. (2001) *Contraction and Convergence*. London: Green Books.

Michaelis, L., Bleviss, D. and Orfeuil J.-P. (1996) Mitigation options in the transportation sector, in IPCC *Climate Change 1995: Impacts, Adaptations and Mitigation of Climate Change*, Scientific and Technical Analyses, Contribution of Working Group II to the Second Assessment Report of the Intergovernmental Panel on Climate Change (IPCC). Cambridge: Cambridge University Press, pp. 680–712.

Michaelis, L. and Davidson, O. (1996) GHG mitigation in the transport sector. *Energy Policy*, **24**(10/11), pp. 969–984.

Ministry of Transport the Netherlands (2002) Pay per kilometer: Progress report, Paper presented at the 2nd Seminar of the EU Imprint-Europe Thematic Network 'Implementing reform on transport pricing: Identifying mode-specific issues', Brussels, 14–15 May.

Mitchell, H. and Trodd, E. (1994) An Introductory Study of Teleworking based on Transport-Telecommunications Substitution. Research project for the Department of Transport. Unpublished, but summarized on the HOP Associates database at www.virtual-mobility.com.

Mitlin, D. and Satterthwaite, D. (1996) Sustainable development in cities, in Pugh, C. (ed.) *Sustainability, Environment and Urbanisation*. London: Earthscan, pp. 23–62.

Mittler, D. (1998) Environmental Space and Barriers to Local Sustainability. Evidence from Edinburgh, Scotland. Paper presented at Planning Patterns for Sustainable Development, International Conference, Padua, Italy, 30 September–3 October.

Mittler, D. (1999) Reducing travel!? A case study of Edinburgh, Scotland. *Built Environment*, **25**(2), pp. 106–117.

Mogridge, M.J.H. (1985) Transport, land use and energy interaction. *Urban Studies*, **22**(4), pp. 481–492.

Mokhtarian, P. (2003) Telecommunications and travel. The case for complementarity. *Journal of Industrial Ecology*, **6**(2), pp. 43–57.

Mokhtarian, P. and Salomon, I. (1999) Travel for the fun of it. *Access*, **15**, Fall, pp. 26–31. Available at http://socrates.berkeley.edu/~uctc.

Mokhtarian, P. and Salomon, I. (2001) How derived is the demand for travel? Some conceptual and measurement considerations. *Transportation Research A*, **35**(6), pp. 695–719.

Muheim, R. and Reinhardt, E. (2000) Car sharing – the key to combined mobility: Small public/private mobility partnership leads the way. *Journal of World Transport Policy and Practice*, **5**(3), pp. 64–77.

Naess, P. (1993) Transportation energy in Swedish towns and regions. *Scandinavian Housing and Planning Research*, **10**, pp. 187–206.

Naess, P. and Sandberg, S.L. (1996) Workplace location, modal split and energy use for commuting trips. *Urban Studies*, **33**(3), pp. 557–580.

Naess, P., Roe, P.G. and Larsen, S. (1995) Travelling distances, modal split and transportation energy in thirty residential areas in Oslo. *Journal of Environmental Planning and Management*, **38**(3), pp. 349–370.

National Economic Research Associates (NERA) (1997) Motor or Modem. Report prepared for the UK Royal Automobile Club, London, November.

National Energy Policy Development Group (2001) *Reliable, Affordable, and Environmentally Sound Energy for America's Future*. Washington DC: Office of the Vice President.

Newman, P.W.G. and Kenworthy, J.R. (1988) The transport energy trade-off: Fuel efficient traffic versus fuel-efficient cities. *Transportation Research*, **22A**(3), pp. 163–174.

Newman, P.W.G. and Kenworthy, J.R. (1989a) *Cities and Automobile Dependence – An International Sourcebook*. Aldershot: Gower.

Newman, P.W.G. and Kenworthy, J.R. (1989b) Gasoline consumption and cities: a comparison of US cities with a global survey,, *Journal of the American Planning Association*, **5**(1), pp. 24–37.

Newman, P.W.G. and Kenworthy, J.R. (1999) *Sustainability and Cities: Overcoming Automobile Dependence*. Washington DC: Island Press.

Ng, K. (2004) A Review of Hong Kong's Transport Policy and Its Sustainability. Unpublished paper prepared for the Sustainable urban Development and Transport Specialism. The Bartlett School of Planning, University College London.

Oak Ridge National Laboratory (2002) *Transportation Energy Data Book*. Oak Ridge, Tennessee: US Department of Energy.

OECD (Organisation for Economic Cooperation and Development) (1988) *Transport and the Environment*. Paris: OECD.

OECD (Organisation for Economic Cooperation and Development) (1991) *Environmental Indicators*. Paris: OECD.

OECD (Organisation for Economic Cooperation and Development) (1992) *Energy Balances of OECD Countries, 1989–1990*. Paris: OECD.

OECD (Organisation for Economic Cooperation and Development) (1993) *Indicators for the Integration of Environmental Concerns into Transport Policies*. Environmental Monograph No. 80. Paris: OECD.

OECD (Organisation for Economic Cooperation and Development) (1995) *Motor Vehicle Pollution: Reduction Strategies beyond 2010*. Paris: OECD, p. 133.

OECD (Organisation for Economic Cooperation and Development) (1997) *Energy Balances of OECD Countries, 1995–1996*. Paris: OECD.

OECD (Organisation for Economic Cooperation and Development) (2002*a*) Global Long Term Projections for Motor Vehicle Emissions (MOVE II) Project. Working Paper on National Environmental Policy, Working Group on Transport, ENV/EPOC/WPNEP/T(2002)8/REV1, October, Paris.

OECD (Organisation for Economic Cooperation and Development) (2002*b*) The Role of Soft Measures in Achieving Environmentally Sustainable Transport, Seminar, Berlin, December. Available at www.oecd.org/pdf/M0001900/M00019258.pdf.

OECD/ECMT (Organisation for Economic Cooperation and Development and European Conference of Ministers of Transport) (1995) *Urban Travel and Sustainable Development*. Paris: OECD/ECMT.

OECD/IEA (Organisation for Economic Cooperation and Development and the International Energy Agency) (1997) *Transport, Energy and Climate Change*. Policy Analysis Series. Paris: OECD/IEA.

Office of the Deputy Prime Minister (ODPM) (2003) *Sustainable Communities: Building the Future*. London: The Stationery Office.

Office of Science and Technology (1998) *The Role of Technology in the Implementing an Integrated Transport Policy*. London: OST.

Office for National Statistics (ONS) (2002) *Teleworking in the UK*. London: The Stationery Office. Available at http://www.statistics.gov.uk.

Office for National Statistics (ONS) (2003*a*) 2002 E-commerce Survey of Business: Value of E-trading. Press release from the Office of National Statistics, 4 December. Available at http://www.statistics.gov.uk.

Office for National Statistics (ONS) (2003*b*) *Social Trends 33*. London: The Stationery Office. Available at http://www.statistics.gov.uk.

Office for National Statistics (ONS) (2003*c*) *Transport Statistics Bulletin: National Travel Survey Provisional Results*. London: The Stationery Office.

Orfeuil, J.-P. (1993) *Eléments pour une prospective transport, énergie, environnement*. Arceuil, Paris: Institut National de Recherche sur les Transports et leur Sécurité (INRETS).

Owens, S (1986) *Energy Planning and Urban Form*. London: Pion.

Oxford City Council (OCC) (2000) *Oxford Transport Strategy Assessment of Impact*. Oxford: OCC.

Oxfordshire County Council (OXCC) (2002) *Oxford Transport Strategy*. Oxford: OXCC. Available at www.oxfordshire.gov.uk/oxford/.

Paul, K.J. (2002) Advocating mileage-based auto insurance. *Conservation Matters*, **8**(3), Spring, pp 31–33.

Peake, S. (1994) *Transport in Transition*. London: Earthscan.

Pearce, D.W. (1991) The role of carbon taxes in adjusting to global warming. *Economic Journal*, **101**(407), July, pp. 938–948.

Peden, M., Scurfield, R., Sleet, D., Mohan, D., Hyder, A.A., Jarawan, E. and Mathers, C. (eds.) (2004) *The World Report on Road Traffic Injury Prevention*. Geneva: World Health Organisation.

Peñalosa, E. (2003) Foreword, Whitelegg, J. and Haq, G. (eds.) *World Transport Policy and Practice*, The Earthscan Reader. London: Earthscan, pp. xxv–xxxi.

Peters, M. and Wilkinson, M. (2000), Suppliers are encompassing the benefits brought by e-commerce, in World Markets Research Centre, *Global Purchasing and Supply Chain Strategies 2000*. London: Business Briefings Limited, pp. 124–127. Available at http://www.wmrc.com.

Pigou, A.C. (1947) *A Study in Public Finance*. 3rd ed. London: Macmillan.

Piore, M.J. and Sabel, C. (1984) *The Second Industrial Divide: Possibilities for Prosperity*. New York: Basic Books.

Porter, M. and Van der Linde, C. (1995) Towards a new conception of environment competitiveness relationship. *Journal of Economic Perspectives*, **9**(1), pp. 97–118.

Prevedouros, P.D. and Schofer, J. (1991) Trip characteristics and travel patterns of suburban residents. *Transportation Research Record*, No. 1328, pp. 49–57.

Priemus, H. and Maat, K.(1998) *Ruimtelijk en Mobiliteitsbeleid: Interactie van Rijksinstrumenten Stedelijke en Regionale Verkenningen 18*. Delft: Delft University Press.

Pucher, J. and Renne, J. (2003) Socioeconomics of urban travel: evidence from the 2001 NHTS. *Transportation Quarterly*, 57(3), pp. 49–77.

Putman, R. (2000) *Bowling Alone: The Collapse and Revival of America's Community*. Boston: Simon and Schuster.

Qi Dong (2003) Mobility, Accessibility and Urban Sustainable Transportation in Emerging Shanghai. Paper prepared for the Sustainable Urban Development and Transport Specialism, Bartlett School of Planning, University College London, December.

Qui, Daxiong, Yan, Li, Zhou, Huang (1996) Status review of sources and end-uses of energy in China. *Energy for Sustainable Development*, 3(3), pp. 7–13.

Rabinovitch, J. (1992) Innovative land use and public transport policy. *Land Use Policy*, 13(1), pp. 51–67.

Rabinovitch, J. and Hoehn, J. (1995) A Sustainable Urban Transportation System: The 'Surface Metro' in Curitiba, Brazil. EPAT/MUCIA Working Paper.

Rabinovitch, J. and Leitman, J. (1996) Urban planning in Curitiba. *Scientific American*, 273(3), pp. 46–49.

RAC Foundation (2002) *Motoring Towards 2050 – An Independent Inquiry*. London: Royal Automobile Club Foundation. www.racfoundation.org.

Reichwald R., Fremuth, N. and Ney, M. (2002) Mobile Communities – Erweiterung von virtuellen Communities mit mobilen Diensten, in Reichwald, R. (ed.) *Mobile Kommunikation*. Wiesbaden: Gabler-Verlag, pp. 523–537.

Replogle, M. (1991) Sustainable transportation strategies for Third World development. *Transportation Research Record*, No. 1294, Washington DC: National Research Council.

Replogle, M. (1992) *Non-motorized Vehicles in Asian Cities*. World Bank Technical Paper Series No 162, Asian Technical Department. Washington DC: World Bank.

Richardson, H. and Gordon, P. (2001) Compactness or sprawl: America's future vs the present, in Echenique, M. and Saint, A. (eds.) *Cities for the New Millennium*. London: Spon, pp. 53–64.

Rietveld, P. and Stough, R. (eds.) (2005) *Barriers to Sustainable Transport – Institutions, Regulations and Implementation in Transport*. London: Spon.

Robinson, J.B. (1982) Energy backcasting: A proposed method for policy analysis. *Energy Policy*, 10(4), pp. 337–344.

ROCOL (2000) *Road Charging Options for London: A Technical Assessment*. Report for the Government Office for London. London: The Stationery

Office, March. Available at www.opengov.uk/glondon/transport/rocol. htm

Rodríguez, D. and Targa, F. (2004) The value of accessibility to Bogotá's bus rapid transit system. *Transport Reviews*, **24**(5), pp. 587–610.

Rogers, R. and Burdett, R. (2001) Lets cram more into the city, in Echenique, M. and Saint, A. (eds.) *Cities for the New Millennium*. London: Spon, pp. 9–14.

Romm, J.J. (2004) *The Hype about Hydrogen: Fact and Fiction in the Race to Save the Climate*. Washington DC: Island Press.

Royal Commission on Environmental Pollution (RCEP) (1994) *Transport and the Environment*. Eighteenth Report of the Royal Commission on Environmental Pollution, Cm 2674. London: HMSO.

Royal Commission on Environmental Pollution (RCEP) (1997) *Transport and the Environment – Developments since 1994*. Twentieth Report of the Royal Commission on Environmental Pollution, Cm 3752. London: The Stationery Office.

Royal Commission on Environmental Pollution (RCEP) (2002*a*) *The Environmental Effects of Civil Aircraft in Flight*. Special Report. London: RCEP.

Royal Commission on Environmental Pollution (RCEP) (2002*b*) *Environmental Planning*. Twenty-third Report of the RCEP, Cm 5459. London: The Stationery Office.

Rubin, J. and Kling, C. (1993) An emission saved is an emission earned: an empirical study of emissions banking for light-duty vehicle manufacturers. *Journal of Environmental Economics and Management*, **25**(3), pp. 257–274.

Rudlin, D. and Falk, N. (1999) *Building the 21st Century Home – The Sustainable Urban Neighbourhood*. Oxford: The Architectural Press.

Rujopakarn, W. (2003) Bangkok Transport System Development: What went Wrong? Internal Working Paper, Department of Civil Engineering, Kasetsart University, Bangkok, p. 14.

SACTRA (Standing Advisory Committee on Trunk Road Assessment) (1999) *Transport and the Economy*. London: The Stationery Office.

Salomon, I. and Mokhtarian, P. (1997) Coping with congestion: Reconciling behavioural responses and policy analysis. *Transportation Research D*, **2**(2), pp. 107–123.

Salon, D., Sperling, D., Shaheen, S. and Sturges, D. (1999) New Mobility: Using technology and partnerships to create more efficient, equitable, and environmentally sound transportation. Institute of Transportation Studies, University of California, Davis. Available at http://database.pat h.berkeley.edu/imr/papers/UCD-ITS-RR-99-1.pdf..

Satterthwaite, D. (1995) The underestimation of urban poverty and its health consequences. *Third World Planning Review*, **17**(4), pp. iii–xii.

Satterthwaite, D. (1997) Sustainable cities or cities that contribute to sustainable development? *Urban Studies*, **34**(10), pp. 1667–1691.

Saxena K.B.C. and Sahay, B.S. (2000) Managing IT for world class manufacturing: the Indian scenario. *International Journal of Information Management*, **20**(1), pp. 29–57.

Schafer, A. and Victor, D. (1997) the past and future of global mobility. *Scientific American*, **277**(4), pp. 58–61.

Schipper, L. (2001) Sustainable Urban Transport in the 21st Century. Mimeo available from mrmeter@onebox.com.

Schipper, L. and Marie-Lilliu, C. (1999). *Transportation and CO₂ Emissions: Flexing the Link – A Path for the World Bank*. Environmental Department Paper No. 69. Washington DC: World Bank. Available at http://www.worldbank.org/cleanair/global/publications/transport_pubs.htm.

Schipper, L., Figueroa, M.J. and Gorham, R. (1995) People on the Move: A Comparison of Travel Patterns in OECD Countries. Discussion paper from the Lawrence Berkeley Laboratory, California.

Schipper, L., Steiner, R., Figueroa, M.J. and Dolan, K. (1993) Fuel prices and economy: Factors affecting land travel. *Transport Policy*, **1**(1), pp. 6–20.

Schleicher-Tappeser, R., Hey, C. and Steen, P. (1998) Policy approaches for decoupling freight transport from economic growth. Paper presents at the Eighth World Conference on Transport Research, Antwerp, July. Available at http://www.eures.de/de/download/antwerp.pdf.

Scholl, L., Schipper, L. and Kiang, N. (1994) CO₂ Emissions from Passenger Transport: A Comparison of International Trends from 1973–1990. Discussion paper from the Lawrence Berkeley Laboratory, California.

Scholl, L. Schipper, L. and Kiang, N. (1996) CO2 emissions from passenger transport – A comparison of international trends from 1973 to 1992. *Energy Policy*, **24**(1) pp. 17–30.

Schwela, D. and Zali, O. (1999) *Urban Traffic Pollution*. London: Spon.

Senft, L. (2003) The Transport Concept of Freiburg. Unpublished paper prepared for the sustainable Urban Development and Transport Specialism at the Bartlett School of Planning, University College London, January.

Shoup, D. (2002) Roughly right or precisely wrong, *Access*, **20**, Spring, pp. 20–25.

Sloman, L. (2003) Less Traffic where People live: How Local Transport Schemes can help cut Traffic. Report prepared under the Royal Commission Exhibition of 1851 Built Environment Fellowship, Transport 2000 and University of Westminster, London.

Smith, T.B. (1973) The Policy Implementation Process, *Policy Sciences*, **4**(2), pp. 197–209.

Social Exclusion Unit (2002) Making the Connections: Transport and Social

Exclusion. Report from the Social Exclusion Unit, Department of Trade and Industry. Available at www.socialexclusion.gov.uk.

Socialdata (1993) *Mobilität Baumt 1 der Stadt Zürich – Verhalten*. Munich: Socialdata.

Southworth, M. and Ben Joseph, E. (1997) *Streets and the Shaping of Towns and Cities*. New York: McGraw Hill.

Spence, N. and Frost, M. (1995) Work travel responses to changing workplaces and changing residences, in Brotchie, J., Batty, M., Blakely, E., Hall, P. and Newton, P. (eds.) *Cities in Competition. Productive and Sustainable Cities for the 21st Century*. Melbourne: Longman Australia, pp. 359–381.

Stavins, R.N. (1995) Transaction costs and tradable permits. *Journal of Environmental Economics and Management*, **29**(2), pp. 133–148.

Stead, D. (1996) Density, Settlement Size and Travel Patterns. Unpublished research note on the National Travel Surveys 1985/86, 1989/91 and 1992/94, Bartlett School of Planning, University College London.

Stead, D. (2000) Unsustainable settlements, in Barton, H. (ed.) *Sustainable Communities. The Potential for Eco-Neighbourhoods*. London: Earthscan, pp. 29–45.

Stead, D. (2000*a*) Trends in transport intensity across Europe. *European Journal of Transport Infrastructure Research* 0(0), pp. 27–39 (this was a trial version of the Journal).

Stead, D. (2000*b*) Relationships between transport emissions and travel patterns in Britain. *Transport Policy*, **6**(4), pp. 247–258.

Stead, D. (2001*a*) Transport intensity in Europe – indicators and trends. *Transport Policy*, **8**(1), pp. 29–46.

Stead, D. (2001*b*) Relationships between land use, socio-economic factors, and travel patterns in Britain. *Environment and Planning B*, **28**(4), pp. 499–528.

Stead, D. and Marshall, S. (1998) The Relationships between Urban Form and Travel Patterns: An International Review and Evaluation. Paper presented at the Eighth World Conference on Transport Research, July 13–17, Antwerp.

Stickland, R. (1993) Bangkok's urban transport crisis. *Urban Age*, **2**(1), pp. 1–5.

Stough, R. and Rietveld, P. (2005) Institutional dimensions of sustainable transport, in Rietveld, P. and Stough, R. (eds.) *Barriers to Sustainable Transport – Institutions, Regulations and Sustainability*. London: Spon, pp. 1–17..

Sutcliffe, A. (1996) Travel for Food Shopping. Unpublished MPhil Thesis in Town Planning, The Bartlett School of Planning, University College London.

Symonds Group (2002) Transport Development Areas Guide to Good Practice. Report prepared for the RICS with ATIS REAL Weatheralls and Gal.com, London, June.

Tayyaran, M.R. and Khan, A.M. (2003) The effects of telecommunications and intelligent transportation systems on urban development. *Journal of Urban Technology*, 10(2), pp. 87–100.

TecnEcon (1996) Central Area Parking Study – Final Report. Prepared for Birmingham City Council, the Department of Transport, and Centro, March.

The Economist (2002) Blowing smoke. *The Economist*, 14 February 2002, p. 49. Available at http://www.economist.com/world/na/displayStory. cfm?story_id=989298.

Toffler, A. (1991) *Power Shift: Knowledge, Wealth and Violence at the Edge of the 21st Century*. London: Bantam.

Toman, M. (1994) Economics and sustainability: balancing trade-offs and imperatives. *Land Economics*, 70(4), pp. 399–413.

Transport and Environment (2003) Congestion Pricing in London: A European Perspective. Paper prepared for the European Federation for Transport and Environment by Stephanis Anastasiades, Brussels, February.

Transport for London (TfL) (2002) The Greater London (Central Zone) Congestion Charging Order 2001. Report to the Mayor, London, February.

Transport for London (TfL) (2003) *Congestion Charging – Six Months On*. London: TfL. Available at www.tfl.gov.uk/tfl/cc_intro.shtml.

Transportation Research Board (1997) Towards a Sustainable Future: Addressing the Long-Term effects of Motor Vehicle Transportation on Climate and Ecology. TRB Special Report 251, Washington DC.

Transportation Research Board (2001) *Making Transit Work: Insight from Western Europe, Canada, and the United States*. Washington, DC: National Academy Press.

Turner, K. (2002) Environmental and ecological economics perspectives, in Van den Bergh, J. (ed.) *Handbook of Environmental and Resource Economics*. Cheltenham: Edward Elgar, pp. 1001–1031.

US Environmental Protection Agency (2002) *Latest Findings on National Air Quality: 2001 Status and Trends*. Research Triangle Park, NC: Environmental Protection Agency.

UNDP (1994) *Non Motorised Transport – Confronting Poverty*. New York: Oxford University Press.

UNDP (1997) Transport and Sustainable Human Settlements: A UNDP Policy Overview. Draft Discussion Paper, Winter.

United Nations Centre for Human Settlements (UNCHS) (1996) *An Urbanizing World: Global Report on Human Settlements*. Habitat Report. Oxford: Oxford University Press.

United Nations Environment Programme (2002) *National Emissions of CO₂ from Transport*. UN Framework Convention on Climate Change (UNFCCC). Washington: UNEP.

UNFCCC (United Nations Framework Convention for Climate Change) (2003) *Caring for Climate: A Guide to the Climate Change Convention and the Kyoto Protocol*. Bonn: Climate Change Secretariat, UNFCCC.

Urban Task Force (1999) *Towards an Urban Renaissance*. The Report of the Task Force, Chaired by Lord Rogers of Riverside. London: Spon.

Urry, J. (2001) Inhabiting the Car. Paper presented at the Barcelona 2001 Conference on the Future of the Car.

US Environmental Protection Agency (2002) *Latest Findings on National Air Quality: 2001 Status and Trends*. Research Triangle Park, NC: Environmental Protection Agency.

Van Essen, H., Bello, O., Dings, J. and Van den Brink, R. (2003) To shift or not to shift, that is the question – The environmental performance of the principle modes of freight and passenger transport in the policy making context, Paper prepared by CE Solutions for Environment, Economy and Technology, Delft, March.

Vasconcellos, E.A. (2001) *Urban Transport: Environment and Equity – The Case for Developing Countries*. London: Earthscan.

Vigar, G. (2001) *The Politics of Mobility*. London: Spon.

Visser, J.G.S.N. and Nemoto, T. (2002) E-commerce and the Consequences for Freight Transport. EU-STELLA project, paper prepared for kick-off meeting, 7, 8 and 9 June in Sienna.

Von Weizsacker, A.B., Lovins, A.B. and Lovins, L.H. (1997) *Factor Four: Doubling Wealth, Halving Resource Use*. London: Earthscan.

Voogd, H. (2001) Social dilemmas and the communicative planning paradox. *Town Planning Review*, 72(1), pp. 77–95.

Wachs, M. (2002) Transportation demand management: The American experience. Why what works is unpopular and what is popular doesn't work. Editorial in the Report on *Sustainable Transport in Sustainable Cities- Why Travel?* The Warren Centre, University of Sydney. Available at http://www.warren.usyd.edu.au/transport/Why%20Travel (bk2).pdf

Wagner, P., Banister, D., Dreborg, K., Eriksson E.A., Stead, D., and Weber, K.M. (2003) Impacts of ICTs on Transport and Mobility (ICTRANS). Institute for Prospective Technological Studies Technical Report. Joint Research Centre, Seville, June.

Warren Centre (2002) Healthy transport, healthy people, Executive Summary. *Sustainable Transport in Sustainable Cities – Why Travel?* University of Sydney. Available at http://www.warren.usyd.edu.au/transport/Healthy Trans_people.pdf

Wegener, M. (1994) Operational urban models: state of the art. *Journal of the American Planning Association*, **60**(1), pp. 17–29.

Whitelegg, J. (1997) *Critical Mass*. London: Pluto Press.

Williams, J (1997) A Study of the Relationship between Settlement Size and Travel Patterns in the UK. URBASSS Working Paper 2, The Bartlett School of Planning, UCL, London. Available at www.bartlett.ucl.ac.uk/planning/urbasss.

Williams, J. (2001) Achieving local sustainability in rural communities, in Layard, A., Davoudi, S. and Batty, S. (eds.) *Planning for a Sustainable Future*. London: Spon, pp. 235–252.

Willson, R. (2001) Assessing communicative rationality as a transportation planning paradigm. *Transportation*, **28**(1), pp. 1–31.

Wilson, R. (2002) *Transportation in America: A Statistical Summary of Transportation in the United States*. Washington DC: The Eno Transportation Foundation.

Winter, J. and Farthing, S. (1997). Coordinating facility provision and new housing development: impacts on car and local facility use, in Farthing, S.M. (ed.) *Evaluating Local Environmental Policy*. Avebury, Aldershot, pp. 159–179.

Wood, C. (1994) Passenger Transport Energy Use and Urban Form. Working Paper, Bartlett School of Planning, University College London, p. 39.

World Bank (1975) *Urban Transport*. Policy Sector Paper. Washington DC: World Bank.

World Bank (1994) *World Development Report 1994: Development and the Environment*. Oxford: Oxford University Press.

World Bank (1996) *Sustainable Transport: Priorities for Policy Reform*. Washington DC: World Bank.

World Bank (1998) *World Development Indicators* (CD-ROM). Washington DC: World Bank.

World Bank (2001) *Cities on the Move*. A World Bank Urban Transport Strategy Review, Washington DC: World Bank. Available at www.worldbank.org/html/fpd/transport/ut_over.htm.

World Commission on Environment and Development (WCED) (1987) *Our Common Future* (The Brundtland Report). Oxford: Oxford University Press.

World Health Organisation (WHO) (1997) Creating Healthy Cities in the 21st Century. Background Paper prepared for the Dialogue on Health in Human Settlements for Habitat II, WHO, Geneva.

Wright, L. (2001) Latin American busways: Moving people rather than cars. *Natural Resources Forum*, **25**(2), pp. 121–134.

WWF (2001) Fuel Taxes and Beyond – UK Transport and Climate Change. Report from the World Wildlife Fund and Transport 2000, London, January. Available at www.wwf-uk.org.

Zoche, P., Beckert, B., Joisten, M. and Hudetz, W. (2002) State of the Art review – Working. Paper prepared for the ESTO Study on the Impacts of ICT on Transport and Mobility, November.

Index

1,3-butadiene 25
24-hour economy 173, 174, 212

Aalborg 74
ABC location policy 114
acceptability 231, 243 (see public acceptability, private acceptability and social acceptability)
accessibility 10, 15–17, 79, 91, 110, 114, 117, 126, 147, 183, 188, 193, 216, 246–247, 252–253 (see political acceptability and public acceptability)
  enhancing strategies 129
  map 200
accessible transport 197
adaptability 245
addiction to the car 6 (see car)
Africa 200
agglomeration cities 14 (see cities)
  economies 15, 54, 176, 238
air pollution 16 (see emissions and individual gases)
  quality 12, 24–26,153
  quality control 89
air transport 58
  travel 20, 148–150, 159, 187, 241
  travel pricing anomalies 149
aircraft noise 148
airports 170
alternative fuelled vehicles 144
  fuels 23, 90, 129, 152, 158, 163,

204 (see petrol and diesel)
anticipatory scenarios 213 (see scenarios and backcasting)
appropriate technology 229
area licensing scheme 137
Asia 201
ASIF equation 51
assessment of risk 245
attitudes 120, 223
Australia 44, 61, 236
average fuel consumption 157
  journey distance 100, 112
  length of haul 165
aviation carbon emissions 148
  policy 150

backcasting 212–213, 215 (see scenarios)
Bangkok 14, 196–197
Bangladesh 200
Barcelona 207
barriers to implementation 9, 70, 240
behavioural factors 120
benzene 25
Bern 235
best available technology 167
  practice 89, 164
bicycle 8, 198, 200, 209, 228 (see cycling)
biodiversity 12
biofuels 163
biomass 66, 162

Birmingham 103
Bogota 3, 204, 206–208
Brundtland 2, 4
Bucharest 74
bus 145
  based systems 201
  lanes 76
  rapid transit (BRT) 201–204,
    206, 208
  services 195
  users 143
business-to-customers 183
busway 199, 202, 210 (see bus)

Calcutta 14
California 31, 66, 67, 117, 160, 164
Canada 21, 61, 63
car 180
  and the city 231
  as an icon 5–7
  based mobility 158
  dependency 16, 154
  driver 29, 116
  free city 248
  free days 208
  free housing 75
  free lifestyles 189
  free location 8, 246
  insurance 138
  ownership 7–9, 19, 20, 26,
    27, 47–48, 62, 88, 120, 142,
    179, 191, 240, 247 (see vehicle
    ownership)
  rental 247
  restricting measures 76
  sharing schemes 75
  trips 106
  use 7–9, 17, 48, 58, 69, 124, 195
carbon consumption 1
  dioxide 20–21, 35, 44–46, 61,
    63, 68, 81, 91–92, 221, 230
    (see greenhouse gas)

efficiency 162
  fixing 30
  leakage 30
  monoxide 24, 34
  sink 30
  tax 32–33, 81, 92, 147, 151,
    230, 249
catalytic converter 18, 25, 63, 157,
  201
cheap oil 225
China 155, 194, 208–209
Ciclovia 209 (see Bogota and bus
  rapid transit)
cities 211, 216, 246, 248 (see
  settlement size)
  in developing countries 193,
    252–253
  in OECD countries 216
city development 229
  economy 231
  vitality and viability 127
city-based cars 165 (see car)
clean car 168 (see car)
Clean Development Mechanisms 34
  (see Kyoto)
  fuels 67, 220, 222 (see alternative
    fuels)
  motoring 242 (see car)
clear zones 8, 127 (see cities, car
  free)
climate stability 154
collective responsibility 79, 95
co-location 109
Communications systems 169
communicative rationality 95
community participation 76
  values 241–242
commuting distance 103
  journeys 185
  trip times 109
compact city 98, 108, 125 (see
  cities, density)

company transport plans 119
comparative analysis 56
competitive advantage 98
complementary effects 188, 238
comprehensive pricing 93 (see
    pricing)
concentration index 103
congestion 6, 15, 67, 69, 71, 88,
    135, 224, 227, 237, 241, 247
    charging 70, 242 (see London,
        electronic road pricing and
        road pricing)
consultation process 243
contraction and convergence 27, 64
    (see flip theory)
contrail formation 149 (see air)
cordon pricing scheme 132 (see
    congestion charging)
corridors 197 (see accessibility)
cost of the technology 168
costs of transport 166 (see pricing)
cross sector implementation 83
culture 6
Curitiba 198–199, 203
customer driven networks 53, 55
customized mobility 181
cycling 59, 69, 75, 109, 194, 250,
    252, 254 (see bicycle and non
    motorized transport)

decentralization of activities 99,
    112–116
    of cities 16
decentralized concentration 125
    responsibilities 93
decision-makers 85
decoupling 9, 41, 44, 55, 157, 219–
    221, 249
demand for travel 108
    management 17, 222, 240
dematerialization 53–55, 66, 161,
    221

demonstration effects 77, 94–96,
    132, 242
density 106, 108–109, 125 (see
    employment density, high density,
    job density, land use density, low
    density, medium density, and
    urban density)
derived demand 187, 234–236 (see
    demand for travel)
desirable city 212 (see scenarios and
    sustainable city)
Detroit 102
developed countries 63 (see OECD)
developing countries 10, 13–14,
    26, 34, 62–63, 191, 201 (see
    non-OECD)
development policies 69–70
    pressures 16
diesel 25, 59, 66, 68, 144, 162, 164,
    230 (see petrol and alternative
    fuels)
direct marketing 183
distance reduction 240 (see travel
    reduction)
distance-based scheme 141
distributional consequences 30,
    140–145, 229

e-business 175–176, 183
e-entertainment 180
e-everything 175, 179–180
e-information 184
e-mail 183
e-marketing 175, 177
e-meeting 184, 186
e-office 183–184
e-publicity 177
e-shopping 181
eco-bus 249
eco-car 7, 10, 67, 221, 223, 230,
    247, 250
eco-labelling 82

eco-taxi 250
ecological disaster 248
  sustainability 226
economic benefits of aviation 150
  competitiveness 61
  development 3, 227
  growth 9, 39, 191, 205, 225
  sustainability 37–38
economics of integration 189
edge city 17, 231
Edinburgh 75
effective governance 229
efficiency increase 239
  of business 241
elasticities 47, 69, 141
electric and hybrid vehicles 162
  vehicles 8, 66, 152
electronic road pricing 135–137,
  207 (see pricing and Singapore)
emerging cities 227 (see cities)
emissions 89 (see air pollution)
  charge 150 (see pricing)
  regulations 250
  standards 223
employment 120, 170
  density 106 (see density)
empty running 167
energy and mineral resources 12
  consumption 20–21, 140
  efficiency 60
  intensity 51
  sector 49
  security 60
  use in transport 124
enforcement 201, 205, 229
Enschede 76
environment development 3
  factors 135
  performance 226
  protection 60
  quality 191
  regulations 219

sustainability 38–39
  tax 147 (see pricing)
equity 25–29, 34, 193–200
escape theory 235–236 (see leisure
  travel)
ethanol 67, 162 (see alternative
  fuels)
EU 13, 21–22, 30–32, 33–34,
  43–44, 45, 49, 52, 56, 61–63, 67,
  80, 138, 140, 151–152, 155, 179,
  181, 214, 223
  Trading Emissions Directive 32
  Transport Policy 44
Europe 42, 131
Eurovignette 139
evaporative emissions 90
excess travel 236
exploratory scenarios 212 (see
  scenarios and backcasting)
externalities 11, 58

face-to-face 180, 186
factor four 41, 97
fair shares 5
feebates 152, 221, 250
fiscal mechanisms 67–69, 253
fixed travel time budgets 188
flexibility 189
flexible location patterns 174
  specialization 54, 221
FlexiTheory 234, 235
flip theory 26, 28 (see contraction
  and convergence)
foresight vehicle programme 160
France 47
Freiburg 122
freight 20, 41–43, 45, 46–47, 50,
  52, 140, 161, 165–166 (see
  logistics and lorries)
  distribution 175, 178
  growth 165
  intensity 165

sector 55, 189
fuel cells 67, 159 (see hydrogen)
  composition 90
  efficiency 90, 151
  price escalator 68, 244 (see
    pricing and tax)
  prices 29, 69
  taxes 29, 137

gasoline consumption 124 (see fuel
  and energy consumption)
GDP 42–49, 50–52
genuine progress indicator 51–52
Germany 20–21, 140, 236
global conventions 84
  emissions of CO_2 246 (see
    emissions, global warming and
    carbon dioxide)
  markets 174
  warming 1, 16, 22, 24, 148 (see
    carbon dioxide)
globalization 17, 53, 60, 170, 173,
  212
glocal 54
governance 3, 204–208
Great Britain 102–103, 105, 165,
  2367 (see United Kingdom)
Greece 138
green consciousness 220
  modes 228, 239 (see non
    motorized transport, walk and
    cycling)
  taxes 29–30
greener products 220
greenfield locations 231
greenhouse gas 33, 61, 151, 157
  (see global warming and carbon
  dioxide)
gridlock 191 (see congestion)
gross mass movement 49
  transport intensity 49
Guangzhou 15

Hague Climate Change Convention
  64
handling factors 165
health 12
healthy transport 241–242
high density developments 198, 202,
  251 (see cities and density)
  speed rail 58, 170 (see rail)
  technology alternative 220
holistic views 245
Hong Kong 15, 123
housing 126, 239
hub ports 177
hybrid vehicle 10, 66, 152, 160, 164
hydrogen 159–163
  fuel cells 66, 158, 162, 223
hypermobility argument 167

Iceland 61
implementation barriers 87
income effects 142
index of sustainable economic
  welfare 53
India 194
individual consumption 5
  interest 95
  mobility 6 (see travel)
  travel decisions 79
industrial organization 166
inequality 145, 195
informal bus services 252 (see public
  transport)
  housing 195 (see housing)
  sector 204, 206 (see employment)
information 251
  and communications technologies
    9, 169–190, 211
  exchange 188
  systems 135
innovation 193, 201–204, 222
  funds 67
innovative policies 92

institutional approaches 80 (see
  organisational structures)
  barrier 71, 78, 147
  coordination 93
  roles 87
institutions 204–208
intelligent car 7
intensity of land use 99–100, 105–
  111 (see cities and density)
interactive planning 76, 77
interchange development 127 (see
  transit oriented development and
  transport development areas)
intergenerational 3
intermodal transport 188
internalization of external costs 189
international travel 48
internet 174, 179, 181–182, 187–
  188, 235, 237
  shopping 172
intragenerational 3
inward migration 194
Italy 47

Jakarta 15
Japan 20, 35, 61–63
job density 109, 111 (see density
  and employment)
Joint Implementation 33
journey frequency 100, 106
  lengths 126
just-in-time production 175–176

kilometre charge 139 (see pricing)
Kuala Lumpur 196
Kyoto 21, 27, 33
  Clean Development Mechanism
    33
  Protocol 21, 61
  targets 63–64

labour force 173

land resources 12
land-use characteristics 99
  density controls 199 (see cities
    and density)
  policy 69, 240
last minute deals 180, 182–183
latent demand 188
lean-burn technologies 24
learning capacity 170
legal and regulatory framework 93
  barriers 72, 140
leisure mobility 234–235
  shopping 179
  travel 237
lifecycle 167
lifestyles 79, 219, 223
Light Rail Transit (LRT) 201, 202
  (see public transport)
limits to growth 39–40
  to travel 187
liveable cities 225
living 179–183
load factors 166
local accessibility 99–100
  Agenda 21 83, 96, 146
  air pollution 246
  air quality 148
  design issues 115
  equity 220
  markets 219
location 100, 112–116, 125
  decisions 188, 245
  of new development 124
logistics 175, 177
  and freight distribution 177
  market 178 (see freight)
  platforms 170 (see freight)
London 69, 102–103, 105, 130,
  154, 207, 242
  congestion charging 48, 131–134,
    141–145
long distance journeys 105, 173, 183

supply chains 178
long-term perspectives 244
lorries 58, 144 (see freight)
lorry road user charging 141
Los Angeles 111
low carbon transport 157
 Carbon Vehicle Partnership 161
 speed limits 237
 technology alternative 219
 density neighbourhoods 199
 income car drivers 144, 231 (see car)
 income housing 199
LPG 163–164 (see alternative fuels)

Maglev 209 (see high speed rail)
management of transport demand 90
Manchester 103
manufacturing systems 175
marginal cost pricing 129, 134
mass movement 49
 transit systems 203, 208 (see rail)
maximum parking standards 118
medium density 216 (see density)
mega trends 169
methane 61 (see global warming)
methanol 66, 158, 160, 162 (see alternative fuels)
metros 203 (see public transport and rail)
Mexico City 194, 203
minibuses 197 (see public transport)
mix of services 125
mixed use 99–100, 111–112, 126, 251 (see land use)
mobile elite 210 (see car)
mobility 88, 115, 167
 car sharing Switzerland 147
 efficiency 70
 limiting strategies 129
modal shift 239

split 165, 220
modification of travel 171
monocentric structures 99
moral responsibility 248
motor industry 80, 84, 145, 160, 251 (see car)
motorcycles 144–145, 195
motorization 13

Nagoya 15
national targets 93
natural capital 37–39, 40
 gas 163–164 (see alternative fuels)
need to travel 108
neighbourhood issues 127
neo-traditional development 116
net mass movement 49, 52
 transport intensity 49
Netherlands 47, 61, 77, 114, 138, 139
network society 15
networking 188
new clean fuels 162 (see alternative fuels)
 development 112 (see land use)
 housing locations 104 (see housing)
 mobility 153 (see car)
 production processes 54
 urbanism 111
New York 102
niche vehicles 66 (see cars)
nitrogen oxides 24, 34 (see emissions)
noise 12, 16
non-motorized transport 193, 228 (see cycles and walking)
non-OECD 82, 87, 157, 227, 252 (see developing countries)
North America 42 (see United States)

Norway 61, 01, 103
Norwegian cities 69
Nottingham 139–140

occupancy levels 46
OECD 13, 17, 19–20, 26, 34–36,
    87, 157 (see developed countries)
oil industry 82, 145
Online Freight Exchanges 177
operation of transport systems 171
opportunity for development 115
organizational change 222
    structures 82–84, 89, 95 (see
        institutional change)
Osaka 15
Oslo 104
Oxford 104, 121
oxidation catalysts 164 (see catalytic
    converters)
ozone 24, 35, 88 (see global
    warming)

packages of policies 89
parasitic disease 226
paratransit 203, 228 (see public
    transport and informal bus
    services)
Paris 105
park and ride 83, 119
parking 114, 117–119, 126, 138,
    251
    charges 138
    provision 99
    standards 113
    supply 100
participation 3, 80, 206
particulate traps 164 (see catalytic
    converters)
particulates 25 (see PM_{10})
partnership 206
Partnership for a New Generation
    of Vehicles 80

passenger travel 43, 45, 46, 52, 55
Pearl River Delta 15
pedal cycle 144 (see bicycle and
    cycle)
pedestrianization 127
pedestrians 116, 252 (see walking)
periphery 196
Perth 105
petrol 25, 68, 144 (see alternative
    fuels, diesel and gasoline
    consumption)
Pew Centre 152
physical barriers 73
    hazards 227
    measures 69–70, 228
    restraint 253
planning measures 85 (see land use)
    systems 229
PM_{10} 35 (see particulates)
policy behaviour gap 72
    packages 56, 216
political acceptability 141, 151–
    153 (see acceptability and public
    acceptability)
    commitment 87
polluting class 253
pollution taxes 147 (see pricing)
polycentric cities 99, 109–110, 137,
    246 (see cities)
poor cities 196, 205
population size 102, 125
Porter hypothesis 98
poverty 195
    reduction 191, 210, 227
precautionary principle 22, 37, 61,
    149, 211, 244
premature congestion 192 (see
    congestion)
price of fuel 129 (see pricing)
pricing 130–141, 222, 229 (see air
    travel pricing, comprehensive
    pricing, cordon pricing, electronic

road pricing, marginal cost
pricing and road pricing)
strategy for aviation 150 (see
aviation)
primary energy consumption 50, 124
private sector 145
transport planning 181 (see car)
production 174–179
productivity 178, 184
professional culture 95
projective scenarios 213 (see
scenarios)
property and land markets 231
rights 39
prospective scenarios 212 (see
scenarios)
proximity 248
public acceptability 72, 77, 134 (see
acceptability and public
acceptability)
discourse 80, 94, 246 (see
communicative rationality)
interest 76
participation 93
policy 60
sector 146
transport 8, 58, 75, 78, 109, 126,
179, 196, 203–204, 219, 224,
230, 239, 245–247, 250–252
(see informal public transport,
light rail transport, paratransit,
rail and high speed rail)
transport innovation 201
transport interchanges 126
transport planning 180
transport trips 106
transport use 69
understanding 84

quality neighbourhoods 127
of life 188, 200, 241, 243, 253–
254

radiative forcing 148
rail 117, 202, 211 (see high speed
rail and public transport)
real time information 190
realistic vision 228
reallocation of road space 127
reasonable travel time 236–237 (see
travel time)
reduce travel 217
trip lengths 55
reducing emissions 87–91
the need to travel 60, 237
regulations 201
regulatory incentives 145–147
relative decoupling 56 (see
decoupling)
released space 239
reliability 237
replacement 180
residential densities 107, 108 (see
density)
resource barriers 71, 75
retail sales 142
reversibility 246
rickshaws 197, 200
Rio de Janeiro 15, 194–195
Rio Summit 21, 61
road accidents 226
pricing 69, 130–131, 135, 137,
245, 250 (see pricing and
electronic road pricing)
safety 16, 227
road space 250
rural lifestyles 183
Russia 20, 22, 64

San Francisco Bay Area 111
Sao Paulo 15
scenarios 93, 212–213
school travel provision 119
scrappage programme 224, 250
selling the visions 230 (see

scenarios)
sequencing of implementation 245
sequential approach 113
sequestration 31
settlement patterns 220
    size 99–100, 102–105, 125 (see
    cities)
Shanghai 209–210
short trips 106
side effects 72
Singapore 8, 69, 135–136, 206–207
    (see electronic road pricing)
Single-centre cities 109
smart car 7 (see car)
    growth 110
Smartcard 137, 250
social acceptability 73 (see
    acceptability)
    and cultural barriers 72
    construct 194
    development 3
    dimensions 175, 199
    equity 3
    implications 253–254
    networks 181
    sustainability 37–38 (see
        sustainability and sustainable
        urban development)
socially inclusive 254
societal benefits of change 244
socio-economic factors 120, 126
solid waste 12
space in cities 249
spatial equity 3
    segregation 195
speed limits 251
sport utility vehicle 152, 162 (see
    car)
stabilization 26
stimulation of more travel 171
stratospheric ozone depletion 148
    (see global warming and ozone)

strong sustainability 37, 39–40, 56,
    248, 254 (see sustainability and
    weak sustainability)
subsidiarity 206
subsidies 81
    to public transport 250
substitution 172, 186, 188, 237
    effects 180, 183
suburbanization 110
superstores 113
supportive national framework 93
Surabaya 15
sustainability 37
    forums 251
sustainable accessibility 70
    cities 9, 19, 77–78, 246, 253 (see
        cities)
    city vision 209 (see scenarios)
    consumption 227
    development 2, 75, 225
    mobility 232
    supply chains 189 (see freight)
    transport 79, 144
    transport planning 233–237
    transport policy 71, 75–77, 153
    transport strategy 87
    transport system 78
    urban development 2, 7–9, 13,
        15, 92, 95, 126, 193, 205–
        206, 233, 239
    urban transport strategy 88–89
    urban travel policies 88–89
Sweden 47, 81, 103, 108
Switzerland 62, 78, 140, 146–147

tag number systems 208
tailpipe emissions 90 (see catalytic
    converters)
targets 82, 85, 214, 218 (see Kyoto)
tax incentives 81, 219, 224, 249 (see
    pricing)
    on aviation fuel 149 (see aviation)

taxis 58, 144
technological arguments 249
    change 169
    fix 110, 168
    innovation 89, 97, 155, 187, 239
    measures 154
    revolution 170, 211
    substitution 249
technology 216, 217, 224, 228,
    246, 251
    policy 66–68, 70
technopoles 170
telecommuting 109
teleconferencing 172
teleworkers 183–185
tiger economies 228
time minimization 236–237
time-based scheme 141
Tokyo 14–15
toll road 131
tradable permits 30–33, 33, 63–64,
    67, 81, 164, 230, 250
traffic calming 128 (see
pedestrianization)
    forecasts 47
    management 228, 247
Trans European Networks 45 (see
    rail and high speed rail)
transaction costs 33
transferability 231
transit oriented developments 115
    (see interchange development and
    transport development areas)
TransMilenio 31, 204, 208 (see
    Bogota)
transport corridors 199, 202 (see
    corridors)
    demand 217 (see demand)
    demand management 85
    Development Areas 115 (see
        interchange development and
        transit oriented development)

efficiency 41, 53
energy consumption 52–53, 99,
101–102, 105, 108, 117 (see energy
consumption)
energy efficiency 50
growth 9
intensity 9, 20, 24, 41, 42–49,
    52–53, 55–56 (see decoupling)
investment 143
policy 69, 216, 238
supply measures 86
system 255
travel awareness 119
    demand 127
    distance 102
    plans 243 (see school travel
        provision and company
        transport plans)
    reduction 75
    time 101, 110 (see commuting
    trip times time minimization)
    time reliability 237 (see
        reasonable travel time and
        fixed travel time budgets)
    time savings 143
trickle-down effects 3
trigger effects 246
trip chaining 114
    distance 114
    frequency 105, 113
    lengths 247, 251 (see reduce trip
        lengths and short trips)
    mode 113 (see car trips and
        public transport trips)
    tour 106

United Kingdom 21, 28–29, 31, 46–
    47, 52, 59–61, 68, 112, 115, 120,
    129, 138, 139–141, 148, 149,
    160–161, 163, 181, 183–184,
    212, 214, 244 (see Great Britain)
United States 20–22, 30, 34, 35,

40, 42–43, 49, 52, 56, 61–64, 66, 80, 102–105, 108–111, 115, 120, 131, 138, 151, 155, 157, 167, 178, 181, 184, 235

urban density 110 (see cities and density)
    development 88, 95
    form 240
    governance 194, 252
    landscapes 16
    poor 193, 197, 199, 201 (see poor cities and poverty)
    renaissance 98
    villages 110
use of space 16
users of resources 6

value density 167
vehicle distance 120
    ownership 13, 20, 26, 192 (see car ownership)
virtual mobility 188, 190 (see information and communications technologies)

visionary leadership 2532
visioning 212–213
visions of the sustainable city 92, 214, 218, 227 (see scenarios)
volatile organic compounds 24, 34 (see emissions)

walking 8, 59, 106, 109, 194, 250 (see non motorized modes and pedestrians)
water resources 12
weak sustainability 37, 40, 56, 249, 254 (see strong sustainability and sustainability)
willingness to change 78
work place parking levies 118, 139–140 (see pricing)
working 183–186 (see employment and commuting trip times)
World Bank 192–193, 195, 201, 210
    economic forum 4
World Wildlife Fund 28

Zurich 74, 78, 138, 146–147